WESTERN WINDOW IN THE ARAB WORLD

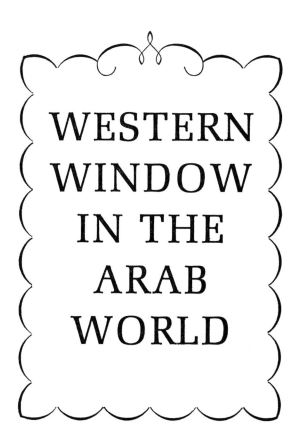

WESTERN WINDOW IN THE ARAB WORLD

By Leon Borden Blair

Foreword by Mohammed El Fasi
Minister of State for Cultural Affairs, Morocco

UNIVERSITY OF TEXAS PRESS
AUSTIN & LONDON

International Standard Book Number 0-292-70083-0
Library of Congress Catalog Card Number 78-131423
© 1970 by Leon Borden Blair
All rights reserved
Typesetting by G&S Typesetters, Austin
Printed by The University of Texas Printing Division, Austin
Bound by Universal Bookbindery, Inc., San Antonio

CONTENTS

ILLUSTRATIONS

FOREWORD

It is always difficult for two peoples of widely differing cultures to find a common frame of reference. Even when they speak the same language, they tend to perceive any given situation in terms of their own traditions and culture. The concept of *Western Window in the Arab World*, or perception through long association, seems valid, for certainly the Moroccan people have through long association gained a unique insight into the mentality of the Americans with whom fortune has placed them in contact. If the present volume departs from the usual format of diplomatic histories, it is nonetheless valuable, for it recognizes that the traditional format does not fit the circumstances for many of the newly independent nations.

Commandant Blair, as he is known to the Moroccan people, was an active and discerning resident of Morocco for many years. He and his family, as did many other Americans, participated in the life of the Moroccan community, and the human understanding thus generated cannot really be described on the printed page, yet it is a potent force which cannot fail to influence the destiny of his country as well as that of Morocco.

Even if one does not share all of the opinions expressed by Dr. Blair, one must admire the depth of his research, the sincere and deep sympathy which he shows throughout this study toward the Moroccan people, and finally and above all, the respect and admiration which he witnesses for our great King Mohammed V and his worthy heir, His Majesty King Hassan II.

Mohammed El Fasi
Minister of State for
Cultural Affairs, Morocco

PREFACE

On December 7, 1941, the United States was hurled into a new stage of national development. Isolationism, which had preoccupied the nation for a decade, receded, and additional prejudices crumbled. Soldiers from New York moved to Texas for training and farmers from Oklahoma went to California to work in burgeoning defense industries. American armies were soon marching on five continents, fighting in spots with strange sounding names—Guadalcanal, Souk-el-Arba, Anzio—and sharing foxholes with Gurkas, Anzacs, Goums, and Tommies. The war years were politically significant as a new generation developed its own ideas and values under the test of fire and steel. The old political order was reestablished after the war, but the old social order could not be put back together again.

The social impact of the United States military establishment did not end with the war. It continues still, but historians and political scientists have made little effort to chart its course or to assess its end. Journalists note the americanization of West Germany and of Japan, and tourists feel at home in the Nile Hilton or the Ramada Inn–Rabat, but a pervasive influence that has contributed much to the americanization of world society passes unnoticed. Since 1946 almost ten million Americans—military personnel and their dependents—have been stationed in foreign countries. Apart from the strategic raison d'être, what has been their impact on the host country? Logic compels the recognition of some influence, positive or negative. Indeed, the Department of Defense has been the only agency of the United States government with enough personnel in daily contact with a foreign people to produce a noticeable transformation. A million Americans have lived in Morocco during the quarter century since November, 1942, when American troops first landed on its beaches. This study concerns their impact on Morocco.

The United States naval base in Morocco was the first foreign base captured by American troops in World War II. Continuously occupied by American forces since November 11, 1942, its history parallels that of the Moroccan independence movement. In reconstructing that history, I have provided an interpretation based on extensive interviews, personal experience, and close examination of French, Moroccan, and U.S. military archives. In a predominantly illiterate society the personal interviews are necessary if the documentary information is to be placed in proper perspective. A reasonable assessment of the degree of influence that the American forces exerted upon Moroccan institutions appears herein. This influence has been denied by Professor I. William Zartman in *Morocco: Problems of New Power* but affirmed by no less an authority than Mohammed V, king of Morocco, in these words: "Your military detachments have been cast in a day-to-day role of contact with various segments of my people. They have imparted to us some of their ways and techniques. . . . The American know-how became a miracle of wonder to our people."[1]

As a lieutenant commander, U.S. Navy, I spent six years from June, 1954, to August, 1960, in the Mediterranean–North African area, first as an aviation technical advisor to the French Navy, next as the U.S. Navy politico-military liaison officer in Morocco, and finally as technical advisor to the Royal Moroccan armed forces. In my first assignment, primarily at French military bases in Morocco, Algeria, and Tunisia, I became acquainted with French military and diplomatic personalities and viewpoints. As politico-military liaison officer from February, 1957, to February, 1960, I worked with French, Moroccan, and United States agencies on specific problems associated with the United States military bases in Morocco, under pressures from officials representing three entirely different cultural viewpoints. In my last assignment, a short but fruitful one, I served with the upper echelons of the Moroccan government, including the royal family, thereby gaining experiences and perspectives on the turbulent postwar years in Morocco.

Morocco's geographic location makes it of crucial strategic importance to the United States. It has received scant attention from

[1] Mohammed V, king of Morocco, as told to Christine Hotchkiss, "Why I Like Americans," *This Week*, September 11, 1960, pp. 33–34.

American scholars, however, perhaps because of its dearth of indigenous historical literature. Morocco is not a lettered society. Tremendous progress in public education since 1957 has produced only 30 percent literacy today. Its newspapers, about a dozen in all, have a combined circulation of less than 150,000. The public records during the era of the French protectorate (1912–1956) are almost exclusively French in origin and language. Anti–French Moroccan intellectuals who might have contributed corrective viewpoints were either in prison or in exile during this era. In either case they were little given to public exposition, as a matter of personal safety. But the French and the Moroccans view events from different perspectives. This study attempts to bridge that gap by using scattered Moroccan sources, supplemented by interviews with participants in the events described, and by American sources to counterbalance the more extensive French-oriented literature.

In the preparation of this work the translations from foreign sources are my own unless otherwise identified. Arabic sources are transliterated according to the French system in use in Morocco. The spelling of proper names, which often varies from source to source when translated, conforms to the individual's own usage and to the general usage in the French press in Morocco.

I am indebted to many people without whose help this study would have been impossible. Mr. Clark Palmer spared no effort to guide me through the maze of the superbly organized United States Air Force Archives at Maxwell Air Force Base, Alabama. Captain Kent Loomis, USN, not only aided my research in the Navy Archives at Washington but also provided valuable information and guidance from his own experience as U.S. naval attaché at Tangier in the early 1950's. Mrs. Lillian C. Kidwell at the American Red Cross Archives in Washington spent many hours searching out Red Cross records dating back to the period before the American landing in Morocco in 1942, and Mr. Carlyle Bennett at the Federal Records Center, New York, was most helpful in expediting research in the records of the U.S. naval activities at Port Lyautey, which are stored there. Nor should the valuable help given by the personnel of the Library of Congress, the New York Public Library, and the Texas Christian University Library remain unacknowledged.

In Morocco Mr. Abdallah Regragui, director of the Bibliothèque

Generale at Rabat, lent his unparalleled knowledge of Moroccan sources unstintingly, and I am particularly grateful to him, not only for the excellent facilities he provided, but also for the counsel and personal friendship that he so graciously extended. Commander R. W. Bennett, the politico-military liaison officer at the naval base, was most helpful in arranging for clerical assistance and the reproduction of certain valuable documents.

Many Moroccans, high and low, shared their knowledge with me. Some of them are identified in the text and footnotes, but the dozens who are not identified provided perspective and corroboration that was invaluable in interpreting the Moroccan independence movement. I am especially grateful to Mrs. Batoul Sbihi for her help in reaching and talking to so many of the "resistants." Mr. Mehdi Bennouna, well known to almost every scholar who has concerned himself with modern Moroccan history, took time to discuss and help unravel the tangled web of Moroccan nationalism and to read and suggest corrections or new interpretations of that portion of the text concerning the birth and growth of Moroccan nationalism prior to the deposition of King Mohammed V in 1953. And at Texas Christian University Dr. Frank T. Reuter, Dr. Donald E. Worcester, Dr. Maurice Boyd, Dr. William C. Nunn, and Dr. George H. Reeves have read the manuscript; I have benefited from their advice. Let all find here an expression of my gratitude.

L. B. B.

University of Texas at Arlington

WESTERN WINDOW IN THE ARAB WORLD

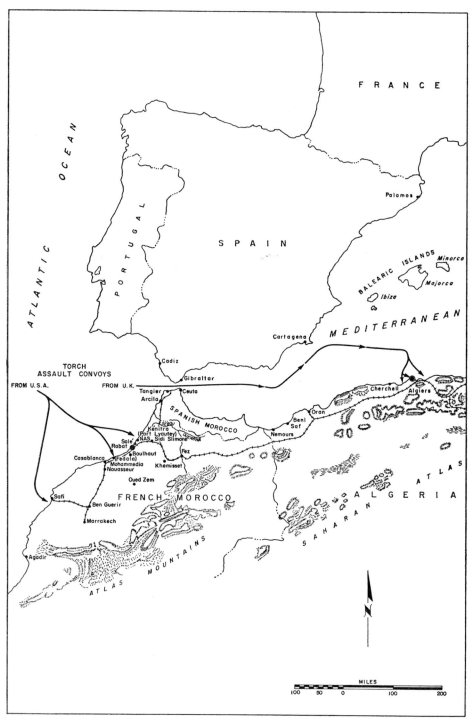

Operation Torch: First Step in the Allied Capture of North Africa

1. Introduction

"CAPTAIN, I SAW A LIGHT"—portentous words by a Moroccan fisherman four hours before dawn on November 8, 1942. There should have been no light. Ships coming out of the Strait of Gibraltar bound for Casablanca, seventy miles to the southwest, would have been farther offshore. Here, a scant mile from the end of the jetty where the Oued Sebou flows into the Atlantic Ocean, the water was too shallow. Nor could it have been a ship entering the Sebou, bound for Port Lyautey five miles upstream. The tide was too low for a ship to cross the bar, and, besides, the ships' masters preferred not to navigate the tortuous Sebou at night; the channel was narrow and treacherous. But the great black shapes were there; the ocean was covered with them. It was a historic moment! The liberation of North Africa and of Morocco had begun. The capture of North Africa was part of an overall strategic plan, and the liberation of Morocco flowed from it as inevitably as the Oued Sebou flows into the sea. The black shapes were the assault ships of

Operation Torch, the first great amphibious operation undertaken by the United States armed forces. The Americans had come to Morocco, an ancient land with a unique people whose complex history, even in the twentieth century, they hardly understood. Such knowledge is essential to an understanding of the events of the next twenty years.

Morocco is a fascinating land. The ancients knew it as the Garden of Hesperides. There, in legend, Hercules sought the golden apples—the tangerines that still grow about the city of Tangier. There Hercules placed one foot on the Jebel Musa and the other on the Jebel Tarik (Gibraltar) and supported the sky. The ancient city of Lixus, which legend says traded with Atlantis, was located just across the river from the present city of Larache, on Morocco's west coast. Barbary pirates sailed from Moroccan ports. Generations of school children have thrilled to the exploits of Robinson Crusoe against the Sallee Rovers. Salé still stands behind its crenelated walls, and its children will guide the curious visitor to the old water gate through which the pirate ships were brought within the protection of the city walls. The Moroccans call their country a land of contrasts: lush farm land and burning deserts, snow-capped mountains and sunny beaches, modern cities and villages little changed from biblical times.

The strategic significance of Morocco is as obvious as its geography. It is the key to the Mediterranean Sea, a crucial theater in the struggle for world power for two thousand years.[1] Located on the northernmost extremity of the African continent with three hundred miles of Mediterranean coastline and eight hundred of Atlantic, it dominates the southern approaches to the Strait of Gibraltar. The principal shipping lanes from southern Europe to West Africa and South America parallel its coast for more than five hundred miles. Great Britain explicitly recognized its strategic importance in the Anglo-French Convention of April 8, 1904, by insisting on Article III, forbidding the fortification of the Moroccan coast between Melilla, held by Spain, and the valley of the Sebou River.[2] Two years later, at the Algeciras Conference, The-

---

[1] The battles of Actium, 31 B.C., Lepanto, A.D. 1571, Navarino, 1827, Gallipoli, 1914, and Malta, 1942, were all challenges to the status quo in the area and were in their time decisive.

[2] The British anxiety is clearly reflected in the extended negotiations dur-

odore Roosevelt threw the weight of the United States behind the Anglo-French entente; he was unwilling to see the status quo disrupted in this critical area.[3] Small wonder that the first objective of Operation Torch was Morocco: it was the most accessible flank of the general European position, the "other leaf of the Gibraltar gate"; in unfriendly hands it would render the position of Western sea power in the Mediterranean untenable, and it might be used by the Axis for a counterblockade in the South Atlantic.[4]

Morocco, Al Maghreb Al-Aksa, land of the last sunset, comprises the westernmost fourth of an area known to the Arab geographers as Al Maghreb Al-Arabi, a unit washed on three sides by salt water and isolated on the south by the inhospitable Sahara. It shares the "island" with Algeria, Tunisia, and part of Libya. On the north, Morocco has several good natural harbors, but the littoral is narrow, cut off from the rest of Morocco by the Rif Mountain chain. On the west, an extended plain rising in steps to the towering Atlas Mountains opens to the Atlantic. This area is the heart of the country. With mountains to the north and east, unbroken except for the narrow Taza Corridor between the Rif and the northern extension of the Atlas Mountains, and an Atlantic coast barren of natural harbors, Morocco has enjoyed an isolation all its own—a factor contributing to the unique character of its people and institutions.

Morocco lies entirely within the temperate zone; in fact, the parallels of latitude that bracket Morocco also pass through Amarillo and Corpus Christi, Texas. Along both the Mediterranean and

---

ing the six months preceding the accord. See France, Ministère des Affaires Etrangères, *Documents diplomatiques français, 1871–1914*, 2. Serie 1901–1911, V, 51, 56, 128, 162, 450, 470, and the text of the accord, pp. 480–494. Lord Lansdowne, British Foreign Secretary, had proposed extending the interdiction as far south as Mazaghan, some two hundred miles to the southwest of the valley of the Sebou.

[3] See George E. Mowry, *The Era of Theodore Roosevelt and the Birth of Modern America, 1900–1921*, pp. 192–196, for a discussion of President Roosevelt's concept of world power. His protestations of slight interest in Morocco did not disarm the French, who suspected American intentions, if not in Morocco, at least in the off-shore islands, specifically, the Canaries. See *Documents diplomatiques français*, IV, 503–504.

[4] "Pertinent Data on French Morocco," a planning document for Operation Torch, dated October 25, 1942, in United States Air Force Archives, file no. 612.610, p. 1.

Atlantic coasts, the climate is superb. Freezing weather is unknown and temperatures above ninety degrees are so rare that their occurrence impels employers to close their business establishments and send the employees home. In the interior, however, furnace-like summer temperatures are the rule rather than the exception. But even there one finds contrast, for only forty miles from Marrakech the thirteen-thousand-foot Toubkal peak rears its snow-capped head. Beyond it, to the east and south, the desert begins.

Although agriculture is still the economic base for the country, Morocco is not well suited for it. The rainfall is seasonal and cyclical, torrential in December and January and almost nonexistent in the latter summer and early fall months. Nor is it uniform from region to region. Ifrane, for example, receives thirty-nine inches per year while Kasba Tadla, less than one hundred miles to the southwest, receives only twenty-five. Because of the distribution of rainfall and the nature of the soils, cereal grains, particularly wheat, comprise the greatest part of the agricultural production. The capriciousness of the climate has affected both the land and the people, nomads by tradition, who have reluctantly accepted a sedentary life.

Morocco has about 200 million acres of arable land, most of it in the Atlantic plains. The arid lands to the east and south of the Atlas Mountains have great agricultural potential when water becomes available, but for the present are deserted except for an occasional oasis. Of the 200 million acres, only some 30 million are considered fertile—and that by Moroccan standards. They are the loams found overlying a limestone base on the low plateaus of the Atlantic plains and in the Taza Corridor, and the alluvial soils deriving from them. The clay-sand content of the loams varies from one region to another, but they are basically the same. They range in color from dark red to brown to black, depending upon the amount and form of the prevalent ferrous oxides. Over the centuries, victims of overgrazing and improper cultivation, the clays have lost their topsoil; in many places even the clays are gone, and the limestone subsoil is exposed. What the *tirs* and the *hamris* lost, however, the *dehs*, the alluvial soils found in the larger river valleys, gained. Of a clay-sand-limestone composition with about 3 percent humus—as contrasted with the norm of 1 percent found in other soils—they comprise the most productive land in the entire country. Such soils along the Sebou River produce most of Morocco's rice.[5] Along the coast the soils are predominantly sand of Marine origin, porous, low in humus and colloidal content, and unsuited to cereal culture, but excellent for horticulture, arboriculture, and forestry plantations.[6]

Most authorities agree that a substantial increase in the Moroccan population occurred under the French protectorate, but their precise figures vary as much as 10 percent. The census is not yet institutionalized in Morocco. Prior to 1936, census takers were few and inexperienced, and they were distrusted by the Moroccans who wondered why the information was needed and what unpleasant consequences were in store for them if they cooperated. Large areas of the country had not been "pacified" until 1934–1935, and many individuals still hiding in the mountains were not included. The census of 1947 was so obviously inaccurate that most statisticians ignored it. Taken in the immediate postwar period, it was systematically padded by French authorities and Moroccan family heads alike, in order to increase their share of food and other necessities being furnished primarily by the United States.[7] Births and deaths were not registered and, except for a few established families, the Moroccans had no family name until the *dahir* (law) of March 8, 1950, provided for the establishment of a civil estate in the Western tradition for individuals. Even that law was not comprehensive; it primarily affected civil servants entitled to family allowances and did not cover the mass of the Moroccan people living in rural areas.[8] The Spanish protectorate and Tangier, with

[5] The commercial production of rice in Morocco began in 1949, and by 1967 covered about thirteen thousand acres. Two long-grain Italian varieties, Stirpe and Patna, and one round variety, Triomphe, of Moroccan origin, account for most of the production. Sixty to 70 percent of the rice produced is consumed in Morocco (interview, Mlah Mchiche, one of Morocco's principal rice producers and millers, at Kenitra, Morocco, May 30, 1967).

[6] See Albert Guillaume, *L'Evolution économique de la société rurale marocaine*, vol. 48 in Institut des Hautes Etudes Marocaines, Collection des Centres d'Etudes Juridiques, for an excellent discussion of the problems of Moroccan agriculture.

[7] Albert Ayache, *Le Maroc*, pp. 281–283, 247–248.

[8] Istiqlal party, *Morocco under the Protectorate: Forty Years of French Administration*, pp. 14–15, denies the validity of published demographic figures showing substantial increase; the population of Morocco in 1912 was estimated by this source at nine million.

about one and a half million inhabitants, were not included in the population figure until the census of 1960, and the American military personnel and their dependents were never included. The following figures are the best approximation available.[9]

1921	4,253,000	1947	8,089,000
1926	4,894,000	1952	8,087,000
1931	5,365,000	1960	11,598,000
1936	6,245,000		

Although the process began earlier and has continued over a longer period, Morocco is no less a melting pot than the United States. It was inhabited in preliterate times by an Ibero-Mediterranean people who called themselves *imazighen*, or free men. They built no cities and left no architectural monuments, but their tongue persists in the Tamazight dialect spoken in the Middle Atlas regions to this day, and it is the root of the Tarifit dialect spoken in the Rif Mountains, and of the Tachelhit dialect of the Schleuh tribes of the Souss Valley. In the fourteenth and thirteenth centuries, B.C., the *imazighen* invaded the Nile Delta where they were known as Lebu or Libyans to the Egyptians. For twelve centuries, until about A.D. 100, the Phoenicians maintained trading colonies on their coasts from present day Melilla to Agadir, and they knew them as Numidians, Getulae, or Moors—as did the Greeks and Romans. After the Phoenicians, for five centuries, Morocco was the Roman province of Mauretania Tangitana. Its capital was Tangier. The Romans called the natives of North Africa *barbares*, or barbarians, the administrative epithet they used for the Parthians, Scythians, and Germanic tribes. Thus when the Vandals and the Goths invaded North Africa, they too were considered the same people. In the seventh century, when the first Arab armies swept across North Africa, they arabicized the term to *baraber*, or Berber, the name by which the natives of the Maghreb are known today.

Foreign invasions of the Berber country have been like water poured on sand. A thousand years of Phoenician civilization and Punic language left hardly a trace, except that some of Morocco's

[9] Ayache, *Le Maroc*, p. 282, for the 1947 figure; Roger Le Tourneau, *Evolution Politique de l'Afrique du Nord Musulmane*, p. 17 for the 1960 figure, and Stéphane Bernard, *Le Conflit Franco-Marocain, 1943–1956*, III, 73, for the others.

Jewish communities were established during the Phoenician period. The Roman civilization with its Latin language and four Christian bishoprics disappeared; even Volubilis, the capital city of 350,000 inhabitants, was abandoned, and the sands of the centuries covered it. Only the olive trees and, perhaps, the tradition of wheat culture remain of the Roman innovations. The Arabs, too, might have lost their identity had they not brought the dynamism of the Islamic religion and the beauty of the Arabic language. The Arabic influence is cultural, not racial. King Hassan II of Morocco is a Sherif, descended from the Prophet Mohammed; his mother is a Berber. Mohammed ben Laabdia, born a Moroccan peasant, is Arab; his father was Spanish and his mother, Arab-Berber. Many of Morocco's Jews are Berbers, converted to Judaism before the Arab conquest. Many of its Arabs are the same Berbers converted to the Islamic religion. Others are the Moriscos, Moors converted to Christianity, before their expulsion from Spain in the seventeenth century. Others quite obviously are Negroes, descendants of the mercenary soldiers brought in from the Sudan by Sultan Moulay Ismael in the seventeenth century. Ethnically, it is as difficult to separate the Arab from the other ethnic sources as to separate the pink from the violet in a rainbow.

Islam is at the same time a religion, a government, and a code of ethical conduct. As a religion, it was readily acceptable to the indigenous population of North Africa, as it was in many areas of the world where conditions similar to those that gave it birth in the Arabian peninsula prevailed. Mohammed preached a religion that satisfied the merchants of Medina and Mecca. It guaranteed their property and allowed them to participate in the direction of their affairs, both spiritual and temporal. It sought to unify the rural tribes and the urban communities into a Moslem community, a concept heartily favored by the commercial interests. And, finally, because of its simplicity, it appealed to the rural nomadic tribes.

Morocco bore a striking resemblance to Arabia in the seventh century. Isolated geographically by seas, mountains, and deserts, it had escaped gradual settlement by other peoples expanding into contiguous lands. Its population was relatively homogeneous with its tribes, sedentary or nomadic, united by ties of blood and by dependence upon the same markets and ports that, dominated by the merchant aristocracy, were the cultural and political centers of the country. Morocco was commercially important in the western Mediterranean. It was, for example, the horse-breeding center for the Mediterranean world.[10] It was, at the same time, a terminal and a crossroads for the caravan traffic of western Africa. Its social and economic institutions were almost identical with those of Arabia; only in such a context can the rapid expansion of Islam into an area impregnated by Christianity for four centuries be understood.

The Islamic religion is simple, tolerant, and profoundly egalitarian. Moslems believe that there is only one God, and that Mohammed is his prophet. They believe in a last judgment, and in a divinely inspired book, the Koran, which provides guidance not only in dogma and ritual, but also in the organization of the community, family, and property, for Mohammed was not only a religious reformer but also a legislator and chief of state. The ritualistic demands are few: profession of faith, prayer five times each day, the *zakat*, a mandatory tax on the Moslem's property (2.5% annually), and, once in a lifetime, a pilgrimage to Mecca for those who can afford it. There is no clergy. Prayers are individual acts, offered wherever the believer may happen to be, but, in practice, the faithful assemble at the mosque and are led in prayer by an imam, a pious Moslem, well instructed in the Koran.

Historically, the whole Moslem community was to have been directed by a caliph who, as prince of the believers, would exercise political authority and, as supreme imam, would provide spiritual leadership. After the death of the Prophet, his followers divided over interpretations of the Koran, and these differences were gradually institutionalized in two different rites: the Shiite and the Sunnite. The latter is divided into four schools of thought: the Hanafite, the Hanbalite, the Shafeite, and the Malekite. Morocco observes the Malekite, the most nationalistic of the four. Although there are other distinctions important to theologians, the political significance lies in the fact that a hereditary king exercises both temporal and

[10] The Greek geographer, Strabo, in the first century A.D., estimated the yearly colt crop in the area to the south and west of Carthage at 100,000— at a time when horses were virtually unknown in Arabia. The question of commerce in horses is examined in Leon B. Blair, "The Origin and Development of the Arabian Horse," *Southwestern Historical Quarterly* 68 (January, 1965): 303–316.

spiritual authority within specified territorial limits. The church and state are concurrent in Morocco, and commonly at Rabat on Friday—the Moslem Sabbath—the king receives foreign ambassadors in the morning, then goes to the mosque at noon to lead the nation in prayer.

The Moroccans—or Berbers—accepted the Islamic religion because it fitted neatly with their existing social and political institutions, and because the acceptance offered substantial practical advantages. As a conquered people, subject to the Arabs, they would not have been exploited, at least not in principle. They would have retained their own institutions, and would have been exempt from military service. They would have paid a reasonable tax.[11] Such were the terms accepted by those Jews who rejected Islam. The majority of the people of North Africa, however, did not desire to escape military service or the booty associated with it. In A.D. 711, less than seventy-five years after the death of the Prophet, the Berber cavalry was the dominant element in the Arab armies that conquered Spain. With the Islamic religion, Moroccans accepted the Arabic language, which gave them access to the Koran.[12]

The Berbers of North Africa were willing to accept the dogma of the Islamic religion, and the Arabic language as a necessary attribute, but rejected the centralized political authority associated with it. In this paradox lies the essence of the "Berber question" about which so much has been written in the last half century. Introspective and fatalistic, the Berbers interpreted their religion pragmatically. The Arab seeking a wife asked if she was of a good family; the Berber, if she was rich. The Arab plagued with locust besieged the central authority for help; the Berber accepted such disasters as the will of God. The Arab subjected himself to the appointed judge, the *cadi*, in civil matters; the Berber rejected the authority of the *cadi* in favor of an elected assembly that would rule, not necessarily according to the Koran, but certainly in accordance with local custom. To say no unique Berber people exists does not deny the existence of a Berber tradition or mentality, but the "Berber question" in recent Moroccan history is best summed

---

[11] See Syedah Fatima Sadeque, *Baybars I of Egypt*, for a description of the fiscal system imposed by the Arabs on conquered peoples.

[12] To the author's knowledge, no religious term has been translated into the Schleuh Berber dialect, and probably to neither of the other two.

up by Mehdi Ben Barka, president of the Moroccan Consultive Assembly in 1958, as "only a relic of the cultural policies of the Protectorate. . . . a product of the school of notables. The Berber is simply someone who has not gone to school."[13]

The Arab-Berber dualism, then, may be described accurately as an urban-rural antagonism. It existed before the protectorate was established, and it produced a revolution in the Rif Mountains in December, 1959, almost four years after the protectorate was dismantled. In the cities and the easily accessible plains of western Morocco, the Arabs were quickly absorbed, but the culture became fundamentally Arabic, commercial, and monetized. In the less accessible regions the people remained illiterate and their culture reflected nomadic or seminomadic traits within a barter economy. These same divisions are also popularly described as the *maghzen*, or "submitted" (to the king's tax collectors) territory, and the *bled es-siba*, or rural areas whose people object to paying taxes and obeying a centralized government. The protectorate regime merely preserved and used the existing antagonisms to divide and rule Morocco.

If the Arab-Berber schism existed in North Africa, at least the people were united in their opposition to their French masters, the *colons*, and the philosophy they represented. Francophiles, enchanted with Paris, stimulated by Montesquieu, Rousseau, and Voltaire, stirred by Emile Zola and Albert Camus, accepted with difficulty the fact of a substantial difference between the metropolitan French and the colonial French. But there always has been a substantial difference. Jules Ferry in 1892, and Albert Camus in 1958, condemned it. Ferry wrote: "It is hard to make the European *colon* understand that other rights besides his own exist in an Arab country, and that the native is not a race to be enslaved and indentured at his whim."[14] Ferry was pleading for educational opportunity for the conquered people of Algeria, the lack of which the *colons* justified by insisting the Arabs were incapable of improvement or education. A half century later, Camus ticked off town after town with ten or fifteen thousand inhabitants where, if any school was

[13] Jean and Simone Lacouture, *Le Maroc à l'épreuve*, p. 83. Chapter 4, "Comment Peut-On Etre Berbère?" pp. 74-79, is an excellent discussion of the whole question.

[14] Quoted in Charles-André Julien, *L'Afrique du Nord en marche*, p. 20.

provided, it was at best a simple one- or two-room structure.[15] In North Africa, Liberty, Equality, and Fraternity were empty words, at least between the French and *les ratons* (little rats), as "indigènes" were called.

Although internal peace had something of an evanescent quality, Morocco had been able to maintain a precarious independence for over a thousand years when the French protectorate was imposed in 1912. It had a rich culture and durable political institutions. Although its economy was not geared to that of Europe, it served its purpose in the rural, decentralized, relatively democratic society that existed in Morocco. Its resources, however, excited the cupidity of Europe. France had cast covetous looks upon Algeria's western neighbor for at least two decades before the world diplomatic situation favored the final grab. Great Britain had to be compensated in Egypt, Italy mollified with a free hand in Tripoli, Germany fended off with concessions in the Cameroons, Spain promised a slice of the booty, and world opinion placated with the promise of a neutralized Tangier guarding the Strait of Gibraltar. Finally, a justification for French seizure had to be found. To important French financial interests, notably of Algeria and Marseilles, the justification already existed—Algeria. Eugene Etienne, deputy from Oran and vice-president of the Chamber of Deputies, argued in 1898 for the "tunisification" of Morocco—penetration, then seizure.[16] The military penetration began in 1900, after the death of Ba Ahmed, grand vizir (prime minister) to Sultan Moulay Hassan until his death in 1894, and then to his son and heir, Abdel Aziz. French troops occupied the Moroccan oases of Gourara and Touat under the pretext of pursuing "desert corsairs." In 1903, Colonel Lyautey enlarged the French "zone of security"—at Moroccan expense.

The economic penetration began in 1903. When his treasury lay emptied by personal extravagances and by laudable but ill-timed fiscal reforms, the young sultan contracted a 22.5 million franc loan at 6 percent interest, subscribed in equal parts by French, English, and Spanish banks. In 1904, he secured a second loan of 62.5 million francs at 5 percent from a consortium of French banks, most of which had participated in the earlier loan. In both, the

[15] Albert Camus, *Actuelles III: Chronique Algerienne, 1939–1958*, p. 60.
[16] Quoted in Ayache, *Le Maroc*, pp. 60–61.

banks retained better than 25 percent of the principal as commission so that Abdel Aziz received a total of only 61.5 million francs from the two. The second was used to pay off the first loan and other pressing debts. The sultan was obliged to pledge 60 percent of his customs revenues toward its repayment and to agree to the creation of a state bank controlled by the consortium. By July, 1904, a French organization had been created for control of the Moroccan ports, and two French cruisers were standing by in Moroccan waters "to protect French interests." On December 10, Theophile Delcassé, the French foreign minister, defined for the Chamber of Deputies a Moroccan policy practically identical with that of the protectorate eventually imposed in 1912. The implementation of that policy, in the face of conflicting European colonial rivalries, preoccupied France for the next eight years. The Algeciras Conference, the "Agadir Incident," and finally the Treaty of Fez became landmarks in the history of diplomacy.[17]

The stated purpose of the various international and bilateral accords concerning Morocco in the early twentieth century was the preservation of its independence and territorial integrity. In agreements with Great Britain on April 6, 1904, France promised not to change the form of government in Morocco. Spain, in a treaty with France on October 3, 1904, affirmed attachment to the integrity of the Sheriffian Empire under the sovereignty of the sultan. Both accords, however, contained secret clauses that envisaged the division and annexation of Morocco. The Act of Algeciras in 1906, enunciated "the triple principle of the sovereignty of the sultan, the integrity of his territories, and equality of economic opportunity for all nations." The imposition of the Treaty of Fez by France upon Morocco brought into operation the secret clauses of the French-Spanish treaty, and on November 12, 1912, the country was divided into a French zone and a Spanish zone. The two countries, having agreed upon a special status for Tangier, arranged with Great Britain at a convention in Paris in 1923 for the International Zone of Tangier.

The Franco-Spanish penetration was never accepted in Morocco, nor, for that matter, in much of the rest of the world. In a phrase presaging the Moroccan position on the United States air bases in

---

[17] Ibid. See Chapter 6, "La fin de l'indépendance," pp. 57–58.

the late 1950's, Moulay Hafid, soon to be sultan, said in 1906 of the Act of Algeciras, "What do I know of it? We were not even consulted. . . ."[18] But Moroccan resistance was in vain. Each act brought greater reprisals. The killing of a French doctor in a riot in Marrakech in March, 1907, resulted in the military occupation of Oujda, three hundred miles to the north, and the riots that broke out in the summer as French engineers started developing the Casablanca port resulted in French occupation of the entire region. Alarmed by the growing unrest he had unleashed, Sultan Abdel Aziz abdicated.

His successor, Moulay Hafid, fared little better. In 1910, he had to contract a third loan to pay for his brother's debts, the port installations, and the indemnity demanded by France for the French victims of their own bombardment of Casablanca, August 5, 1909. He called upon French forces to suppress protest riots in the vicinity of Fez—and discovered too late the price, the Treaty of Fez, which he signed March 30, 1912. His actions produced a truly nationalist revolution against him, the imam, who had sold a part of Dar El Islam to the Christians.[19] The revolt that broke out on April 17, with a mutiny in the Moroccan army was soon suppressed, but it forced the abdication of Moulay Hafid in favor of his younger brother, Moulay Youssef.

The French actions were hardly more popular outside of Morocco than within. Twice German opposition to them led Europe to the brink of war, in 1906 and again in 1911. In France, Jean Jaures, head of the Socialist party, denounced the French penetration in the press, in the National Assembly, and in such international conventions as the Congress of Stuttgart, September, 1907, declaring the actions costly, brutal, and unnecessary.[20] In Spain the mobilization of reservists on July 10, 1909, for intervention in northern Morocco provoked riots almost revolutionary in nature. Labor unions protested the Treaty of Fez with general strikes in

[18] André P. G. A. Tardieu, *La conférence d'Algéciras; Histoire diplomatique de la crise marocaine (15 janvier–7 avril, 1906)*, p. 551.

[19] Fritz Weisgerber, *Au seuil du Maroc moderne*, p. 272. Dr. Weisgerber's study of the Moroccan resistance to French penetration is the most complete yet made.

[20] See Ayache, *Le Maroc*, pp. 57–58, for an account of international opposition to French actions in Morocco.

Rome, Leghorn, and Buenos Aires. In France, 100,000 Parisians marched from Place d'Anvers to Place de la Concorde.[21] The United States refused to recognize the new order created by the treaty.

In the acquisition of its colonial empire, France had used various formulas to describe its new territories: possessions, colonies, protectorates, and, later, mandates. In both Tunisia and Morocco, the protectorate formula was used. In fact, the Treaty of Bardo (1881) and the Convention of Marsa (1883), which established the French protectorate in Tunisia, served as the pattern for the Treaty of Fez. The protectorate formula, according to General Lyautey, the first French resident-general, was the only one with a chance to succeed in Morocco. It left the people with the illusion of independence, he said, but was supple enough to permit maximum economic development—"the primary objective of any colonial establishment." Control, rather than direct administration, achieved that objective and was less expensive.[22]

The Treaty of Fez authorized France to institute in Morocco such judicial, educational, economic, financial, military, and administrative reforms as it deemed useful; to occupy such territory as it deemed necessary for the maintenance of order and the security of commercial transactions; to exercise all police powers on Moroccan territories or territorial waters; to provide for Morocco's defense; and to represent it in foreign affairs. The previous investments of the French banks were guaranteed, and the sultan was forbidden to contract any future loan for public or private use, either directly or indirectly, or to grant any concession without authorization from the French government. The government of France obligated itself variously to maintain the respect and traditional prestige of the sultan, to protect the exercise of the Moslem religion and religious institutions, and, in the same article, provided for the alienation of the northern third of the nation. France was to be represented in Morocco by a resident-general who, uncontrolled by the French Assembly or government, would exercise all of the powers granted France by the treaty and would be the only

[21] M. Toudelas, "L'Espagne au Maroc," *Cahiers Internationaux: Revue internationale du monde du travail* (Paris), no. 71 (December, 1955).

[22] Jean Dresch, "Lyautey," *Les Techniciens de la colonisation, XIX–XX siècles*, pp. 133–156, quotes Lyautey's report of November 18, 1920, and of June 16, 1915, on these points.

intermediary between the sultan and any foreign government, including that of France.[23] The sultan was stripped of the attributes of sovereignty—that is, the responsibility for internal government, for the conduct of foreign affairs, and for defense. He retained only negative powers. He could refuse his assent to laws proposed by the resident-general and thus prevent their operation, and he could refuse to invest appointees to their offices in the Moroccan government—powers that remained unused until the mid-century.

The first high commissioner and resident-general in French Morocco, Louis Hubert Gonzalve Lyautey, was fifty-eight years old when, on April 27, 1912, he was appointed to the post. He had spent most of his adult life in colonial administration and "pacification," first in Indo-China, next in Madagascar, and then in Algeria where, in 1903, along the ill-defined frontier, he began the military penetration of Morocco. His strategy was not conventional; there were no Isandlwanas, no Omdurmans, no Herreros campaigns. His was "the strategy of the creeping tendril,"[24] interposing French forces and influence between centers of resistance. He avoided open conflict when possible. He sought submission by paring away the support of potential opponents. He was never able to bring all of the French zone under control, but he left few lasting scars associated with his name on the Moroccan consciousness. And he was able, before his resignation in 1925, to bring under French control all of the useful parts of the country—the plains and the regions connecting the principal cities. For the most part, more conciliatory than some of his subordinates, Lyautey was content to isolate the desert and mountain tribes and wear them down cheaply and gradually.[25]

[23] The text of the treaty is found in France, *Journal Officiel*, July 27, 1912, and in Bernard, *Le Conflit Franco-Marocain*. III, annex 1.

[24] Quoted in Maurice Beaumont, *L'Essor industriel et l'imperialisme colonial, 1878–1904*, XVIII in *Peuples et Civilisations*, 358.

[25] The Ouled Haha tribe, to the south of Casablanca and east of Mogador, was pushed into resistance by the French insistence on flying the French flag above the Moroccan. It took four years to subdue the sling-shot–armed Ouled Haha. According to Mohammed Ben Barka, who related to the author at Kenitra, Morocco, May 9, 1967, the story of his tribe's resistance, the slingshot was an effective weapon in the broken, brushy Ouled Haha country. To emphasize, Ben Barka, now sixty-seven years old, stepped out into the yard, picked up a rock the size of a teacup, whirled it about his head a couple of times, and

Politically as well as militarily, Lyautey's policy was "divide and rule." Aristocratic and royalist himself, he supported the sultan publicly and deferred to him socially, but he sought to institutionalize the political and economic opposition to the sultan's government on racial lines, Berber against Arab. As the price for Berber cooperation, he abandoned the less useful parts of Morocco, the mountains and the deserts, to the grand caids, the most famous of whom was Thami el Glaoui. The authority of the grand caids was virtually absolute; they paid only nominal homage to the sultan. In a further attempt to wean the Berber-speaking tribes away from the authority of the sultan, Lyautey promulgated in 1914 the first Berber *dahir* that authorized a village council to act in local civil affairs rather than the *cadi*, or Koranic judge.

Apologists for French policy in Morocco deny the charge that their "civilizing" mission envisaged the division of the people on racial lines; the Moroccan people were already divided, they insist. If true, the protectorate officials did little to fuse the disparate peoples into a single nationality, and nowhere is the failure more obvious than in educational policies, which, Lyautey felt, had to "take into account the social classes so each one kept its place." There were to be schools for all classes. Instruction was to be of practical nature (preapprentisage), and "like all Moroccan instruction, given almost exclusively in French."[26] Access to education and the subject matter had to be strictly controlled by the state, for, Lyautey thought, "people have a right to liberty only after they have earned it, and to choose freely the education one desires constitutes precisely the most delicate of liberties, reserved to the most advanced peoples. To give the Moroccans access to generalized education in lycees and universities will be the work of time."[27]

Educational policies during the protectorate underwent many convolutions, but one aspect, the restricted access, never varied. On the eve of World War II, about 2 percent of the Moslem Moroccan

---

knocked a dent three-quarters of an inch deep in a eucalyptus tree some fifty yards away.

[26] Louis Lyautey, *Paroles d'action: Madagascar, Sud-Oranais, Oran, Maroc (1900–1926)*, p. 462.

[27] Eugène Guenier, *Maroc*, p. 16.

children of school age were in school.[28] As an indication of the result of the restricted access, in 1959 there were only eighty doctors of Moroccan nationality in a nation of ten million people.[29] The denial of educational opportunity was a persistent grievance of the Moroccan people and a proximate cause of the eventual revolution.

Lyautey recognized the desirability of associating a Moroccan elite with the protectorate regime, and, to that end, he created primary schools in the principal towns for the children of the "notables," and a high school at Fez where students who had completed the primary cycle might receive a mixed French and Arab-Islamic education. For the best of those graduated at Fez, he organized a special section of the Institute des Hautes Etudes Marocaines at Rabat, thus providing university-level education. But for whatever the reason—fear, hostility, or caution—few Moroccan students were ever admitted to the institute, and the Moroccan section was abolished by Lyautey's successor, Theodore Steeg.[30] The primary function of the institute remained the preparation of French candidates for positions in the Moroccan administration and, toward the end of the protectorate, for the justification of French colonial policy in Morocco.

The Treaty of Fez obligated the French resident-general to safeguard the respect and traditional prestige of the sultan, but from the beginning the policy of the grand caids, the derogation of the authority of the *cadi* inherent in the Berber *dahir*, and, finally, the isolation of the Berber-speaking tribes contravened the obligation. For the latter, Lyautey created Franco-Berber schools: "French in instruction and life, Berber in recruitment and surroundings; French instructors, Berber students. Consequently, no foreign intermediaries." In such schools, "all teaching of Arabic, any intervention by Moslem teachers, any Islamic manifestation was rigorously put down."[31] At the Franco-Berber College at Azrou in the 1930's,

---

[28] Ayache, *Le Maroc*, pp. 312–324, gives an excellent statistical analysis of the educational policies of the protectorate.

[29] Youssef Ben Abbes, *Conférence Nationale de la Santé*, p. 16.

[30] Le Tourneau, *L'Afrique du Nord Musulmane*, p. 180 n.

[31] Paul Marty, "La politique berbère du protectorat," *Bulletin du Comité de l'Afrique française*, July, 1925, quoted in Ayache, *Le Maroc*, p. 316.

students were recruited only from the groups speaking the Tachel-hit, or Schleuh, dialect (one of the three Berber dialects). They wore only native robes and were instructed in French with only ninety minutes per week of instruction in Arabic. A student who wrote his name Ahmed ben Lahcen was reprimanded for using Arab terminology instead of the proper Berber form, Ahmed ou Lahcen.[32] In attempting to arrest the arabicization of Morocco and channel it toward French culture, the College of Azrou produced administrators with a good knowledge of French and Berber, but not of Arabic. Residency officials thus fanned the flames of Moroccan nationalism.

By the end of 1925, Marshal Lyautey's star had set in Morocco. After nine years' experience in Algeria, Le Patron, as he liked to be called, deemed French policy something less than an unqualified success, and he had no desire to see the pattern repeated in Morocco. He opposed an immigration policy that would attract low-class, indigent settlers. He opposed direct administration by French officials, preferring instead a few key officials who shared his devotion. He found such administrators in his civil controllers and officers of the Service des Affaires Indigenes. In developing the ports, railroads, roads, mines, and cities, he destroyed nothing and modernized little; instead, he built anew alongside the old. His policies were self-defeating. He built a magnificent infrastructure in Morocco—capital flowed in and industry multiplied. The coastal cities expanded explosively. But the social development of the Moroccan people did not keep pace, and the gulf widened between the traditional and the new. Moroccan resentment grew against the patronizing attitude of the French officials, and in France the newly elected Cartel des Gauches regarded their aristocratic, military pro-consul in Morocco with increasing reserve. When the Rif revolt threatened the French zone, Lyautey demanded substantial military reinforcements; his policy of restricted immigration reaped its bitter harvest. The reinforcements were furnished grudgingly, sparingly, and late. Lyautey was relieved of military command by Marshal Pétain. On September 27, 1925, Lyautey offered his resignation; it was accepted, and two days later he was replaced by Theodore Steeg, a civilian and ex-governor-general of Algeria.

[32] Lacouture, *Le Maroc à l'épreuve*, pp. 84–87.

Steeg, in reversing Lyautey's policies, set the stage for the revolution that culminated in independence for Morocco in 1956. Dissidence was nothing new in Morocco. The entire history of the protectorate was one military operation after another, but the sporadic violence originated in the rural areas as resistance to the modernizing innovation of the French. The resistance movement lacked national leadership and cohesion until Steeg's policies spawned it in a group of young, Arabic-speaking, well-educated, urban intellectuals. All were influenced by news, smuggled in via the British Post Office in Tangier, of the nationalist movements in Egypt, Turkey, and other parts of the Middle East and India. Near Rabat on the night of August 1–2, 1926, ten of these young nationalists met in the garden of Hadj Mohammed ben Mustapha Guessous and organized the resistance movement. The organization consisted of a cultural society, the Supporters of Truth, and a clandestine society, the Moroccan League. Ahmed Balafrej, who has figured large in Moroccan history for a quarter century, was elected president. He was eighteen years old, and a nephew of Guessous. The organization invited recruits to join the Supporters of Truth, and the new members, after they had proven themselves, were admitted to the clandestine Moroccan League—the political-action arm of the nationalist movement.[33] Henceforth the violence was to

[33] See Mahdi A. Bennouna, *Our Morocco: The True Story of a Just Cause*, pp. 33–43, for an account of the birth of the movement and the names of the organizers. Mr. Bennouna, now director-general of Maghreb Arabe Presse, the largest news agency in North Africa, in an interview with the author at Rabat, May 11, 1967, recounted the history of *Our Morocco*. It was printed clandestinely, sixteen pages at a time, on a hand press because the power drain of an electric press would betray the operation, with type stolen a few letters at a time from three different presses. Since a French type box uses fewer of the letters *w*, *c*, and *f*, than an English-language type box, several different type faces were used, giving the finished page a rather uncommon appearance. Of the two thousand copies printed, only about one thousand were circulated; the rest were seized in Paris, Rabat, and Tangier. The Moroccan police, while cleaning out a storeroom in 1960, found three hundred of the copies confiscated in Rabat and returned them to Mr. Bennouna, one copy of which he gave to the author.

The account of the birth of the Moroccan nationalist movement contained in Nevill Barbour, *Morocco*, pp. 161–163, is an obvious, unacknowledged quote of *Our Morocco*, pp. 33–34.

John P. Halstead, *Rebirth of a Nation: The Origins and Rise of Moroccan*

be centered in the cities, for the new leaders knew little of rural life and less of the nomadic mountain tribes. Their objective was the preservation of a Moroccan personality in a modern world.

The Moroccan League spread rapidly. Mohammed bel Hassan Ouezzani joined immediately. Hadj Abdeslam Bennouna organized a branch in Tetuan that was operating by August, 1926. By January, 1927, a branch was operating in Tangier and the movement had become nationwide. While the Moroccan League was organizing in Rabat, a second group led by Allal El Fassi and Mohammed Gazi started a clandestine movement known as the Students' Union, the objective of which was purification of the Islamic religion. The Students' Union directed its attacks principally against Sheik Abdelhay Kettani, who was both a religious and a political leader in Morocco. In April, 1927, the Students' Union and the Supporters of Truth learned of each other and the two movements coalesced. A national political party was thus born. In 1929, it was officially named the National Action Committee. Following the arrest of El Fassi, Balafrej, Abdelatif Sbihi, and other nationalist leaders, precipitated by their outcry in 1930 over the "second" Berber *dahir*, the National Action Committee was split into two parts, one for French Morocco and the other for Spanish Morocco. The Spanish zone element was in charge of propaganda activities abroad, especially in Egypt and the other Arab countries.[34]

Within a year, the flame of nationalism had spread beyond the borders of Morocco. In 1927, Ahmed Balafrej, then a student at the Sorbonne, and Mohammed El Fasi organized the Association of Moslem North African Students in Paris, with permanent headquarters at 16 Rue Rollins, in the Latin Quarter. Ostensibly organized to provide material aid to needy students from Morocco, Algeria, and Tunisia, it was in fact a nationalist organization and

---

Nationalism, 1912–1944, attributes the origin of Moroccan nationalism to the Salafiyya, a fundamentalist religious reform movement with Mohammed bel-Arabi al-Alaoui as its foremost proponent in Morocco (pp. 120–126) and minimizes the secular and student influence (p. 131). He differs with Bennouna concerning the original nationalist organizations (pp. 166–168); however, both Bennouna and Balafrej affirm the accuracy of *Our Morocco* and the present account based upon it (letter, Mehdi Bennouna to the author, dated Rabat, October 1, 1968).

[34] Bennouna, *Our Morocco*, p. 46.

for many years the only one espousing the concept of a Maghreb, or unitary North African State. The association held annual congresses beginning in August, 1931, at Tunis; in 1932 at Algiers; and in September, 1933, at Paris, because the scheduled congress at Fez was forbidden by the resident-general.[35] Balafrej, El Fassi, Taibi and Mohammed Benhima, Reda Ahmed Guedira, Moulay Ahmed Alaoui—the roster of the North African Students Association reads like a ministerial roll in the governments of an independent Morocco twenty-five years later.

Although the student intellectuals provided the inspiration and direction for the nationalist movement, the scouts provided the shock troops. Even though authorized by a residential decree in December, 1927, scouting did not get under way in Morocco until 1931. By 1933, Tangier, Rabat, and Casablanca had sections of scouts, and Marrakech and Fez were organizing sections. In December, the Rabat section recruited a new honorary president, five-year-old Prince Hassan; its members were therefore called the "Hassani scouts." They played a preponderant role in the riots in Rabat in 1936.[36]

The role of the scouts, viewed in the traditional concept of the American Boy Scouts, is incomprehensible. The Moroccan scouts were—and are—adults, a majority of them twenty to thirty years old. Their organization and training were paramilitary. Their activities were less concentrated on camp-outs and nature studies than on honor guards at the funerals of martyred nationalists, pickets at strikes, and militants in demonstrations, nationalist or otherwise.[37]

The young Moroccans regarded the inevitable consequence of the protectorate policies as a modern state, dominated politically and economically by the French, who would rely for popular support upon the Jewish and Berber elements of the population. In an increasingly apostatized nation, the Arab-Islamic influence would be submerged and Morocco would become simply an appendage of

[35] Robert Rezette, *Les Partis Politiques Marocains*, pp. 76–77.
[36] Ibid., p. 78.
[37] "Le Scoutisme musulman," Part 1 in Centre d'études de politique étrangère, *Entretiens sur l'évolution des pays de civilisation arabe*, points out that this concept of scouting is common to all Moslem countries, particularly those in which obligatory military service does not exist.

France in which the natives would be privileged to work for the
white man "and one day become really useful men."[38] The issue
upon which El Fassi and his colleagues launched their campaign
for reform—not yet independence—was the Berber *dahir* of 1930.
They found support in Moroccan intellectual circles, especially
from scions of the wealthier urban classes educated at Karaouine
University, who were being systematically squeezed out of their
traditional governmental posts by French personnel. They found
support among the artisans and shopkeepers. The artisans, a third
of the urban population, were suffering from the competition of
imported manufactured goods and from the loss of traditional markets in Senegal and Algeria. Many of them had abandoned handi-
crafts to become workers in the industries created in the mid-1920's
in Morocco, and they now found themselves out of work. The shopkeepers, squeezed on the one side by increased taxes and administrative regulations and on the other by the decreased purchasing
power of an impoverished clientele, were in desperate circumstances.

Their tactics were nonviolent. In the mosque on Friday they
would pray that God might not permit the division of the Moroccan nation.[39] Then they would parade through the streets. Such
demonstrations took place in Rabat, June 20, Salé, June 27, and
Fez, July 4, 1930. Following the Fez demonstration, the resident-
general authorized a delegation to visit Rabat to discuss their grievances. But the young leaders were excluded from it, and the
delegation, comprising three doctors of Koranic law and four merchants, thought it prudent not to discuss political matters. The
unrest continued. In attempting to stifle it, residency officials arrested several of the suspected leaders and had several of the dem-
onstrators publicly whipped. By autumn a superficial calm had

[38] The following quotation is from L. Sonolet and A. Peres, *Moussa et Gi-
Gli: Histoire de deux petits noirs*, chapter on "Rights and Duties," the book
found in the library of the Lycée Abdelmalek as Saadi, Kenitra, Morocco: "It
is an advantage for the native to work for the white man because the Whites
are better educated, more advanced in civilization than the natives, and because,
thanks to them, the natives will make more rapid progress, learn better and
more quickly, know more things, and one day become really useful men."

[39] The actual text of the prayer, according to Bennouna, *Our Morocco*, p. 45,
was: "Oh Merciful God! We request Your Mercy in whatever Destiny may
bring, Oh Merciful God! Do not separate us from our Berber brethren."

been restored in Morocco, but May 16, 1931, was observed as a day of national mourning, and the independence movement steadily gained strength thereafter. In denying overtures toward reform, the residency crystallized the discontent and transformed it into sentiment for independence.

To the French, the new order of complaints seemed insincere, picayune. The suppression of the Moroccan section of the Institut des Hautes Etudes Marocaines was more symbolic than damaging; very few students were involved. The new immigration policy was rational: Morocco was underpopulated; the new lands being opened were not claimed by anyone—they were communal tribal lands for the most part, and the tribes affected were not yet complaining. The new colonists, using modern agricultural methods, were infinitely more productive, and the Moroccans could only benefit from the example. The flood of French technical personnel was necessitated by the modernization of the Moroccan economy, and was not the advantage obvious? The Berber *dahir* of May 16, 1930, picked by the young nationalists as their cause célèbre, was only a codification and extension of Lyautey's Berber *dahir* of 1914. The first had removed the Berber-speaking Moroccans from the civil jurisdiction of the *cadi* and the second from the penal jurisdiction of the sultan. Neither the sultan nor his advisors had objected to either, perhaps because neither power had ever been effectively exercised among them before. The program of the Apostolic Vicar of Rabat to convert the "irreligious" Berbers to Christianity was not an action of the residency; religious freedom was guaranteed to all—by the Koran, too—but if it resulted in the pacification of the Berbers, was that not good?[40]

The appearance of a nationalist press tended both to internationalize the movement and to lend it cohesiveness at home. In Paris, in 1932 a group of Moroccan students in which Ahmed Balafrej was prominent launched *Maghreb*, a monthly review, under left-wing French auspices. Never authorized in Morocco, it was distributed

[40] Le Tourneau, *L'Afrique du Nord Musulmane*, p. 183, quotes Guiraud, a member of the residency juridical commission: "The Berbers can be conquered. The conquerors will be missionaries. Speak to them of Jesus; their legends are full of the name of the Savior." The evangelistical campaign had one notable success, Mohammed Ben Abdeljalil, of a prominent Arab family of Fez and the brother of the nationalist leader, Omar Ben Abdeljalil.

clandestinely. Polemical in tone and not particularly accurate in
its facts, the review did advance a doctrine that became fundamental in the Moroccan argument for independence—that the
Treaty of Fez was an international convention and therefore subject to the jurisdiction of the League of Nations.[41] In August, 1933,
the weekly *L'Action du Peuple* also made its appearance in Fez
with a French publisher, but strongly influenced by Mohammed
bel Hassan Ouezzani. Initially authorized by the residency, it supported the Moroccan nationalist position and increasingly attacked
government officials and policies. It was suspended on May 16,
1934, after attacking the decision to transfer the direction of Moroccan affairs from the Ministry of Foreign Affairs, which properly
had cognizance of relations with a sovereign, foreign state, to the
Ministry of Colonies. Despite the protests and explanations of El
Fassi and Ouezzani, the residency refused to renew the authorization. Meanwhile, two Arabic-language publications, *Es-Salaam*, a
monthly review, and *El Hayat*, a weekly newspaper, began publication in the Spanish zone (in December, 1933, and January,
1934), and were circulated surreptitiously in the French zone.
From 1938 to 1943, Abdelatif Sbihi published *La Voix Nationale*,
a French-language weekly newspaper, in Casablanca and Rabat,
adroitly sandwiching nationalist news into effusive praise of the
French protectorate.

In a country with 90 percent illiteracy, the press was less important in spreading nationalist sentiment than the "grapevine."
El Fassi was an especially good organizer and propagandist. He
organized reunions on appropriate occasions, such as the anniversary of the Berber *dahir*, and formed "Koranic schools," so designated to avoid the interdiction of private schools, to spread the
doctrine of nationalism.[42] As an example of his tactics, he launched
an effective campaign against the French tobacco monopoly. Tobacco, the schools taught, was forbidden by the Koran. Whether
to create another focus for nationalist pride or to enlist the support
of the young sultan—the effect was the same—El Fassi and his

41 Reliance on collective action through the United Nations is characteristic
of the Moroccan foreign policy to this date.

42 Le Tourneau, *L'Afrique du Nord Musulmane*, p. 193, indicates that ten
such schools were organized in Fez in 1933–1934 for about five hundred students
and for about eighty adults in an auxiliary course.

colleagues, in November, 1933, launched the idea of an annual Fête du Trône to commemorate the accession of Sidi Mohammed. When he appeared in public, they saluted him with the acclamation "king," rather than the traditional "sultan," and they hailed his young son, Hassan, as the crown prince, a title never before used in Morocco. Thus the nationalists heralded their cause before the non-Arabic-speaking world. When speaking Arabic, the Moroccans seldom used any title other than *malek* for their ruler. The connotation of hereditary authority was more closely akin to the authority acquired by conquest or coup. Whether a legitimate distinction or not, the use of the new title became an audible measure of protest.

By 1934 the National Action Committee had substantial membership in Fez, Rabat, Port Lyautey, and the Spanish zone, but, significantly, not in Casablanca or in the rural areas still under control of the grand caids. The time had come, its leaders decided, to come into the open. On December 1, they simultaneously presented a 134-page document called a *Plan of Reforms* to the sultan, the resident-general, and the French premier, Pierre Laval. It was a clear challenge to the "racial, partial, obscurantist, anti-liberal colonizing, and assimilative"[43] policies of the protectorate. It did not ask for independence; but it did demand an end of direct French administration and participation of French nationals in the public life of the country, the application of a single code of law to all Moroccans, the access of all Moroccans to a modern education, an end to official French colonization in Morocco, and nationalization of the principal national resources and means of production. It was a document that perhaps lacked proportion, covering as it did both basic policy and such details as the design of the Moroccan flag and decorations. Its accuracy was challenged, but it became a plan of action for the young nationalists.

The *Plan of Reforms* was summarily dismissed by French officials, both in Morocco and in Paris. Its promoters hoped for a more sympathetic hearing from Leon Blum's Popular Front government, elected in May, 1936, but were disappointed. Marcel Peyrouton,

[43] *Plan de Réformes Marocaines, élaboré et présenté à S. M. le Sultan, au Gouvernement de la République française et à la Résidence Générale au Maroc par le Comité d'Action Marocaine* (no place of publication or name of editor, 1935).

bête noir of the nationalists, was removed as resident-general, only to be replaced by General Noguès, a member of the Lucien Saint cabinet when the Berber *dahir* was promulgated in 1930. On October 19, 1936, when Ouezzani and Omar Ben Abdeljalil called on the Socialist undersecretary of state for foreign affairs, Pierre Viénot, to request implementation of the *Plan of Reforms*, they were politely shown the door.[44] In March, 1937, the Blum government, concerned primarily with domestic problems in France, announced "the pause," an action that the resident-general in Morocco signaled with a decree abolishing the Moroccan National Action Committee.

Meanwhile, the nationalist movement seemed to be breaking apart, not on doctrine, but on personalities and tactics. In the Spanish zone, the National Reform party, led by Abdelkhalak Torres, had worked in close liaison with the Moroccan Action Committee in the French zone until after the outbreak of the Spanish civil war. The nationalists first offered their support to the republicans; their price was independence for the Rif. Their demand refused, Torres came to agreement with Franco, and the National Reform party took a fascist bent. The republicans countered by supporting Mohammed Mekki Naciri, a refugee from the French zone, who founded the Moroccan United party in Tetuan in early 1937. The rivalry was personal; both were committed to independence. In the French zone, the movement split similarly between the followers of Allal El Fassi and Ouezzani. El Fassi, from an ancient and illustrious family, was educated in the traditional forms at Karaouine University at Fez. He favored an absolute monarchy, a theocracy guided by a reformed and enlightened Islamic code. He would depend upon a mass following to achieve the desired reforms, if not by persuasion, then by violence. Ouezzani, regarded by El Fassi as an upstart and from a less illustrious family, was also a

[44] Le Tourneau, *L'Afrique du Nord Musulmane*, pp. 193–195, points out that, far from being obscurantist, French influence and example were responsible for the Moroccan demand for modernization and that, as for access to higher education, thirty-three Moroccan students were in school in France in November, 1933—nine from Fez, fourteen from Rabat, five from Meknes, two from Marrakech (sons of Thami el Glaoui), and one each from Salé, Casablanca, and Tangier.

descendent of the Prophet, and he was wealthy. He had received a modern education in France and envisaged a form of parliamentary democracy that he thought could be realized by diplomacy brought about by a reasoned presentation of the Moroccan position in the press in order to influence French and world opinion in Morocco's favor. Thus, by 1937, the nationalist movement appeared to be fragmented in four parts.

The breakup was more apparent than real. All four factions recruited vigorously. El Fassi's group had more success than the others, for he had given his group an administrative structure—an annual national congress, a council that met quarterly, and a permanent executive committee. In February, 1937, probably as a demonstration of strength, his group enforced a Friday "blue law" in Fez; all shops remained closed for a "day of rest." In July, the El Fassi group emerged under a new party name as the National Party for the Realization of Reforms, and the Ouezzani group was known as the Popular Movement. The residency could cope with the mercurial situation only with force when the first real test of strength came in September. The explosive issue was the diversion of the Bou Ferkane River from the native quarter of Meknes in order to irrigate surrounding farmland. The stream had been used for washing clothing, and in some cases for domestic uses, but, more important, most of the mosques used the water to fill their basins so that the faithful might perform the prescribed ablutions before prayer. Now the basins remained empty. The riots that broke out in Meknes on September 1 spread to Port Lyautey, Salé, Rabat, Casablanca, Khemisset, Marrakech, the Middle Atlas, and Oujda by the end of October. They were put down by the police, gendarmerie, and army; they left more than thirty Moroccans dead and more than one hundred wounded. Allal El Fassi was arrested, deported to Gabon, and not permitted to return until 1946; Omar Ben Abdeljalil, Ahmed Mekour, Mohammed Lyzadi, Ouezzani, and other leaders were placed under surveillance in various military posts in the Moroccan Sahara. A troubled calm returned to Morocco.

The detente lasted until after the defeat of France in June, 1940, and the installation of the Vichy regime, events that seemed to stupify and sadden the Moroccan people. On September 3, 1939, the sultan had publicly declared his support of France "without reserve, bargaining, or recoil before any sacrifice."[45] After France's defeat, the Moroccans wondered what was to become of them. They soon found out. While British propaganda eulogized the Atlantic Charter and the liberalism of the British colonial regime, Vichy policies became more restrictive, the taxes increased, and the exceptionally good harvests of 1941–1942 were requisitioned to feed European populations. To add insult to injury, different rationing standards were applied to the European and the Moroccan populations. When the Americans landed on the Moroccan shores, November 8, 1942, the discontent was latent, but present—a fact little understood by the Americans. What they did right insofar as the North African peoples were concerned, they seemed to have done more by instinct than by design.

[45] Le Tourneau, *L'Afrique du Nord Musulmane*, p. 204.

2. "Allo, Maroc, Ici les Americains"

NORTH AFRICA REPRESENTS an ambiguous chapter in American foreign affairs, an irreconcilable antipathy between idealism and practical politics, between long-range vision and the exigencies of the
moment. The United States never recognized the French protectorate in Morocco, yet from its first involvement in North Africa in
1940, it gave tacit recognition and claimed the protection of its authority for the next quarter century. The crisis came in 1942, and
of all the Allied policy makers, only President Franklin D. Roosevelt seems to have looked beyond the end of the war to an inevitable
change in the status of the British and French colonies. Peace in the
future, he told Winston Churchill at the Atlantic Conference in
August, 1941, depended on fulfilling colonial aspirations, and Article III of the Atlantic Charter pledged respect for the right of all
people to choose their form of government and to exercise the sovereign rights of which they had been deprived. Churchill's assent
was grudging at the time,[1] and in 1945, his famous statement, "I did

[1] Elliott Roosevelt, *As He Saw It*, pp. 36–43.

not become Prime Minister to preside at the liquidation of the British Empire," seems to have more accurately expressed his real feelings. As for the French, a cardinal objective of their foreign policy from the signing of the armistice with Germany in 1940 almost to the present day has been the preservation of the French imperial influence.[2] Roosevelt's underlings were persuaded to play the French game, and the policies that they initiated still inhibit relations between the United States and the nations of North Africa.

The French debacle in the summer of 1940 was more than a military defeat. It was a national humiliation compounded of ineptness, confusion, and a lack of the will to fight. The army, the pride of France, capitulated with hardly a fight. Unbloodied divisions sat in the Maginot Line, unused fighter planes at Tours, and unused antitank guns in depots throughout France. General Erwin Rommel's Seventh Panzer Division lost only thirty-five men killed and fifty-nine wounded while capturing more than ten thousand prisoners and vast quantities of equipment. General Maxime Weygand, the seventy-three–year–old commander of the French army, called for an armistice and labeled as "dishonorable" Premier Reynaud's proposal to transfer the government to North Africa and continue the war. A dispirited France, its ego deeply scarred, turned to eighty-four–year–old Marshal Pétain for its salvation, and on June 21, 1940, an armistice with Germany was signed.

The authoritarian Pétain government, sternly repressive in domestic matters, pursued an equivocal foreign policy in which the flight of the government to North Africa or adherence to De Gaulle's Free French government-in-exile were always possibilities. Pétain and most of his colleagues considered a German victory over Great Britain inevitable. Vice-Premier Pierre Laval, frankly pro-German, favored open collaboration with Germany, even as an ally against Britain.[3] General Weygand and Admiral Darlan, the

---

[2] See, for the 1940 attitude, United States State Department, *Documents on German Foreign Policy, 1918–1945*, series D, vol. X, doc. no. 163; vol. II, doc. nos. 20, 149, 566; vol. XII, doc. no. 490.

[3] The Italians, particularly, were concerned lest the French "slip over to the Italian-German side," and thus obtain more favorable peace terms with respect to North and West Africa. Axis strategy envisaged Italian annexation of Tunisia and part of Algeria, while Spain was to get the rest of Algeria and French

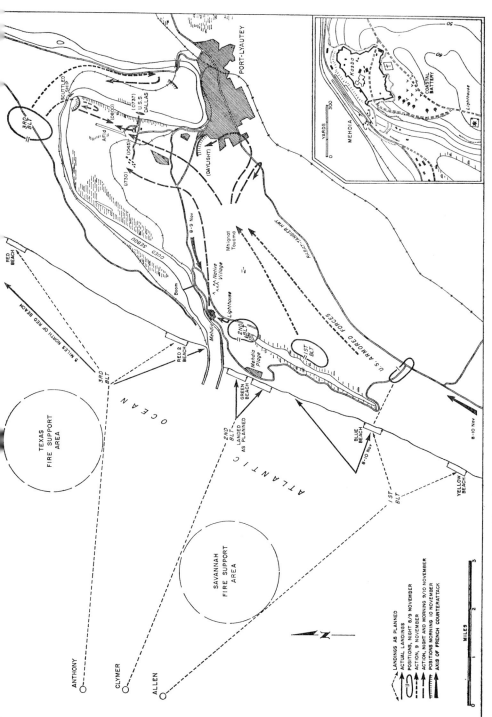

The Capture of Port Lyautey, November 8–10, 1942

other Vichy personalities important to the future of North Africa, were anti-German, but also anti-British. Pétain himself kept avenues open in all directions; he collaborated to the degree he deemed necessary with the Germans, but he repeatedly assured Ambassador William D. Leahy, Counselor of the Embassy Robert Murphy, and even Admiral Darlan of his friendship toward the United States.[4]

In the uneasy game of power politics, Marshal Pétain held one trump card—the French fleet—and he used it to good advantage. Hitler and Mussolini both doubted the ability of the Axis forces to capture it, and they were prepared to make substantial concessions to keep it from escaping and perhaps falling into British hands.[5] General Huntziger, head of the French Armistice Commission, argued to the Germans that only the army had been defeated, that the fleet and air force were still intact, and that France would continue the war rather than accept dishonorable terms involving concessions to the Italians.[6] His arguments were effective. On June 22, Mussolini notified Hitler that he would forego occupation of Corsica, Tunisia, and Djibouti, "as we had intended at Munich" on June 18, in order to make the armistice terms more palatable to the French government and thus prevent its flight to Algiers.[7]

The potential threat of the French fleet concerned not only Rome, Berlin, and London, but Washington as well, and it caused the United States to adopt the highly unpopular "Vichy Policy," the consequences of which are still being felt. In the fall of 1940, President Roosevelt became alarmed lest the fleet fall under German control, and he wrote to Admiral William D. Leahy, then governor of Puerto Rico, asking him to accept the post of ambassador to France. Roosevelt thought that Leahy's military background might enable him to gain Marshal Pétain's confidence and possibly influence the higher officers of the French navy who were openly

Morocco. See Hitler-Ciano conversation, Berlin, July 8, 1940, in *Documents on German Foreign Policy*, vol. X, doc. no. 129.

[4] William D. Leahy, *I Was There*, pp. 24, 485; Robert D. Murphy, *Diplomat among Warriors*, p. 58.

[5] *Documents on German Foreign Policy*, vol. IX, doc. no. 479.

[6] Ibid., doc. no. 522.

[7] Ibid., doc. no. 525. The apparent soft policy toward France was for propaganda purposes, Hitler said. At the peace treaty, which had to be delayed to avoid giving the British a pretext for occupying French Africa, France was to be treated as the "eternal enemy of Germany." See ibid., vol. X, doc. no. 129.

hostile to the British.[8] In his letter of instructions to Ambassador Leahy, dated December 20, he was more explicit as he revealed the other side of the coin—a willingness to help France maintain authority in its North African possessions.[9] The Vichy regime lasted only four years, and its influence was speedily erased in France after the Allied landings. But Admiral Leahy and Robert D. Murphy, architects of the "Vichy Policy," exerted tremendous influence on American foreign policy long after Marshal Pétain had disappeared from the international scene. Leahy became chief of staff to Presidents Roosevelt and Truman, and Murphy served ultimately as assistant secretary of state.

Robert D. Murphy became important to the North African policy of the United States, not from any special competence but from circumstances. A career foreign service officer since 1917, he was counselor of the U.S. embassy in Paris in the summer of 1940 and followed the French government to Vichy as chargé d'affaires. In the fall of 1940 he gained direct access to President Roosevelt when the latter dispatched him on an inspection tour of French North and West Africa with orders to report directly to him. Roosevelt used Murphy's report as the basis for his African policy.[10] At Vichy, Murphy won the respect and confidence of Ambassador Leahy, a circumstance that stood him in good stead during the near decade that Leahy served as chief of staff to the president. In September, 1942, Roosevelt appointed him to General Eisenhower's staff for Operation Torch, and the amicable relationship established during their year together in North Africa continued throughout their subsequent public careers. Murphy's ability to avoid the pitfalls inherent in such confused lines of responsibility is mute testimony to his skill as a diplomat.

Murphy shared with other United States policy makers a lack of understanding of the twenty million "natives" who lived in North Africa. During his ten years in the American embassy in Paris prior to the outbreak of World War II, Murphy confessed, he paid almost no attention to France's African empire.[11] President Roosevelt chose him for the 1940 inspection trip because of his

[8] Leahy, *I Was There*, p. 6.
[9] Ibid., appendix I, pp. 443–446.
[10] Murphy, *Diplomat among Warriors*, pp. 68, 70.
[11] Ibid., pp. 66, 70.

knowledge of the European political situation, and because he was a Catholic. Roosevelt said a Catholic might have more influence with Vichy personalities such as General Weygand.[12] In "boning-up" for his mission, Murphy found little help in State Department archives, and he gained most of his preliminary information from a congeries of foreign documents, many of them still untranslated. The remarkable aspect of Murphy's North African experience is not his lack of preliminary knowledge, but his lack of understanding twenty years later. He spent forty months in North Africa, recording his experiences in his autobiographical *Diplomat Among Warriors*, published in 1964. He mentions the names of only two of the "natives," Habib Bourgiba and Ferhat Abbas. The latter, he said, was a "moderate and reasonable man, and his organization made no difficulties for our military operations later when he might have hampered us seriously. I was disappointed after the war when Abbas . . . became involved in one of the longest and most unhappy wars in French history [the Algerian Revolution]."[13]

Measured by the limited objective set in the winter of 1940, the "Vichy Policy" was successful. The French fleet did not come under German control, and France maintained its authority and some military capability in its North African possessions. It was a precarious authority, subject to abnormal pressures that did not erupt for yet another decade. The Germans expected a nationalist revolution and a request for German protection in French Morocco in 1940.[14] In November, Laval expressed his concern for the ill effects that events in Europe were having upon the native population in

---

[12] Ibid., p. 68.

[13] Ibid., p. 123. Roosevelt's knowledge was little better. In a press conference following the Casablanca conference, he referred to the "Riffian Empire of Morocco," an apparent allusion to the Rif Mountains in Morocco, instead of the "Sheriffian Empire of Morocco," the proper title, and one which indicates that the ruling dynasty descended from the Prophet Mohammed. Roosevelt concluded that much ink had been spilled in the United States about Morocco by people who "don't know one blessed thing about it. You have to go there to understand it" (*The Tide Turns*, 1943 vol. in *The Public Papers and Addresses of Franklin D. Roosevelt*, ed. Samuel I. Rosenman, pp. 84–86). The Franklin D. Roosevelt Library, Hyde Park, letter dated April 27, 1967, to the author advised that the allusion to the Riffian Empire is "correct as printed."

[14] *Documents on German Foreign Policy*, vol. IX, doc. no. 397, June 7, 1940.

Morocco.[15] Admiral Leahy reported the natives "restless"[16] in 1941 because of food shortages and German propaganda.

The Italians, perhaps because of their own colonial position in North Africa, were also concerned. They generously allocated French troop strength to maintain internal order in the French North African colonies—an Italian responsibility as determined by the Armistice Commission. In the summer of 1940, the United States naval attaché found 125,000 combat-trained men on active service and 200,000 in reserve in Morocco and Algeria.[17] These forces became a primary objective of Allied strategy. With them, Leahy pointed out to Roosevelt in May, 1941, a small army equipped with modern weapons, including aircraft, could "hold North Africa, insure control of the Mediterranean Sea, and shorten the duration of the war by half. . . . Today, the vulnerable spot [in the German expansion plan] is North Africa," he declared.[18] His estimate was perhaps a bit optimistic.

The problems actually encountered in rearming French colonial troops for modern technical warfare in 1943 were inherent in the origin and experience of the troops. For example, 83,000 Moroccan troops comprising four regiments of *tirailleurs* (infantry) organized in twenty battalions and two regiments of *spahis* (cavalry) were in the French army at the time of the armistice. They served under French field-grade officers and were integrated into French divisions. Although 6 percent of the adult Moslem male population of Morocco volunteered for army service, 74.28 percent of those came from rural communities and tribes, while only 7.14 percent came from an industrial milieu. They were not technically adept. From the standpoint of hardihood and courage, however, Moroccans of the Atlas Mountains were second to none.[19]

"The French African policy of the United States Government," asserts Robert Murphy, referring to his conversations with President Roosevelt in the fall of 1940, "became the President's personal policy. He initiated it, kept it going, and resisted pressures against

[15] Ibid., vol. XI, doc. no. 343.
[16] Leahy, *I Was There*, p. 458.
[17] Murphy, *Diplomat among Warriors*, p. 67.
[18] Leahy, *I Was There*, appendix 19, pp. 458–459.
[19] *Revue de la France d'Outre-mer*, Numéro Spécial, *Maroc, Terre d'avenir*, 1948, p. 132.

it until 1942 when French North Africa became the first major battleground where Americans fought Germans."[20] The decision to launch Operation Torch was not in fact quite that simple or straightforward. The strategy was British. Operation Gymnast in 1940–1941 was a British plan to support General Weygand in North Africa with four divisions, if he would accept them—which he would not. On December 16, 1941, Winston Churchill proposed Operation Super-Gymnast, a joint British-American amphibious landing in North Africa. His memoirs detail the involved campaign to persuade the Americans to accept his peripheral strategic concept, closing the ring as he called it.[21]

President Roosevelt wanted an invasion of continental France in 1942, and the United States Joint Chiefs of Staff concurred. Hitler remained the number one enemy in the American view, and the appropriate strategy was the opening of the second front in Europe, thus bringing American troops in contact with the Germans at the earliest possible opportunity and taking the pressure off the Russians. Only when technical difficulties, shortages of landing craft and shipping, made the invasion of Europe in 1942 impractical did Roosevelt consent to the North African invasion— against the advice of his Joint Chiefs of Staff.

Both General Marshall and Admiral King opposed the Operation Torch concept, Marshall because he thought it would divert from and delay the invasion of continental Europe, and King because it would take urgently needed naval forces and shipping from the Pacific.[22] The "strong surge of feeling in the powerful second rank of the American staff" against the North African strategy that Churchill noted was perhaps explained by Presidential Chief of Staff Leahy as the fear "of some of our officers that Great Britain wanted to confine Allied military effort in Europe to the Mediterranean area in order that England might continue to exercise control thereof regardless of what the terms of peace might be."[23] Roosevelt opted for the British strategy as against the latent "Vichy

[20] Murphy, *Diplomat among Warriors*, p. 68.
[21] Winston S. Churchill, *The Hinge of Fate*, pp. 23–24.
[22] Ibid., "Decision for Torch," pp. 432–449, discusses the pro and con of the Torch strategy.
[23] Leahy, *I Was There*, p. 157.

Policy" when circumstances precluded the preferred American strategy.

An essential element of the French African policy of the United States government both before and after the landings was the preservation of French authority over the "native" population, although the justification shifted from political to military, from preservation of the greatest possible measure of independence for the Vichy regime in the face of mounting Axis pressure to security for the Allied lines of communication running through Morocco and Algeria. From the outbreak of the war until the French-Axis armistice in 1940, French Morocco had rallied to the support of France. After the armistice, the Moroccans became restless. They resented the repressive Vichy social and economic measures. Abdelatif Sbihi editorially denounced General Auguste Noguès' concentration camp for Jews at Bou-Denib and warned that non-Jewish Moroccans risked similar accommodations if General Noguès deemed it necessary.[24] Marshal Alphonse Juin interpreted the Moroccan disaffection in politico-military terms. He said the Moroccans were disillusioned by "the humiliating spectacle of the protector suddenly taking its turn at being protected."[25] The American plans were fraught with political significance.

The Murphy-Weygand Agreement prepared the way for American entry. During a hurried inspection trip to North Africa in the winter of 1940, Murphy and the Vichy high commissioner for North Africa, General Weygand, agreed that the interests of both their countries would be served by placating the local populations. The draft agreement was worked out in Algiers with Secretary-General Emmanuel Monick and Director of Economic Services Léon Maréchal representing Morocco. By its terms Vichy officials would be permitted to use French funds frozen in the United States to buy nonstrategic goods and ship them through the British blockade to North Africa. Distribution was to be supervised by a group of American control officers serving as vice-consuls, in order to see that nothing fell into the hands of the Axis.[26] Murphy cabled the

[24] *La Voix Nationale*, November 5, 1942.

[25] Alphonse Pierre Juin, *Mémoires*, II, 145.

[26] René Richard and Alain Serigny, *La bissectrice de la guerre: Alger, 8 Novembre 1942*, p. 42; Murphy, *Diplomat among Warriors*, p. 81.

draft agreement from Lisbon, January 17, 1941.[27] It was approved in the United States in February, ratified at Vichy on March 10, and remained in effect until the Allied landings in November, 1942. While in effect the economic aspects of the treaty were co-ordinated by Mr. Paul Guerin, son of the president of the Moroccan railways system. He worked out the details of the purchases with the State Department and obtained the "navicerts," authorizations to traverse the blockade, from the British Ministry of Economic Warfare representatives in Washington. In March the tanker *Frimaire* sailed from New York for Casablanca with a cargo of motor fuels, the first shipment under the agreement.[28]

Seven French ships were employed to transport the supplies. Three tankers, the *Frimaire*, the *Lorraine*, and the *Scheherezade*, each made one trip. They all carried low-grade motor fuels, an item so controversial that shipments were soon suspended. Four cargo ships, the *Ile d'Ouessant*, the *Ile de Noirmoutier*, the *Ile de Re*, and the *Aldebaran*, began operations in July, 1941. With simultaneous departures, two ships at a time shuttled from North African and United States ports—a compromise arrangement. The Germans had insisted that only French ships interned in the United States could be used, and the United States, reluctant to lose control of ships already in the bag, insisted that ships still available to Vichy be used. With the simultaneous departures, the status quo was maintained.[29] The ships brought North African products: cork, tartar, olive oil, and red squill,[30] and took back cargoes of cotton cloth, sugar, tea, agricultural machinery, and other goods. The last departure from the United States was in July, 1942, by the *Ile d'Ouessant* and *Ile de Noirmoutier*. The *Ile de Re* and the *Aldebaran* were in New Orleans when the Allied forces landed in North Africa and the Murphy-Weygand Agreement was terminated by events. Under the agreement, French Africa got

[27] Murphy, *Diplomat among Warriors*, p. 81.

[28] Henry Villard, "Action in North Africa," *American Foreign Service Journal* 19 (December, 1942): 637 ff. Mr. Villard was chief of the African Section, Department of State.

[29] Paul Auphan and Jacques Mordal, *The French Navy in World War II*, trans. A. C. J. Sabalot, p. 177. Paul Auphan was the French navy minister under the Vichy regime.

[30] Red squill is a rodenticide, made from a plant that grows profusely in Morocco.

40,000 gallons of liquid fuel, 1,800 tons of coal, 20,000 tons of sugar, some cotton goods, nails, binder twine, insecticide powders, and miscellaneous other items.[31]

The control officers, provided for in the agreement to supervise distribution of the supplies in North Africa, were recruited in the New York area in the spring of 1941. For the most part they were selected by the War and Navy Departments on the basis of their knowledge of France and the French language. They were divided into groups and assigned to the consulates at Casablanca, Algiers, and Tunis, with Ridgeway B. Knight and Leland L. Rounds serving independently at Oran.[32]

The French government limited the number of control officers serving in North Africa to a maximum of twelve at any one time. Even so, the difficulties inherent in the program reduced deliveries to the extent that it became difficult to justify the presence of any. Many Washington officials resented any traffic with Vichy, particularly after Laval returned to power in 1942, and they expressed their disapprobation in a particularly cogent fashion—a refusal to issue export licenses. Frequent changes in the Vichy regime were reflected in Washington by delays in shipment, "pending clarification." The Vichy officials, too, were under severe pressure from the Germans who insisted on the abrogation of the economic agreement and expulsion of the control officers. Finally, in August, 1942, Admiral Leahy intervened, and a White House directive started the supplies flowing once more,[33] too late for the Murphy-Weygand Agreement, but helpful in providing supplies for the civilian population through other channels after the invasion.

[31] Auphan and Mordal, *French Navy in World War II*, p. 117.

[32] Villard, "Action in North Africa," p. 637 ff. The control officers were Sidney L. Bartlett, Charles Denby Wilkes, W. Stafford Reid, John Crawford Know, Ridgeway Brewster Knight, John Ellington Utter, Leland L. Rounds, Donald Q. Coster, all of New York City; David W. King, Chester, Connecticut; Harry A. Woodruff, Bedford Village, N.Y.; John H. Boyd, Wesson, Mississippi; Franklin O. Canfield, Washington, D.C.; and Kenneth Pendar, Sharon, Connecticut. Mr. Bartlett, Mr. Wilkes, Mr. Canfield, and Mr. Coster resigned within the year and were replaced by Gordon H. Browne, Cambridge, Massachusetts; George R. Hull, Buffalo, N.Y.; and William Douglas Reed and Harry P. Blank, Jr., both of New York City. Mr. Paul Cuthbert was originally assigned to Dakar but was subsequently transferred to Casablanca.

[33] Ibid., p. 690.

By virtue of their diplomatic status, the control officers were able to travel freely about North Africa, and their activities were almost open intelligence gathering. They "established contact with patriotic Frenchmen and anti-Axis elements,"[34] apparently oblivious to the antithetical nature of the two criteria. When planning for Operation Torch began in the summer of 1942, the control officers provided much of the information. Vice-Consul John C. Knox from Algiers, Rounds from Oran, and Paul Cuthbert from Casablanca were called to London for conferences with General Eisenhower's staff. Murphy also attended, and both he and Cuthbert went on to Washington.[35] Ardently pro-Vichy and anti-De Gaulle,[36] they misjudged the temper of the "patriotic Frenchmen," who not only failed to rally to the Allied side, but actually fought against their liberators.

The weakness in Murphy's planning was inherent in his organization. For an essentially military coup, he put together a politico-civilian group that lacked both military experience and influence in the French military organization. His famous "Group of Five" consisted of Jacques Lemaigre-Dubreuil, the neck that turned the Murphy head, Lieutenant Colonel Louis Jousse, Jacques Tarbé de Saint Hardouin, and Colonel A. S. Van Hecke, and probably Henri d'Astier de la Vigerie, Jean Rigault, and José Aboulker. The group was apparently a very informal one, and authorities seem not to be able to agree on its exact composition.[37]

The "Group of Five" military staff included General Charles Mast, on the French army staff at Algiers; Major Dartois, French air force; and Commander Pierre Barjot, cashiered in 1940 from the French navy for his pro–De Gaulle activities. Lieutenant Colonel Jousse commanded the military garrison at Algiers. Colonel Van Hecke[38] was not on active duty; he was the chief of the Chan-

[34] Ibid., p. 642.

[35] Ibid.

[36] See Kenneth W. Pendar, *Adventures in Diplomacy; Our French Dilemma*, for an example.

[37] See Auphan and Mordal, *French Navy in World War II*, pp. 212–214; Richard and Serigny, *La bissectrice de la guerre*, pp. 37–44; and George F. Howe, *Northwest Africa: Seizing the Initiative in the West*, p. 189, for variations.

[38] Auphan and Mordal, *French Navy in World War II*, pp. 212–214; Howe, *Northwest Africa*, p. 189, identifies him as Colonel Jean Van Haecke; Richard

tiers de Jeunesse, a youth organization. No major French military commander was included or apparently desired; when in mid-October, 1942, Admiral Darlan sent Colonel Chrétien to establish contact with the Americans, Consul-General Felix Cole rejected his overtures on the advice of the "Group of Five."[39]

Lemaigre-Dubreuil was without doubt the dominant personality in the group. He set the policy for North Africa and selected the personnel to implement it. Associated with a group of economic collaborationists,[40] he was able to move with relative freedom in both occupied and unoccupied France and in North Africa. He was an astute businessman, married to the heiress of the Lesieur vegetable-oil industry, a royalist with a passion for plotting and, long before the war, deeply involved in political opposition to the financial policies of the Third Republic. He was unpopular with the French of both Vichy and De Gaulle persuasion, but he played an essential role vis-à-vis the Americans,[41] for he extracted from Robert Murphy the promise that the United States would restore France "in full independence and all grandeur and extent of territories that it had held before the war in France and its colonies,"[42] a promise incorporated in the Murphy-Giraud Agreement of November 2, 1942.[43] President Roosevelt, who planned for extensive

---

and Serigny, *La bissectrice de la guerre*, pp. 37–44, as Von Ecke; and Harry C. Butcher, *My Three Years with Eisenhower*, p. 107, as Van Heck.

[39] Auphan and Mordal, *French Navy in World War II*, pp. 212–214; see also Butcher, *My Three Years with Eisenhower*, pp. 145, 178a.

[40] Waverly Root, *Casablanca to Katyn: The Secret History of the War*, p. 161.

[41] Interview, Marcel Peyrouton, Casablanca, Morocco, May 23, 1967. Peyrouton, secretary-general of Algeria in 1930, resident-general in Tunisia in 1933 and again in 1940, resident-general in Morocco in 1936, Ambassador to Argentina in 1941, and governor-general of Algeria in 1943, said that he was chosen for the latter post by Lemaigre-Dubreuil, but was not given authority commensurate with his responsibility.

[42] Richard and Serigny, *La bissectrice de la guerre*, p. 52.

[43] Ibid., p. 68. The text of the agreement is in annex 2, on p. 217. Signed by Robert Murphy and General Charles Mast for General Henri Giraud, it provided for: (1.) Restoration of France in full independence, with all territories possessed before the war in France and overseas. (2.) Restoration of French sovereignty as soon as possible over all territories, metropolitan and colonial, over which the French flag flew in 1939. (3.) Restoration of France to the position occupied before the armistice in the United Nations (The United States to consider and treat France as an ally). (4.) Reinstallation of French administra-

reductions in the French empire, chided Murphy for going overboard with his promises. "Your letter may make trouble for me after the war," he said.[44]

Murphy's roseate political reports from North Africa created an aura of optimism in Washington that in turn was reflected in military planning. Brigadier General Walter B. Smith, Eisenhower's new chief of staff, arrived in London on September 7, and, with the Washington outlook, announced: Torch "will be a pushover." He said that President Roosevelt would handle the political angle with the French, "and he's a master." He reported that "the American fifth column in French Morocco is expected to be effective, for important French leaders, both military and civil, will actively support the American invasion."[45] On September 10, Leahy and Murphy discussed the possible attitude of French military commanders in North Africa, and agreed that Murphy might be able to align large parts of the French army with an American invasion effort provided "competent authority," presumably President Roosevelt, gave assurance that administration of the French colonies would be left in French hands. Leahy later observed that the plan "didn't work out as successfully as anticipated."[46] It should have been obvious even then that no overwhelming pro-Allied sentiment existed among the North African French, either civilian or military, and that the "native question" was the root of their inquietude.

The historical record did not support the Washington optimism. In 1940, General Huntziger had protested against the establishment of a German control commission in Casablanca because, he said, the Arabs respected primarily the power and might of the European power that ruled them and the German presence might be misconstrued by the Moroccan tribes.[47] Murphy himself noted that

---

tion in all territories liberated without any mixing of foreign authority in anything touching the exercise of French sovereignty. (5.) Transfer to French command of the Allied troops in North Africa, once the debarkation was completed and the necessary bases secured. (6.) Extension of lend-lease to reequip the French army. (7.) Facilitating the purchase and delivery of goods necessary to the civil population on the world market.

[44] Murphy, *Diplomat among Warriors*, p. 168.

[45] Butcher, *My Three Years with Eisenhower*, p. 91.

[46] Leahy, *I Was There*, p. 114.

[47] *Documents on German Foreign Policy*, vol. XI, 1940, doc. no. 671.

most of the French were complacent under the armistice, that they wanted no part of the war, and that they generally approved of Marshal Pétain and Laval. As for the military, General Noguès told him in October, 1942, "If Morocco becomes a battleground, it will be lost to France."[48] Murphy was given no basis for expecting anything but resistance from either General Noguès or Admiral Michelier, commander of the French navy in Morocco.

There is little doubt that General Noguès was hostile to Murphy's overtures; whether that hostility was more than a personality clash is not clear. The evidence is overpowering that Noguès planned reentry in the war, but not in Morocco. Ambassador Marcel Peyrouton, a collaborator of Noguès before and after the American landing, said, "He spoke to me of it more than twenty times."[49] Colonel Adrien Feste said, "General Noguès told the Americans many times, if you come with a commando, I will fight and push you into the sea; if you come with an armored division, I will welcome you on the beaches with flowers, and will march at your side."[50] Colonel Feste was engaged in training *goums*[51] after the armistice in 1940. Disguised as *mehalla cheriffian*, and presented to the armistice commission as tribal police, they trained daily with their automatic weapons and even held field maneuvers. These troops fought well in Tunisia in 1943. Other units were disguised as, for example, garrison companies or transport units. Munitions were hidden in mines, farm buildings, caves in the mountains, and *kasbahs*. One mine, with the mouth caved in for concealment, contained seven hundred tons of munitions.[52] Colonel Feste laid the effusion of blood during the landing squarely at the door of "that damn fool, Murphy,"[53] for his failure to give Noguès timely warn-

48 Murphy, *Diplomat among Warriors*, pp. 109–110, 112.

49 Interview, Marcel Peyrouton, May 23, 1967.

50 Interview, Colonel Adrien Feste, French Army (Retired), May 23, 1967, at Casablanca. Colonel Feste at the time was a liaison officer on General Mathenet's staff and was privy to the defense plans at Port Lyautey. He is now manager of General Tire Company, Casablanca.

51 A *goum* is a Moroccan troup unit consisting of about two hundred infantrymen, two French officers, and seven noncommissioned officers.

52 Richard and Serigny, *La bissectrice de la guerre*, pp. 205–210, presents documentary evidence relating to the camouflage of men and materials as proof that the spirit of resistance to the Axis guided Noguès and all of North Africa.

53 Interview, Colonel Feste, May 23, 1967.

ing of the invasion. Ambassador Peyrouton was only slightly less vehement.

Murphy and Leahy pinned their hopes on General Henri Giraud, the nominee of Jacques Lemaigre-Dubreuil.[54] He would, Murphy said, participate in the African campaign only if given command, "a matter of guaranteeing French sovereignty and demonstrating American acceptance of it."[55] The rationale probably more accurately reflects the imperatives of Lemaigre-Dubreuil than Giraud, for Giraud demonstrated almost total disinterest in political questions throughout his career. It is significant that Murphy was not in direct contact with Giraud; he made his arrangements through the intermediary of the "Group of Five."

In choosing Giraud as their front man, the Allies by-passed General De Gaulle. They also rejected General Weygand and Admiral Darlan, both of whom had indicated support for an Allied invasion, provided it was strong enough to ensure success, for they anticipated a German counterinvasion. Weygand, then seventy-five years old, had committed himself by the armistice not to fight against the Germans, while Giraud had not. Admiral Darlan, because of his anti-British attitude and because of his collaboration with the Germans, was suspect. Ironically, it was Darlan and not Giraud—whom Darlan termed "a good divisional commander, nothing more"—whose name was magic to the French military forces in Algeria and Morocco in 1942, and it was ultimately General De Gaulle whose authority prevailed in North Africa and France.

Although Murphy was permitted to go ahead with his plotting, the military estimates anticipated the possibility of resistance by the French navy. The sea forces were made up of career servicemen, loyal not to Vichy, but to their service. The French navy, the estimates concluded, would obey the orders of their anti-British commanders who were inclined to regard Anglo-Saxon seapower

[54] Jacques Lemaigre-Dubreuil, "Giraud et De Gaulle à Alger," *Revue de Paris*, July, 1949, p. 94, said he met Giraud at Lyon, May 19, 1942, and decided he was the one to sponsor an American landing. Richard and Serigny, *La bissectrice de la guerre*, p. 41 n., states that Lemaigre-Dubreuil did not know Giraud personally and picked him from a photograph as the Hollywood image of a French general most likely to appeal to the Americans.

[55] Murphy, *Diplomat among Warriors*, p. 117.

(including American) as a threat to their colonial empire. As for the French army, there was more hope. With a broader base in the population of metropolitan France and less dominated by traditionalist elements in its command structure, the army was more inclined than the navy to favor the United States, which, after all, had not participated in the British actions against the French colonies. Moreover, the army harbored a growing resentment of the Germans, who were systematically depriving it of its weapons. An invasion, predominantly American, might meet some degree of welcome from the French army.[56]

The Americans were aware of the attitude of both the French and the "natives" in Morocco. A large element of the French civil population, the governmental functionaries, was considered "neutral . . . content to jog along on their salaries and pensions."[57] They could ill afford to do otherwise. Allied sympathizers in the intellectual and professional classes lost their status. In Port Lyautey an ex-teacher kept pigs, and an ex-police chief worked as a waiter in order to live.[58] Generally, the French were unaware of the United States goals in the war; censorship of radio and the press coupled with their own provincialism left them apathetic. They shared the suspicion that the United States was trying to dismember the French empire.[59]

Gaullism was never a serious threat to the Vichy status quo in Morocco, because initially it lacked leadership and always lacked organization. Potential leaders decamped either to Great Britain or the United States. C. W. Krijanowsky, a Tsarist Russian naval officer who had settled in Casablanca in 1929, was a Gaullist. Unwilling to accept Pétain's armistice, he connived with a fellow Russian, Theodore N. Komaroff, the port director at Port Lyautey, to seize the 19,000 ton Polish school ship, *Wilya*.[60] On July 3, 1940,

[56] "History of the Twelfth Air Force," I, part I, 2–3, in United States Air Force Archives, file no. 650.01, vol. I.

[57] Ibid.

[58] Brigadier General Arthur R. Wilson, "Report of Operations in North Africa, 8 Nov.–Dec., 1942," p. 32, Modern Military Records Division, National Archives and Records Service, Alexandria, Va., file no. 95 TF 3-9.30, Western Task Force.

[59] Ibid.

[60] Mr. Komaroff remembers the ship as the *Iskza*, another Polish ship in-

he set out for England with 620 Poles and "some French officers in Polish uniforms." His crew was a polyglot lot, mostly Scandinavian from interned ships. The Poles and French were good soldiers, Krijanowsky said, but they were not seamen. Evading French navy patrols that had orders to sink him, he refueled at Gibraltar and joined a 25–ship convoy headed for England before breaking down off the coast of Spain. The convoy continued without him. Krijanowsky ignored the orders of the British convoy commander to head for a Spanish port and internment. He proceeded alone at his best speed of four knots for Liverpool. Sailing unscathed through a British minefield laid after he left the convoy, he arrived on June 22, much to the surprise of the Admiralty. The Admiralty presumed he had been sunk.

Krijanowsky's odyssey did not end at Liverpool. In November, 1940, he was back in Morocco as an agent of De Gaulle. But sentiment had so hardened against the British after their attack on Mers-el-Kebir that his efforts to organize a De Gaulle faction in the French military forces were ineffective. He was able to relay information through the American consul in Casablanca, but De Gaulle, who was getting his intelligence information through the British, paid little heed. Betrayed for fifteen hundred francs, Krijanowsky was arrested on June 21, 1941, and shipped off to France where he was tried and imprisoned for the duration of the war, not for treason or espionage, but for insulting the examining judge.[61]

Morocco had a significant military force in 1942, but it was under French command. The Moroccan regiments were at full strength; young Moroccans, eighteen to nineteen years old, volun-

---

terned at Port Lyautey at the same time, which also escaped to England (letter to the author, dated Paris, July 1, 1967).

[61] Interview, Commandant C. W. Krijanowsky, 3 Rue Jacquard, Casablanca, Morocco, May 23, 1967. As a lieutenant commander in the Russian Aeronavale, he was in charge of mining the Kiel Canal and Danzig Bay. In 1919 Admiral Kolchak appointed him to the German Control Commission. When the Kolchak government collapsed, Krijanowsky went to France. In April, 1945, the American army released him from Dachau, and he served in the French army in Germany until demobilized, December 31, 1945. The American consul, Mr. Green, put the author in contact with Mr. Krijanowsky, as a "reliable and knowledgeable person."

teered for the French colonial forces in order to escape conscription for labor in Germany.[62] Within this element, particularly among the young officers, there was a strong nationalist sentiment, but since the sultan had given no indication other than whole-hearted support of France, there was little possibility of defection by Moroccan forces.[63]

The disaffection potential was high in the Moroccan civil population. Imports from France had ceased, and the Moroccans were suffering distressed living conditions. Local authorities were requisitioning grain, and flour was in short supply in an area that normally produced a surplus. Building, except for military purposes, was forbidden. Wood, cement, brick, and nails were unobtainable, and cotton goods virtually so. Railroad service was reduced and the equipment was in bad condition. Electric service was curtailed. The cost of living was high and rising rapidly.[64] Military planners paid lip service to the "uncritical admiration of many Moroccans for the prestige of the United States" as an "asset of which the most must be made,"[65] but the United States was already committed to support of the French colonial position. The Moroccan population, largely illiterate and dependent upon the censored radio broadcasts for news, was hardly aware that the United States was at war.[66]

It must be reiterated that the United States objective in Morocco was short term and military, not political. It was to secure French Morocco with the view of occupying Tunisia as quickly as possible, and to establish a striking force in French Morocco capable of ensuring control of the Strait of Gibraltar by moving into Spanish Morocco. The possibility of Spanish intervention, or of German intervention through Spain, was considered a real threat.[67] The

[62] Wilson, "Report of Operations in North Africa," p. 32.

[63] Interview, Colonel Serghini Embarek, Royal Moroccan Army, in Madrid, May 3, 1967. Colonel Serghini, then sous-lieutenant, was in a Moroccan regiment at Agadir in 1942, and later fought in the American Fifth Army in Italy.

[64] "Pertinent Data on French Morocco," a document dated 25 October, 1942, in USAF Archives, file no. 612.610, p. 7.

[65] Ibid.

[66] Wilson, "Report of Operations in North Africa," p. 33.

[67] Wesley F. Craven and James Lea Cate, eds., *Europe: Torch to Pointblank. August 1942 to December 1943*, vol. II of *The Army Air Forces in World War*

Spanish forces anticipated an Allied landing in either North Africa or Portugal in November. At the time of the landing, Spanish forces in Morocco were deployed from Larache north to the International Zone of Tangier, for the beach at Arcila was considered a logical target. But the Spanish army had absolutely no plans for any offensive action in the French zone.[68]

The plans for Operation Torch envisaged three amphibious landings on the Moroccan Atlantic coast, one at Safi, one at Fedala, and one at Mehdia Beach. The armored forces landing at Safi were to support the investment of Casablanca by preventing reinforcements from coming up from the south. The main forces for the capture of Casablanca, gateway and terminus for the railway to Algeria, were to land at Fedala. The landing at Mehdia Beach had a double objective. The first was to capture the airfield, the most modern in North Africa and the only one in Morocco with concrete runways. The second objective was to liberate Port Lyautey, three miles south of the field. Port Lyautey was Morocco's third most important port[69] and it also served as a way station on the Casablanca-Algeria railway.

In many respects, the Mehdia Beach landing was potentially the most difficult of the three. The Safi and Fedala landings had the advantage of somewhat protected harbors, but Mehdia Beach was open to the sea and usually had a pounding surf. It was backed by difficult terrain, and the tactical assault had to be tailored to the specific objective of capturing the airfield. Hopefully, P-40 fighter airplanes catapulted from the escort carrier, the U.S.S. *Chenango*, could be based there by the end of D day to provide support for the main assault on Casablanca.[70]

II, pp. 68, 76. See also "History of the Twelfth Air Force," vol. I, part I, annex 8, paragraph 12, in USAF Archives, file no. 650.01, vol. I, for a discussion of the possibility of strategic bombing in southern Spain.

[68] Interview, General Mohammed bel Kacem Mezziane, Royal Moroccan Army, in Madrid, Spain, May 3, 1967. General Mezziane, Moroccan ambassador to Spain, was a lieutenant general in the Spanish army in 1942, and was in command of the Larache division.

[69] Op-32-F112 Secret Memo, dated December 4, 1942, in Port Lyautey, N.W. Africa Base Maintenance file, in U.S. Navy Archives, indicates that Port Lyautey handled 282 ships with a gross tonnage of 281,000 tons in 1937, and handled 78,500 tons of imports and 95,000 tons of exports.

[70] Howe, *Northwest Africa*, p. 147.

The airfield was located in the broad, U-shaped, bend of the Sebou River, about three miles from the mouth. The site was chosen and the base developed for seaplanes. The river bend provided excellent landing areas, no matter what the wind direction might be. Francesco de Pinedo had used it on his flight from Rome to the United States in 1927 as had Italo Balbo in December, 1931, with his flight of fourteen Savoia-Marchetti seaplanes, on his flight from Rome to Rio de Janeiro. The Club de Tourisme Aerien de Port Lyautey used a grass landing field there as early as 1932. The French navy took control in 1936 and began construction of a permanent installation, including the hangar and barracks. Construction of a hard-surfaced runway was begun in 1940 and the first combat plane, a Dewoitine 520, landed in April, 1942.[71] The airfield was therefore a prime target.

Although only sixteen feet above sea level itself, the airfield was dominated from the west by a high, fortified ridge south of the river and by precipitous bluffs about one hundred feet high north of the river. Except for the surf, the beaches themselves presented no potential obstacle, but they were backed by low dunes of marine sand, impassable for wheeled vehicles. A swampy lagoon, about five miles long and four hundred yards wide, separated the dunes from the ridge overlooking the field. To the south of the lagoon, a secondary road pierced the almost sheer face of the ridge and joined the paved highway three miles inland, connecting Port Lyautey with Rabat. At the north end of the lagoon and ridge, a narrow shelf not more than one hundred yards wide gave access by rail and road to the airfield and Port Lyautey. Two 75-mm. guns mounted on railway flatcars and manned by naval crews provided defensive fire power at the river's mouth. The ridge, which terminated in a sheer drop of two hundred feet to the river, was surmounted by an old Moorish fortress, the Kasbah, which mounted two 5-inch guns also manned by naval crews. The fortifications had been extended to the southwest of the Kasbah by entrenchment and by concrete emplacements in which were mounted four 155-mm. Grandes Puissances Filloux rifles. The latter actually contributed nothing to the defense of Mehdia Beach; their blocks had been removed

[71] "United States Naval Air Station Command History," dated September 8, 1959, in U.S. Navy Archives, Washington, D.C.

and sent to Meknes in order to prevent their use against the invasion "when it came."[72]

Surprise was a fundamental premise of the strategy for Operation Torch, but somehow word leaked out—too soon for surprise to be militarily effective and too late to permit a political compromise.[73] General De Gaulle, who knew of the plans for the invasion of North Africa on September 18, 1942, announced that he expected to be named commander in chief, for "any invasion of French territory not under French command is bound to fail."[74] On November 7, Henri Recoing, director of public works for the city of Port Lyautey, had searchlights mounted with their projectors turned skyward to welcome the invasion forces, but at 8:30 P.M he was advised to cancel his preparations; French military forces would resist any landing.[75] President Roosevelt told his 876th press conference, held in Washington on February 2, 1943, that the four hundred French troops manning the Kasbah at Mehdia Beach were told the night of November 7 that the Americans were going to land, and the troops cheered. About two hours later, Roosevelt added, the commander of the Kasbah garrison, who had assumed there would be

[72] Interview, Colonel Feste, May 23, 1967. Mr. Boniface, who lived at Mehdia Beach immediately below the guns told the author in an interview at Mehdia Beach, May 25, 1967, that the guns were fired. (Howe, *Northwest Africa*, p. 163, said they were used.) Mr. and Mrs. Boniface operated a restaurant at the northernmost edge of the town of Mehdia Beach, not fifty yards from Green Beach upon which the 1,268 men of the Second Battalion Landing Team, Sixtieth Regimental Combat Team, debarked. Eyewitnesses to the actual landing, they described it and the subsequent events in a tape-recorded interview with the author, who retains possession of the tape.

[73] Conclusive evidence as to the degree of surprise achieved must await release of French documents—in about twenty years according to Ministère des Armées, "Marin," Etat-Major letter no. 402, dated Paris, April 24, 1967, to the author.

[74] Lucian K. Truscott, Jr., *Command Missions: A Personal Story*, p. 78. According to Butcher, *My Three Years with Eisenhower*, p. 89, that page of his diary containing the first Torch directive to General Eisenhower to "clean up the North African coast" was discovered missing on September 7, and Butcher speculated that "all hope of attaining surprise is already in vain."

[75] Interview, Mrs. Jeanne Mortier, Kenitra, Morocco, May 21, 1967. Mrs. Mortier is the daughter of M. Manin, leader of the Gaullist faction in Port Lyautey, and a friend of Recoing, both now deceased. Recoing alerted Manin to the changed plans and the latter departed immediately with friends "on a hunting trip" and did not return until late Sunday night (November 8).

no opposition to the landing, got definite orders from his general to oppose it.[76]

Allied strategy envisaged the deposition of the Vichy authorities and therefore made no attempt to arrange with them for an un-opposed landing. The French, for their part, considered American violation of French neutrality unthinkable, and they failed to take elemental military precautions.[77] On November 7, General Alphonse Juin, French commander in chief in North Africa, sent out a general alert to his forces for 8 A.M., November 8, based on a French navy estimate that the Allied convoy in the Mediterranean was bound, not for Tripolitania, but for Algeria.[78] Abdallah Ibrahim and four companions, fishing off the mouth of the Sebou River an hour or so before midnight, discovered the invasion armada. They returned to the dock within fifty yards of the flatcars upon which the French navy guns were mounted. Although they did not specifically alert the French authorities, the presence of the ships was common knowledge along the waterfront within minutes after their return.[79] Nevertheless, Admiral François Michelier did not alert his forces in Morocco until 1:30 A.M., November 8, and did not consider the situation urgent until 2:27, even though he and General Noguès had been advised about midnight by General Marie Bethouart that the landings were taking place. Michelier and Noguès thought they were confronted with a Gaullist putsch, combined perhaps with minor operations against the coast to stir up dissidence in Morocco.[80] In retrospect, the savage fighting in Morocco resulted not from incompatibility of objectives, but from political misjudgments.

Probably no successful operation in the annals of military his-

---

[76] Rosenman, ed., *The Tide Turns*, pp. 61–62.

[77] Auphan and Mordal, *French Navy in World War II*, p. 288. Rear Admiral Auphan, French navy minister in 1942, said no one in Morocco suspected that an American force was approaching the Moroccan coast, because a shortage of aviation gasoline had caused the French Aeronavale to discontinue the surveillance of the Moroccan sea approaches.

[78] Ibid., p. 217; Samuel Eliot Morison, *Operations in North African Waters: October, 1942–June, 1943*, vol. II in *History of United States Naval Operations in World War II*, p. 121.

[79] Interview, Abdallah ben Ibrahim, May 13, 1967, at Mehdia Beach, Morocco.

[80] Auphan and Mordal, *French Navy in World War II*, p. 288.

tory was as thoroughly fouled up as Operation Torch, particularly
in the Goalpost phase (the capture of Port Lyautey). The tactical
execution of the assault was as bad as the political planning. Brigadier General Lucian K. Truscott, Jr., who commanded Goalpost,
described the landing as chaotic[81]—the kindest thing said about it.

In the planning stage the army and the navy had differed on
their concepts of amphibious warfare. For example, the navy concept envisaged landing lightly equipped assault forces in the initial
waves of landing craft, leaving the heavy logistic support for later
waves. Thus a maximum force would be available for securing the
beachhead, and its numbers would not be depleted by the necessity
of unloading equipment. Greater unit integrity, and therefore
greater combat efficiency, could be maintained on a beachhead un-
encumbered by equipment needed to set up base camps at a later
day. The army favored getting the troops ashore accompanied by
unit equipment. Then if enemy submarines or aircraft decimated
the convoy, troops ashore had a fighting chance for survival. The
disagreement was fundamental, for it affected the manner in which
the transports were to be loaded.[82]

A second major area of disagreement concerned the question of
command. Both the army and the navy were involved about equally in Operation Torch. Was there to be an organically unified
command or a temporary partnership? Admiral Henry Kent
Hewitt, the commander of the amphibious force, Atlantic Fleet,
was charged with the responsibility of putting some 34,000 men
ashore on the Moroccan coast, but those men remained under the
command of Major General George S. Patton, Jr., commander of
the western landing force, and completely independent of Admiral
Hewitt until the expedition was actually embarked and under way.
During the transit supreme command was vested in Admiral
Hewitt, but on November 9 the responsibility was again split, with
Admiral Hewitt retaining responsibility for naval operations and
General Patton assuming command of the troops ashore.[83] Within

---

[81] Truscott, *Command Missions*, p. 113.

[82] Morison, *Operations in North African Waters*, p. 27.

[83] The organization, training, and employment of the forces employed in
Operation Torch are treated from a navy point of view in Morison, *Operations
in North African Waters*, and from an army point of view in Howe, *North-*

such a no man's land, many decisions were left unresolved: training problems, for example, and such operational problems as naval gunfire support for troops ashore. With more time the command problems might have been resolved, but there was little time. General Patton was not ordered to his command until August 24, and Brigadier General Truscott, not until September 19. Both had to assemble staffs after they themselves had reported for duty.

For an operation of such complexity, the forces employed were woefully unprepared. Of the thirty transports and cargo vessels used for Operation Torch, only fourteen were in commission and assigned by August 1, 1942. Only ten of those had been in commission more than one year, and none were in satisfactory condition for amphibious warfare. All had to undergo modification. Several did not arrive in time to participate in the rehearsals, held August to October at Solomon Island in Chesapeake Bay, and even these landings in smooth and protected waters were unrealistic. Landing craft were in short supply and many of those actually delivered did not have engines installed until mid-October.[84] Captain Harry Butcher, in his diary entry of September 7, noted that General Eisenhower was frustrated by the "continued delay of the U.S. Navy to specify the number and type of escort vessels it could supply for *Torch*."[85] Three thousand men were needed to man the landing craft; there was little time to train raw recruits who had never seen salt water, and there were few others available. Their training had been geared to a shore-to-shore operation—a cross-channel landing—and it was not until late August that emphasis was shifted to ship-to-shore training. The lack of training was manifest during the landings on the Moroccan coast.

The gods of war and weather favored the American venture. In an area where surf conditions were unfavorable four days out of five, the Allied planners had unwittingly picked the calmest day in forty years—the sea was like a mirror.[86] It was a dark night; the thin sliver of a new moon low on the southern horizon betrayed

---

west Africa. Truscott, *Command Missions,* contains an excellent commentary, particularly on deficiencies.

[84] Morison, *Operations in North African Waters,* pp. 23–33.

[85] Butcher, *My Three Years with Eisenhower,* p. 91.

[86] Interview, Mr. and Mrs. Boniface. May 25, 1967.

little. In the darkness, however, the northern attack force, approaching the unfamiliar estuary of the Sebou River, lost its way. It was unable to find the beacon submarine *Shad*, which had been on station off the beach since November 4, and it had not compensated for the northerly set of the current that prevailed along this coast. In the darkness and under conditions of radio silence the invasion armada lost two hours in fruitless maneuvering as its various components sought assigned positions. These were the two precious hours of darkness General Truscott had counted on for the cold-steel assault upon the Mehdia Beach defensive positions. The troop transports were not in position as planned at 11:00 P.M. (November 7); the U.S.S. *Susan B. Anthony* did not reach her position until 12:40 A.M.[87]

The plan of attack for Mehdia Beach provided for 9,079 officers and men, divided into three battalion landing teams (BLT) and supporting forces, to land at five points on the Atlantic beaches, two north and three south of the mouth of the Sebou River, at 4:00 A.M., November 8. But the attack did not go according to plan. The lack of training was painfully evident as the troop transports tried to get their boats into the water. The U.S.S. *Clymer* was ready to go by 2:00 A.M., but the U.S.S. *Allen* and the U.S.S. *Anthony* were delayed by some two hours. Only one BLT, the second, from the U.S.S. *Clymer*, hit its assigned beach (at 5:30 A.M.). The third BLT, from the U.S.S. *Anthony*, was assigned two beaches about three miles apart (Red Beach and Red Beach 2) north of the river mouth. The first wave landed south of Red Beach 2, and the second wave, five miles north of Red Beach. The third BLT saw little action except in arduous march through the sand dunes while under attack from French aircraft. Because of navigational errors, the U.S.S. *Allen* contingent, the first BLT, landed one to three miles north of its assigned Yellow and Blue beaches, and the second wave landed ahead of the first.[88] With most of its troops out of position, the invasion was off to a bad start.

There is something beguiling about psychological warfare, and in the North African invasion almost everyone tried his hand at it. President Roosevelt led off at 1:30 A.M., a few minutes after the

[87] Morison, *Operations in North African Waters*, pp. 118–124.
[88] See Howe, *Northwest Africa*, pp. 150–159, for details of the composition of the attack force, and for the difficulties encountered.

landings in Algeria, with a broadcast over BBC stating the American objectives and asking French support.[89] His broadcast was repeated at thirty-minute intervals the rest of the night. General Eisenhower followed with a broadcast and leaflet drop in the populated areas, giving instructions to both military and civilian elements of the North African population who wanted to avoid conflict.[90] At 4:00 A.M., H hour on the Moroccan coast, the U.S.S. *Texas* transmitter began broadcasting: "Allo, Maroc. Allo, Maroc, ici l'emmeteur des forces americains au Maroc," and giving instructions in French to the local population.[91] General Truscott, too, tried his hand. At dawn on November 8 he sent two officers ashore to deliver a personal letter to the local French commander. Truscott, in President Roosevelt's words, outlined the reasons for the landing and concluded with a plea for the avoidance of bloodshed.[92]

There is little evidence that anyone in a position of authority in Morocco heard the broadcast of either President Roosevelt or General Eisenhower, and the broadcasts certainly failed to lessen resistance.[93] The U.S.S. *Texas* had the wave lengths to itself until about 10:00 A.M., November 9, when Radio Maroc began to warn of a "clandestine radio," and to warn listeners not to believe its "propaganda." Thereafter, listeners were treated to two stations on the same frequency: Radio Maroc, playing records and denouncing its competitor, and the U.S.S. *Texas*, broadcasting news and propaganda and playing the national anthems of France and the United States.[94] On November 13, the U.S. broadcasts were transferred ashore to the new Armed Forces Radio Station, established with equipment lent to the U.S. Army by Moroccan radio "hams" in Casablanca, since it was unable to find its own equipment in the

[89] Morison, *Operations in North African Waters*, pp. 70–71. Richard and Serigny, *La bissectrice de la guerre*, pp. 125–126, contains the text of the French version of the message.

[90] Butcher, *My Three Years with Eisenhower*, pp. 173–174.

[91] "Final Report of Western Task Force, 7–11 November 1942," annex 5 (G-2 report), section 6 (psychological warfare report), in Modern Military Records Service Archives, Alexandria, Virginia, file no. 95 TF 3-2 Western Task Force.

[92] "History of the Twelfth Air Force," vol. I, part I, annex 19, p. 79.

[93] Ibid., p. 14.

[94] "Final Report of the Western Task Force."

jumble being unloaded from the transports.[95] General Truscott's
ill-starred attempt produced the first casualty—and the first Medal
of Honor winner—in the North African campaign.

Colonel Demas T. Craw, a swashbuckling air officer, embarked
on the U.S.S. *Allen* with General Truscott, was familiar with the
projected peace overture. He persuaded Truscott to enlarge the
mission, originally intended for the French-speaking G-2 officer,
Major Pierpont M. Hamilton, to include himself. General Truscott
was reluctant to risk the loss of his air expert, but finally capitulated, concluding that, after all, Colonel Craw was "indestructible."
At first light at 6:00 A.M. in class A uniforms with boots shined
and campaign ribbons in place, they landed on Green beach with
a radio-equipped jeep and a driver named Corey. Mounting an
American, a French, and a white flag on their jeep, they set out for
Port Lyautey.

The artillery duel between French and American guns had already started. The last words General Truscott heard from Colonel
Craw were: "Damn it, we're being shelled by both you fellows
and the French."[96] The commander of the French naval gun crew
at Mehdia declined to furnish an escort for Craw and Hamilton.
The noncommissioned officer in charge told them he had no men
to spare, but he did permit them to pass through his lines on the
road to Port Lyautey.[97] At the top of the steep incline where the
road comes up from the river shelf to the plain overlooking the
airfield (near the southwestern perimeter of the U.S. Naval Air
Station), they ran upon an outpost manned by Moroccan soldiers
who, startled by this strange-looking vehicle flying a white flag,
their battle flag, opened fire. Colonel Craw was killed, and Hamilton and Corey taken prisoners. The French investigation that followed determined that it was simply an unfortunate mistake,
compounded of uncertainty, surprise, and lack of experience on

[95] Interview, Lucian Ben Simon, one of the lenders, at New York, April 13,
1963. When the Armed Forces Radio Service was being dismantled after the
war, it was impossible to distinguish between Ben Simon's equipment and that
of the army; therefore, all of it was sold to Ben Simon as surplus, and he
moved it to Tangier to establish Radio Tangier.

[96] General Truscott's account, contained in "History of the Twelfth Air
Force," vol. I, part I, annex 19, p. 79.

[97] Ibid.

the part of the soldiers. "If the post had been manned by French soldiers, it would never have happened," the investigator concluded.[98]

General Truscott's first objective, the capture of the air field at Port Lyautey, was so important that Allied planners envisaged the use of paratroopers to "destroy, eliminate, or neutralize the French Air Force actually present."[99] The Fifty-first Troop Carrier Wing, flying out of St. Eval in southern England was earmarked for the job. It is perhaps just as well that the paratroopers were shifted to objectives in Algeria, for the operation went "sour."[100] Security was so tight that the pilots were not told their destination until thirty minutes before takeoff, hardly time to find it on the map. The weather was bad over Spain, and the navigation beacons in the Mediterranean were on an unexpected radio frequency. The thirty-nine planes, after their fifteen-hundred-mile flight, scattered all over the North African coast, landing in dry lake beds and fields—three of them in Spanish Morocco. Only twenty planes remained serviceable.[101] The Twelfth Air Force, putting the best possible face on the matter, conceded that, as a precise military operation, the paratroop venture was a failure, but said that it "accidentally accomplished" the vital part of its mission, for it "so confused the French Air Force that they dispatched no missions against the convoys, but were completely occupied in defending their own airdromes."[102]

Although the French army did fight at Port Lyautey, it did so more from discipline than from conviction. Colonel Lavisseur, a much-decorated officer in World War I, commanded a regiment

[98] Interview, Colonel Adrien Feste, May 23, 1967. Colonel Feste was a member of the board of investigation.

[99] Major General George S. Patton, Jr., letter dated October 10, 1942, to Brigadier General John K. Cannon, in "History of the Twelfth Air Force," vol. I, part I, annex 12.

[100] Butcher, *My Three Years with Eisenhower*, p. 187.

[101] "History of the Twelfth Air Force," vol. I, part I, annex 15, p. 40. Captain William H. Raymond, Jr., one of the pilots who landed at Einzoren, Spanish Morocco, commented on the Spanish troops who interned him, described the twelve horse-drawn 37-mm. guns, the four hundred "very efficient Moorish cavalrymen," and the poor equipment. The supposed "Spanish menace," which had so disturbed the higher headquarters, was apparently overdrawn.

[102] Ibid., annex 19, p. 31.

of Foreign Legion cavalry at Port Lyautey. When his regiment encountered the first American troops, Colonel Lavisseur met with the American commander and told him: "I have orders to hold this position until nightfall, and I will obey . . . but if you are not in a hurry . . . we will not fight for nothing and we will reserve our ammunition for the common enemy, the German." The American battalion commander concurred, and the two units held their position, the soldiers exchanging American cigarettes for French wine. At nightfall the French withdrew, and the Americans took the position without firing a shot.[103]

Many of the frustrations experienced by the western task force were inherent in the divided command and the differing concepts held by the navy and the army. For example, the French defensive position in the Kasbah, overlooking Mehdia Beach, held up the advance of General Truscott's forces and delayed the capture of the airfield for three days. During that time, the battleship *Texas*, the heavy cruiser *Savannah*, and three destroyers, the *Roe*, *Kearney*, and *Ericsson*, all earmarked for fire support, were waiting offshore. In addition, the auxiliary aircraft carrier *Sangamon* had two air groups available upon call. There is no doubt but that the Kasbah could have been reduced to dust in a matter of minutes, but, according to the Torch plan, the fire-support ships were limited to replies to offshore fire unless called upon by the forces ashore. General Truscott distrusted the accuracy of naval gunfire and called for it only when his situation became desperate; then it was effective.[104] General Truscott's distrust was perhaps reinforced by his appreciation of Allied policy—avoid hostilities if possible. Since he was out of contact with his higher headquarters, the decision rested squarely with him.

The western task force was also plagued by communications difficulties from the very moment the debarkation began. General Truscott was obliged to go by scout boat to the transports during the unloading to find out what was going on, and he lost contact with his units as soon as they were ashore. In the early afternoon of November 8, lacking exact information, he went ashore and found

[103] Interview, Colonel Feste, May 23, 1967.
[104] See Howe, *Northwest Africa*, pp. 154–155, and Morison, *Operations in North African Waters*, pp. 117–118, 132, for a discussion of the naval gunfire support problem.

landing craft broaching in the surf, spilling men and equipment into the sea; no beach party to direct the landing boats; no shore party to unload them; transports beyond the range of the beachmaster's signal lamps; men lost, wandering about hunting for their units; battalion and company commanders out of contact with their subordinate units; and few heavy weapons landed for defense against expected opposition. The failure to neutralize or capture the French coastal defense guns forced the transports to move back out of range so that the round trip for the landing craft was lengthened to more than thirty miles. And the sea was no longer a mirror—a pounding surf had come up. By nightfall General Truscott's whole force was in a precarious position.[105]

The communications chaos extended up the line of command. General Patton was not only out of contact with General Truscott at Mehdia Beach and Major General Ernest N. Harmon, commanding the force that had landed with little opposition at Safi, but also out of communication with General Eisenhower's headquarters at Gibraltar. Patton and Eisenhower had different code books and were not able to decode each other's messages.[106] When General Eisenhower sent a reconnaissance plane from Gibraltar, the U.S. Navy shot it down only a stone's throw from the U.S.S. *Allen* off Mehdia Beach.[107] Finally on November 12, General Eisenhower sent H.M.S. *Welshman*, a 37–knot fast minelayer, to Casablanca to find "lost WTF" (Western Task Force). But the battle was already over. The Americans had won.

The campaign for Morocco, with all of its heroic episodes and dreary mistakes, had dragged on for three days. The airfield at Port Lyautey, named Craw Field, was to have been captured by 11:00 A.M. on D day. It did not fall until November 10, and then its runways were dangerously pitted and the turf so soft that the heavy American fighter planes could not land safely on it. Of the seventy-seven P-40's launched from the U.S.S. *Chenango*, one crashed at sea, one flew off into the fog and was never heard from again, and seventeen cracked up on landing. None saw action. The P-39's flown down from England encountered adverse winds and were

[105] Morison, *Operations in North African Waters*, pp. 121–128; Howe, *Northwest Africa*, p. 160; and Truscott, *Command Missions*, pp. 109–116.

[106] Butcher, *My Three Years with Eisenhower*, p. 188.

[107] Truscott, *Command Missions*, p. 109.

forced to land, most of them in Portugal where they were interned.[108] The United States Navy had its inning with the French navy off Casablanca; it fought professionally and well. The United States Army, in spite of its mistakes, won a military victory on shore because it had overwhelming material superiority and a will to win, both of which the French army lacked. French spokesmen after the surrender called the French resistance a *baroud d'honneur*, a token resistance.[109] It was an expensive token, for it cost France far more than the 1,469 casualties suffered by the American forces, and it demonstrated French military impotence to the whole Moroccan nation. Morocco had become a battlefield, and France had lost it.

[108] History of the Twelfth Air Force," vol. I, part I, p. 16; Craven and Cate, *Army Air Forces in World War II*, p. 60.

[109] Interview, Marcel Peyrouton, May 23, 1967.

3. Souvenir of the G.I.— Chewing Gum

ALTHOUGH THE EVIDENCE points to a well-founded suspicion among French officials that an American invasion was imminent, the civilian populace, both French and Moroccan, was taken by surprise. Even after the landings were under way, business in Port Lyautey was being conducted as normal. The Allies did not seek support from local Gaullists, nor was any pro-Allied organization in evidence. Whatever the vice-consuls might have done elsewhere, they had no impact in the Port Lyautey area, and they apparently made no attempt to influence the "natives" in any part of Morocco.

Marius Boniface, who described himself as a "sort of mayor" of Mehdia Beach, was a neighbor and close friend of René Malevergne, the Sebou River pilot who was spirited out of Morocco in October, 1942, by the United States Office of Strategic Services (OSS). Malevergne was a key figure in the Mehdia Beach landing, yet Mr. Boniface, wakened at four o'clock in the morning, November 8, by the noise of motors offshore, wondered from what army came the soldiers whom he could dimly make out on the beach across the road from his house.[1]

In Port Lyautey, Mrs. Charles Manin customarily left home about mid-morning to go to the market. She met a neighbor, Mrs. Lucien Gameler, who told her that an American army had landed at Mehdia Beach during the night. Mrs. Manin was the wife of a known Gaullist sympathizer, and she had been warned that the Vichyites had planned an action for this date to "unmask" the Gaullists. She was understandably wary.

"Non, c'est pour rire" [You're kidding], she replied.[2]

Mrs. Gameler assured her that she was not kidding; her husband, who was in the French army, had been called during the night. The two ladies hastened through their shopping and returned home, but they waited almost forty-eight hours before they received any authoritative news over known radio stations.

Mr. Mohammed Zizi, a Moroccan merchant of Kenitra (Port Lyautey), has vivid memories of the American landing.[3] On Saturday the manager of a Port Lyautey trucking company telephoned him to rent his truck, a "well-used" Chevrolet. The deal made, Zizi sent the truck with a driver to Mehdia where it was loaded with cases of canned fish. It returned to Port Lyautey before leaving early the next morning for Rabat. Just north of Sidi Bouknadel, about ten miles south of Port Lyautey, it was stopped by "some soldiers, I don't know who," the driver said. The driver fled, abandoning his truck.

General Truscott told the story from the American point of view in his autobiographical *Command Missions.* The First Platoon, Company A, Sixtieth Infantry, Lieutenant Jesse Scott commanding, was detailed to establish a roadblock on the Rabat–Port Lyautey highway. Their weapons carrier stuck in the sand, and Sergeant Augusta "made arrangements" with a Moroccan man for the use of his truck. They used it for only a few minutes, and the surviving part of the company had only a fleeting glimpse of it before a French tank opened fire and destroyed it.[4]

Mr. Zizi harbors no ill feelings. "C'est la guerre," he shrugged.

[1] Interview, Mr. Boniface, Mehdia Beach, Morocco, May 25, 1967.

[2] Interview, Mrs. Jeanne Mortier, Kenitra, Morocco, May 21, 1967.

[3] Interview, Mr. Mohammed Zizi, Kenitra, Morocco, May 19, 1967.

[4] Lucien K. Truscott, Jr., *Command Missions: A Personal Story*, pp. 96–107.

Besides, in a few days an American officer came to see him, took all the necessary information, and six months later the U.S. Army replaced his Chevrolet with a brand new Dodge truck.[5]

In the Rabat *medina*, the old native quarter of the city, there was little visible evidence of the forty years of the French protectorate. The streets were narrow in the traditional fashion of Moroccan cities, bordered with drab, windowless walls pierced here and there with small doors. Behind one of those doors, as in many of the Moroccan homes in the *medina*, lay a courtyard that, with its graceful arches and fanciful carved plasterwork, might have been transposed from a scene in the *Arabian Nights*. It was the home of Sheik Kettani, and there the elite of Rabat's Moroccan society met to drink tea and discuss current events.

Mohammed Bargach was an habitué of Sheik Kettani's "salon." His family had lived in Rabat more than six centuries since their expulsion from Spain. (Bargach is a variation of the Spanish name, Vargas.) The men who frequented the sheik's salon were an optimistic lot, and they competed to see who would be the first each day to bring a morsel of good news. This day of November 8, 1942, Mohammed Bargach hurried to the rendezvous. Today he would be first, and indeed he had good news, for his English-speaking son, Ali, had just heard the president of the United States announce by radio that American troops were landing in Morocco. Breathless when he arrived at about eight o'clock, he called for silence from the eight or ten men assembled there in order that he might divulge momentous news.

"If you are going to tell us about the American landings in Morocco, save your breath," someone told him. "We have been talking of it for two hours."[6]

Another small but important segment of the Moroccan population was surprised by the landing—the German-Italian Armistice Commission. Headquartered at the Anfa Hotel in Casablanca, it numbered about 150 members, 60 in Casablanca, and the others

[5] Interview, Mohammed Zizi.

[6] Interview, Ali Bargach, Rabat, Morocco, May 20, 1967. Mr. Bargach was editor of *Al Alam*, Morocco's largest Arabic-language newspaper, for ten years, and is now in the export-import business in Rabat and Casablanca. His brother, Ahmed Bargach, has served as governor of Casablanca, and as minister of *habous* (religious properties) in the Moroccan national government.

scattered in small detachments about Morocco. Consternation reigned in Casablanca, November 8, when Allied warplanes appeared overhead.

"Where are the French aviators?" the German aviation colonel demanded.

"You took their airplanes away from them," the French liaison officer replied.[7]

The ten-man unit of the commission at Fedala was captured by the American landing forces, but in spite of the elaborate plans of Vice-Consul David W. King,[8] the main body at Casablanca escaped to Fez, from whence General Noguès permitted it to leave by air for Axis-held territories.[9]

The surprise was no less at the higher echelons of the Moroccan government. Shortly after the landings began, at about five o'clock in the morning, King Mohammed V received a telephone call from Fedala, presumably from the pasha, advising him that the landings were taking place. He had understood from the French-language broadcast of the BBC that unusual events were taking place in Algeria. Now, in Morocco!

The king awakened several of the palace retainers who were constant friends as well as employees, and together they waited on an outside balcony until daylight. The sky was overcast at the palace with a 2,400-foot ceiling. They could hear airplanes overhead, but whether French or otherwise they did not know, for none came down through the overcast near the palace. The question was soon resolved, however, for the planes began their attack on the military airfield, a half-mile east of the spot where the king's party waited. When a spent bullet hit the wall over their heads, they went inside.[10]

Perhaps the most far-reaching event of that crowded day took place at the home of Mohammed El Fasi, the tutor of thirteen-year-old Prince Moulay Hassan, the king's eldest son. El Fasi,

<hr/>

[7] R. Lauriac, "La guerre secrète au Maroc," *La Vigie Marocaine*, January 8, 1946, a serialized account beginning December 31, 1945.

[8] George F. Howe, *Northwest Africa: Seizing the Initiative in the West*, p. 92.

[9] Ibid., pp. 127, 141.

[10] King Mohammed V gave this account to the author at Rabat, November 20, 1957. The palace retainers, who asked that their names not be used, gave the author substantially identical accounts at Rabat, May 17, 1967.

unbeknown to the king, was an active member of the militant nationalist group. He met on Sunday night November 8, with Mohammed Ghazi and others of nationalist persuasion and decided that the moment of their liberation was at hand—not liberation from the Germans, of whom they knew little, but liberation from the French.

The next morning El Fasi identified himself to the king as a member of the nationalist movement, told him of the meeting the night before, and urged him to take a position in favor of the Americans. Specifically he urged him not to leave Rabat to go to Fez as the resident-general was urging. "His Majesty was thirsty for news of the nationalist movement," El Fasi recalled. "He questioned me as to my associations, and I told him. Finally, he agreed to join us in the struggle. His refusal to leave Rabat was the first open indication given by His Majesty that he was with us."[11]

Mr. El Fasi's account is consistent with the historical record. Marshal Juin, commander in chief of the French forces in North Africa at the moment of the debarkation, and later resident-general in Morocco, has said that King Mohammed V was "faithful to the policy of cooperation until after the Allied debarkation in North Africa."[12] However, the king's change of heart apparently came before the debarkation and had deeper significance than can be explained by political events. It emanated from profound religious convictions of which only the king's intimates were fully aware or can, even now, fully appreciate.

King Mohammed V, asked in 1947 who had been his "tutor" in nationalism, gave this account:

I had read, and talked, and studied, but the turning point came in 1941 after a particularly trying experience with General Noguès, who insisted that I apply the Vichy anti-Semitism laws to my Jewish subjects. I slept badly. I had a dream in which my father appeared. I recognized my father, and I knew he was dead and was appearing to me in a vision. He counseled me to be patient with the foreigners in Morocco and not to risk the throne and my family.

Then suddenly another person appeared, tall, handsome, and im-

[11] Interview, Mohammed El Fasi, Rabat, Morocco, May 26, 1967. Formerly minister of national education in the Moroccan government, at the time of the interview president of University Mohammed V, at Rabat.

[12] Alphonse Juin, *Mémoires*, II, 144–145.

posing. He told me: "Do not listen to your father. It is your duty to protect your people. That is why you are here. You will suffer much, but, with God's help, you will win."

Then the figure faded away. My father was still there. His brow was beaded with sweat, and he appeared very uneasy. I asked him who the other man had been.

"That was the Prophet," he said.[13]

Whatever the philosophical background of Mohammed V's conversion to the nationalist point of view, it appears that his conversation with Mr. El Fasi was significant in translating resolution into action. He immediately canceled orders given earlier that morning for a car to take his children to his farm thirty-five miles east of Rabat. "We will stay here," he told the chauffeur. "The Americans will not harm us."[14] Later in the day he "took a position in favor of the Americans"; he had the palace chamberlain telephone General Noguès and tell him to stop the fighting. "The French Army can wade in the waters and fight outside our territories. The lives of my subjects must be protected."[15] The king reminded General Noguès that he, too, had declared war on the Axis on September 3, 1939, and that he had not signed an armistice.

On the basis of available evidence, it is difficult to evaluate the significance of the last statement. Was it a forthright assertion of sovereignty, or simply emphasis for his demand that the fighting be stopped? It was probably the latter, for, although the French welcomed the declaration of support in 1939, France never conceded and the king never otherwise claimed the authority to make war and peace until the Treaty of Fez had been abrogated in 1956.

The moment that the first American soldier set foot on Moroccan soil, the problem of the relationship between the G.I. and the Mo-

[13] Interview, Mehdi Bennouna, Rabat, May 11, 1967. The king told the story to Mr. Bennouna in the summer of 1947, just prior to the latter's departure on a propagandizing mission to the United States. Several of the king's close associates indicated to the author in May–June, 1967, that they also had heard the story from King Mohammed V.

[14] Interview with the chauffeur, who asked that his name not be used, at Rabat, Morocco, May 17, 1967.

[15] Mahdi A. Bennouna, *Our Morocco: The True Story of a Just Cause*, p. 59. His account was confirmed by Mohammed El Fasi, and by Dr. Sadani, Moroccan minister of state for African affairs, in interviews at Rabat, May 28, 1967.

roccan people was transformed from a theoretical one to a practical one. That relationship developed empirically, emanating from instinct, for the G.I. had little practical guidance. Quite obviously the vice-consuls had oriented their activities toward the French minority, regarding the Moroccan majority in the usual stereotypes. General Patton, for example, had opposed a landing at Rabat because he wanted to "avoid stirring up the natives in their holy city of Rabat."[16] Rabat, the political capital, was not a "holy city" any more than Casablanca, Fez, Marrakech, or Tangier. General Patton's preconception is quite evident in his memoirs, in which biblical metaphors fall like rain.[17]

Concerning the "natives," the G.I. received conflicting instructions. He was advised on the one hand to avoid the native people insofar as possible, because their water was contaminated, their food was not sanitary, and their houses were infested with vermin and live fleas.[18] On the other hand, he was advised to treat the country Arabs with friendly confidence, to accept their food, and to participate in their social life.[19] The latter memorandum also advised airmen forced down in Morocco to avoid Frenchmen and rich, city Arabs who, from fear of the French or because they were employed by them, might be inclined to betray the downed airmen.

Seemingly, the confidence in the country Arab was not misplaced. All pilots and crewmen of the Twelfth Air Force carried a message from President Roosevelt in Arabic and English, based upon the apparent assumption that someone would be able to read one of the two. The message read:

To all Arab Peoples: Greetings, and peace be with you. The bearer of this letter is a soldier of the United States government and a friend of all Arabs. Treat him well, guard him from harm, give him food and drink, help him to return to the nearest American or British soldiers,

[16] Samuel Eliot Morison, *Operations in North African Waters, October, 1942– June, 1943*, p. 115.

[17] See George S. Patton, Jr., *War As I Knew It*, pp. 12–13, 15, 47–48.

[18] "Pertinent Data on French Morocco," a document dated October 25, 1942, in USAF Archives, file no. 612.610, p. 7.

[19] "Miscellaneous Material Dealing with the Moroccan Landings," in the USAF Archives, file no. 651.430-1, September–December, 1942.

and you will be liberally rewarded. Peace, and the mercy of God be upon you.

Franklin D. Roosevelt
President of the United States[20]

Lieutenant Colonel Roland F. Wooten, of St. Stephens, South Carolina, made good use of the message. He crash-landed near an Arab community and was surrounded by Arabs who thought him French until he produced the president's message. A spokesman for the Arab group expressed pleasure that the Americans had come and described the sufferings of the village, pillaged of everything useful for shipment to Germany or Italy. He accepted a gold coin from Wooten, but said it was not necessary to pay for their help, for it would be given with pleasure.[21]

The realization that the Americans were "different" did not long escape the Moroccan people, high and low. The king registered his "immense satisfaction" with the American soldiers whom he had seen on November 10, near Casablanca, playing with Moroccan children.[22] Youssef Omar, born "about 1922" in the Tata tribe in Morocco's Souss Valley, came to Kenitra in the 1930's to work for a French establishment and was there when the landings took place. "I did not care one way or the other," he said. "The Americans meant nothing to me . . . but I could see a difference. They played around with the Moroccan kids—gave them gum and candy."[23] Thus, the uncoached G.I. seems to have touched upon a sensibility that is peculiar to the Moroccan mentality as well as the American.[24]

The American troops who reluctantly stormed ashore at Mehdia Beach and elsewhere in North Africa were not veteran soldiers. They were civilians in uniform—farm boys, artisans, students. They had never been shot at before and, significantly, knew no

[20] "History of the Twelfth Air Force," vol. I, part I, annex 19, p. 30 in USAF Archives, file no. 650-01, vol. I.

[21] Ibid., p. 48.

[22] To General Patton, reported in *La Vigie Marocaine*, November 18, 1942.

[23] Interview, Youssef Omar, Kenitra, Morocco, May 5, 1967. Youssef Omar has worked for the United States armed forces since 1942.

[24] Frantz Toussaint, "Chants of War of Islam," *Revue d'outre-mer*, numéro spécial, *Maroc: Terre d'avenir, 1948*, p. 132, indicates the Moroccan mentality: "I am a generous victor who never pillages or burns an encampment. I do not cut off the heads of my enemies. I respect their women. I caress their children."

one who could tell them what war was like. They were three thousand miles from home, and their sense of isolation was the greater because their families did not even know where they were. They reacted to their novel circumstances, some with craven fear, some with bravado, but by and large with credit to their country.

The Boniface family at Mehdia Beach was the first to establish contact, then friendships, with the American soldiers. Within minutes after the first G.I. set foot on Mehdia Beach, Mr. and Mrs. Boniface, standing on their veranda, were challenged: "Are you Italian or German?"[25] Mr. Boniface assured his challenger that he was a French civilian who lived at Mehdia Beach, and he was thereafter treated with courtesy and consideration. Before the day was over, Mrs. Boniface was "mothering" scared, homesick G.I.'s. She found one hiding in her cellar who followed her to her back door begging, "Madame, I am scared. Take me prisoner." Then an artillery shell burst close at hand, and the scared G.I. was killed.

Mehdia Beach, occupied by the Americans on November 8 and never retaken by the French forces, presented the first civil-affairs problems encountered by the U.S. Army. General Truscott had established his headquarters in the casino with a field hospital alongside. The troops had taken over many of the unoccupied beach houses for shelter. However, sixteen French families were living in Mehdia Beach.[26] Their food normally came from Port Lyautey, but Port Lyautey was cut off, and by Monday they lacked bread, meat, vegetables—almost everything except wine— for refrigeration was virtually nonexistent, and housewives shopped daily for their needs. Mr. Boniface, officially director of Mehdia Beach, went to the American headquarters to seek relief. He was well received, he said, and the Americans were sympathetic. Ra-

[25] The source of information for the American occupation of Mehdia Beach as discussed in the next two pages was the interview with Mr. and Mrs. Boniface, at Mehdia Beach, May 25, 1967. The persistent expectation of an Axis presence, particularly in the Port Lyautey area, is in itself a commentary on intelligence procedures within the Allied forces, for René Malevergne, embarked with the Northern Task Force, lived at Mehdia Beach, and his wife and children were there during the landing. Germans or Italians were never garrisoned or lived at Mehdia Beach or Port Lyautey, information obviously known to Malevergne.

[26] Truscott, *Command Missions*, p. 116, states that Mehdia Beach was unoccupied at the time of the landing.

tions in the form of pork and beans, tomato and fruit juices, and C-rations were issued on the basis of the list of inhabitants Mr. Boniface provided.

"It was a little adventure," Mrs. Boniface recalled, "for even with a dictionary it was not possible to translate the labels—but we survived. We amused ourselves [the ladies] competing to see what we could make out of these strange things."

The list of Mehdia Beach inhabitants that Mr. Boniface provided for the American headquarters contained the names of two French sailors. The American commander objected that he could not permit hostile forces behind his lines, but accepted Mr. Boniface's assurance that the sailors had no inclination to fight against the Americans and that they would not attempt to escape, since their wives and children were there. They were arrested and paroled to Mr. Boniface.

The Ninth Division, the Boniface account concluded, remained for some three months before moving on, and Mehdia Beach returned to "the state we are now in"—half of its population American military personnel and their families. Mehdia Beach was no longer only a summer resort; it had become a year-round residential suburb.

In Port Lyautey, a garrison town for its entire corporate existence, circumstances were different from those at Mehdia Beach. The town witnessed three days of fighting, time for hostility toward the invaders to crystallize. Civilian and military families alike watched the French army—their husbands, fathers, and neighbors —moving through town leading pack horses, moving up toward the sound of artillery fire, moving up "to the butchery," one observer remarked.[27] The local hospital was filled with wounded, and a warehouse next to the French military headquarters was filled with the unburied bodies of the dead. The stench hung over the entire town.[28] The final assault on the airfield launched from the U.S.S. *Dallas* on November 10 took place in full view of the town. René Malevergne, the port's ex-chief pilot, had brought the *Dallas* through the boom at the river's mouth and up the tortuous, ob-

[27] Interview, Mrs. Jeanne Mortier; the observer was her father.
[28] Interview, Mrs. Hélène Walton, née Campillo, Kenitra, Morocco, June 4, 1967. She was working as a secretary at the French headquarters at the time of the invasion.

structed channel to launch the commandos against the airfield. And while French soldiers were fighting and dying, the automobile of the American consul at Casablanca, a shiny new Plymouth bearing diplomatic license plates, moved with impunity about Port Lyautey, driven by French army officers.[29] Understandably, the people of Port Lyautey were confused.

Despite the differing circumstances, the reaction of people in Port Lyautey and throughout Morocco was substantially the same as that of the people of Mehdia Beach: first apprehension, then curiosity, then acceptance. After the fighting was over, the Americans were encamped at the southwestern edge of the city near the Mimosas Café. Theirs was not a well-planned camp; tents were pitched at random, and the soldiers were still in battlefield dress. The inhabitants of the town flocked out to see them as if to the zoo. And they were not disappointed. One soldier, with his canteen held high, greeted them: "This water is from America! This water is from America!" The two Port Lyautey men who spoke English, Angelo Ligiardi and René Malevergne, were in great demand as guides and exponents.

Anna Campillo, whom her friends called Nony, was seventeen years old when the Americans came to Morocco. She lived with her parents, three sisters, and one brother at the western edge of Port Lyautey adjacent to the American encampment. What was her most vivid memory? "I think it was the silence of the American vehicles," she said. "All of the French vehicles were *gasogen* [converted to burn charcoal], and they were very noisy. The American vehicles were almost upon you before you ever heard them."

"I was never afraid," Nony recalled, "although we had heard terrible things about American soldiers—that they were a rough, tough sort, like the Foreign Legion. . . . One day, on the street in the middle of town, one of them grabbed me and kissed me—not an ordinary kiss, but mmmm. I couldn't breathe. Another time,

[29] According to Colonel Adrien Feste, interview, Casablanca, May 27, 1967, General Marie E. Bethouart, Robert Murphy's nominee as commander of French forces in Morocco after the landing, arrested General Georges Lascroux, whom he was to replace, and sent him to Meknes in the car in the custody of the Guillaume brothers, both lieutenants in the French army. General André Dody, commanding at Meknes, released Lascroux and arrested the Guillaume brothers. Colonel Léon and Feste took the car to go to Port Lyautey, and continued using it until after the armistice, November 11.

some of them came down the street in a jeep, and one of them reached out and slapped a girl's face. She had never even seen him before. . . . That wasn't nice, do you think?"[30]

The Campillo home quickly became a rendezvous for the American G.I.'s, a situation explained in part by the elder Campillo's hospitality and in part by the presence of four eligible daughters, two of whom subsequently married American servicemen. The men came as individual suitors, and as group visitors, often with food for Mrs. Campillo to prepare for them, and sometimes because they were homesick. Mrs. Campillo mailed many letters to mothers in the United States with the message, "Your son had dinner with us last night . . . He is in good health, but very busy . . . He will write when he has time."[31]

Corporal Jimmy Longcup personified the G.I.'s humanitarian instinct for the Campillo family and their friends. A polished New Yorker, he was older than the average G.I., and perhaps more inclined to individual initiative. He came to the Campillo home looking for a bottle of liquor. He noted a child, the Campillo's son, ill of pneumonia aggravated by malnutrition. Longcup left, but soon returned with "a truckload" of food. "Until my brother was out of danger . . . until New Year's Eve, 1942, he took over our home. He was stricter with us girls than my father; every boy that came around—French, too—received his careful scrutiny. His outfit went to Tunisia, and Jimmy lost an arm there. He was shipped home, and we never knew what happened to him, but we will never forget him. He saved my brother's life."[32]

Most people in Morocco, whether French or Moslem, associate the coming of the G.I. with "better times." Although vegetables were always available, bread was not, and meat, fats, soap, and a wide range of comfort commodities were both scarce and rationed after 1940. "After the war," Mr. Campillo used to say, "I am going to get a plot of good land, well watered, with lots of fertilizer, and grow carrots. Then I am going to stomp them into the

[30] Interview, Mrs. Nony Nourani, née Campillo, Kenitra, Morocco, May 21, 1967. The author interviewed dozens of individuals in May–June, 1967 who lived in Port Lyautey during the 1940's, and the foregoing is a composite, except where an individual is directly quoted.

[31] Ibid.

[32] Interview, Mrs. Helène Walton.

ground."[33] He was that tired of carrots. After November, 1942, the rationing continued, but more commodities were available from supplies put into the normal distribution channels by the U.S. Army, the black market, and gifts from individual soldiers.

The social impact of the G.I. upon the local community was immediate; indeed it is illogical to think that the arrival of so many new people in a relatively small community would not have an immediate and profound impact. Fathers and mothers no longer needed to plead with their high-school-age children to "study your English; you never know when you will need it." They needed it now. Before the month was out, the American Red Cross leased a ballroom across from the Continental Bar in downtown Port Lyautey, and conducted twice-a-week dances for the American soldiers and "nice girls" from the local community. On other nights the center was open to soldiers and their guests, whoever they might be.

The twice-a-week chaperoned dances were adequately financed and featured good bands; they gave Port Lyautey an ambiance it had never had before. Girls of good reputation in the community who desired to attend were picked up at their home by a U.S. Army bus (which had an armed escort) between seven and eight o'clock and returned with the same precautions between eleven and midnight. They could neither come nor return by other means, but what they did later, or on other nights, was not the concern of either the Red Cross or the U.S. Army.[34] The town rapidly became U.S. Army oriented.

The arrival of the American soldiers produced another, less salubrious, social change in Port Lyautey. Prior to their arrival, Port Lyautey's red-light district had been carefully restricted to the *medina* quarter of the city; afterwards, prostitution spread to the European quarter. The U.S. Army was both consciously and unconsciously responsible. From the commanding general on down, the G.I. heard: "Leave the Arab women alone. Stay away from them. Stay out of the *medina* at night. You risk more than a new, virulent type of venereal disease—you risk a cut throat, or worse."[35]

---

[33] Ibid.

[34] The Campillo girls changed clothes after the dances, then queued up for the rationed items.

[35] General Patton relates in *War As I Knew It*, pp. 13–14, his conversation with King Mohammed V on November 16, 1942, in which he assured him that

The enterprising Madame Suzon, newly arrived in Port Lyautey from the French Congo, provided joy without risk (of getting one's throat cut). She assembled a bevy of Spanish, French, and Jewish girls and opened a brothel almost at the gate of the army encampment. Her girls were medically inspected by U.S. Army doctors, and she continued to operate until at least 1946, although she changed locations after the departure of the Ninth Infantry Division in January, 1943.[36]

The black market, the other *bête noire* of the commander of an overseas American base, probably arrived in Morocco with the invasion force. It found fertile ground in the "shortage of food and practically everything else, including toilet paper, that you could name."[37] By 1944 it had reached significant proportions. One culprit estimated that "at least ninety percent of all hands were dealing in the black market,"[38] and another that "practically everyone was engaged in dealings in the local black market."[39] At the upper echelons of command, there was no problem because it was not called "black market" when the base commander supplied the local dignitaries with scarce commodities in order to cultivate "good will" and social acceptance. The G.I., however, could see little difference in principle between such operations and his own money-making deals.

At Port Lyautey the black market had two sources of supply, the base "ship's store" and smuggled goods. The ship's store items

---

orders "had been issued in forceful language prior to our departure from the United States and would be enforced" to assure respect for Moroccan institutions. On pages 23–24, he reported his conversation with the grand vizier concerning the "proper hanging" of miscreants, such as rapists.

[36] Captain William E. G. Taylor, USN, in a letter to the author dated Washington, D.C., May 1, 1967, said that when he assumed command of the U.S. Naval Air Station at Port Lyautey in the early summer of 1945, "I inherited from my predecessors [a brothel] in the Medina at Port Lyautey, which I took over completely for the station personnel under the supervision of our medical officers."

[37] Captain William E. G. Taylor, USN, letter to the author, dated Washington, D.C., July 28, 1967.

[38] Sworn affidavit, Lloyd Earl Phillips, dated July 26, 1944, in the Truman C. Penney papers, Walnut Creek, California.

[39] Sworn affidavit, Edward David Bonham, dated July 27, 1944, in the Truman C. Penney papers, Walnut Creek, California.

were "hotter" than the smuggled ones because they were more readily identifiable. Generally speaking, however, only personnel from the aviation squadrons were able to smuggle in profitable quantities. Lloyd Earl Phillips, attached to the Naval Air Transport Service at Port Lyautey, dealt in the black market. He bought suit material in Natal, Brazil, through an intermediary, a mechanic for American Export Lines, to whom he paid a 100 percent markup. The material was flown to Port Lyautey on one of the giant Coronado seaplanes, and Phillips sold it either in Rabat or Port Lyautey. On one typical "deal" he paid two hundred dollars for thirty meters of suit material, which he sold in Rabat for eight hundred dollars. Sometimes he worked as a middleman, buying sheets flown in from Patuxent River, Maryland, on the R5D transport planes for ten dollars each and reselling them for twenty. For a time he dealt in watches bought by squadron mates for him in "hock shops" in the United States, but the English flooded the market with watches from Gibraltar and he did little better than break even. In fact he lost most of the proceeds from the watches to a pickpocket and the rest in a crap game.

Phillips had no difficulty in selling almost anything. People were "just begging to buy articles on the black market, especially clothing. . . . It seemed every Arab kid in town knew someone because they all wanted to know if we had business." Before he left Port Lyautey in July, Phillips had made arrangements with "Jimmie, a Frenchman working for NATS," to sell his merchandise for him, and he used Navy transportation to haul it into town.[40]

The black market operations at Port Lyautey reflected not only the opportunity associated with the wartime shortages in Morocco, but also the undisciplined character of the American personnel. Neither Phillips nor Bonham expressed any remorse for their participation; they justified it by insisting that "everyone, even the officers" were similarly engaged. Both said they were sorry to have lied about their involvement when initially asked about it. They were representative of the personnel sent to Port Lyautey who were, generally speaking, not the navy's most impeccable in conduct. Thirty-seven men temporarily attached to the Naval Air Station committed a total of 62 offenses for which they were punished

[40] Lloyd Earl Phillips affidavit. Phillips was not punished for his black-market dealings because of the assistance he gave in breaking up the traffic.

either at disciplinary captain's mast or court-martial, and 106 men permanently attached committed a total of 248 offenses. Captain Penney explained that while some of the offenses were cases of "going by the book with no allowance for civilians in uniform," the majority were the consequence of an unfortunate navy policy that permitted one command to transfer its unwanted personnel to another command—and Port Lyautey was the end of the line.[41]

That great international sport of gouging the G.I. did not immediately assume major proportions in Morocco. This practice awaited the end of the war and the arrival of American women and children, for the soldier did not need housing or facilities. General Patton noted that money initially had little value, for there was nothing to buy.[42] The soldier spent his money in restaurants and bars, and he was not less gullible than countless ones who came after him; he, too, bought ordinary sparkling wine at champagne prices,[43] which perhaps explains the absence of drunkenness amongst American soldiers on liberty in Morocco.[44] He could not afford enough of it to become inebriated.

The Moroccan intelligentsia did not wait long to pass judgment on the American forces. *La Voix Nationale*, on January 10, 1943, "saluted with joy the arrival of the American troops" as a step toward the recovery of Morocco's "full function in the concert of nations." Another writer concluded that the Moroccans were "reassured and seduced by the courtesy of the Americans," who had become in a few short weeks "a source of prosperity for the present and hope for the future"—these "allies whom we hope to make our friends."[45]

---

[41] Brig Reports, in the Truman C. Penney papers. The Naval Air Station existed to provide services and facilities for the operating forces, and by far the greater part of the personnel at Port Lyautey were attached to Fleet Air Wing Fifteen and to Naval Air Transport Service.

[42] Patton, *War As I Knew It*, p. 18.

[43] *La Voix Nationale*, February 10, 1943.

[44] Patton, *War As I Knew It*, p. 19, said he had seen only one drunk soldier (by November 19).

[45] El Mathar, "Chewing Gum," *La Voix Nationale*, January 10, 1943. El Mathar was a pseudonym for Reda Ahmed Guedira, who as minister of national defense, minister of information, minister of agriculture, foreign minister, and president of the Council of Ministers has played a dominant role in Moroccan politics since 1955.

Interestingly, at a time when newspapers all over the world were stressing the military aspects of the American invasion of North Africa, *La Voix Nationale* wrote of American idealism. "America was born of an act of faith: of indestructible optimism and unshakable confidence of the first settlers—who came to escape injustice."[46] It voiced approval of the Atlantic Charter, but said it would be meaningless without the history of the United States.[47] It paid homage for the Moroccan people to the American troops, who "were respectful of their fellowman, treated women with respect, treated children with touching humor, paid their bills, and were filled with a sense of human dignity. . . . The prolonged usage of liberty," the editor concluded, "constitutes a surer sense of responsibility than severe coercion."[48]

Although *La Voix Nationale* did not subscribe in 1942–1943 to the set of values current in the United States and Great Britain, its point of view was representative, consistent, and important. It provided a prophetic view of the future. For example, Reda Guedira saw the Allied debarkation presaging a "liberal democratic economy" in North Africa; twenty years later, he was director of the ministerial cabinet and in a position to implement such a policy in Morocco.[49] The United States ought not to have been surprised by, nor fearful of, the Moroccan independence movement, for it was modeled upon the American experience.

[46] *La Voix Nationale*, March 20, 1943.
[47] Ibid., January 20, 1943.
[48] "Remerciements à l'armée américaine," Ibid., March 10, 1943.
[49] In an interview at Rabat, May 20, 1967, Mr. Guedira explained his concept of a liberal democratic economic system as one in which private initiative and capital played the major role and the state, a coordinating role, exercising control only in such key sectors as ports, highways, and airports, the same policy to which he had referred in *La Voix Nationale*, April 20, 1943.

4. Civil Affairs: "A Can of Worms"

THE ESTABLISHMENT of an American presence in Morocco posed a critical question—one that was never resolved. To use Carl Becker's aphorism, it was home rule, but who was to rule at home? Allied policy makers, who saw the American presence as a short-term one, were little concerned with home rule, but were vitally concerned with the conflict between United States and French imperatives, and with the political infighting in both the French and U.S. camps. President Roosevelt arrogated to himself the dominant policy role, but seemed unable to make up his mind whether the role of the U.S. Army in North Africa was military occupation or not.[1] Nor did he have the time to devote adequate attention to the day-to-day political developments. Lacking positive and consistent guidance, U.S. policy backed and filled, blown by the winds of expediency.

[1] See Robert Murphy, *Diplomat among Warriors*, pp. 145, 169, for conflicting statements.

In the first place, United States military strategists had never wanted to enter North Africa. Once in Africa, they wanted to pull out as quickly as possible, return to England, and launch a cross-channel attack. Their concepts had been subordinated to a centuries-old British strategy—the protection of their Mediterranean lifeline. And for two years Americans fought in the Mediterranean, a traditionally British sphere of influence. By following British strategy, American ideas concerning French territories automatically became obsolete. Whatever might have been President Roosevelt's personal convictions on colonization, he was obliged to go along with the British policy, which envisaged a strong central French authority as necessary to ensure the tranquility of North Africa.

Nor did he ever resolve the conflicts within his own government over who should direct "civil affairs," that all-embracing term for other than tactical military operations in occupied territories. The distracting, debilitating controversies chiefly involved the United States Army, the Office of Lend-Lease Administration and its subordinate agencies, and the American Red Cross.

The position of the army was clear: Operation Torch was a military operation, and almost every problem in North Africa, insofar as the United States was concerned, was related to it. Confronted with the threat that a hostile population would pose for its supply lines running through Morocco and Algeria, the army sought to placate the as yet uncommitted citizenry of North Africa by alleviating the economic distress the war had entailed. General Eisenhower was not particularly concerned with the long-range political significance of his decisions; he regarded the North African native simply as a laborer who would be quiet and not disrupt military operations if given an increased allotment of food and clothing.[2]

The Office of Lend-Lease, dominant among the half-dozen agencies operating under the secretary of state in the field of civil affairs,[3] was charged with the responsibility of financing and pro-

[2] George F. Howe, *Northwest Africa: Seizing the Initiative in the West*, pp. 57–58.

[3] See Harry L. Coles and Albert K. Weinberg, *Civil Affairs: Soldiers Become Governors*, pp. 41–42. This source contains an exhaustive treatment of civil affairs administration and planning in World War II.

curing supplies for the occupied areas. It was a temporary agency, without administrative experience or tradition, and without operating personnel, and it was not particularly effective in North Africa. It was politically potent at home, however, and it hampered military operations by complaints to the White House that the United States Army planned to control the postwar world, ruling it by armed force, instead of establishing a "civilian democratic free world."[4]

The Office of Lend-Lease was not able to discharge its asserted responsibilities in North Africa until after mid-1943. It sought to ban the American Red Cross from the theater and hire away its personnel.[5] Rebuffed, it then tried to borrow from the army, which, accustomed to feeding, housing, providing for the health of, and dispensing justice to masses in camps larger than many cities, refused to do for another agency a job that it felt better able by reason of experience to do itself.[6] But war would not wait for the resolution of departmental infighting in Washington; the requirements of the civilian population in North Africa were met from military supplies.[7] General Patton exchanged sugar, tea, cloth, and other commodities for Arab labor,[8] and, at the request of General Noguès, provided the French with 185,000 gallons of gasoline for agricultural use and 190 cubic meters of diesel fuel for the fishing fleet.[9]

The Red Cross position was analogous to that of the army. It had supplies and an experienced organization for distributing them— and it was the object of the same petty jealousies and carping criticism. Lend-Lease begrudged shipping space for Red Cross sup-

---

[4] By letter dated January 8, 1943, Secretary of Interior Harold L. Ickes forwarded to President Roosevelt a memorandum from an aide, Saul K. Padover, concerning the U.S. army school at Charlottesville, Virginia, for civil administrators, urging him to put a stop to army plans that he thought would lead to "the worst kind of trouble, notwithstanding who may win the war." Letter and memorandum in the Franklin D. Roosevelt Library, Hyde Park, New York.

[5] File no. 973.08 French Africa-War Relief, North Africa Section, pp. 1, 9, in the American Red Cross Archives, 1725 E. Street, N.W., Washington, D.C.

[6] Coles and Weinberg, *Civil Affairs*, p. 56.

[7] *Logistical History of NATOUSA-MTOUSA*, pp. 331–332.

[8] George S. Patton, Jr., *War As I Knew It*, p. 18.

[9] *La Vigie Marocaine*, December 19, 1942.

plies,[10] and, unwilling to share its responsibility, refused the Red Cross offer of aid in the distribution of Lend-Lease supplies.[11] The essence of the conflict, however, was the attempt of the political agencies of the United States government to divert Red Cross supplies from relief aid to French commercial channels.[12]

The internecine conflict in the American camp was compounded by French pressures. Jacques Lemaigre-Dubreuil and the *groupements*, cartels managing trade and distribution, sought to reestablish prewar channels of production and distribution. They wanted the available shipping used for production items: machinery, coal, gasoline, and kerosene.[13] The dust had hardly settled from the landing before *La Vigie Marocaine* launched an editorial plea for agricultural machines, "more essential than weapons."[14] The French objected to direct relief, particularly to the Arab population.[15] Chief of [French] Services of Production Igonet opposed free distribution of Red Cross layettes, which, he said, went to the black market. He recommended selling them through commercial channels,[16] and Fred K. Hoehler, who headed Lend-Lease activities in North Africa, recommended holding them for the European population, which he said would use them more advantageously than the "indigenes."[17] William H. Giblin for the Red Cross indignantly rejected both recommendations: "I cannot understand," he said, "how the United States or the Allies can plan a world wide relief program without including as an integral part of the plan the voluntary free will offerings of the American people. It is a traditional characteristic of the American people which is known in almost all parts of the civilized world."[18] Although the French were unable to secure modification of Red Cross policy concerning the layettes, their insistence on the primacy of commercial channels over

[10] "Summary Report by Hugh Buckner Johnson," file no. 973.08, French Africa–War Relief, North Africa Section, Appendix, doc. no. 1.

[11] Ibid., pp. 1–3.

[12] Ibid., and p. 25.

[13] Waverly Root, *Casablanca to Katyn: The Secret History of the War*, p. 198.

[14] *La Vigie Marocaine*, December 4, 1942.

[15] "First Quarterly Report, March 31, 1943," in American Red Cross Archives, file no. 973.08, French Africa–War Relief, North Africa Section, appendix, p. 19.

[16] Hoehler to Giblin letter dated March 24, 1943, in ibid., pp. 11–13.

[17] Hoehler to Frank Wheeler cable dated June 30, 1943, in ibid., p. 38.

[18] Giblin to Richard F. Allen cable dated June 17, 1943, in ibid., p. 38.

donated relief did prevail.[19] On March 31, 1943, Mr. Hoehler terminated the free distribution of milk in the schools, despite Red Cross protests that school would continue for another month and it had six hundred tons of powdered milk on hand. Since the protests were unavailing, the Red Cross delivered the remaining milk to Mr. Hoehler. If it spoiled, as the Red Cross considered probable, it would spoil in his hands.[20] The Red Cross relief operation in North Africa that ceased in August had lasted for about ten months, and since it was so closely associated in the public mind with the U.S. Army, in the coincidence of arrival if nothing else, the favorable reaction redounded to the army's credit.[21]

In fact, the plight of the North African population seems not to have been as desperate as the Americans were led to believe. When Dr. George K. Strode, from the Rockefeller Foundation, surveyed the North African situation for the Red Cross, he found little or no starvation and little evidence of deficiency disease.[22] But the operation did serve the military objective of placating the local populations, and it was long remembered. The free milk program alone served 799,200 people through 149 local agencies and 6,400 volunteer workers who operated 2,085 distribution points in thirteen major cities (over 20,000 population) in Morocco.[23] In addition, the Red Cross distributed clothing and blankets, over ten tons in December, 1942, alone; conducted massive inoculation programs; and even distributed 27,200 rubber nipples, one at a time upon a doctor's prescription.[24] The money value of the aid to North Africa given by the Red Cross was $700,221.24, of which $398,812.56 was in government-furnished material.[25]

[19] Ibid., and Hoehler to Frank Wheeler cable dated June 20, 1943, in ibid.

[20] Giblin to Allen cable dated June 17, 1943, in ibid.

[21] See Giblin to Allen letter dated April 14, 1943, in ibid., pp. 22–24, in which Giblin stated: "The actual direction and administration [of relief] seem to have become the complete responsibility of the military."

[22] George K. Strode, "A Brief Report and Recommendation on the North African Survey of Civilian Relief," in ibid., pp. 4–5.

[23] "Foreign War Relief Operations," Senate Document No. 228, 78th Congress, 2d Session.

[24] William E. Stevenson to Norman H. Davis cable dated December 7, 1942, pp. 1ff., and "First Quarterly Report, March 31, 1943," in American Red Cross Archives, file no. 973.08, French North Africa Appendix.

[25] "Foreign War Relief Operations," Senate Document No. 228, 78th Congress, 2d Session.

Although the relief operation of the American Red Cross in North Africa terminated in 1943, its presence did not. The first Red Cross service club overseas was established at Port Lyautey in November, 1942. By the end of the fiscal year, June 30, more than two hundred were in operation, providing U.S. soldiers with meals and lodging, recreational opportunities, welfare, and personal services.[26] The service clubs operated until after the war and were reinstituted during the Korean conflict. Their impact was probably longer lasting than the relief operation. Matrons today in Port Lyautey recall "what fun we had at the Red Cross Club" during the war.

The dissension in the American camp was of minor import when compared with that in the French, which, although it polarized around General De Gaulle, was more fundamental than a personality clash. French dissension caused General Eisenhower more headaches than any tactical phase of Operation Torch.[27] Who was to rule in North Africa and in France—a legitimist, defeatist, collaborationist regime, intent on protecting such vested interests as Nazi Germany vouchsafed, or what appeared to be an equally totalitarian[28] but anti-Nazi "Fighting French" one? The United States chose neither. Instead it sought to create a third force, less tainted with collaboration, but also untainted with dissidence, to which, hopefully, the French in North Africa would rally. General Henri Giraud was the American choice to head it, and American authorities stuck with him long after it became apparent that he was a loser.

Giraud's French backers had driven a hard political bargain in his name, but General Giraud was unable in fact to deliver. He found little support in North Africa until covered with the "legitimist" mantle of Admiral Darlan. There is little doubt, in retrospect, that the Allies could have had the support of Admiral Darlan from the outset, and they did have his loyal and effective cooperation after November 8. He strained his own legitimacy pretensions, perhaps spurred by General Mark Clark's threat to arrest him and

---

[26] *American Red Cross Annual Report for Year Ending June 30, 1943*, p. 23.

[27] According to Butcher, *My Three Years with Eisenhower*, p. 198.

[28] President Roosevelt's view is indicated in the remark, recorded in Elliott Roosevelt, *As He Saw It*, p. 73: "Elliott, De Gaulle is out to achieve one man government in France. I can't imagine a man I would distrust more."

anyone else who failed to cooperate. He interpreted Pétain's enigmatic "You know you have my full confidence"[29] as authority to cease fire. His orders were obeyed, and he rallied French West Africa to the Allied cause—the same French West Africa that had beaten off De Gaulle at Dakar. Under the pressure of events, he found sufficient authorization for his further actions in Marshal Pétain's message of 3:00 P.M., November 13, advising that Pétain and Laval agreed on the accord with General Clark, but could not reply officially until the Germans had been consulted.[30]

Under the claimed authorization, Darlan entered into his far-reaching accord with General Clark (the Darlan-Clark Agreement of November 22, 1942). There was little new in it; it simply consolidated the promises contained in the Murphy-Giraud correspondence and the principal terms of the draft armistice for Darlan's signature. It guaranteed French control of the North African infrastructure, but permitted the Allied forces to use it and gave them extraterritorial privileges while there. It set up censorship on press, radio, telegraph, mail, and other organs of public expression, and it provided for rearming and retraining eleven French divisions, equipping nineteen air squadrons, and reequipping the French navy.[31]

General Eisenhower accepted responsibility for the agreement because, he said, "existing French sentiment in North Africa does not even remotely resemble prior calculations."[32] He urged Washington not to upset by precipitate action the equilibrium that he had established. Eisenhower's acceptance of the status quo was a military expediency, an attempted recovery from erroneous intelligence estimates (minimizing the possibility of French resistance), and it had the effect of "theoretically saving the difference between the 18,000 casualties [which would have resulted if

---

[29] René Richard and Alain de Serigny, *La bissectrice de la guerre: Alger, 8 Novembre 1942*, p. 82.

[30] Paul Auphan and Jacques Mordal, *The French Navy in World War II*, trans. A. C. J. Sabalot, pp. 246–247.

[31] The text of the agreement is contained in Richard and Serigny, *La bissectrice de la guerre*, pp. 226–230, and Howe, *Northwest Africa*, contains an excellent discussion of the factors involved in its conclusion. See also Murphy, *Diplomat among Warriors*, p. 141.

[32] Quoted in Howe, *Northwest Africa*, p. 268.

French resistance had continued], and the 1,800 actually suffered."[33]

The public outcry in the United States and Great Britain against any deal smacking of collaboration forced President Roosevelt to issue a qualified denouncement of the agreement as "only a temporary expedient, justified solely by the stress of battle."[34] It had, Roosevelt said, accomplished two military objectives; it had saved American, British, and French lives, and it had gained time for the attack on Tunis and Tripoli by making a mopping-up period in Morocco and Algeria unnecessary. Thereafter Roosevelt walked the tightrope of public opinion, his position always suspect because of the strict censorship that existed in North Africa, until delivered from his dilemma by Darlan's assassination.

From the whole affair Admiral François Darlan emerges a somewhat pathetic figure. He had devoted his life to the service of France and had felt obliged to work within the Vichy regime to protect the French people, insofar as he was able, from the Germans. His critics had nothing for which to reproach him after he joined the Allied cause. A realist, he recognized President Roosevelt's statement as the end of the line, and in a letter to General Eisenhower he announced his readiness to retire from political and military life when the Allies considered he had nothing further to contribute—"when the lemon had been squeezed dry"—but he pointed out that only his name had been able to rally Generals Giraud, Noguès, and Boisson, and Admiral Michelier to a common cause. Such statements as President Roosevelt's, he said, which undermined his prestige while leaving him in the key position of responsibility, did the Allied war effort no good.[35]

Darlan's death on December 24 will perhaps always remain a mystery. His assassin was Fernand Bonnier de la Chappelle—at least that much is certain—but at whose instigation he acted is uncertain. After the assassination, the twenty-year-old ex-member of Colonel Van Hecke's Chantiers de Jeunesse was tried by French

[33] Butcher, *My Three Years with Eisenhower*, p. 201.
[34] Minutes of Roosevelt's Press Conference #861, of November 10, 1942, in the Franklin D. Roosevelt Library, Hyde Park, New York.
[35] Admiral Darlan's letter, dated November 21, 1942, is quoted in Butcher, *My Three Years with Eisenhower*, pp. 206–207.

court-martial, convicted, and immediately shot, hopeful to the last that the American high command would intervene to save him.[36] General De Gaulle implies in his memoirs that the Allies liquidated their "temporary expedient" after having made use of it, but the evidence is equally persuasive that the Gaullists were responsible. Whether an Allied plot, a royalist plot,[37] or the work of a deranged mind, only De Gaulle stood to benefit—and he did benefit from the removal of Darlan from the political scene.

With Darlan out of the way, De Gaulle moved swiftly to consolidate his political power, using General Giraud as his own temporary expedient. On December 25, he called upon Giraud to meet him either in Algeria or Chad to organize a provisional government for metropolitan France and her overseas territories.[38] Such a proposal was clearly not in accord with Allied political plans, and Giraud demurred. On January 1, De Gaulle addressed another appeal to Giraud and on January 2 made a public statement calling for a provisional central power that would include "Fighting France." Neither appeal produced the desired results, but the lines were clearly drawn.[39]

General De Gaulle attended the Casablanca conference with President Roosevelt, Prime Minister Churchill, and Giraud, but only because Churchill threatened to withdraw British support from him if he persisted in his refusal to come. He achieved nothing. He found Giraud "stubborn," unconcerned with political problems, and hostile to the "elementary, popular, revolutionary character of the resistance in France."[40] President Roosevelt, in a protocol signed by himself and Giraud, ratified all of the provisions

[36] *The War Memoirs of Charles De Gaulle: Unity, 1942–1944*, trans. Richard Howard, II, 75. De Gaulle, pp. 72–76, gives a detailed account of the "seething discontent" in North Africa that he said united diverse political groups in opposition to Darlan. Butcher, *My Three Years with Eisenhower*, pp. 226, 335, implies that De Gaulle procured the assassination.

[37] *Memoirs of Charles De Gaulle*, II, 72–73, indicates that the Count of Paris pretender to the French throne, was in Algiers gathering his followers at the time of the assassination, and Marcel Peyrouton, in an interview with the author at Casablanca, May 27, 1967, said flatly that the assassination was part of a royalist plot.

[38] *Memoirs of Charles De Gaulle*, II: *Documents*, p. 117.

[39] Ibid., pp. 120–121.

[40] Ibid., pp. 85–96.

of the Murphy-Giraud agreement except the one conferring the Allied command upon Giraud after the landing had been secured.[41] De Gaulle fulminated—as he often did—against "dictation from Washington."

In March, 1943, "Washington" still insisted that "no supreme political power should be set up now to exercise control over the French people. No provisional government should be created or recognized, and any political activities should be kept to the minimum dictated by necessity."[42] By June, however, De Gaulle had won his point, and the French Committee of National Liberation was set up with De Gaulle and Giraud as cochairmen to "direct the war effort . . . exercise sovereignty in all territories not occupied by the enemy, and administer and defend French interests."[43] Vichyites were to be purged. Peyrouton in Algeria had seen the handwriting on the wall and resigned on June 1. De Gaulle ordered him to hand over his functions to his secretary-general and report as a captain in the Colonial infantry to the general, commander in chief in the Levant—this ex-resident-general and ex-ambassador. Noguès in Morocco and Boisson in West Africa were to be relieved of their posts and functions and were ultimately tried for their Vichy sins.[44]

The struggle was characterized by its bitterness. President Roosevelt viewed De Gaulle's success with alarm, and each treated the other with cavalier contempt. General Eisenhower intervened with a refusal to continue arming French forces unless their commander in chief remained responsible to the Allied commander in chief, and a compromise resulted—for a time—with Giraud retaining command in North and West Africa, and De Gaulle elsewhere in the French empire. With the departure of Boisson and Noguès, however, all of North Africa fell into the De Gaulle camp.[45] By October, Roosevelt had lost faith in Giraud as a check

[41] The text of the Anfa Protocol, so-called from the name of the hotel at which the conference was held, is contained in Richard and Serigny, *La bissectrice de la guerre*, pp. 231–232; see also Herbert Feis, *Churchill, Roosevelt, and Stalin: The War They Waged and the Peace They Sought*, p. 137.

[42] Cordell Hull to Anthony Eden, at Washington, March 22, 1943, cited in *The Memoirs of Cordell Hull*, II, 1215.

[43] *Memoirs of Charles De Gaulle*, II: *Documents*, pp. 179–180.

[44] Ibid., pp. 173, 175, 312–313.

[45] Ibid., II, 129–134.

on De Gaulle, and Eisenhower had lost faith in Giraud's ability to organize the French armed forces. The Committee of National Liberation was reorganized to provide for only one chairman (De Gaulle) with a power of veto. Giraud remained for a time as commander in chief, but resigned from the committee November 8, 1943, exactly a year after the invasion.[46] Thus matters continued, De Gaulle asserting the authority of a chief of state and President Roosevelt protesting, but acquiescing, until August 25, 1944, when Eisenhower and General Koenig, for the Committee of National Liberation, exchanged letters that comprised an agreement on civil affairs. Eisenhower said: "I have been authorized to deal with the French Committee of National Liberation as the *de facto* authority in France which will assume the responsibility for the administration of the liberated areas of France."[47] The British and French Foreign Offices signed identical accords.

The political maneuvering in London and Algiers was important because it determined the political future of all of North Africa, but local events in Morocco took quite a different turn from those in Algeria. In Algeria the settlement following the American-British landing was predominantly a diplomatic one that left few scars. In Morocco it was predominantly a military one, and the French hierarchies felt compelled to justify their resistance. On October 8, General Noguès had minimized the threat: "Local dissidence," he said, then, "a weak landing."[48] It was not until November 11 that he called out the reserves, and by then armistice talks were already under way.

General Maurice Mathenet at Port Lyautey led the way. He refused General Truscott's demand that the French forces be disarmed,[49] but pledged them not to fight against the Allies. The two

[46] Feis, *Churchill, Roosevelt, and Stalin*, p. 316.

[47] Ibid., p. 322. This agreement was superseded by the Bidault-Caffrey Agreement of February 16, 1948.

[48] *La Vigie Marocaine*, November 9–11, 1942.

[49] "Minutes of Armistice Meeting, General Mathenet and General Truscott, at Mehdia, November 11, 1942," in the possession of Colonel Adrien Feste, Casablanca, Morocco, and examined by the author, May 27, 1967. The crux of the matter of disarming French troops was indicated in the remark of General Koeltz, quoted in Richard and Serigny, *La bissectrice de la guerre*, p. 224: "Above all, the indigènes must not learn that the troops are unarmed."

generals reached an agreement whereby the French forces kept their arms and returned to barracks in areas not occupied by the Americans. Arrangements were made for the exchange of prisoners and burial of the dead and for the American occupation and use of the port. French officials were to continue their normal functions but were to take no action prejudicial to the U.S. forces. General Truscott promised not to interfere with the civil economy of the area and to pay fair prices for anything he requisitioned.[50]

Six hours later, at 2:00 P.M., General Noguès met General Patton at the Anfa Hotel in Casablanca. The State Department had provided Patton with alternative sets of conditions, one to be applied if the French did not resist, another if they did. Patton read the terms of the latter. Seeing Noguès' anger and mortification, he tore up the document that would have "virtually abolished the protectorate, thus infuriating all patriotic Frenchmen,"[51] and appealed to Noguès' "soldier's honor" as the guide for their future collaboration. Patton thus assumed the role of an independent policy maker in Morocco, and the policies actually followed were not the same as those in Algeria.

General Noguès explained the French resistance to the American invasion, even when the consequences were overwhelming and evident, thus: "We fought to uphold our honor."[52] Madame Har-

---

[50] "Final Report of Western Task Force on Operation Torch, November 8–11, 1942," II (annexes) in file no. 95-TF3-0.3 Western Task Force, in Modern Military Records Service Archives, Alexandria, Virginia; see also, Truscott, *Command Missions*, pp. 122–123.

[51] Murphy, *Diplomat among Warriors*, p. 151. Charles R. Codman, who was Patton's aide in 1942, called the decision to tear up the conditions of the armistice and appeal to "soldier's honor" intuitive but correct, in "Le Maroc français," *La documentation française; Articles et documents*, August 20, 1952.

[52] *La Vigie Marocaine*, November 12, 1942. In a paradoxical commentary on "soldier's honor," General Patton relates in *War As I Knew It*, pp. 19–20, the "touching and significant gesture" of French General Henri Martin, defeated in France in 1940, and at Safi by American troops commanded by Major General J. W. Anderson, Third U.S. Infantry Division, in 1942. General Martin brought the flag of his Sixty-seventh Division to General Anderson and asked him to remove the crepe with which it was decorated "as a sign that the shame of the division had been removed by the fighting which General Martin had done [against the Americans]." General Martin then cut the crepe in two and gave half of it to General Anderson.

doin, wife of the French minister for civilian affairs, spoke in the same sense of the French, "so ashamed of themselves that they had no pride, and the women were more ashamed than the men . . . so digusted with the men that they would not live with them." Madame Hardoin insisted that the French soldiers were delighted with the prospect of fighting "in a friendly manner" with the Americans. General Patton observed that a war costing four thousand casualties in three days was hardly a "friendly" sort of war.[53]

Honor satisfied, General Noguès worked after the armistice on the principle "if you can't beat them, join them." Patton wanted security for his troops and for the line of communications to Algiers and Tunisia. Noguès provided that, and in return Patton allowed him to call the tune in Morocco. President Roosevelt's message to the sultan, to have been delivered on D day, was not delivered, because Noguès did not like its tone. He felt that it might make the sultan feel more independent.[54] His proclamation to Morocco on November 12 specified that military commanders would retain their commands; that a state of siege still existed in Morocco; and that neither assemblies nor manifestations would be tolerated. He urged the populace to stop party partisanship and to rally around Pétain, "who saved us at Verdun, and His Majesty the Sultan, who supports France completely and loyally."[55] The next day, after consultation with Patton and his staff, Noguès announced that there would be no change in the political and economic structure of Morocco.[56] He validated United States and British money until December 31 at seventy-five francs to the dollar, twenty-five above the current market.[57]

Although the U.S. forces had established contact with the royal

[53] Patton, *War As I Knew It*, pp. 18–19.

[54] Murphy, *Diplomat among Warriors*, pp. 152–153; Howe, *Northwest Africa*, p. 95; Kenneth W. Pendar, *Adventures in Diplomacy; Our French Dilemma*, pp. 97, 99, 122–124. According to Department of State letter to the author, dated Washington, August 1, 1967, that refers to Consul General H. Earle Russell's report of November 24, 1942, the message was delivered by Vice-Consul Ernest Mayer to M. du Gardier, chief of the Residency Diplomatic Cabinet at Rabat, shortly before 7 A.M. on November 8, for transmission by Noguès personally to the sultan.

[55] *La Vigie Marocaine*, November 12, 1942.

[56] Ibid., November 13, 1942.

[57] Ibid., November 15, 1942.

palace earlier,[58] General Patton did not call upon the sultan until November 16, at which time he was presented by the ubiquitous General Noguès. On November 18, during the Throne Day celebration, they made a second call. Patton noted that he was now accorded precedence after Noguès; during the first visit, he sat immediately to the sultan's right. In the ensuing *pourparler*, Patton said he "became more and more impressed with the fact that the United States was playing too small a role, so . . . without asking anyone's permission," he put his foot in his mouth with an extemporaneous speech in which he made fulsome references to the "French Government of Morocco." If the sultan noted the faux pas, he apparently forgave it. He invited Patton to tea that afternoon but General Patton was unable to go.[59]

In the weeks that followed, Patton was wined and dined by General Noguès, but he never regained primacy vis-à-vis the Moroccans. He appeared as a part of Noguès' retinue. The local press noted that when the two generals called on the sultan during Aid el Kebir (Feast of the Lamb), December 19, "General Noguès took a place in Major General Patton's command car, thus marking the close ties which unite the two Commanders in Chief."[60] Patton, who had been invited with his division commanders and forty officers directly by the sultan, was also invited to provide the escort of honor. He remarked that "the escort of honor had a profound effect on the populace, it being the first time I ever heard the Arabs cheer."[61] The sultan remarked somewhat wryly when the entourage arrived at his palace that "the traditional Moroccan holidays now become French national holidays."[62]

Patton and the entire American high command were roundly

[58] Palace retainers who were in the sultan's service in 1942 remember fondly an American Colonel Swersky, from San Francisco, who served as liaison officer at the palace after November 10.

[59] Patton, *War As I Knew It*, p. 16. General Harmon represented General Patton at the afternoon reception. Habitués at the Riad Palace noted the great bronze doors to the garden were strangely closed. The changed routine was shortly explained. A panther had escaped from the royal zoo and was loose in the garden. Captain Laforest, a young French officer in the sultan's service, shot it just as His Majesty was receiving General Harmon.

[60] *La Vigie Marocaine*, December 20, 1942.

[61] *Patton, War As I Knew It*, p. 24.

[62] *La Vigie Marocaine*, December 20, 1942.

criticized for political naïveté and indifference. On November 8 the residency forces had rounded up all anti-Vichyites they could find. The jails were full and remained full long after the Allies were in ostensible control.[63] General Béthouart and Colonel Pierre Mangin, who had attempted the pro-Allied coup in Morocco during the night of November 7–8, were in custody, and probably escaped the firing squad only through the intervention of General Eisenhower. In Algeria, Henri d'Astier, Father Cordier, and Henri, José, and Rafael Aboulker, the nucleus of the pro-Allied *putsch*, were imprisoned. New anti-Jewish measures were promulgated that would exclude those of Gaullist persuasion from the army. By limiting Jews to noncombat units, they were excluded from the politically and socially desirable status of war veterans.[64] Anti-American and anti-Allied literature was distributed openly in Morocco, sabotaging American-Arab relations by charging that the Americans were living off the country. Patton took no action against such excesses and justified his inaction on the grounds that the anti-Darlan-Noguès groups had neither the personnel nor the positions to control Morocco.[65]

President Roosevelt was aware of the situation, certainly after the Casablanca conference, for he told his press conference that U.S. Secret Service agents in Casablanca felt that the Moorish population represented "a very slim risk" to his safety, but that they took elaborate precautions "when they encountered our French brethren."[66] Roosevelt made no changes, Robert Murphy said, because he "could see during his visit to Morocco how valuable it

[63] Interview, Cyril Barton Smith, at Casablanca, May 23, 1967. Mr. Smith, a former British consular official in the employ of the American Consulate on November 8, was one of those arrested. Because of his diplomatic status he was released November 11, but the others, less favored were held "for weeks," Smith said.

[64] Root, *Casablanca to Katyn*, pp. 158–193, quotes Giraud's anti-Jewish Orders nos. 582-MGP-CAB, and 40C-MGJ-CAB; also an article by William Stoneman, *Chicago Daily News*, February 8, 1943, on the reprisals and on the anti-American propaganda. Butcher, *My Three Years with Eisenhower*, pp. 223–224, his entry dated December 17, 1942, remarked the anti-American literature being distributed by Noguès "pro-Nazi staff."

[65] Howe, *Northwest Africa*, pp. 177–178.

[66] *Public Papers of Franklin D. Roosevelt. The Tide Turns*, ed. Samuel I. Rosenman, pp. 57–58.

was to retain the support of local French administrators, even though some of them proclaimed support of the Vichy regime."[67]

Roosevelt appears not only to have misread the Moroccan tableau, but also to have been sympathetic toward Noguès personally. He told a press conference after his return from Casablanca that the Moroccans "like the French who are there over them . . . they want no change." He said that Noguès was not pro-Vichy or pro-Nazi, just pro-Noguès, and, as for changing the regime, "it is better to keep a nice quiet position in Morocco than to chase rainbows as to the future of France."[68] In May, General Noguès sent Roosevelt an album of Moroccan stamps and took the occasion in a lengthy letter of transmittal to thank him for bringing "your powerful country into a war which will save us while it is saving the world." Affirming his identity with the Allied high command, he chided Roosevelt for failing to support Giraud against "professional politicians and propagandists who surround De Gaulle," infiltrating Giraud's entourage, and creating disturbances among the natives and producers. Such people, Noguès insisted, had only one aim: "to organize a government in Africa in order to impose it afterwards on France."[69]

The State Department warned the president that a direct communication to General Noguès might be inadvisable, since it was Noguès who had given the order to fire on American troops, and he might well be out of office by the time a letter arrived.[70] Roosevelt nevertheless wrote, thanking him for the stamps, but even as the letter was being written, De Gaulle was coming to power in North Africa. The letter arrived June 24, several days after Noguès'

[67] Murphy, *Diplomat among Warriors*, p. 170. Walter Lippman, in "Today and Tomorrow," January 19, 1943, quoted in Root, *Casablanca to Katyn*, pp. 187–188, attributed the muddle in North Africa to "the bad judgment of Robert Murphy who took his political coloring from those with whom he associated." Butcher, *My Three Years with Eisenhower*, p. 245, also noted that Murphy was being much criticized in the United States for his bad advice to Eisenhower.

[68] Press Conference #879, February 12, 1943. Minutes in the Franklin D. Roosevelt Library, Hyde Park, New York.

[69] Noguès to Roosevelt letter, dated Rabat, May 12, 1943, in the Franklin D. Roosevelt Library, Hyde Park, New York.

[70] Memorandum from Stanley Woodward to Major General Watson, dated June 4, 1943, in the Franklin D. Roosevelt Library, Hyde Park, New York.

departure for asylum in Portugal. The U.S. consul at Rabat forwarded it to Lisbon for delivery.[71]

President Roosevelt established direct contact with King Mohammed V while he was in Morocco in January, 1943, for the Casablanca conference. He had written to him shortly after the landing to thank him for his cooperation, and the sultan had replied that Morocco "had no disagreement with the United States, whose chivalrous and liberal principles are known to us," and as long as "our prestige, our religion and our traditions [are] respected by your troops, they [will find] only friends and collaborators." Then he added: "The first contacts between peoples who do not know each other well enough are marked by hesitation and reticence, but progressively, as reciprocal understanding is established between them, they are followed by esteem and friendship which create a cooperative effort for all"[72]—a prescient afterthought.

At Casablanca, Roosevelt extended an invitation to the sultan to be his guest for dinner on January 22, 1943, but did not extend the invitation through the French resident-general. In bypassing him, Roosevelt departed from the procedures that had governed previous American actions in North Africa and tremendously encouraged the nationalists, for his action fitted neatly with their concept of international law. Their reasoning ran thus: The United States had a valid treaty of friendship and commerce with Morocco; the United States had never recognized the Treaty of Fez; Morocco had surrendered certain prerogatives by the Treaty of Fez; but the United States' presence in Morocco was not by agreement, but by right of conquest—France had been unable to fulfill her treaty obligations to Morocco; therefore, it was perfectly proper and normal for the two chiefs of state to meet directly, without a French intermediary.[73]

In view of the historical aftermath, it is difficult to take President Roosevelt's promises that evening very seriously. Why should

[71] U.S. Consul, Rabat, letter to secretary of state, dated Rabat, June 29, 1943, in the Franklin D. Roosevelt Library, Hyde Park, New York.

[72] The text of the president's letter, dated November 23, and the sultan's reply, dated November 25, 1942, both sent by cable, and the original of the sultan's letter, in Arabic, delivered to General Patton, are in the Franklin D. Roosevelt Library, Hyde Park, New York.

[73] Allal El Fassi, *Livre rouge et documentaires*, p. 82.

this dinner-table conversation be regarded as a solemn engagement on the part of the United States to seek Moroccan independence? Roosevelt had done no serious preparation for postwar peace settlements elsewhere in the world. He came to Casablanca to plan military strategy. Even the dinner itself was a happenstance; a time-filler while Churchill tried to get De Gaulle to Casablanca to meet with Giraud.[74] Roosevelt did express sympathy for Moroccan aspirations for independence; suggested the use of American capital, technicians, and business procedures in developing Morocco's economy, particularly its mines; and invited the sultan to visit him in Washington after the war.[75]

That Mohammed V was pleased and honored by President Roosevelt's gesture was unmistakable. He accepted in principle the invitation, and sent Mrs. Roosevelt a jeweled crown and two bracelets, family heirlooms, as a memento of the meeting.[76] To the president he was quite open in his criticism of the protectorate policies, deploring the lack of trained scientists and engineers among his countrymen. He thus sounded again the note that characterized the whole Moroccan independence movement. He expressed a keen desire to obtain the greatest possible aid in securing modern educational and health standards for his country.

The Moroccans took Roosevelt seriously; after all, he was the leader of the coalition upon which the future of the world turned, and they took his encouragement to the sultan as a promise of American support.[77] When Robert E. Sherwood visited Morocco in April, he found wide discussion of and support for an American university, modeled after the American University at Beirut, to be founded at Fez, the cultural heart of Morocco. Sherwood relayed this information to Roosevelt, suggesting that such an institution,

[74] Robert E. Sherwood, *Roosevelt and Hopkins: An Intimate History*, pp. 688–690.

[75] Accounts of the dinner are contained in ibid., in Murphy, *Diplomat among Warriors*, pp. 172–173, and Roosevelt, *As He Saw It*, pp. 109–112. *Public Papers of Franklin D. Roosevelt. The Tide Turns*, p. 59, confirms the invitation to visit the United States.

[76] On display at the Franklin D. Roosevelt Museum, Hyde Park, with a copy of the president's letter of thanks to the sultan, dated February 15, 1943.

[77] According to Robert Rezette, *Les partis politiques marocains*, p. 137, Roosevelt told King Ibn Saud that he had assured Mohammed V of his support for independence after the war.

financed by private subscription, be established as a monument to the American landings in North Africa, and as a token of gratitude for the friendly cooperation given American troops by the Moslem population.[78]

Sherwood's suggestion fell on deaf ears in Washington. Cordell Hull opposed it. Recalling the slow growth of the American University at Beirut, he said that a ready-made education institution, as proposed, could not succeed in Morocco, that it would be regarded as a United States propaganda effort, and that the Moroccan population would not accept an expensive modern university. He expressed doubt that funds could be raised privately. Most cogently, however, he concluded that the French protectorate officials would not admit foreign religious or philanthropic activities in Morocco, and that, as long as the French controlled, it would be impossible to establish or to maintain any alien cultural or educational mission. That ended that—at least to the mid-1960's.[79]

Proceeding on the assumption of American support and sympathy, the Moroccan nationalists sought to broaden their contact with the Americans. Many levels of Moroccan society were already in contact with the U.S. forces when Abdelatif Sbihi, editor of *La Voix Nationale*, formed the Roosevelt Club in the summer of 1943. Its objective was to establish social contact with the American military personnel present in Morocco, to discuss and examine American political and economic concepts, and to try to determine to what degree American ideas might contribute to Moroccan independence. An obvious corollary was to generate American understanding of the Moroccan people and their problems, and, hopefully, support for the independence movement.

The membership of the Roosevelt Club was exclusively Moroccan–American, or more accurately, exclusively Moroccan with as many high-ranking American officers as could be induced to asso-

[78] Robert E. Sherwood, Office of War Information, letter to Franklin D. Roosevelt, dated May 5, 1943, in the Franklin D. Roosevelt Library, Hyde Park, New York.

[79] State Department memorandum, signed C. H., to the president, dated June 10, 1943, in the Franklin D. Roosevelt Library, Hyde Park, New York. In 1965, the United States proposed the establishment of an American University at Tangier, and it is now under construction.

ciate with the predominantly anti-French, Moroccan nationalist membership. The American "membership" was obviously a transient one—friends of Sbihi, friends of Guedira, friends of Bargach. The Moroccan membership was permanent and the club lasted, at least in name, until independence was achieved in 1956.[80]

The significance of the Roosevelt Club lay not in what it contributed to the achievement of independence but in the formulation of ideas that were important after independence. Its members for the most part became political independents, or at least few of them joined the Istiqlal party, and they have dominated the Moroccan government since 1960.[81]

Initially intended as a formalized club with headquarters in Rabat and Casablanca, the association became a nebulous group, headquartered wherever Abdelatif Sbihi happened to be living, first in Rabat-Casablanca, then Tangier after 1944, New York in 1947, and then Malaga, Spain. Wherever he was, he remained firm in his belief in the usefulness of American-Moroccan liaison. The Roosevelt Club lost its cohesiveness and perhaps extended its influence as it became internationalized. Certainly the repression in French Morocco, which scattered its members, also scattered its ideas. Reda Guedira, for example, who left Morocco in 1946 to study law in Paris, became the club delegate there.

The French also took Roosevelt seriously. Where the Moroccans had responded to his gambit with searching interest, the French

[80] Abdelatif Sbihi was a personal friend of the author from 1956 until his death in 1963 and discussed the Roosevelt Club many times. The foregoing information was confirmed in interviews in May, 1967, in Rabat, with Mehdi Bennouna, Ahmed Reda Guedira, Boubker and Batoul Sbihi—all ex-members.

[81] Members of the Roosevelt Club (and offices they have held in the government of Morocco after independence) include Abdelatif Sbihi, member of the National Consultive Assembly, and ambassador to Norway and to Argentina; Ahmed Reda Guedira, minister of national defense, minister of information, minister of agriculture, foreign minister, director-general of the Cabinet of Ministers, and minister of higher education; Rachid Moline, minister of state for public function; Dr. Ben Bouchaib, minister of state; Mfaddel Cherkaoui, director of His Majesty's Military Cabinet, president of the Senate, undersecretary of state–interior; M'hamid Bargach, minister of development, vice-governor, Bank of Maroc, and delegate to the Promotion Nationale; Mohammed Bargach, Royal Cabinet; His Royal Highness Moulay Hassan, brother of King Mohammed V; Mokhtar Aherdane, of Tangier; Mehdi Bennouna, cultural attaché, Royal Cabinet, and director of Maghreb Arabe Presse (private).

responded with outraged indignation. General Noguès, apprehensive about American designs on the French empire, was sullen.[82] General De Gaulle lashed General Giraud with the fact that he found nothing to criticize in Roosevelt's rendezvous with the sultan.[83] General Juin attributed the sultan's adherence to the nationalist movement to the encouragement given him by President Roosevelt at Anfa.[84] Noguès, Giraud, De Gaulle, and Juin formed and led French opinion on North Africa for better than two decades, and their resentment of American policies that "did not tally very well with the French protectorate," to use De Gaulle's words, has embittered Franco-American relations to this day.

A year of feverish political activity in Morocco, 1943 was marked by increased militancy on the part of the Moroccan nationalists, a hardened French attitude as General De Gaulle eliminated his opponents, and by an accelerated withdrawal of the United States from the political considerations of North Africa. For a time, it appeared that the Moroccans might be able to work out their problems with General De Gaulle, who had been in contact with Allal El Fassi in exile in Gabon as early as 1941. De Gaulle hoped to use El Fassi in a coup against Vichy to bring Morocco into the Fighting French fold.[85] The Torch planners had also been eyeing El Fassi—perhaps he might prove useful in raising a revolt if Spain should prove hostile.[86] But Spain was not hostile, and De Gaulle, suspicious of any contact between El Fassi and a foreign power, broke off contact. El Fassi remained in exile.

By the fall of 1943, almost all of the Moroccan political activists had abandoned the idea of achieving Moroccan independence through evolution. First General Giraud and then General De Gaulle were obviously determined to exploit the colonies as much as possible in the effort to resurrect France. That was the tenor of all their pronouncements, and the degree to which they succeeded is perhaps measured in a statement by Marshal Juin in 1948: "Morocco furnished the largest number of soldiers during the war. The

[82] Murphy, *Diplomat among Warriors*, p. 173.

[83] *Memoirs of Charles De Gaulle*, II, 93.

[84] Alphonse Pierre Juin, *Memoires*, II, 144–145.

[85] Allal El Fassi, *The Independence Movements in Arab North Africa*, trans. Hazem Zaki Nuseibeh, pp. 208–212.

[86] William L. Langer, *Our Vichy Gamble*, pp. 319–320.

native units benefited from an admirable French training. I can say that never in the course of our history have we had a more useful instrument of war than that which came out of North Africa in 1943."[87]

The final blow to Moroccan aspirations came out of the Conference of Brazzaville, opened on January 30, 1944, by General De Gaulle with the pledge that France would lead the sixty million colonials down the road to integration in the French community,[88] and closed with a final report that stated: "The objectives of the civilizing work accomplished by France in the colonies reject all idea of autonomy, all possibility of an evolution outside the French block of the Empire. An eventual constitution, even in the distant future, of self-government in the colonies is rejected."[89]

The Brazzaville declaration was in fact anticlimactic; the Moroccans had already seen the handwriting on the wall and, by December, had formed a new, united political party, the Istiqlal party. The guiding spirit was Ahmed Balafrej, the president in 1926 of the Supporters of Truth Society. The objective was clear and simple: the independence of Morocco and its entry into the concert of nations. Undoubtedly Morocco would have demanded its ultimate independence, but the American presence precipitated the demand. According to Mehdi Bennouna: "The very fact of the Americans coming, not at the invitation of France, but whether or no; the spectacle of the Americans feeding, clothing, and rearming the French made us realize that this powerful master was, after all, not such a powerful master."[90]

On January 11, 1944, the Moroccan nationalists declared for independence in the *Manifesto of the Istiqlal Party*. One of the writers explained the circumstances under which it was drafted: "We knew that we must have foreign support if we were to succeed; therefore, we thought it proper to declare before the opinion of the world our grievances and our demands. We were uneasy about the position of the United States, because we were not sure

---

[87] *Revue de la France d'outré-mer*, Numéro Spécial, *Maroc, Terre d'avenir, 1948*, p. 131.

[88] *Memoirs of Charles De Gaulle*, II: *Documents*, p. 250.

[89] Quoted in Georges Hardy, *Histoire sociale de la colonisation française*, p. 235.

[90] Interview, Mehdi Bennouna, May 11, 1967.

about their attitude vis-à-vis France, but we decided to chance it. A small group met at my house in Fez and we came up with the manifesto."[91]

The *Manifesto* denounced the protectorate as failing to observe the terms of the Treaty of Fez, of imposing a direct, oppressive rule upon the Moroccan people for the benefit of the French community, of monopolizing the resources of the country, and of excluding the Moroccans from the economic benefits as well as from all public and private liberties. It recalled the contributions of Morocco in both world wars, and called upon the Allies to fulfil its promises of the Atlantic Charter and other international proclamations, and to admit Morocco to the United Nations.[92] Fifty-six representatives of sections of the Istiqlal party signed it.

A new era in Franco-Moroccan relations had begun. Those Moroccans who had been uncertain of the attitude of the United States soon learned it was disavowal. Copies of the *Manifesto* were delivered to the sultan, to the resident-general, and to the consuls-general of the United States and Great Britain. According to M'hamid Zeghari, "The French officials asked when the *Manifesto* was presented if the Americans were associated with the movement. When in the course of the next ten days it became apparent they were not, the French repression was brutal. I spent five months in prison myself."[93]

On January 29 arrest orders were issued for all of the prominent members of the Istiqlal party. Ahmed Balafrej was exiled to Corsica. Mohammed Ben El Arabi El Alaoui and Ahmed Bargach were dismissed from the Moroccan government. French military forces equipped with American weapons occupied the principal cities to suppress the outbreaks of violent protest, and American officials raised not a voice against the brutal repression of nationalist manifestations. According to French sources, of the thousands arrested 387 Moroccans were condemned and imprisoned. According to

[91] Interview, M'hamid Zeghari, Kenitra, June 1, 1967. Mr. Zeghari was minister of agriculture.

[92] The text is contained in El Fassi, *The Independence Movements in Arab North Africa*, pp. 215–217; in a publication of the Istiqlal party, *Documents: 1944–46*, and in Roger Le Tourneau, *Evolution Politique de l'Afrique du Nord Musulmane*, pp. 208–209.

[93] Interview, M'hamid Zeghari, Kenitra, June 1, 1967.

Moroccan sources, the figure was ten times that. "All this happened in the presence of the United States armies and authorities and only one year after the famous meeting between President Roosevelt and His Majesty Sidi Mohammed V. But the Allies wanted 'peace and order' in Morocco."[94] A new era in American-Moroccan relations had also opened—one of bitterness.

[94] Mahdi A. Bennouna, *Our Morocco: The True Story of a Just Cause*, p. 63.

5. The War Years

AMERICAN MECHANICAL INGENUITY, machines, and attitudes toward mechanization attracted and excited great numbers of the Moroccan people, and, in the final analysis, probably had a longer-lasting effect than the limited human contacts over the period of the two decades after the landings. Many Moroccans had served in the French armed forces, almost without exception in the infantry. Their French weapons were generally of World War I vintage, and, under the pressure of the Armistice Commission, even those were scarce. The civilian community, predominantly rural, had even less exposure to mechanization than the soldier. Neither the military nor civilian communities had seen or heard of ships that came up on the beach, opened giant jaws, and disgorged trucks, tanks, and field guns. They had seen airplanes, of course, but had no concept of aircraft-carrier-based aviation. They therefore watched with curiosity the arrival in Morocco of this large, superbly equipped army that was able to crush the French forces far more efficiently and speedily than had the Germans. To many Moroccans, it was that simple. They were unable to recognize the changed circumstances.

Moroccans familiarized themselves with the Americans in two ways. Moroccan troops who fought against the Americans in November, 1942, were fighting with them against the Germans before the year was out. They were given American weapons as rapidly as they were able to learn to use them. But for the illiterate, technically untrained Moroccan, the conversion to modern weapons and the strategy dictated by those weapons was a slow process. For the most part, Moroccan infantry units were simply attached to French or American mechanized units. This pragmatic solution had far-reaching effects. It placed the Moroccan soldier in daily contact with his American counterpart and allowed him to contrast French attitudes, of which he had considerable knowledge, with American attitudes. The decision favored the Americans

Embarek Serghini summed it up this way: "To the American G.I., son-of-a-bitch and ol' buddy mean the same thing in a different time situation. He will say—to American or Moroccan; it doesn't matter—'Hey, you sons-a-bitches, get a move on! Shake it up!' And five minutes later, 'Well, ol' buddy, let's go see what delicacies they got for chow tonight.' But when the French Sergeant-Chef says, 'Patate, bouge ta graisse, flémard' [the approximate equivalent of the first phrase], we took it for the insult it was meant to be."[1]

The Moroccans saw a certain practicality in the American attitude, as well as a rude egalitarianism. "My company was attached to an American tank unit in Italy," Colonel Serghini continued. "When we were moving, and under conditions in which we did not expect combat, our tanks would come along. We would move off to the side of the road, of course. The tank commander would stop and yell: 'Hey, hop on and ride. No use wearing yourself out walking.' A French tank commander would never do that. But when we got up to the front, we knew where our tanks were and they knew where we were—and we weren't all tired out from walking."[2]

[1] Interview, Colonel Embarek Serghini, at the Moroccan Embassy, Madrid, Spain, May 3, 1967.
[2] Ibid.

Although shared military experiences made a lasting impact on Moroccan soldiers, many of whom later came into positions of leadership, the Moroccan population at large was treated to a vastly greater learning experience as the Americans established bases from which they not only fought a war, but also trained and reequipped the French military forces. Headquarters for the American forces remained in Casablanca until the end of the war, and Casablanca served as the depot for the receipt and assembly of American armament for the French and Moroccan soldiery, but Port Lyautey and Agadir became the principal American operating bases.

Craw Field, at Port Lyautey, became a United States operational base within three hours after its capture at 10:30 A.M., November 10, and has remained as such continuously since then. It operated under U.S. Army command until February 15, 1943, at which time it passed to the U.S. Navy and the U.S. Naval Air Station was placed in commission. The U.S. Army, Twenty-first Engineers, Second Battalion assumed initial responsibility for completion of the airfield, and passed it along to the 120th Naval Construction Battalion when the navy took over the field.

The first order of business was to rehabilitate and extend the facilities for handling airplanes. When the Americans took over, they found two hangars, one 450 by 200 feet, and the other, 165 by 111, with ninety offices, sanitary facilities, and machine and carpenter shops. A control tower and aerological office were completed and in operation. Buoys were anchored in the river for mooring seaplanes, and a twenty-ton crane for lifting them out of the water had been installed.[3] The base, however, was only about half completed by French standards and was grossly inadequate for the scale of operations envisaged by the Americans. The runways, taxiways, aprons, and hardstands were only partially completed. The field had obstruction lights, but no runway or taxiway

[3] The information in this and subsequent paragraphs concerning initial construction at Port Lyautey is taken from R. Moore, Jr., and Raul Tunley, "A Short History of the United States Naval Air Station at Port Lyautey, French Morocco," a typed manuscript based on the notes of Lieutenant Colonel W. R. Macleod, USA, of the army intelligence unit that landed at Port Lyautey. The manuscript, undated, but apparently written in early 1944, is in the files of the public affairs officer, U.S. Naval Training Command, Morocco.

lighting. Storm and sanitary sewers were installed, and a sump pump provided for field drainage, but extensive runway drainage was needed. Malaria control was virtually nonexistent. Only one road on the base, that from the runway to the main road, was paved.

In order to speed construction, the United States assumed the contractual obligations of the French navy, more than thirty of them, and agreed to pay for the water and electricity furnished by the local authorities of the city of Port Lyautey, but use of the field and its facilities was to be rent-free. For the vastly expanded construction program, the U.S. Army supplied most of the materials and all of the specifications, but drew heavily on local labor— practically all of the force already working on the base, plus an augmentation recruited by French subcontractors.

Within the next few months, the runways had been enlarged, the east-west one from 132 by 3,440 feet to 167 by 4,990, and the north-south one from 116 by 3,440 feet to 151 by 4,885—obviously not jet airfield size, but adequate for the planes of World War II. The taxiway system was repaired and extended from 4,275 to 25,100 feet. The 285,000-square-foot felt-asphalt apron was repaired, and an additional one (112,000 square feet) built. Seventy-eight hardstands, fifty of pierced steel planks and twenty-eight of concrete with bar-rod footings, were added to the parking system. The whole complex was lighted and a drainage system installed. A small-boat dock and a clipper dock were built to facilitate seaplane operations.

As soon as the airfield was operational, the engineers turned their attention to service facilities. Only seven permanent buildings had existed on the base at the time of capture, exclusive of barracks and mess halls. Many were completed in the next few weeks: laundry, barber shop, tailor shop, cobbler shop, post office, and living quarters. Most of the new construction was the familiar World War II quonset hut, but the warehouses and the terminal and office building for the Naval Air Transport Service were of masonry or reinforced concrete construction. The roads on the base were widened and paved. Three wells were drilled and a pumping station installed to provide water for the expanded facilities. A base hospital was set up in the ex-isolation ward of the French government-owned hospital in town, leased for eighty dollars per month, and

supplemented with seven quonset huts and a 30-by-50-foot warehouse, all new construction. By the middle of the summer, 1943,
the United States Naval Air Station, Port Lyautey, had attained
the form that it was substantially to maintain until 1951. It was
still "temporary" in appearance and boasted—or deplored—253
tents that served as living quarters. The cost of all labor and material in the initial expansion program was $1,900,347.[4]

Although it resulted in little if any direct contact with the natives, the U.S. Army signaled its presence in the Moroccan community with an effective malaria control program that went far
beyond ditching and draining the airfield. Arabic-speaking French
women, hired by the army, went into the villages near American
troop concentrations and into the native quarter of Port Lyautey,
thoroughly and frequently spraying the *noullas*, round thatch-
roofed huts, to kill the malaria-carrying mosquitoes. With the own-
er's consent, they put "little fish" [*Gambusia assina*] in the open
water wells to eat the mosquito larvae. The ladies carried out the
control program, fraught with a potential for misunderstanding
and ruinous rumor, with tact and discernment, their efforts unmarred by a single unpleasant incident.[5]

The economic impact of the American troops in Morocco, their
numbers reduced by half when the combat units moved out at the
end of December, 1942, was felt more intensely in 1943 than in
1942. The combat units had been self-contained; they needed little
in the way of provisions from the local community, and their soldiers had little time or inclination to patronize the local establishments. The fifteen thousand remaining troops adjusted rapidly to
the new and foreign environment however, and business in the
local bars and restaurants picked up. In addition, the U.S. forces
purchased many materials locally, aggregate for the runway and

[4] Ibid. The breakdown of the expenditures was as follows:

Runway extensions	$308,258.00
Hardstands	269,667.00
Taxiways	190,616.00
Naval air transport service	29,900.00
Hospital improvements	29,300.00
Barracks	214,183.00
Seaplane ramp	19,965.00
Malaria control	10,862.00

[5] Interview, Mrs. Jeanne Mortier, Kenitra, May 21, 1967.

road construction, for example. The economic benefits flowed primarily to the French. Arab labor, for example, accounted for less than 2.5 percent of the total expenditure at Port Lyautey, but the French contractors did use it, and, as Moroccan economy improved, the situation of the Arab worker improved. Unemployment dropped. Rationing restrictions were eased. Previously unobtainable commodities appeared on the market, and living became easier for the native population.

The French residency sought to minimize the contact between the Americans and Moroccans by interposing its own officials when circumstances would otherwise bring the two peoples together. For example, to prevent disrupting the local labor market, the French were conceded the right of supplying local labor for the American forces. They proposed an Arab laborer only if the position was not acceptable to a Frenchman, another European, or Moroccan Jew. To cite another example, in April, 1943, the U.S. Navy commander of an advanced operating base at Agadir provided facilities for distributing U.S.-supplied cotton cloth to children in the Franco-Moroccan and Jewish schools in the area. The teachers apparently required the children to write letters of thanks; in any event, a number of letters, remarkably similar in content, were forwarded to President Roosevelt. Without exception, they thanked the pasha of Agadir, General de Brigade Chatras, the French civil controller at Agadir, and finally, the Americans.[6]

The distribution of cloth at Agadir was a part of a nationwide distribution of 200,000 meters, three meters per child, on the occasion of the Fête de Mouloud. The distribution passed unnoticed by the French press in Morocco, although *La Voix Nationale* devoted its entire front page to pictures of the "largesses Americaines."[7] Editor Sbihi did not confine his reporting to the cloth distribution; he recapitulated the evidence of "American sincerity": 14,000 tons of sugar at the end of March—as much as the combined February and March consumption—that permitted raising the sugar ration to 750 grams (27 ounces); and 2 million liters of petro-

[6] The letters are in the Franklin D. Roosevelt Library, Hyde Park, N. Y., attached to President Roosevelt's letter of July 16, 1943, to Mr. C. D. Jackson, Psychological Warfare Board, Allied Forces Headquarters, asking him to extend his thanks for the letters.

[7] *La Voix Nationale*, April 20, 1943.

leum products released on March 10, 75 percent to the Moslem population. The petroleum products ration, 30 percent above pre-war consumption, was necessitated because of the shortage of candles. Finally, he noted daily distribution of free milk by the American Red Cross.[8] The circulation of *La Voix Nationale* was not large, but newspapers themselves were rather recent innovations in Morocco; the bulk of the population still depended on the "grapevine," and they undoubtedly knew why things were looking better.

The direct economic impact of the American presence in Morocco was felt to any extent only in Casablanca and Port Lyautey. The social impact was felt throughout Morocco, for in the coastal cities to which great numbers of them had migrated, the Moroccans from the interior came in contact with the Americans. The Moslem population of Port Lyautey increased by two-thirds between 1941 and 1945.[9] Not only did the migration create a Moroccan proletariat in the coastal cities, but also it tended to break down the old Franco-Berber solidarity, for many of the migrants came from the Berber tribes whose chiefs had been the backbone of French support, particularly in the South. The Berbers, especially of the Schleuh and Haha tribes, proved to be mechanically apt, industrious, and generally more stable than the Arab population of the coast. Although they maintained their tribal identity, and returned to the tribe for a wife when they were ready to marry, they tended to establish permanent domiciles and seek advancement in one place instead of floating from job to job and city to city.[10] Freed

---

[8] Ibid.

[9] According to Stephane Delisle, "Le prolétariat marocain de Port Lyautey," in Jean d'Etienne, Louis Villeme, and Stephane Delisle, *L'évolution sociale du Maroc*, p. 115, the population of Kenitra (renamed Port Lyautey in 1932) was:

	European	Moroccan	Total
1912	600	500	1,100
1920	2,204	2,363	4,567
1936	5,684	11,912	16,601
1941	6,954	19,709	26,663
1945	7,550	28,648	36,198
1949	8,938	54,264	63,202

[10] Robert Montagne, "Naissance et développement du prolétariat marocain," in Centre d'études de politique etrangère, *Industrialisation de l'Afrique du Nord*, pp. 215–216.

from the direction of their tribal chieftains, they came to represent a new political force in Morocco.

Mohammed Ben Barka is a case in point. He is Berber, from the Ait Malal faction of the Ait Aissa tribe in the southern Atlas Mountains. His father was one of the tribal notables, impoverished by the exactions of the grand caid, and Mohammed would have succeeded to his position—and debts—had he not left the tribe to come to Port Lyautey. He worked for a French-owned brewery. Illiterate himself, he was determined that his children would be educated. The eldest, now thirty-five years old and an employee of the U.S. Navy for the past fourteen years, received about six years of formal schooling. He married a girl from the parent tribe in 1958, and has two small children. The second son completed his baccalaureate and is now an honor student in an American university. The family lives in a paid-for modern home, comparable to and across the street from one occupied by an American military family. The Ben Barka family, in a quarter century, has evolved from a tribal society to a middle-class urban one.[11]

Mr. Ben Barka estimated that at least twenty other Moroccan employees of the Naval Air Station had enjoyed similar success, a generalization that was confirmed by Mr. Carl Yazi, the industrial relations officer for the navy base. Even individuals not touched directly took vicarious pleasure in recounting a neighbor's good fortune. When asked how the presence of the Americans in Kenitra (formerly Port Lyautey) had affected the community, M'hammed Amraoui replied, "I have a friend, Abbas Mahrouma, whose brother worked on the base. With the money he made he built a house in Kenitra, a two-story structure with two stores on the ground floor. His father is a tailor and uses one of the stores. He rents the other one, and they live upstairs. Halima—I do not know the rest of her name—is not married. She worked as a domestic servant for an American family. With what she made she also built a house over a store. She rents out the store and lives upstairs."[12]

Life not only became better for the Moroccans after the Americans came, it also became more exciting. Their presence brought

[11] Interview, Mohammed Ben Barka, Kenitra, May 13, 1967.

[12] Interview, M'hammed Amraoui, a Moroccan student, at Fort Worth, Texas, March 26, 1967.

the war closer to home—not the deprivation and death, but the more heroic and glamorous aspects of a war going well. Navy amphibious patrol planes began operations against the German submarines operating in the Atlantic approaches to the Strait of Gibraltar on November 13, 1942. By the end of 1943, eight squadrons of over four thousand officers and men were flying thousand-mile patrols out into the Atlantic and occasional missions into the Mediterranean.[13] The operations were shrouded in secrecy, but the local populace could not fail to see the river full of moored Catalina seaplanes, nor fail to hear the night-and-day roar of the four-engined Liberators taking off and landing at the airfield. Occasionally, they grieved with the Americans when one of the planes failed to make it. Hélène Walton vividly remembers the crash of a Liberator: "We had just come home from a dance at the Red Cross when we heard a terrible noise . . . ran outside . . . a plane had crashed just behind our house and was burning. To this day, I can still hear the men screaming. My father tried to get them out, but the flames spread too fast. He helped take out the bodies the next day, and my mother used to take flowers to their graves until after the war was over and their bodies were taken back to the United States."[14]

The antisubmarine patrols did not stop the merchant shipping losses. Ten ships, totaling 52,042 tons, were sunk in the Moroccan Sea Frontier Area of responsibility,[15] which extended from 26° 10′ north latitude to 35° 00′, and westward to the "chop line," beyond which protection was furnished by U.S.-based forces.[16] The Moroccan-based navy planes probably sank twenty German submarines by December 20, 1943, at a cost of five planes and thirty-six men lost in training accidents and thirteen planes and sixty-two men lost operationally.[17] The losses were heavier after July, 1943,

[13] "Diary of Fleet Air Wing 15, December 1, 1942, to March 16, 1944," in Moore and Tunley, "A Short History." The patrol squadrons were 73 and 92, equipped with PBY-5A's; 127 and 132, equipped with PV's; 111 and 112, equipped with PB4Y's, and two squadrons of the U.S. Army Air Force 480th Group, equipped with B-24's.

[14] Interview, Mrs. Hélène Walton, Kenitra, June 4, 1967.

[15] Moore and Tunley, "A Short History."

[16] "Commander Moroccan Sea Frontier War Diary," December 7, 1943, in U.S. Navy Archives, Washington, D.C.

[17] Moore and Tunley, "A Short History."

for the German submarines stayed on the surface and fought back,[18] and long-range Focke-Wulf-200 planes started flying protection for the German forces.

In April, 1943, the British were persuaded to give up the base they had established the previous November at Agadir, and Fleet Air Wing 15 used it for the rest of the war to extend antisubmarine coverage southward. The army engineers built a 5,200-foot all-weather runway, but all functions were under tents until September, 1943, when a limited construction program was instituted, most of which was completed by the end of December.[19]

The southward extension of the operating area brought the United States forces in conflict with Spain. On October 26, 28, and November 1, Spanish planes based in the Canary Islands attacked U.S. Navy patrol planes and inflicted some damage to the planes, but no casualties resulted from the attack. The potentially dangerous situation was resolved through diplomatic channels,[20] and the patrols continued unmolested. Actually the Spanish had cause for alarm, for the American strategy included seizure of the Canary Islands and the establishment of an advance base there for antisubmarine patrols. Material for the base was stockpiled at Port Lyautey, but the project was "delayed and delayed because of some high level diplomacy,"[21] and finally abandoned.

Although flight schedules and operational areas were classified as secret, sailors will brag, and the news of success was generally an ill-kept secret. Patrol Squadron 73 made its first attack on a submarine on November 22, 1942. The results were inconclusive, but the presence of the planes forced a change in German tactics; earlier, the submarines had been selective in their attacks—no use wasting a torpedo on a trawler. After December 1, the submarines

[18] Ibid.

[19] GG, SOS, NATOUSA confidential dispatch dated September 14, 1943, quoted in FAW 15 Diary in ibid., authorized construction of water-storage facilities, three bathhouses, and twenty-eight buildings (20 by 100 feet) for operations, communications, barracks, and warehouses.

[20] "Commander Moroccan Sea Frontier War Diary," November 13, 1943.

[21] Truman C. Penney letter to the author dated Walnut Creek, California, August 11, 1967. Captain Penney was commanding officer of the Port Lyautey Naval Air Station from March 6, to September 3, 1944.

remained submerged, and sank all ships that they could reach.[22] The commander of the Moroccan Sea Frontier was obliged to furnish a naval escort for the fishing fleet, a daily practice that, according to his war diary, continued until November 26, 1944. The operational antisubmarine patrols continued until June 6, 1945. Their work became easier and more effective after June 4, 1944, for the capture of the German submarine U-505 by the U.S.S. *Guadalcanal* made a complete set of German code books available to the U.S. Navy, a happy circumstance that saved countless lives.[23]

In early 1944, as the news began to leak out that the navy planes could find and destroy a submarine even though it remained underwater, the admiration of the community, particularly the younger set, knew no bounds. School children besieged their teachers with questions as to how it was done, and the teachers had no answers.[24] But that it was being done was obvious. Observers at Tangier could watch the planes flying their clover-leaf patterns two hundred feet above the surface of the water in the Strait of Gibraltar, dropping their float-lights each time the plane passed over the submarine, and, when the course and speed of the submerged submarine had been determined with a dozen or so float-lights, attacking with retro-firing rockets. Shortly thereafter, a giant oil slick appeared—if the attack was successful—and surface ships gathered up debris, bodies, and, sometimes, survivors. The MADCATS, Catalina patrol planes equipped with Magnetic Anomaly Detectors, were one of the most sophisticated weapons systems developed in World War II.

The people of Port Lyautey did not have to go to Tangier to wit-

[22] "Commander Moroccan Sea Frontier War Diary," November 19, 1942–June 30, 1943.

[23] Truman C. Penney letter dated August 11, 1967.

[24] M. Challot, a teacher at the Lycée Mixte de Port Lyautey during the war, asked the author in September, 1959, to explain the concept and procedure, and said that his interest dated from the wartime questions.

The MADCATS had their greatest success in the Strait of Gibraltar because of the restricted area through which the German submarines had to pass. Other detection equipment, mostly sonic, was ineffective because the submarines cut their engines and floated through in one of the saline currents always present in the strait. The different density between the waters of the Atlantic and those of the Mediterranean produced two currents, one in each direction, at different depths.

ness American technical competence. They only had to visit the river bank where American crews and liberated Norwegian seamen who had been interned at Port Lyautey worked to clear the channel of ships sabotaged, both to prevent their capture and to render the port unusable. There were fifteen ships sunk November 8–10, by order of Captaine de Fregate Caderet, the French navy commandant at Port Lyautey.[25] Salvage operations began December 18, and by January 19, 1943, six of the ships had been raised and repaired and the others moved for salvage later, or destroyed. The quay had been repaired and extended to take six ships alongside at one time. Eleven locomotive cranes, five of 2.5-ton capacity, and six of 3-ton capacity, were operating. Ten warehouses and three sheds provided 135,000 square feet of covered storage, and thirty thousand barrels of fuel, mostly black oil and diesel, but some gasoline, were stored in the port area. The bar at the mouth of the Sebou had been dredged so that vessels of 19-foot draft (vice 17) could enter the river. The port was busier than ever before in its history.[26]

Without doubt the American undertaking that had the most profound effect upon the population of Morocco, French and Moroccan, civilian and military, was the rearmament of the Franco-Moroccan armed forces. The United States had obligated itself by the Murphy-Giraud Agreement of November 2, 1942, to deliver the matériel to organize and modernize the French forces.[27] The level of armament was fixed by the Casablanca conference at six infantry divisions, two armored divisions (later raised to three), and two

[25] Th. N. Komaroff, "Compte rendu de l'attaque de Port-Lyautey les 8,9 et 10 Novembre, 1942," copy furnished by Mr. Komaroff to the author, July 1, 1967, from his personal papers. Mr. Komaroff was director of the port. The ships included: *St. Emile*, 1,269 tons, in the bend of the river; *Batavia*, across the channel from the *St. Emile*; *Hilde*, 1,595 tons; *Belgien*, 1,979 tons; *Hebe II*; *Alphee*; *Ailette*—all in the channel below the port. The *St. Hugues* and several ships whose names are not given, unable to move under their own power, were sunk at their moorings, and, finally, the two port tugs, *Chergui* and *Texel*, were sunk above the port.

[26] "Commander Moroccan Sea Frontier War Diary," dated December 18, 1942, and "Brief History of Port Lyautey," prepared by the chief of naval operations (OP-441H), dated April 9, 1951, in Port Lyautey file, U.S. Navy Archives, Washington, D.C.

[27] René Richard and Alain de Serigny, *La bissectrice de la guerre, Alger, 8 Novembre 1942*, p. 219.

colonial divisions. The 100,000 troops allowed by the German-Italian Armistice Commission, plus an additional 80,000 reserves camouflaged in the Chantiers de Jeunesse and other paramilitary organizations were immediately available, and, in all, over one million men were available in North Africa for military service.[28] By midsummer, 1943, matériel was pouring into Morocco at a fantastic rate—over 850,000 tons between March, 1943, and mid-June, 1944. Sixteen Liberty Ships entered the port of Casablanca in one day of August, 1943, and during the whole period the port averaged six to ten ships each ten days.[29]

The massive influx of matériel created problems. The Americans distrusted the French—and made their distrust felt. The French, for their part, regarded the young American army with condescension, even while conceding material superiority. American military personnel, concerned with rearmament, doubted the ability of the French units to rapidly absorb the new weapons and adapt to their use—a well-founded fear, as time demonstrated. The French army, unable to absorb the matériel because it lacked sufficient technical specialists, complained that the Americans were loading them down with useless luxuries. "A division does not need a laundry company," General Juin said. "The soldiers can wash their own."[30] Spare parts were especially sensitive items. A one-year supply came with the basic equipment. The French opened the containers and issued the spare parts upon receipt because, they said, they did not have the personnel or time to inventory them. Most of the spares were lost or discarded before they were used. The matter became so critical that, on November 10, 1943, the American authorities stopped delivery of additional equipment and refused to resume until the French created a supply service.[31] The same problem did not exist with respect to the French navy, for the auxiliary vessels supplied to the French carried their spares on board.[32]

[28] Georges Marey, "Le réarmament français en Afrique du Nord, 1942–1944," *Revue politique et parlementaire* 193 (October, 1947); 48–49.

[29] Ibid., p. 56. American Lend-Lease was terminated by the Blum-Byrnes Agreement of May 28, 1946. The total value of deliveries to September 1, 1945 was U.S. to France, $2.25 billion; and France to the U.S., $870 million. Ibid., p. 140.

[30] Ibid., pp. 45, 56.

[31] Ibid., p. 57.

[32] According to "Commander Moroccan Sea Frontier War Diary" entries, the

American specialists supervised the distribution of the flood of matériel. John Labbancz was one of them. He came to Morocco on December 24, 1942, in the Thirty-seventh Air Depot Group, and as a soldier and civilian he has remained in Morocco ever since. He described the aircraft assembly line at Camp Cazes for the P-40's, then successively, P-39's, P-38's, P-47's, and P-51's. The airplane fuselages came in huge crates, the center section on a skid, and the wings fastened to the sides of the crate. One end of the crate was opened, the plane slid out, the wings were attached and engine installed, and the plane was almost ready to fly. The Thirty-seventh Air Base Depot Group turned out twelve to fifteen planes per day, but "could never top the British," Mr. Labbancz said. "They always hit twenty or better a day."[33]

The planes flew off to war, and the crates, by some devious routes, made their way to the *bidonville*—those haphazard slums built of tar paper and wood and roofed with flattened-out tin cans, which grew up like cancerous sores on the outskirts of Casablanca and Port Lyautey. Neither the French nor the American authorities approved of the new housing developments, and, according to Labbancz, the theft or the failure to report the theft of lumber of any sort was a court-martial offense, but "Hell, they had to live someplace." There was no doubt as to where the material was coming from. Every shingle on the roof proclaimed its origin: GULF, TEXACO, ESSO, SCHLITZ, BUDWEISER, SPAM. And if some builder might have wanted a rain gutter or a downspout, he could have found a matching decor in the local tin market, the cans soldered end to end. "Made in USA" entered the language of Morocco at Casablanca and Port Lyautey in 1943.[34] To many Moroccans, *Amriki* (American) became synonymous with excellence. Mohammed Ben Barka said he was eighteen years old before he knew that the green-striped watermelon (the Tom Watson variety) sold in the local markets was called *dallah Amrikani* because the seeds

---

following vessels for coastal antisubmarine patrol and harbor service were furnished: to the "North African Government" on November 12, 1943, the SC-1335; and to the French navy, the YMS-23 and 77 on March 5, 1944, and the SC-519 on March 27—all three received by Capitaine de Vaisseau Roques, Commander, Coastal Defense.

[33] Interview, John Labbancz, Kenitra, May 21, 1967.

[34] Marey, "Le réarmament français," p. 52.

came from America, and not because it was the best melon to be found in Morocco.[35]

Functional words, too, entered the Moroccan language. Arabic has little or no technical vocabulary; besides there was no time to translate. American words were simply incorporated in the French and Moroccan language: jeep, tank, bulldozer, weekend, G.I., and many others less acceptable, for the American associates of the Moroccan who lived in the *bidonville* did not usually represent the highest level of American culture. But, whether he could pronounce it or not, the American demonstrated the substance of fraternity and equality.

The pervasiveness of the Moroccan-American contact, rather than the discovery of some Machiavellian plot, caused the French officials to suspect a greater rapport than actually existed. While G.I. Joe helped Mohammed—his generic name for any Moroccan man—steal lumber, Colonel Swersky, asked to supply a set of piston rings for King Mohammed V's Buick automobile, said, "Hell, let's change the motor," and did so in three hours. At the lower echelons of contact, neither the G.I. nor the Moroccan was interested in politics; at the higher echelons, they were too discreet to talk about such topics. The upper-echelon contact did exist, despite General Noguès' determination at least to monitor it if he could not avert it entirely. On January 12, 1942, the sultan and his cabinet visited the U.S.S. *Wainwright* in the harbor at Casablanca, and on January 13 he gave a luncheon for General Patton and other American officers.[36] On June 25, 1943, at Oujda, General Mark Clark staged a fire-power demonstration for the king, who so far abandoned protocol when General Clark entered as to rise and go forward to meet him.[37] The king's contacts with the Americans were more frequent than twice yearly. According to Dr. Sadani, of the Moroccan Foreign Office, they were "very frequent. His Majesty had a *laissez-passer*, and he could go anywhere in the American lines without General Noguès' even knowing about it."[38] Captain William E. G. Taylor, the commanding officer of the Naval Air Station at Port Lyautey, "accepted and returned many invita-

[35] Interview, Mohammed Ben Barka, Fort Worth, Texas, February 12, 1967.
[36] "Commander Moroccan Sea Frontier War Diary," January 12–13, 1943.
[37] *La Voix Nationale*, July 19, 1943.
[38] Interview, Dr. Sadani, Rabat, May 28, 1967.

tions to receptions and dinners with the Sultan." At the official functions, he never had an opportunity to speak with him, but at the informal functions, "a large group sat on banquettes around three sides of the sultan, conversations were general in nature, usually in French, infrequently in English. No controversial subjects were ever brought up."

Captain Taylor was wary in his relations with the Franco-Moroccan community. He knew that "something very mysterious had been going on in Morocco," for he was instructed by Admiral William A. Glassford, Jr., who commanded the U.S. naval forces in the Mediterranean, to "improve the relationship between the Naval Air Station and the French in Morocco." He was given no specifics and assumed that the hostility, so great that "there had nearly been an armed invasion of the [naval air] station" before he took over command, was associated with the Vichy-Gaullist conflict.[39]

Actually, Captain Taylor and Captain Truman C. Penney, his predecessor, were caught in a three-way conflict of interest. In the spring of 1944, the French officials in Morocco saw their authority slipping away from them. They were alarmed on the one hand by the De Gaulle purge of ex-Vichy sympathizers, and on the other by resurgent Moroccan nationalism (the Istiqlal *Manifesto* of January 11, 1944). American intelligence sources warned Captain Penney of the possibility of a revolt by the French army in Morocco against the De Gaulle takeover and advised him to take precautions against forcible seizure of the base by French military units. Captain Penney's defensive preparations included continuous armed patrols around the perimeter of the base, entrenched defensive positions within the perimeter, and plans to seize the Harbor Entrance Control Post at the mouth of the Sebou River—

[39] Letters, Captain Taylor to the author, dated Washington, D.C., May 1 and July 28, 1967. Captain Taylor was assigned a French naval liaison officer shortly after he assumed command, and it was from that source that the reference to the "armed invasion" came.

On the question of Franco-American hostility, Captain T. A. Turner, USN (Ret.), who was commander, Fleet Air Wing 15 and commanding officer of the Naval Air Station from June 26, 1943, to March 6, 1944, stated in a letter to the author dated Jackson, Mississippi, April 27, 1967, that "our relations with the Moroccans and French couldn't have been better. I sensed some strain between the Moroccans and the French Civil Service Administrators but believe this resentment aimed mainly at the taxes imposed by the French government."

its guns could fire at point-blank range upon the station. His greatest concern, however, was the French army regiment stationed in Port Lyautey. The pasha of Port Lyautey, Sherif Moulay Hassan El Ouezzani (whose intelligence service was as good as his own, Captain Penney said), advised him not to worry about the French regiment, the Arabs would "take care of it."[40] The tension eased as the French discovered that the Americans were not backing the Istiqlal, and no overt act disturbed the uneasy calm.

Whatever the circumstances, relations with the French speedily improved. Captain Taylor said he "tried very hard to be helpful whenever possible" in relieving the distressed economy, but he kept aloof from anyone except the top officials with whom he felt obliged to associate. He conducted his official business "through channels" —French channels, and refused to receive members of the Roosevelt Club, "a leftist group of agitators . . . for obvious reasons."[41] For his efforts in putting Franco-American relations "back on the track," Captain Taylor won the plaudits of the French navy.[42] If U.S. Navy personnel had been involved in political activities—and it was never established that there was such involvement—he had taken them out, and, to the best of Captain Taylor's knowledge, "the only problems that the succeeding C.O.'s had were with the French navy which, understandably, wanted to take the Naval Air Station back for its own use."

The war years in Morocco telescoped colossal change into a relatively short time span. The personnel level stabilized for the Americans at something over ten thousand in mid-1943 and remained there for the rest of the war. About four thousand were naval personnel, concerned with antisubmarine warfare, primarily, and with resupply problems for naval units operating in the Mediterranean area. The army personnel, including air force, were

[40] Truman C. Penney letter to the author dated August 11, 1967. According to Rear Admiral George T. Owen, letter to the author dated Treasure Island, Florida, September 29, 1967, the idea of a French seizure of the Naval Air Station was "ridiculous," but he said "the French would have liked to see some incident which would demonstrate ill will between the Arabs and the Americans." RADM Owen commanded Fleet Air Wing 15, based at Port Lyautey, from March 6, 1944, until "six days after peace was declared."

[41] Captain Taylor letter to author, dated Washington, May 1, 1967.

[42] Admiral Mariani, *Marine au Maroc*, letter to Captain Taylor, dated Casablanca, August 29, 1946; copy furnished to the author by Captain Taylor.

concerned, after the initial invasion, with rearming the French forces, and with resupplying units in Italy and then France. Almost all of the American personnel in Morocco were male and were either not married or were not accompanied by their dependents. Their recreational interests were either touristic or social and, in the latter case, involved contact for the most part with French girls, for they were not inclined to try to bridge the cultural gap to the distaff side of the Moroccan community. The American contact with the Moroccan community during the war years was "man to man." On September 3, 1945, the navy held a "victory dance" at Rabat's largest hotel for its personnel and about three hundred "nice" girls from the area. About one thousand guests partook of the free beer, food, and entertainment, and the navy then turned its attention to demobilization and the peacetime problems associated with its Moroccan infrastructure.[43]

[43] "Commander Moroccan Sea Frontier War Diary," September 3, 1945.

6. Reestablishment of the French Colonial Regime

SEVERAL FEATURES CHARACTERIZED the political evolution of Morocco in the immediate postwar period. Faced with the problems of peace in Europe and the Pacific, American diplomatic interest in North Africa waned. The G.I., preoccupied with demobilization, lost much of his curiosity about foreign lands and peoples. He stayed close to his quarters on the base, and the cultural rapport he had developed with the local community was lost.[1] French of-

[1] The lack of concern for the local community largely resulted from the unstable personnel situation. According to "A Brief History of Port Lyautey," prepared by Op-441H, dated April 9, 1951, in the Port Lyautey file, U.S. Navy Archives, the Naval Air Station at Port Lyautey counted 4,191 officers and men in April, 1945, and the number climbed during the next two months as the Army Air Transport Command staged its United States bound personnel through the port. By the end of the summer, the flood had ebbed. On August 31, the total of army, navy, and coast guard personnel had dwindled to 2,359, and by November 30, to 839, at which point it stabilized. See "U.S. Naval Air Sta-

ficials, profiting from American absorption elsewhere, sought to reestablish their old colonial regime but met resistance from an increasingly militant group of nationalists to whom King Mohammed V gave support and leadership. Had it not been for the United States Navy's need for a Moroccan link in its world-wide communications system, Morocco might have become merely a historical memory for the Americans.

The constant problem for French officials during the war and thereafter was to recoup primacy vis-à-vis the Americans, no easy matter, for French prestige had been destroyed by the ease with which the Americans had occupied Morocco. American military authorities, however, accepted the subordinate role assigned them by protectorate officials. As Rear Admiral Paul L. Dudley, who was in command of the Naval Air Station in 1946–1947, explained the function of Capitaine de Corvette (Lieutenant Commander) Henri Glaziot, his French navy liaison officer: "I never doubted that he was put there to watch every move we made. So what? We had no argument with the French. They were in control of Morocco— there was no doubt about it. He was personable and efficient. I never made a move outside of my command without him. He arranged my hunting trips, accompanied me to social functions, and generally made himself as indispensable as possible."[2]

The French policy toward the Moroccan nationalist movement was not consistent, but it reflected internal tensions in French political circles rather than concern for American or other viewpoints. Gabriel Puaux, who succeeded General Noguès as resident-general on June 5, 1943, considered that "all of us here represent France, which will judge us, and as for us, we keep our eyes fixed on our far off native land."[3] He was not able to suppress the nationalist spirit, however. Although he exiled or imprisoned the leaders of the new Istiqlal party on charges of Nazi collaboration, he failed to

---

tion Command History," dated September 8, 1959, and "Logistics Report, U.S. Naval Air Station, Port Lyautey, Northwest Africa base maintenance file," both in the Port Lyautey file, U.S. Navy Archives for the composite report of the personnel situation.

[2] Interview, Rear Admiral Paul L. Dudley, September 11, 1967, at Washington, D.C.

[3] Address to the Government Council, reported in *La Vigie Marocaine*, January 31, 1946.

outlaw the party and new leaders emerged to continue the agitation. General De Gaulle sought to abate the unrest by an appeal to King Mohammed V during the latter's state visit to France in June. De Gaulle proposed concrete reforms to be accomplished in stages and dates to be agreed upon jointly. But De Gaulle fell from power and in the next six months the colonial reforms of the Fourth Republic slipped into a state of paralysis.

During the entire independence movement, the conflict was not in fact between France and Morocco, but between the French colony in Morocco and the imperial palace. As one close observer of the Moroccan drama remarked, it was not France on trial but the concept, acknowledged or not, of exploitation of the Sheriffian Empire for the benefit of a few.[4] Despite the perhaps sincere desire of De Gaulle and of Resident-General Eirik Labonne, who succeeded Puaux in March, 1946, the protectorate policies remained repressive and exploitative in practice.

Despite myriad indications to the contrary, Moroccans, high and low, persisted in the belief that the United States understood and sympathized with their plight even if it did not give outright support to their cause. When Gabriel Puaux released 387 members of the Istiqlal party from prison in July, 1944, the nationalists attributed his action to American intervention.[5] There is no evidence to justify such wishful thinking, and in forums where the United States might properly have considered Moroccan demands, such as the United Nations Conference at San Francisco in March, 1945, or the Potsdam Conference, which considered the future of Tangier, the United States was silent.[6]

Although Eirik Labonne, the new resident-general, proposed a substantially liberalized regime that he intended to be free of foreign influence in Morocco, it had little chance of success. French

[4] Pierre Corval, "Les forces en présence," *La Nef: Maroc et Tunisie*, p. 69, and Jean Lacouture, "Polémiques en surface, malaise en profondeur," ibid., p. 89.

[5] Charles-André Julien, *L'Afrique du Nord en marche*, p. 352.

[6] The text of the appeal to the United Nations, dated March 8, 1945, and the protest of "big power" dictation of the future of Tangier at the Potsdam Conference, dated August 2, 1945, are contained in Istiqlal party, *Documents, 1944–1946*, pp. 16–22. See also Julien, *L'Afrique du Nord en marche*, pp. 352–353, and Roger Le Tourneau, *Evolution Politique de l'Afrique du Nord Musulmane*, pp. 217–218, on this question.

agricultural and industrial interests opposed his program, and lesser officials of the protectorate sabotaged it.[7] Nationalists denounced it as a consolidation of a colonialist program that had demonstrably failed for thirty-four years. And finally, the state of the French and Moroccan economy simply did not permit dispensing with American aid. Disposition of war-surplus matériel was a typical postwar problem. France and the French in Morocco cast covetous eyes on the huge stocks of American trucks, jeeps, and tractors standing unused in depots in France and Morocco. In May, 1947, five ships brought more than 750 trucks, ranging from jeeps to tractor-trailers, and spare parts worth 25 million francs from France to Casablanca. Title to more than 2,000 jeeps, 1,000 Dodge trucks, and several hundred GMC trucks was transferred to the French government, which sold the equipment to individuals at prices marked up to four times the actual value. When the Association des Anciens Combattants protested the markup, the prices on jeeps were reduced, but truck prices were increased to compensate for the decline.[8] Nor did the American dominance end after the initial infusion of surplus equipment, for the users in Morocco still expressed preference for American equipment after the resumption of French manufacturing. "Is this how we are to understand the practice of an economic policy?" M. de Peretti, president of the Rabat Chamber of Commerce, challenged the purchase by protectorate officials of five hundred U.S. tractors "almost identical to tractors made in France."[9]

The French in Morocco were haunted by the suspicion that Americans were trying to replace them in their privileged economic position, and they were not reassured by the absence of overt action. For them the danger existed as long as any American presence was maintained. Both *Espoir*, the Communist daily newspaper, and *Le Petit Marocain*, historically a right-wing daily but at that time temporarily under Communist control, charged that the Americans

[7] Ibid., pp. 355–364. Stephane Bernard, *Le Conflit Franco-Marocain, 1943–1956*, I, 75–76, details the machinations of Civil Controller Boniface and the director of interior, Colonel Jean Lecomte, to thwart the Labonne program; see p. 74 n. for a résumé of LeComte's career after 1948.

[8] *La Vigie Marocaine*, January 24, March 14, May 10, July 30, 1947.

[9] Ibid., March 10, 1947. The author discovered in the spring of 1967 that substantial quantities of the spare parts were still on sale in Casablanca.

intended to return to Morocco—if indeed they ever left.[10] As if to confirm their suspicions, the United States Navy held on to its base at Port Lyautey. The French government responded to the powerful Moroccan French lobby by pressuring the United States to evacuate. French motives were mixed, reflecting a combination of chauvinism, economic nationalism, and Communist influence in the French National Assembly.

American diplomatic officials were sympathetic to the French position. They insisted that the United States was in the process of evacuating its bases in Morocco. The Naval Air Station at Port Lyautey had been placed in "reduced operational status" on January 15, 1947,[11] and all but two of thirty major African bases, including Camp Cazes at Casablanca, had been abandoned by March 15.[12] The diplomats implied that complete evacuation would follow the completion of such administrative details as reburial of the American dead in military cemeteries at Casablanca or in the United States.[13] The diplomatic protestations were misleading, although that was not the intent, for the U.S. Navy had no intention of evacuating.[14]

The navy concern was not for maritime or aviation facilities, but for its communications facilities at Port Lyautey, the only adequate

[10] Kenneth Campbell analyzed the French fears as expressed in the Moroccan press in the *New York Times*, May 21, 1947, p. 13. *Le Petit Marocain* was a part of the right-wing Mas trust except for the period 1945–1950, when it followed the lead of the Communist party. See Bernard, *Le Conflit Franco-Marocain*, III, 126, for an explanation of the changing direction and editorial policy of *Le Petit Marocain*.

[11] Air Logistics Directive 95-NN-46 of December 31, 1946, in the Port Lyautey: Shore Establishment file, Office of Aviation History, Navy Department, Washington, D.C.

[12] The *New York Times*, March 15, 1947, announced the abandonment.

[13] *La Vigie Marocaine*, March 8, 1947, reported the American plans to rebury their dead at Casablanca or to return the bodies to the United States if the families so desired.

[14] The information concerning the United States Navy maneuvers to retain its base at Port Lyautey was given to the author by Rear Admiral Paul L. Dudley, USN (Retired), in an interview, September 11, 1967, at Washington, D.C. RADM Dudley, then a captain, was commanding officer, NAS, Port Lyautey, a technical advisor to Ambassador Jefferson Caffrey at Paris, and a member of the technical subcommittee that worked out the Navy-to-Navy Agreement of September 15, 1947.

link between the continental United States and the Philippines, and indispensable for ships operating in the Mediterranean. Senior officers vividly recalled the difficulties of operating during World War II from the limestone caves of Malta, where the U.S. Navy "was always on hind tit."[15] They insisted upon retention under United States control of a communications site in the North African area. In early 1947 Admiral R. L. Conolly, commander of U.S. naval forces in the eastern Atlantic and Mediterranean, flew to Washington and impressed upon Secretary of the Navy James Forrestal the urgency of the navy need.[16] In June, Ambassador Jefferson Caffrey was directed to open negotiations at Paris for indefinite retention by the United States of its facilities at Port Lyautey.

The ambassador's efforts met with slight success. The political differences were irreconcilable. The first round of negotiations produced a "White Paper" that vaguely recognized French sovereignty (over Moroccan territory) and agreed that the Americans would evacuate, but did not fix a date. Then the negotiations deadlocked; neither government would make further concessions. Admiral Conolly suggested that diplomatic discussions be abandoned and the question treated as a technical one to be settled by the two navies, the formula that eventually was adopted.

In suggesting such a disposition, Admiral Conolly was confident that he could come to agreement with the French navy. Admiral H. M. Nomy, the French vice-chief of naval operations, and Admiral Pierre Barjot, the French navy commander in Morocco, were both strongly pro-American. As in the United States, the French armed forces were engaged in an interservice fight over the organi-

[15] Captain J. A. H. Tuthill, USN, commander of the U.S. naval communications facilities, Port Lyautey, 1958–1960, usually began his briefings of visiting congressmen with a résumé of the difficulties at Malta, and the need for retention of Port Lyautey. The author attended many such briefings.

[16] Forrestal does not mention this specific matter in his diary, but see his report of March 13, 1947, to the Senate Foreign Relations Committee "in general terms on the importance to the United States of the Mediterranean," and the navy's role there, in *The Forrestal Diaries*, Walter Millis, ed., pp. 257–258. The gravest threat at the time was the conflict inherent in the communist pressure on Turkey and Greece. The U.S. Navy had deployed a squadron to the eastern Mediterranean, and Forrestal well understood the support requirements thus necessitated.

zation of the postwar French military establishment. The navy, its budget cut, could ill afford at that time to operate a Naval Air Station at Port Lyautey. It feared losing the best airfield in North Africa to the French air force more than it feared sharing it with the U.S. Navy, since the latter was willing to help pay for maintaining and operating it.

A naval technical subcommittee was appointed to work out the details.[17] It met "off and on for about three months, generally in disagreement."[18] but finally hammered out the "Port Lyautey Base Technical Agreement between the United States Navy and the French Navy" signed at Paris on September 15, 1947, by Admiral Conolly and Admiral Nomy. The disagreements were not on principle but specifics. Both navies agreed that the airfield and seaplane base would pass to French flag and command, but the Americans desired a specific enclave within the base that would be under United States control. The French wanted to control the facilities that they would furnish to U.S. Navy users. The French-built aircraft hangar and the bachelor officers' quarters were two major items in dispute.

The subcommittee compromised; the French navy received the hangar and the American navy, the B.O.Q. The French navy assumed full operational and financial responsibility for the airfield and seaplane base, agreeing to furnish facilities free of charge to the U.S. Navy for specified units and missions. The U.S. Navy kept its territorial enclave and assumed financial responsibility for construction of such facilities therein as it might need. The details of the transfer of command were to be determined by the French and American commanding officers at the base. The agreement was to be effective as long as required by the occupation of Germany and ex-enemy nations in Europe.[19]

The actual transfer was remarkably smooth, Rear Admiral Dudley recalled. In July, 1947, the French navy moved in personnel who worked alongside American counterparts in order to familiar-

[17] The subcommittee was composed of Rear Admiral V. H. Ragsdale, USN, Admiral Conolly's chief of staff, Dudley, and Assistant Naval Attaché Jordan, for the United States Navy, and Admiral Nomy and two other French officers, whose names RADM Dudley did not recall, for the French navy.

[18] Interview, RADM Dudley, September 11, 1967.

[19] The text of the agreement is in the U.S. Navy Archives, Washington, D.C.

ize themselves with the installation. On January 1, 1948, command of the base was passed to the French, and the United States Naval Air Station was redesignated U.S. Naval Air Activities.[20] Dudley resolved the thorny issue—the status of the American enclave—without agreement and without reference to higher authority. As the American flag was hauled down at the hangar where the change-of-command ceremony took place, another one was raised within the American enclave on the hill. Admiral Barjot, visibly displeased by the action when it was brought to his attention by the French liaison officer some days later, accepted the *fait accompli*. The change of status made little difference in the base routine. French and American personnel had worked side by side in the airfield control tower and in the other aviation facilities; they continued to do so, although the authority and responsibility relationships were reversed.

Moroccan reaction to the Franco-American technical agreement was interesting. American diplomatic and military authorities had deferred to the French residency officials almost from the date of the landing in 1942. The substantial Moroccan-American contact at the soldier-citizen level had been broken at the end of the war when the G.I.'s went home. Although dependents of American personnel began to arrive, the first on December 31, 1946, they were few in number and they lived on the base.[21] Nevertheless, the Moroccan nationalists considered the American presence a safety factor for themselves and opposed the French demand for evacuation with a plea for the Americans to remain in Morocco.

The Moroccans were strongly influenced by the American anticolonial tradition, but they also had seen a practical demonstration of American good-neighborliness. During the week of July 11–18, 1946, a series of mysterious fires occurred in the Arab quarter of Port Lyautey. Three fires on July 11, one at noon, another at 5 P.M. in the Douar Saknia *bidonville* in the Senailhac district, and a third one at 7:30 P.M. on the other side of town, destroyed six hundred homes and left some three thousand people homeless. Not a

---

[20] Op 56 B Conf. Memo, ser. 01 P 56, of January 21, 1948, and SecNav letter, ser. 50 P 24 of February 17, 1948, in "A Brief History of Port Lyautey."

[21] Ibid. As of May 1, 1948, the personnel count at Port Lyautey was 58 officers, 723 enlisted men, 409 civilians (including 13 Americans), and 106 dependents, plus 1 marine officer and 39 enlisted men.

single house occupied by Europeans was touched.[22] Other fires on July 13 and July 15 destroyed additional homes.[23] On each occasion the pattern was roughly the same with multiple fires in widely separated districts. American firefighting equipment was dispatched from the base each time and for all practical purposes fought the fire alone. On July 17 the Société Nord Africaine des Oléagineu burned,[24] the only European-owned property to be touched by the fires. French and American fire trucks fought the blaze.

Concerning this series of events, Captain W. E. G. Taylor, USN, then in command of the Naval Air Station, said:

> During a sirocco [hot wind from the desert], a large section of the thatched huts—part of the native section outside the Medina proper—caught fire. As we had the only adequate water supply and fire equipment plus bulldozers, we did our best to put out the fire—first using water, then by bulldozing a fire break to prevent the spread of the fire. Our enlisted men saved nearly a dozen Moroccan babies who were abandoned in these huts by their fleeing parents, but we were successful in saving only about a third of the hut area . . . We provided food for the refugees and also turned over to them lumber from an abandoned Italian prisoner of war camp, to rebuild houses. This lumber was a gift.[25]

French authorities made no serious inquiry as to the origins of the fire, or if they did, never made public the findings. The Port Lyautey police arrested Larbi ben Said, who had been taken prisoner in 1940 while serving in an engineer's company of the French army and released "at liberation." About him the police report said that little was known except that he was "anti-French." His motives, the report concluded, were personal. His fifteen-year-old girlfriend had been reproached by her mother for "light conduct." Larbi ben Said set fire to a neighbor's house in revenge and the fire spread, the report said. Another conflagration was explained in a similar vein: Two Moroccans disputing over a car set fire to each other's house.[26]

The official explanations satisfied few. King Mohammed V vis-

---

[22] *La Vigie Marocaine*, July 12, 1946.

[23] Ibid., July 13, 15, 1946.

[24] Ibid., July 18, 1946.

[25] Letter to the author, dated Washington, July 28, 1967.

[26] *La Vigie Marocaine*, July 19, 1946.

ited Port Lyautey "privately" on July 18,[27] and "I told him the French set the fires," one of the victims said. "The *bidonvilles* were on land owned by the A.F.C.A. [a French company], which wanted it cleared so they could sell it. The authorities wanted the arms hidden in the *douar* destroyed. They therefore agreed that burning would clear the land and destroy the arms."[28] Rear Admiral Dudley, who assumed command of the U.S. Naval Air Station the week following the fires, said he had heard the rumors but did not believe the French authorities, most of whom he knew personally, were capable of such gross inhumanity, nor was the political situation sufficiently strained at that time to make such action even expedient.[29] The more affluent Moroccans of the Port Lyautey community generally shared that opinion.

Whether the French set the fires or not, a substantial number of militant Moroccans believe they did. The people who lived in the *medina*, many of whom joined the nationalist movement in the 1950's, regarded the Americans, sailors like Aviations Chief Machinist Mate Dawson, the fire chief, as heroes. Even the French-controlled press accepted the official explanation with skepticism. *La Vigie Marocaine*, April 16, 1947, noted that "another *noualla* in the medina burned last night," and editorially wondered "with some uneasiness if the rest of the Port Lyautey *bidonville* will not end up burned this year. The first of six *noualla* fires coincided with the first relocations into the modern apartments of the new city for *indigènes*." *Le Petit Marocain*, April 29, 1947, commenting on the 1946 fires and the apathy of the administration in investigating them, said, "The *bidonvilles* of Port Lyautey belonged to a society which paid dearly for the land . . . by some strange irony, the day after the fire, the administrator of the society in question was decorated with the Legion of Honor." And finally, the lumber given by the U.S. Navy to rebuild the houses never reached the victims. The French authorities used it to construct barracks on city-owned

27 Ibid., July 18, 1946.
28 Interview, Arbab Ahmed, alias Ahmed ben Djilali, alias Sam, at Kenitra, Morocco, May 15, 1967. Arbab Ahmed was active in the Liberation Army and in the terrorist activities in Port Lyautey in 1953–1955. The same opinion was expressed, one reason or the other or both, by some fifty individuals of the "proletariat" class during the author's visit to Port Lyautey in May, 1967.
29 Interview, RADM Dudley, September 11, 1967.

property near the port to house two thousand homeless Moroccans,[30] and M. Ortola, a local builder, used the newly cleared land to construct permanent apartments.

Against such a background, the crisis of 1947 erupted. King Mohammed V had become incontestably the head of the nationalist movement. He had openly supported denunciation of the protectorate by the crowds that greeted him during his visit to Marrakech in February–March, 1945,[31] and he regarded the reforms proposed by Labonne as no different from the program proposed by General Noguès in 1942 for the exploitation of Morocco for the benefit of France.[32] To prevent enactment of those aspects of Labonne's program that would strengthen French control, the king resorted to his one effective weapon, a negative one, that he used frequently during the next six years. He refused to sign the decrees prepared by the resident-general. Robert Montagne, author and observer of Moroccan life and politics for over twenty years, said the king's conduct was predictable. He prepared and encouraged political agitation that led to political crisis, retreated when rupture with France threatened, but resumed his indefatigable opposition when calm returned.[33]

In the contest for world opinion that began in October, 1946, and reached a crescendo during his visit to Tangier in April, 1947, King Mohammed V played a starring role, and he planned it carefully.[34] He had no forum in French Morocco and no access to foreign diplomats, even those of the French government, except through the offices of the resident-general. The censored French press in

[30] Stephane Delisle, "Le Prolétariat Marocain de Port Lyautey," in Jean d'Etienne, Louis Villème, and Stephane Delisle, *L'Evolution sociale du Maroc*, p. 124.

[31] Julien, *L'Afrique du Nord en marche*, p. 352.

[32] Robert Montagne, *Révolution au Maroc*, p. 195.

[33] Montagne, *Révolution au Maroc*, pp. 199–200. The specific issue that led to the crisis of 1947 was the right of Moroccan workers to organize labor unions, favored by the king, but opposed by protectorate officials because of the potential as a political force. See Public Relations Service of Morocco, *News Bulletin*, no. 9 (June 1, 1952): 6–8, for a French view of the history of the labor movement in Morocco.

[34] Interview, Mehdi Bennouna, Rabat, May 11, 1967. See Mahdi A. Bennouna, *Our Morocco: The True Story of a Just Cause*, p. 75, for an account of the beginning of the propaganda campaign. For personal reasons Mr. Bennouna changed the spelling of his first name after *Our Morocco* was published.

Morocco closed its eyes to political events. It had mentioned neither the Istiqlal *Manifesto* of January 11, 1944, nor the resulting visit of René Massigli, De Gaulle's commissioner for foreign affairs, to the king on January 28, nor the riots at Fez, February 1–3. It had ignored the political reforms proposed by the resident-general. The king's appeal had to be made in a setting free from French control and in a positive context that would evoke the support of an already conditioned body of public opinion. Within his own realm, in Tangier, he would have freedom of action, and he was confident of the support of the Arab League and of the benevolent neutrality of the United States and Spain.[35]

The League of Arab States had been created on March 22, 1945. Great Britain supported it as a guarantor of peace in the Middle East. An Egyptian nationalist, Abderrahman Azzam Pasha, became its permanent secretary-general. The League's objective was clearly stated in its organizational pact as the liberation of all the Arab countries from foreign imperialism.[36] Moroccan nationalists were in contact with it from the beginning. One of them, Mehdi Bennouna, returned to Morocco from Palestine and Egypt in the summer of 1945 and became a trusted confidant of the king. He served as a principal liaison link between the king and the nationalist movement in the Spanish zone of Morocco, which in turn maintained open contact with the Arab League in Cairo.

Although the Tangier visit was planned and discussed at the palace in early 1946, the requisite residential permission was not forthcoming until the fall when Ambassador Labonne called upon the king to urge the signature of certain *dahirs*. The king replied that he could not approve laws affecting the entire nation until he had affirmed his authority throughout its breadth and again proposed a visit to the international city of Tangier, a part of his realm in which he had never set foot. Labonne demurred, citing "international complications"—wishful thinking on his part, for the Istiqlal party leadership had already ascertained that the members

[35] Montagne, *Révolution au Maroc*, pp. 201–202, confirms Bennouna's account of the planning of the Tangier visit, as well as the intent.

[36] Robert Rezette, *Les Partis Politiques Marocains*, pp. 150–153, has an excellent discussion of the relations between the Arab League and Morocco, and the role played by the Bennouna family. See also, Bernard, *Le Conflit Franco-Marocain*, III, 319–327.

of the International Control Commission would interpose no objections to the visit.[37] After several weeks of diplomatic backing and filling the date of the visit was finally set for April 9, 1947.

French *colons* understood that the visit was a nationalist propaganda device, and they undertook to prevent it by precipitating an incident forcing its cancellation.[38] This episode shocked and angered the king. It was a "last straw" that removed any doubts as to his course of action at Tangier.[39] His progression through the Spanish zone of Morocco was tumultuously acclaimed, and his entry into Tangier was triumphal. At the diplomatic reception on April 10, he declared that Morocco must reclaim its rights and realize its aspirations. In a private tête-à-tête with the American consul he expressed the hope that the rumor of evacuation of the American base at Port Lyautey was unfounded.[40] In his speech at the *mendoub*'s [governor's] palace he eulogized the Arab League, affirmed Morocco's attachment to the Islamic religion, and predicted a brilliant future for a unified Morocco. In a radio speech the next day he denounced the division of Morocco into zones of foreign influence and at the mosque, as *imam*, preached of religious ties as a powerful stimulant to progress, culture, and knowledge. At a press conference on April 12, he again proclaimed Morocco's solidarity

[37] Mehdi Bennouna told the author, May 7, 1967, at Rabat, that the King's visit was carefully planned and timed, that the American consul at Tangier was fully informed at all times, and that he [Bennouna] had discussed the final details with him only three days before the visit.

[38] According to Bernard, *Le Conflit Franco-Marocain*, I, 73–74, 85, based upon his interviews with two residents-general and one secretary-general of the protectorate, the French police provoked an incident in Casablanca resulting in the deaths of 1 European, 3 Senegalese soldiers, and 57 Moroccans (according to the proresidential *La Vigie Marocaine*, April 8, 1947), or a total of 813 persons, overwhelmingly Moroccan (according to the *New York Times*, July 8, 1947).

The controlled press, reflecting the attitude of the residency, treated the matter as simply an unfortunate incident, and Robert Montagne, *Révolution au Maroc*, p. 204, suggested that this massacre in the *quartier réservé* (red-light district) was provoked by the Istiqlal party, but the weight of the evidence indicts Civil Controller Phillipe Boniface, acknowledged leader of the French *ultras* in Casablanca.

[39] Interview, King Mohammed V, January, 1958, at Dar-es-Salaam, the king's country residence, near Rabat.

[40] Interview, Mehdi Bennouna, May 7, 1967. Mr. Bennouna was the king's interpreter at the tête-à-tête.

with the other Arab countries, again demanding that Morocco be restored to full sovereignty.

Publicly, as well as in private diplomatic conversations, the visit had a significant pro-American aspect that is usually overlooked. The French reaction generally has been accepted as the measure of importance, but the Roosevelt Club[41] staged the most impressive demonstration in its history at the luxurious El Minzah Hotel on April 11–12. Most high officials of the king's entourage, including his brother, attended. Abdelatif Sbihi, Ahmed Balafrej, and Mehdi Bennouna made speeches, Sbihi in Arabic and Spanish, Balafrej in French, and Bennouna in English. All paid tribute to President Roosevelt and to the "correct" deportment of the United States military forces in Morocco—a backhanded slap at the French forces. Since the El Minzah Hotel could not accommodate the crowds, loudspeakers were mounted outside and the speeches broadcast to literally thousands of the people of Tangier.[42]

At Tangier the sovereign not only introduced himself to the world as an able and articulate defender of his nation, but also presented a son and a daughter who were from that time forward to attract world attention in their own rights. Both Prince Moulay Hassan and Princess Lalla Aisha spoke to audiences in Tangier during the visit, the prince in much the same terms as his father, but the princess, speaking in English part of the time, urged closer contact with Western civilization, and the study of the English and French languages. She said that Morocco, an Arabic and Islamic but also a Western nation, stood at a crossroads.[43] The speeches of the prince and princess were not isolated expressions of individuality, but carefully considered parts of the entire gambit, carefully orchestrated by the king himself.[44] The play for the support of the Arab League and the repudiation of the protectorate attracted much attention, but at Tangier King Mohammed V was proposing more than Moroccan independence; he was proposing a

[41] See pp. 98–99.

[42] Interview, Mehdi Bennouna, Rabat, May 7, 1967.

[43] *Le Petit Marocain*, April 12, 1947.

[44] Princess Aisha told the author in August, 1959, at Rabat, that she had been assigned a duty to perform by her father, and that, although she found the publicity associated with her role as emancipator of the Moroccan woman personally distasteful, she would do her duty, even as her father did his.

revolution that would profoundly change the social and political structure of Morocco after independence had been attained. He anticipated a change free of the xenophobia that characterized nationalist movements in Egypt and the Middle East; indeed the king spoke of Morocco as a *trait d'union*, a bridge, between the East and the West.

The Tangier visit, which revealed the rupture between the resident-general and the king, marked a turning point in Franco-Moroccan relations. Partisans of the protectorate, professing surprise at the king's statements, reacted angrily,[45] probably not so much to his ideas as to his emergence on the world stage. The implication was unmistakable that he had chosen Tangier as his podium only because he was not free to speak out in Rabat, an impression that Allal El Fassi confirmed when he told *Paris-Presse*, April 23, 1947, that the king's position was not new, but that his voice previously had been stifled by the resident-general. The French delegation to the Tangier Control Commission did nothing to allay the charge of censorship when it moved to suspend the nationalist paper in Tangier, the *Voix du Maroc*, for printing "inflammatory and tendentious material"—pictures of the Casablanca massacre.[46] Perhaps because it was no surprise, the French press in Morocco did not immediately comment on the king's declarations in Tangier, and, when it did, it gave the usual economic inventory of roads, ports, and railroads.[47]

The official reaction was not long in coming. On May 14 Ambassador Labonne was recalled. He had been appointed in the first place only because the government of Felix Gouin in Paris could not decide between Generals Jean Leclerc and Alphonse Juin. General Juin was named to replace him. Labonne's enemies had pre-

[45] Robert Montagne, *Révolution au Maroc*, p. 204, rhetorically asked if it was possible that "our country would accept without reaction such manifestations of ingratitude and independence." See Allal El Fassi, *The Independence Movement in Arab North Africa*, trans. Hazem Zaki Nuseibeh, pp. 266–283, for details of the preparation and course of the visit, and Rezette, *Partis Politiques Marocains*, p. 174, and Marcel Peyrouton, *Histoire Générale du Maghreb*, p. 261, for additional comment.

[46] *New York Times*, July 8, 1947, p. 8. Paul H. Alling, United States minister in Tangier abstained from voting.

[47] *La Vigie Marocaine*, April 15, 1947.

vailed, led by Colonel Lecomte, his director of the interior at Rabat, and by Pierre-Henri Teitgen, minister of armed forces at Paris, both exponents of a policy of force in handling colonial peoples.[48] The king's speech was only a pretext, for the decision to return to a policy of force in the colonies had already been made. Even as King Mohammed V spoke at Tangier, the governor-general at Algiers "in full accord with the authorities in Paris" warned Messali Hadj to put an end to his "appeals to violence" in Algeria.[49] Labonne recognized that his failure to secure the enthusiastic cooperation of the king had placed him at the mercy of his opponents, and he told him on the train taking them both back to Rabat that he expected to be recalled and to be replaced by General Juin. He warned the king to anticipate his own deposition "shortly."[50]

The press in France interpreted Juin's appointment as a return to a policy of firmness.[51] *L'Epoque*, a Paris daily, blueprinted the actual course of events when it reported that the Moroccan monarch would be asked politely but firmly to quit obstructing French plans and sign the decrees put to him, but that, if he refused to do so, "We will not hesitate to replace him by another."[52] Based upon rumors from London, Moroccan nationalists in Cairo openly expressed the fear of the deposition of Mohammed V by the French.[53]

Nationalists heard in the news of General Juin's appointment the death knell of their hopes for a peaceful solution to the Franco-Moroccan problem. Following the Tangier visit, during which the various North African nationalist groups had been able to consolidate their positions, Allal El Fassi went to Paris for another attempt at direct negotiations. He found the French attitude unchanged. France would not consider Moroccan independence outside the French union, but would consider granting autonomy within it, provided French settlers in Morocco were given the rights of citizens and French continued as a second official language in administration, business, and education. The Treaty of Fez would be

[48] Bernard, *Le Conflit Franco-Marocain*, I, 71, 87.
[49] *La Vigie Marocaine*, April 12, 1947.
[50] Bernard, *Le Conflit Franco-Marocain*, I, 86.
[51] *La Vigie Marocaine*, May 15, 1947.
[52] Quoted in Bennouna, *Our Morocco*, p. 77.
[53] Bernard, *Le Conflit Franco-Marocain*, I, 95.

modified only to the extent that France and Morocco still constituted a politico-strategic unit.[54] When he heard that General Juin had been appointed resident-general, El Fassi prudently did not return to the French zone. Instead he joined Abdelkhalak Torres in Cairo, and they embarked upon an ambitious program of propaganda to attract world sympathy to the Moroccan cause.

The western arm of the Moroccan propaganda offensive reached towards the United States. Mehdi Bennouna returned to Rabat for several weeks of planning with the king and then departed for Washington. He was present behind a screen when the king received the new resident-general shortly after his arrival on May 28, 1947. Although the encounter was amiable on the surface, the gulf separating Juin and Mohammed V was obvious. The resident-general resolutely refused to listen to talk about "legitimate aspirations of the Moroccan people," and fourteen times during the audience cut the king off when he attempted to raise the question.[55] Bennouna was thus given a firsthand insight into the problem and then dispatched to the United States, his expenses paid from the king's private funds.[56]

Mr. Bennouna arrived in Washington on July 7, 1947, and registered with the Department of Justice as the representative of the five most powerful nationalist parties of French and Spanish Morocco, Algeria, and Tunisia. He was careful to point out that the Communist party was not associated with the nationalist bloc, a premise evidently accepted by the United States, since its vice-consul in Tangier had issued him an affidavit in lieu of a passport so that he might come.[57] Bennouna announced plans to open an office in New York and to present an appeal to the United Nations pro-

[54] Bennouna, *Our Morocco*, p. 76.

[55] Interview, Mehdi Bennouna, Rabat, May 11, 1967, discussing the reference in *Our Morocco*, p. 78, to this audience.

[56] Ibid.

[57] General Juin sought to discredit the Moroccan nationalists by branding them as Communists, the same individuals whom Puaux had imprisoned in 1944 as Nazis, and his French opponents as "all fellow travelers." See Centre d'études marocaines, *Morocco: Truth versus Fiction*, for examples. The Istiqlal party recognized the danger inherent in the charge of communist affiliation and devoted much attention to refutation. See, for example, Abderrahman Anegai in the *New York Herald Tribune*, July 7, 1953. See also Rezette, *Partis Politiques Marocains*, pp. 201–206.

testing the French and Spanish regimes in North Africa. Direct negotiations had failed, he said, and if the United Nations failed to act, revolution would follow.[58] He was able to present a memorandum to the secretary-general on September 29, but the Moroccan *démarche* was ignored, and it was not until 1951 that the General Assembly took up the Moroccan question.[59]

Juin's appointment was well received by both the French and Americans in Morocco. The French saw him as one of themselves, Algerian-born and married into an old and prominent Algerian family, "Juin, the African." They counted upon him to protect the status quo. In fact, Civil Controller Phillipe Boniface approvingly noted that Juin's appointment was a step "twenty years backward."[60] The Americans knew him as a capable general who had commanded the French Expeditionary Force in Italy in 1943, served as chief of staff for the French armed forces in 1944, participated as a member of the French delegation in the San Francisco conference to organize the United Nations in 1945, and represented France at the London conference on common defense matters in 1947. Rear Admiral Paul Dudley explained the relationship of the American military community in Morocco with General Juin thus: "He was a very charming man personally, and we had absolutely no difficulties with him. We did not get involved in Moroccan politics. The Arabs with whom we associated socially, a protocol contact only, made no secret of their dislike of him—when he was not around, but they feared him just the same."[61] Since the American interest was primarily strategic and only superficially political, there was no reason to become involved in politics.

The new resident-general moved swiftly to reestablish French control. He had authority from Premier Ramadier and Foreign Minister Georges Bidault in Paris to threaten the king with deposition if he refused to cooperate and, if threats were insufficient, to

[58] *New York Times*, July 8, 1947, p. 8.
[59] Bernard, *Le Conflit Franco-Marocain*, III, 330.
[60] *La Vigie Marocaine*, May 27, 1947.
[61] Interview, RADM Dudley, Washington, September 11, 1967. RADM R. A. Macpherson, who was executive officer of NAS, Port Lyautey, 1949–1950, in a letter to the author, dated Corpus Christi, Texas, September 15, 1967, confirmed continuance of "most excellent" relations with the French and Moroccan authorities after Dudley's departure.

actually depose him.[62] He used that authority sparingly. It was not until February, 1951, that he actually issued an ultimatum—sign the *dahirs* or else. In the interim he sought to establish French Moroccan cosovereignty in fact if not in name.[63]

The Juin program was fourfold. It aimed at repressing nationalist agitation by the arrest or exile of its leaders and the censorship of its press.[64] It sought to abate the nationalist appeal by improving the economic conditions of the Moroccan masses.[65] It proposed a series of "democratic reforms" designed to undercut the authority of King Mohammed V and to assure the rapidly increasing French community a regime of cosovereignty in which they would dominate.[66] And finally, it sought to deprive the nationalist movement

[62] Bernard, *Le Conflit Franco-Marocain*, I, 94.

[63] See *Le Monde*, May 29, 1949, for the declaration of M. Coste-Floret, Minister of France d'Outre-Mer, to the National Assembly that the protected states had become associated states, members of the French Union, without the necessity of changing their legal relationship with France. See also General Juin's declaration of November 18, 1949, to the Academy of Colonial Sciences, quoted in Julien, *L'Afrique du Nord en marche*, pp. 365–366, 373, that a condition of cosovereignty existed in Morocco.

[64] See Albert Ayache, *Le Maroc*, pp. 98–103, for a discussion of the historical development of the state of seige imposed in Morocco on August 2, 1914, and maintained throughout the remaining years of protectorate rule, and for the formal censorship imposed August 29, 1939, and also maintained until Morocco regained its independence.

[65] Juin provided additional employment by increasing the number of "mixed" companies engaged in exporting fruits, grains, and phosphates. The mixed companies joined French and Moroccan capital, but the majority and the control was always French. Jacques Lucius, "L'Evolution économic recente du Maroc," Centre d'études de politique étrangère, *Industrialisation de l'Afrique du Nord*, p. 274, points out that in Moroccan companies with a capital of over 100 million francs, Moroccans held less than 5 percent of the stock, and Europeans in Morocco, more than 35 percent. Fifty-five percent was held in France, and 5 percent was held abroad, not in France. The bond issues for railroads and other public service utilities were all held in France. See also Bennouna, *Our Morocco*, p. 94, and Bernard, *Le Conflit Franco-Marocain*, I, 83, on Juin's economic policies.

[66] See Rezette, *Partis Politiques Marocains*, pp. 41–44, for a detailed analysis of the proposed electoral reforms that would result in the creation of a legislative organ of government in which half the members would represent the half million French citizens in Morocco and the other half would represent the seven million Moroccans.

of royal leadership by destroying the prestige of King Mohammed V.[67]

Juin's policies encountered opposition from "Old Morocco Hands," Frenchmen whose inspiration and experience stemmed from Marshall Lyautey, as well as from the nationalists. They protested his senseless exploitation and regimentation of the Moroccan masses in order to build an acceptable façade for his regime,[68] but the protests were unavailing. Juin deported the Frenchmen to metropolitan France, and the old Moroccan nationalist leadership prudently remained beyond his grasp. Ironically, his reforms were responsible for unifying opposition against protectorate policies and producing new leaders within Morocco from the economic interests with which he sought to buttress the protectorate.[69]

King Mohammed V was obliged to move cautiously. The strength he had envisioned in the Arab League was a mirage. Preoccupied with the war against Israel and the coup against King Farouk in Egypt, it had degenerated into a squabbling group of provincial representatives. There was no unity and little strength. As Charles-André Julien remarked, "If the Sultan had to make his Tangier speech again, he surely would modify the hierarchy of values."[70] Nor had the overture to the United Nations been more successful. Without the assurance of external diplomatic support, the king avoided a decisive confrontation. He deferred action on proposed laws. The 1947–1948 budget lay on his desk almost a year. He appointed committees to study other measures; their deliberations

[67] See Montagne, *Révolution au Maroc*, p. 217, Julien, *L'Afrique du Nord en marche*, p. 369, Le Tourneau, *L'Afrique du Nord Musulmane*, p. 228, Allal El Fassi, *Independence Movement in Arab North Africa*, pp. 332–336, Georges Vaucher, *Sous les cèdres d'Ifrane: Libres entretienes avec Hassan II, roi du Maroc*, pp. 172–173, for consistent accounts of the Farfrah pamphlets questioning the legitimacy of King Mohammed V and therefore his right to the throne.

[68] Pierre Parent, *The Truth about Morocco*, trans. Eleanor Knight, pp. 32–34, 72. *The Truth about Morocco* is a compilation of a series of articles Parent wrote for *Al Istiqlal* in 1951–1952.

[69] See Julien, *L'Afrique du Nord en marche*, pp. 373–377, and Rezette, *Partis Politiques Marocains*, p. 50, for accounts of the formation of and controversies in the National Consultative Assembly, which resulted in Mohammed Laghzaoui and others from the Moroccan commercial community joining the nationalists.

[70] Julien, *L'Afrique du Nord en marche*, p. 372.

were interminable. Meanwhile he prepared fresh appeals to the president of France and to French public opinion.

General Juin was not deceived. The showdown was inevitable, and he prepared for it. Categorically denying that the protectorate had failed in any respect, he encouraged immigration from France to augment the French colony. It grew enormously between 1947 and 1952.[71] Capital flowed in, some attracted by the apparent stability that the Juin reforms promised, and some fleeing from the political and economic turmoil of postwar France. Profitable investment of the new capital was assured by Juin's four-year plan, announced in January, 1949, to step up agricultural and mineral production, to create new manufacturing complexes in Morocco, and to rebuild the Moroccan public utilities.[72]

General Juin lost some of his popularity with the French government after 1948, but, in his own words, "A government in its state of agony had no power to remove me from the residency."[73] He relied for support upon the recent European immigrant class, a flooding tide of government clerks and industrial workers. The stream began about 1929 when Resident-General Theodore Steeg first recruited immigrants from France, and the immigration grew to a torrent during the war years. As their capitalist kin developed new industries, they preempted the place in the factory or the lower-salaried job in the Moroccan government that might have gone to a Moroccan under the old Lyautey policy. It was this group, financially insecure themselves and therefore resolutely hostile to the nationalist movement, that made inevitable the revolution that began in 1950.[74]

[71] Bennouna, *Our Morocco*, p. 83, gives the increase between 1947–1951 as 300,000 to 425,000; Ayache, *Le Maroc*, p. 250, shows the increase, 1947–1952, as 325,000 to 410,000.

[72] Ayache, *Le Maroc*, p. 126.

[73] Quoted in Bennouna, *Our Morocco*, p. 85, from Juin's speech of May 5, 1951.

[74] See Bernard, *Le Conflit Franco-Marocain*, III, 97–99, for an analysis of the lower-class European attitude of exaggerated racism.

7. The Paradox of Long- and Short-Term Diplomacy

THE POSTWAR DECADE IN MOROCCO was characterized by diplomatic striving and, when that failed, by violence. General Juin's objective was the transformation of Morocco into a modern state within the French Union, a sort of "independent associated state like Vietnam,"[1] but the massive reentry of United States military personnel in 1951 negated any possibility of success. Had the Communist aggression in Korea, half a world away, been less blatant, the American presence in Morocco probably would have continued to pass unnoticed, and the Moroccan quest for independence would have taken a different turn.

Renewed American interest in Morocco reflected a basic change in military strategy. Since 1945 the United States had demobilized the most powerful fighting machine the world had ever seen, and Secretary of Defense Louis A. Johnson sought further economies.

[1] Mahdi A. Bennouna, *Our Morocco: The True Story of a Just Cause*, p. 79.

United States strategy, based upon monopoly of the atomic bomb and Strategic Air Command delivery capability, minimized the significance of foreign bases. The Soviet Union jarred the United States complacency, however, with the explosion of an atomic bomb of its own in the summer of 1949, and on June 25, 1950, North Korean troops launched a surprise invasion of South Korea. The United States, with only ten below-strength divisions, was confronted with a limited war in which the use of the atomic bomb was inexpedient and for which its conventional military forces were woefully unprepared. It began frantically rebuilding a balanced military establishment. In the evolving new strategy, Morocco became of major strategic significance, the site of four new U.S. Air Force bases and a vastly expanded Naval Air Station. The construction and utilization of those bases meant the return to Morocco of a dominant American influence that precipitated the Moroccan war for independence.

United States basic policy in 1950, unchanged since 1942, envisioned maintenance of the pre-World War II status quo in Western Europe against a threat from the East, the strategy of world power centered in the Atlantic community rather than in the "heartland" of Eurasia. France was a key factor. Humiliatingly defeated and occupied by the Axis powers in 1940, its liberation and restoration to prewar grandeur became an essential element of United States strategy in 1942, and considerations that did not contribute directly to the defeat of Nazi Germany received little attention. In 1950 the threat was from the Soviet Union, but France, although economically prostrate and handicapped by a succession of weak governments, retained its strategic importance. Recognition by the United States of Moroccan nationalism, or even of the sovereignty of Morocco, would have become a political issue in France and would have delayed the rebuilding of a military defensive infrastructure upon which the defense of the Atlantic community would depend. The United States therefore tacitly recognized the French protectorate and negotiated directly with France without extending any notification to Morocco for its air bases there. In the face of the exigencies of the moment such a short-term policy was perhaps justifiable, but it has weighed heavily on United States foreign policy since 1957. The agreements reached "for the life of NATO" were invalidated within the decade and the U.S. Air Force bases had to be evacuated by 1963. For a time it appeared the Naval Air Station would suffer a similar fate, damned by the same agreements.

The U.S. Navy build-up in Morocco presented few of the problems associated with the U.S. Air Force bases. No new agreement was necessary, and the Naval Air Station already possessed facilities that were not in use. The navy problems were primarily administrative, budgetary, and technical rather than political. They were quickly resolved. By July 1, 1950, the command structure had been reorganized with military command vested in the commander in chief of the U.S. naval forces in the eastern Atlantic and Mediterranean and management control in the chief of naval operations in Washington. The personnel complement was increased from 1,978 on June 30, 1950, to 3,895 (2,244 military, 994 civilian employees, and 657 dependents) by February 28, 1951.[2]

The United States Air Force designated the construction of its Moroccan air bases a "crash program" to be accomplished as quickly as possible without regard to cost. The initial directive that the air force sent to the U.S. Army Corps of Engineers in November, 1950, asked for five fields to be ready for operations by midsummer, 1951. Four existing fields were to be rebuilt, and a new one constructed. Only four were ever built, and they were all new, but the cost was so inordinate that Congress spent almost two years investigating air force construction practices.[3]

In the final analysis, the monetary cost was probably less signifi-

[2] "A Brief History of Port Lyautey," dated April 9, 1951, in the U.S. Navy Archives, Port Lyautey file. Rear Admiral Thurston B. Clark, then a captain, was the navy commander at Port Lyautey at the time. In a letter to the author, dated St. Mary's City, Maryland, November 2, 1967, he said that he "worked in complete harmony with the French Navy until about 1952 using only a two-page technical agreement that . . . no one ever seemed to be able to find to guide our relationships." He said the French recognized that the Americans were there by conquest and not agreement, and that he "kiddingly" reminded them of it when the French commandant asked him to shorten the new American flag pole so the American flag would not be higher than the French. Captain Clark told him, "out of the question," but that he would interpose no objection if the French wanted to increase the height of their flag pole.

[3] Ibid., February 28, 1952, p. 52. The full investigation is in "Investigation of Military Public Works, Moroccan Air Base Construction," in *Hearings*, Subcommittee of House Committee on Appropriations, 82 Cong., 2d Sess., 1952, Parts 4 and 4–2.

cant than the diplomatic cost. Crash diplomacy can be expensive too. The air force plans were not coordinated with the navy. The chief of naval operations was not even aware of the air force intentions until after the air force negotiating mission, George Brownell, Kenyon C. Bolton, and Pierpont M. Hamilton, arrived in Morocco to make arrangements for sites. After they arrived, "none of these fellows even deigned to favor me with a courtesy call," recalled Captain Thurston B. Clark, commanding officer of the Naval Air Station and the senior United States military officer in Morocco. He discovered their presence when they tried to use the navy communications system without his authorization. Their mission "resembled a poorly conducted clandestine operation," he said. "They started on the left foot and stayed on the left foot throughout."[4]

The negotiations took about four months. According to John P. Perry, deputy secretary of the air force for installations, the principal difficulty with the French revolved around the location of the bases,[5] but that was only one aspect of the larger question. The protectorate officials were concerned about the potential effect of a large American community in Morocco upon the independence movement. The agreement finally concluded in Paris was signed by Brownell, Bolton, and Hamilton for the United States on December 22, 1950.[6] It permitted the United States to construct at its own expense, upon land provided by the French government without cost to the United States, certain specified facilities for use by the U.S. Air Force. The facilities were to revert to the French

[4] Rear Admiral Thurston B. Clark, letter to the author dated November 2, 1967.

[5] "Moroccan Air Base Construction," Part 4-2, p. 10.

[6] A copy of the agreement is contained in "History of the Fifth Air Division," January 14, to June 30, 1951—Annex, in USAF Archives, Maxwell AFB, Alabama.

I. William Zartman, in *Morocco: Problems of New Power*, p. 24, and in "The Moroccan-American Base Negotiations," *Middle East Journal* 18 (1964): 27–40, erroneously identifies this agreement as the Bidault-Caffrey Agreement and must be used with caution lest the Moroccan agreement be confused with a Bidault-Caffrey Agreement of February 16, 1948, which pertained to the occupation of Germany and Austria. Robert Schuman was the French foreign minister on December 22, 1950, and Jefferson Caffrey was United States ambassador to Egypt.

King Mohammed V gave young Prince Hassan his first sports car for his fourth birthday, July 9, 1933. The two shared a common interest in high-performance automobiles for almost thirty years.

Port Lyautey in 1943; *foreground,* native *nouallas; center left,* the European city; sabotaged ships in the port; *upper right,* the Central Prison. (Official U.S. Navy photograph)

The Second World War brought the Moroccan monarch in close contact with American military commanders. General Mark Clark conducted a fire power demonstration at Oujda on June 25, 1943, for the sultan, *center*, and General Noguès, *left*.

Mohamed ben Miloudi ben Maati, *left*, and two uniformed soldiers of the Liberation Army; photo taken near Khemisset in early summer of 1955.

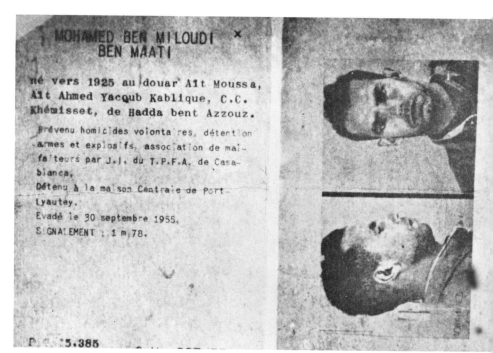

MOHAMED BEN MILOUDI ✕
BEN MAATI

né vers 1925 au douar Aït Moussa,
Aït Ahmed Yacoub Kablique, C.C.
Khémisset, de Hadda bent Azzouz.

Prévenu homicides volontaires, détention
armes et explosifs, association de mal-
faiteurs par J.I. du T.P.F.A. de Casa-
blanca,
Détenu à la maison Centrale de Port-
Lyautey.
Évadé le 30 septembre 1955.
SIGNALEMENT : 1 m,78.

D... 5.385

Ben Miloudi does not deny his criminal record: willful homicide, possession of arms and explosives, and association with criminals—but, he explained, the French authorities considered anyone who participated in
the revolution a common criminal.

A group of naval reservists visit the Andalusian pavilion in the garden of the king's palace near Rabat, February, 1959.

The holy city of Moulay Idriss, near Meknes, was founded in the eighth century by a descendant of Ali, son-in-law of the Prophet Mohammed. The tomb of the city's founder is under the pyramid roof in the foreground. (Official U.S. Navy photograph)

King Mohammed V had a carpet woven with
the message in Arabic, "souvenir of friendship
to the people of Minnesota." Commander Sam
Goad, USNR, presents the carpet to Governor
and Mrs. Orville Freeman.

Moroccans inspect a picture display showing navy aid and friendship in
action during the Agadir disaster. The display was a part of Friendship
Day, May 4, 1960. (Official U.S. Navy photograph)

A naval reservist presents a pair of cowboy boots to Princess Amina, youngest daughter of King Mohammed V.

Princess Aisha opens the little league season at the Naval Air Station, Kenitra, May 1, 1960. (Official U.S. Navy photograph)

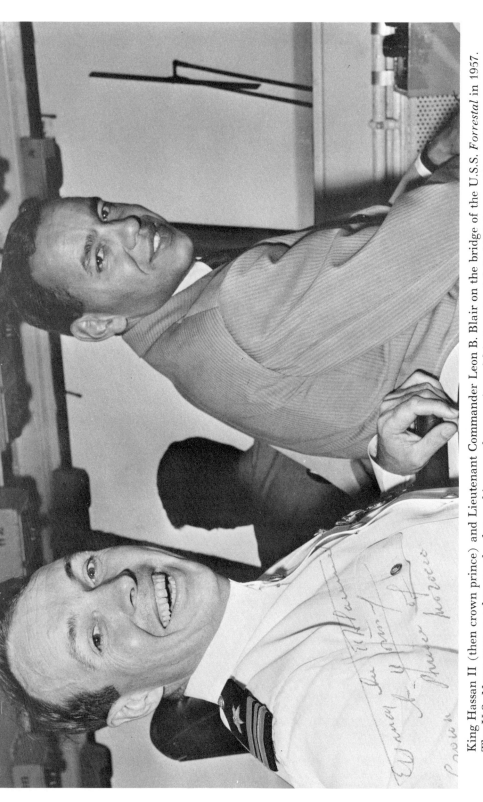

King Hassan II (then crown prince) and Lieutenant Commander Leon B. Blair on the bridge of the U.S.S. *Forrestal* in 1957. The U.S. Navy gave a salute to the future king on the occasion of his twenty-eighth birthday and investiture as crown prince. (Official U.S. Navy photograph)

government without compensation to the United States at the end of the life of NATO, or earlier if both nations agreed to terminate the arrangement. The United States was to be permitted the use of an American principal contractor for the construction, but was obligated to procure materials and services in Morocco if they were available in the necessary quantities and at competitive prices. A French liaison mission was to "aid and advise" in the construction, and the bases were to remain under French flag and command. The agreement, twelve articles long, subjected the United States to French control with respect to relations with Morocco and the Moroccan people, but accorded to military personnel and "persons accompanying the United States Armed Forces" substantially the same privileges they enjoyed in France under a Status of Forces Agreement.

Neither King Mohammed V nor any agency of the Moroccan government was notified of the negotiations in progress or of the agreement, thus providing the basis for subsequent Moroccan refusal to recognize the legal existence of the bases. The failure to advise the king was no simple oversight. The American negotiators recognized the potential difficulty and asked that the king be consulted, but, according to Assistant Secretary of State George V. Allen, "the French . . . failed to do so."[7]

Edwin A. Plitt, the United States minister at Tangier, was to have notified the sultan of the intention of the United States to build air bases in Morocco. Several months after construction had actually begun he called upon Resident-General Juin to suggest that out of courtesy the sultan should be told of the United States plans. Rear Admiral Thurston B. Clark was present with Mr. Plitt. He said: "The General listened politely but fidgeted visibly; the fuse was obviously short. When Mr. Plitt had finished, the General stood up and with some apparent agitation and considerable emphasis replied, 'Mr. Minister, you must know that I am the Foreign Minister of the Sultan. I am the protector of Morocco. The passing of military matters to the Sultan is my business and mine alone. Au revoir, Messieurs!' The message was clear."[8]

[7] "Relinquishment of Consular Jurisdiction of the United States in Morocco," *Hearings on S. J. Resolution 165*, Senate Committee on Foreign Relations, 84 Cong., 2d Sess., 1956, p. 5.
[8] Rear Admiral Thurston B. Clark, letter to the author, dated November 2,

As a part of the price for the new accord, the terms of which were less favorable to the United States than the Navy to Navy Technical Agreement of September 15, 1947, the United States agreed to supplant the navy agreement with a new one consistent with that just negotiated for the air force. The "Agreement between the United States of America and the Republic of France regarding new construction and increased use of facilities at Port Lyautey, French Morocco, by the U.S. Navy"[9] contained a saving clause, however, for it validated those provisions of the 1947 Navy Technical Agreement that were not in conflict. It thus gave the U.S. naval base a claim to legitimacy that *had* been recognized by King Mohammed V when an independent Morocco justified nonacceptance of the Franco-American agreements of December 22, 1950, on the grounds that Morocco had not been consulted in the first place.

Construction of the air force bases began on January 10, 1951, and two fields had nine-thousand-foot runways available for use eighty-three days later, but the construction program dragged on for four more years. Mr. Perry explained the delay in the construction program and the costs that considerably exceeded estimates by citing French insistence on placing the American bases in isolated locations, well away from population centers, after they became aware of the number of American personnel involved.[10] Colonel George T. Derby, resident engineer in Morocco for the U.S. Army Corps of Engineers, said the French were obsessed by the "fantastic" fear that the United States intended to send in armed forces and take over their restive protectorate,[11] a theme reiterated ad infinitum in the French press.[12]

1967. RADM Clark said the fact that he was on excellent terms with General Juin was probably the reason that Plitt asked him to accompany him to the meeting.

[9] Authenticated copy of the text, unsigned and dated simply December, 1950, forwarded by CINCNELM Serial 00011 of January 5, 1951, in U.S. Navy Archives, Washington, D.C.

[10] "Moroccan Air Base Construction," Part 4-2, p. 10.

[11] Ibid.

[12] See for example, Robert de Louis, "Une chose dont on parle . . . l'invasion américain au Maroc n'est pas un myth," *Maroc-Monde*, January 24, 1953, pp. 1, 5, in which he charged that fifty thousand Americans, many with their families, intended to colonize Morocco, and that, he said, accounted for the anti-

The changes invalidated most of the early planning, and the Corps of Engineers was forced to negotiate for sites, obtain land, arrange for equipment and construction companies, and build all at the same time. Speed was of the essence. Mistakes were made that pyramided costs. Construction begun at Ben Guerir was abandoned because of the inability to find a suitable water supply, and the men and equipment were shifted to Mechra Bel Ksiri. That site was abandoned after the expenditure of $143,000 in nonrecoverable costs when the air force added a requirement for the base to accommodate medium bombers and the terrain proved unsuitable for such use. The base at Ben Guerir was then completed. The water supply was adequate after all. At Sidi Slimane and Nouasseur the runways were built before field drainage systems were installed—a calculated risk, according to General Lewis A. Pick, chief of Army Engineers—and heavy rains ruined the foundations. The loss amounted to two to three million dollars.[13] Unsound accounting practices, theft, kickbacks, French taxes on U.S. materials —the abuses were myriad—almost doubled the $300 million estimated cost.

As a matter of practical fact, the cost and the difficulty over the selection of sites were less important than the persistent difficulties over operational matters after the bases had been completed. For example, the French imposed a ceiling on American personnel that was never adequate either for the construction of the air force bases or their operation after completion. The French dilemma, Colonel Derby continued, was "a garrison which would not interfere too much with their political situation and would still be a minimum garrison that would be workable from the Air Force point of view to operate those fields." The conflicting criteria were never reconciled.

The French justified their decision to admit only 130 American administrative and construction personnel to Morocco during the initial phases of the construction program with the argument that additional personnel would upset the local economy by increasing the competition for locally available goods and by raising the wage

French, anticolonial attitude of the United States government. See also A. Gros, *New York Times*, July 25, 1952, p. 3, for the charge that the United States sought to establish its own protectorate in Morocco.

[13] *New York Times*, February 22, 1952, pp. 1, 6.

scale—from ten to about thirty-five cents an hour for Moroccan
labor. The lack of personnel made it impossible for the American
contractor to receive, inventory, and check his incoming matériel,[14]
and the restriction was not lifted until April 22, 1951. The Air
Force Technical Agreement No. 1, signed at Paris, May 2, 1951, by
General Lauris Norstad for the USAF and General Charles-Fran-
çois Lechères for the French air force allowed the United States to
station 7,400 air force personnel in Morocco, but, to compensate,
allowed the French substantial control over American personnel
and policies.[15]

The Norstad-Lechères Agreement conceded control of the employment and salary scales for locally hired civilian personnel to
the French, and it was soon apparent that the French authorities
were less concerned with keeping wages down than in maintaining
the three-to-one differential between wages paid to French and
Moroccan employees, and in securing the better-paying jobs for
French nationals.[16] The wage differential was incorporated in the
French-approved salary scales and was for the purpose, so William
Atwood charged in the *New York Post*, of making "the exploited
natives feel that the Americans they have admired so long are no
better than their French masters."[17] The job discrimination was
enforced by arbitrary "security-risk" determinations against individuals whom the French wished to exclude from employment.
American authorities were denied access to French investigative
reports or even the criteria upon which the security determinations
were made.[18]

[14] Brigadier General Orville E. Walsh, Division Engineer, Mediterranean
Division, U.S. Army Corps of Engineers, testimony in "Moroccan Base Construction," Part 4, p. 2, and Part 4-2, p. 74.

The U.S. Navy, and not the French, imposed a limit of one hundred construction and supervisory personnel on its prime contractor, the Steers-Grove Construction Company, in order to keep down costs, but the navy program was well
under way before the air force agreement was even negotiated (Rear Admiral
Clark letter to the author, dated November 2, 1967).

[15] Text in "History of the Fifth Air Division," January 14–June, 1951, annex.

[16] *New York Times*, February 9, 1952, p. 5, and February 10, 1952, p. 9.

[17] "Your World," *New York Post*, June 25, 1951.

[18] Interviews, Youssef Omar and Mohammed Ben Barka, Kenitra, May 5,
1967. Youssef Omar was initially hired in 1951 at 300 francs an hour but his
wages were reduced to 135 francs an hour a few months later at the request of
the French, he was told. Mohammed Ben Barka was denied a security clear-

Initially successful, the French control system broke down as the labor demand began to exceed the supply of Europeans applying for employment at the American bases. By February, 1952, the Atlas Construction Company, the prime contractor for the air force bases, employed about 3,700 United States nationals including approximately 400 U.S. designers and architects and 125 uniformed men of the Corps of Engineers. In addition nearly 10,000 French and Moroccan employees were working on the five air force bases.[19] Atlas operated trade schools to train Moroccan workers as carpenters, truck drivers, tractor operators, and mechanics. Overall, the training program was successful, and the development of local unskilled laborers into craftsmen resulted in substantial savings in the ultimate cost of the bases but the American supervisors were forced to adapt to a way of thinking that they had not previously encountered.[20]

Russel Hope described the somewhat chaotic conditions that existed as construction work attained its full growth in 1952:

We were expanding so fast that almost every night we made up a new list of positions to be filled. I would go down to the gate at eight o'clock with the list. There would be probably three hundred Moroccan men waiting there. I would announce, 'Seventy-five electricians.' Every hand would go up. When we had enrolled the electricians, I would call for thirty plumbers. Again every hand would go up, and so on until the positions had all be filled. The next day it would be the same thing.

Those people didn't know a coaxial cable from a pipe wrench. We had to train them. They were skillful with their hands and eager to learn and to please, but you don't train a craftsman in two months or even two years. I could teach one to splice a coaxial cable, and he would do a good job. But don't get yourself into a bind and shift him to splicing power cables. Pfft! Three times out of ten, he will use a coaxial splice.[21]

---

ance by the French for suspected nationalist activity. (He was a member of the Istiqlal party.) He was later hired by the U.S. Navy at Port Lyautey. The existence of the French labor policies was confirmed by C. F. Kaslowski, one of the American labor supervisors at the time, in an interview with the author at Kenitra, May 21, 1967.

[19] *New York Times*, February 9, 1952, p. 5.

[20] "Moroccan Air Base Construction," Part 4-2, p. 55.

[21] Interview with Russel Hope, Kenitra, June 1, 1967.

The Moroccans learned something about the American mentality too. At first they were inclined to resent the generic name of Mohammed for all Moroccan males and Fatima for all females. Then they discovered that the Americans usually called each other "Hey Mac," if they did not know the name, and they came to accept the informality as an American characteristic without class significance. They apparently liked the American mentality, for many of those unskilled laborers became craftsmen and are still employed by the U.S. Navy at Kenitra (formerly Port Lyautey). They have learned to speak, read, and write English; they have adopted Western dress and have bought small two- and three-acre farms in the vicinity, or have built or bought houses in town. They speedily accepted another American attitude. Almost as a way of life, they were accustomed to making a gift to someone from whom they expected to ask an accommodation—even one so prosaic as employment. But the Americans not only did not demand bribes, they considered them illegal! They said so in three languages on posters in all of the employment offices, and they fired anyone guilty of accepting "kickbacks" or peddling "influence."[22]

The French were not able to regain control of American-Moroccan relations until 1953, although they never relinquished the principle. Their control agency was the French Liaison Mission in Morocco, an arm of the Central French Liaison Mission in Paris, provided for in the basic agreement of December 22, 1950, to perform specified functions associated with construction contracts let in Morocco. The Norstad-Lechères Technical Agreement of May 2, 1951, recognized the need to coordinate questions of local procurement, customs, finance, and jurisdiction with local civilian authorities because of the obvious impact on Moroccan economic and social life of the large funds, quantities of material, and numbers of personnel that the Americans proposed to employ, but coordination control was to be exercised through joint agreement between the air force commanders in Morocco. Any disagreements that could not be resolved locally were to be forwarded to the chiefs of staff of the two air forces, and then if still unresolved to the foreign minister and the secretary of state. Progressively, through a series

---

[22] "Moroccan Air Base Construction," Part 4, p. 636.

of supplementary agreements and interpretations, American prerogatives were whittled away, and control channeled into the liaison mission. Each concession by the air force served as a precedent for similar demands on the navy.

The disputes were acrimonious. General Olds, commander of the Fifth Air Division at Rabat, rejected the French interpretation of the Norstad-Lechères Agreement that U.S. Air Force acceptance of the French air force as an intermediary between U.S. forces and the civilian element applied to his relations with the American press, or that he was obligated to have a representative of the French air force present if he talked to an American newspaperman.[23] Major General Hutchinson, commander of the Seventeenth Air Force, contested the French interpretation of the Norstad-Lechères Agreement, which would put his forces "completely at the mercy of foreign control" in the distribution of aviation gasoline through the U.S.–built pipeline network in Morocco. That dispute was referred to "higher authority," and, failing of resolution, was sent back to Morocco where the resident-general refused to accept a solution parallel to that found in metropolitan France because of the "political situation in Morocco."[24]

Other disagreements concerned the procurement of labor and services in Morocco. Hutchinson reluctantly accepted the French proposal to take over the employment, administration, and pay of local personnel on an indirect hire basis, but the negotiations broke down on the question of administrative costs to be charged to the United States.[25] When the French Liaison Mission attempted to dictate on the question of bus transportation for U.S. Air Force employees, Hutchinson notified it that he would award the contract to the lowest bidder offering satisfactory service, and that no further discussion was necessary.[26] He opposed the Liaison Mission's attempt to take over all procurement for the U.S. Air Force on the local market, and that question was referred, not to the chiefs of staff of the two air forces, but to the Central Liaison Mission in

[23] *New York Times*, February 10, 1952, p. 9.
[24] "History of the Seventeenth Air Force," April 25 to June 30, 1953, II, App. 2, ex. 32, in USAF Archives file no. K-573.01.
[25] Ibid., ex. 33.
[26] Ibid., ex. 38–40.

Paris. Colonel Frank B. Elliot, USAF, noted in his reply that the Liaison Mission concept worked well in France, but the difficulties arose from "the delicacy of the political situation in Morocco."[27]

When the Liaison Mission advised the Corps of Engineers and Atlas Construction Company that American doctors employed by Atlas would have to request and receive permission from the local authorities in order to practice, or be prosecuted for practicing medicine illegally, the district engineer replied that the suggestion "constituted an unwarranted invasion of his prerogatives . . . not countenanced by any agreement. . . . They were another of the many and repeated attempts by your mission to interfere with or exercise control . . . through the medium of a legalistic and technical application of Cherifian dahir to which you contend the prime contractor is completely subject without regard to the international agreements," he added. He stated his intention "to resist the action with any and all means at his command, . . . and to intervene in any court action as an official act of the United States."[28]

The commander of U.S. naval activities at Port Lyautey also protested the entrance of the French Liaison Mission into all fields as the sole agency competent to deal with civil matters affecting the U.S. Navy in Morocco. Such an interpretation, he said, would exclude the French commandant of the Base Principle Aeronavale "through whom, by the Technical Agreement of June 12, 1951, I am required to maintain liaison with the civil authorities." He protested that, if successful in its attempts to control labor, supplies, and services, the French Liaison Mission would have become an agency of control and not of the liaison for which it was organized, and that the military effectiveness of the U.S. Navy in Morocco would be seriously impaired.[29]

In fact the resident-general intended to do precisely what was charged—to twist the various agreements out of the context understood by the negotiators on both sides to serve an antinationalist

[27] Ibid., ex. 34–37.

[28] Ibid., I, 120.

[29] ComNavActs, Port Lyautey, letter to the resident-general, dated April 23, 1953, quoted in ibid., p. 128. The date is in error; he refers to the Technical Agreement of June 11, 1951, signed in Paris by Rear Admiral Walter F. Boone and Vice Admiral H. M. Nomy, which parallels the Norstad-Lechères Agreement.

political purpose. General Guillaume's Residential Directive No. 300/DN of February 9, 1952, directed the French Liaison Mission "to expand its activities to centralize and control all matters concerning the U.S. Armed Forces in Morocco."[30] In attempting to centralize and control American activities in Morocco, protectorate officials at first attempted to prevent contact between the Americans and the Moroccan population; that was the objective of isolating the base, and of General Juin's circular letter to pro-French tribal chieftains forbidding fraternization between Moroccans and the American troops. El Abed Bouhafa, secretary of the North African Liberation Committee, in a letter to President Truman, charged that Juin also told the chieftains the United States was in full accord with his colonial policy; that the Americans were coming back to Morocco to cooperate with French forces in the maintenance of peace and order in the face of a threatened Communist coup; and that the Americans were under orders to assist the French in suppressing any possible nationalist uprising.[31] In a further attempt to quarantine the Moroccans against American influence, residency officials limited the Armed Forces Radio Service to one hundred watts output on its broadcast antennas and forbade the broadcast of news or discussion of French Morocco.[32]

A part of the French resentment of the Americans undoubtedly emanated from American intrusion into what the French considered their private economic preserve. According to the residency, less than a dozen American businessmen were active in Morocco before World War II, but thousands of G.I.'s stationed in Morocco

[30] French Liaison Mission letter signed DeBlesson, to Captain T. B. Clark, ComNavActs, Port Lyautey, of April 10, 1953, in ibid., p. 128. Clark, in his letter to the author of November 2, 1967, said that in view of the *grande pigou* (French for "screwup") that the air force was experiencing in its construction program, it was little wonder that they felt compelled to exercise control; the air force was not. Those were the circumstances, Clark said, that led to creation of the French Liaison Office and "ensnarled" the navy too.

[31] *New York Times*, May 31, 1951, p. 11. Rear Admiral Clark, letter to the author dated November 2, 1967, said he knew of no ban on fraternization issued by General Juin. He said that Mr. Housson, the "chef de territoire" at Port Lyautey, "deeply resented" American friendships and associations with the Arabs and "conjured up imaginary crises" in order to impose "innumerable" curfews. Clark said he suspected that the rumor of an antifraternization ban stemmed from those circumstances.

[32] "History of the Seventeenth Air Force," April 25–June 30, 1953, I, 130.

observed the immense commercial possibilities of the Moroccan market, and they stayed, or came back after the war. Citing the "most favored nation" provision of the Treaty of Meknes (1836), they claimed commercial equality with French citizens. The French contended that the Treaty of Algeciras, guaranteeing equal economic opportunity in Morocco to all nations, was modified when various European powers recognized preponderant French influence in Morocco following the Franco-German confrontation in 1911, and further, that the Breton Woods Charter in July, 1944, gave France the right to protect the Moroccan currency. In March, 1948, General Juin had authorized liberalization of the import regulations for American businessmen, but in December, under pressure from French business interests, he rescinded the concessions.[33]

A group of thirty-seven of the Americans organized the American Trade Association of Morocco and challenged the authority of the protectorate. They protested to the U.S. secretary of state that maximum import duties fixed by treaty were 12.5 percent, but that the French authorities added arbitrary taxes and currency discounts, and used other devices to charge as much as 150 percent of the valuation, and that United States funds furnished by the Economic Cooperation Administration were being used to freeze out American businessmen trying to trade in Morocco. Both State and ECA denied competence, each insisting that the protest was the affair of the other, and the French Foreign Office denied the charge that French officials were conniving with French business interests to freeze out the Americans as "utterly false."[34]

Finally, Robert E. Rodes, commander of the American Legion Post in Casablanca and president of the American Trade Association, appealed to Congress to withhold the $3.2 million in Marshall Plan funds allocated to Morocco as long as France continued to violate international treaties. Congress responded with the Hickenlooper Amendment to the U.S. Foreign Aid Act of August 28, 1950, which gave the president discretionary authority to withhold the funds, but French pressures were sufficient to prevent President Truman from invoking it. In fact, Mr. Rodes charged, Secretary

[33] Resident-General, Public Relations Service of Morocco, *News Bulletin*, no. 8 (May 15, 1952): 6–8.

[34] *New York Times*, March 15, 1949, p. 14, March 16, 1949, p. 24.

of State Acheson tended to favor French interests rather than those of Morocco or of United States citizens.[35]

Faced with the threat of losing Marshall Plan aid, France brought suit against the United States in the International Court of Justice, seeking a legal definition of her treaty status in Morocco. In a decision handed down August 27, 1952, the court affirmed the sovereignty of Morocco and held valid the jurisdiction of American consular courts in cases involving Americans. It held invalid General Juin's attempts to favor French commerce and declared that United States importers had the same rights as the French, but it rejected the American contention that its citizens were not subject to Moroccan laws to which the United States had not consented—a concession granted by the Treaty of Meknes.[36]

It is not difficult to sustain the charge that French pleading before the International Court was knowingly deceptive. In seeking to invalidate American consular jurisdiction, France argued that the courts in Morocco were actually Moroccan courts, although staffed with French personnel. The court agreed, although it did affirm consular jurisdiction in cases involving American citizens. While the case was before the International Court, however, another French prosecutor presented a case against an American sailor in Port Lyautey, charged with a hit-and-run accident. Elmer Keil contested the jurisdiction of the French court, asserting the validity of the Treaty of Meknes. The French prosecutor appealed the question of jurisdiction to the Cour de Cassation (Supreme Court) in Paris, which held that, although Keil was an American citizen, he was also a serviceman and as such was subject to the Bidault-Caffrey Agreement and therefore to *French* jurisdiction. He was tried in Tribunal de Paix at Port Lyautey, convicted of seven different violations, and sentenced to four months in prison (suspended) and fines totalling 200,000 francs ($57.00).

[35] Ibid., October 27, 1950, p. 28.

[36] See Department of State, *American Foreign Policy, 1950–1955*, II, 2296–2297; *Department of State Bulletin*, July 30, 1951, p. 79, October 29, 1950, December 11, 1950, pp. 951–953, January 8, 1951, p. 79, and December 17, 1951; International Court of Justice, *Reports of Judgements, Advisory Opinions and Orders*, 1951, pp. 178–213; and Joseph M. Sweeny, *Department of State Bulletin*, October 20, 1952, pp. 620–623, for a summary analysis of the background and implementation of the court decision.

In asserting French, not Moroccan, jurisdiction the prosecutor cited a top secret diplomatic agreement that was read in open court and subsequently published in one of the daily newspapers.[37] The document pertained to the occupation of Austria and Germany and did not even mention Morocco or French overseas territories. Dr. Richard Carl Medford, the navy base legal specialist, said there must have been top-level agreement to extend the Bidault- Caffrey Agreement to Morocco, for otherwise there would have been inevitable diplomatic repercussions to the Keil case decision and the revelation of the contents of the document, but that the navy was never informed, either before or after the fact.[38]

The French sought to exclude American business interests from Morocco for political as well as economic reasons. They resented the support American firms gave to the nationalists. While the level of support may be debatable, the fact is not. The Coca-Cola Company had Moorish nationalists on its board, and both Coca-Cola and Pepsi-Cola furnished free refreshments to nationalist gatherings.[39] The French read something more than a conventional advertising motivation into the gesture. They were suspicious of the contact of Under Secretary of State George C. McGhee and the U.S. minister at Tangier, Edwin A. Plitt, with the nationalists.[40] Resident-General Guillaume said he could not understand why the

[37] See *La Vigie Marocaine*, May 16, 1952, p. 1, for the hostile article hailing "the breach opened in the capitulatory regime by the Bidault-Caffrey agreement, which for the first time has now been applied in Morocco."

[38] Interview, Richard Carl Medford, Ph.D., Naval Air Station, Kenitra, May 28, 1967. According to a Department of State letter to the author, dated Washington, October 25, 1967, an agreement was signed at Paris, November 6, 1950, by United States Ambassador David Bruce and Secretary-General of the Ministry of Foreign Affairs Alexandre Parodi for France, establishing a line of communications across France, and this agreement with its annexes, still classified "Secret," extended the Bidault-Caffrey Civil Affairs Agreement of February 16, 1948, to govern the status of United States forces in French North Africa. The 1950 agreement was superseded by an agreement of December 8, 1958, between France and the United States, published as *Treaties and Other International Acts Series 6132*.

[39] *New York Times*, February 10, 1952, p. 9; Stephane Bernard, *Le Conflit Franco-Marocain*, III, 341–342; Robert Rezette, *Les Partis Politiques Marocains*, p. 212.

[40] *New York Times*, October 13, 1950, p. 11, erroneously identifies the minister at Tangier as Edwin A. Platt.

Department of State wanted its people to listen to the nationalists; his police would furnish them any information they wanted on the local political situation. He rather plaintively asked why the United States would not send people who would look at Morocco strictly as a strategic piece of real estate and not get mixed up in local political considerations.[41] The French-owned press was entirely hostile, charging that the Americans wanted to take over the country.[42] *La Croix* (February 21, 1951) opined that Morocco could continue to exist only as an American colony if granted independence, and *L'Eclaireur Marocain* (November 8, 1952) expressed disdain of the American "double gospel" of political liberty and material comfort as naïve. "Americans can not imagine," it declaimed, "that even the modest Moroccan looks down upon them."

The return of the Americans to Morocco placed the nationalists squarely on the horns of a dilemma. What should their position be? On the one hand, they favored the dilution of French influence and the renewed interest of the United States in Moroccan conditions. On the other hand, they resented the high-handed French action in bargaining away their territory and their sovereignty without so much as a notification to their sovereign. They equivocated. Ahmed Balafrej proclaimed Moroccan solidarity with the West, "especially the United States." He said that Morocco had become familiar to thousands of American homes because their sons, husbands, and fathers were stationed there, and he appealed to the United States to use its influence with France to secure Moroccan freedom.[43] Perhaps more significantly, nationalists like Mehdi Bennouna, Mohammed Abdesselam El Fasi, and Abderrahman Menebhi became employees of The Voice of America

[41] *New York Herald Tribune*, December 17, 1951.

[42] "History of the United States Air Force, Europe," January–June, 1954, supplement no. 1 (Intelligence Summary) dated October 15, 1953, in vol. IV, appendix VII P, file no. 570.01, USAF Archives.

[43] Moroccan Office of Information and Documentation, *Free Morocco*, no. 2 (May 25, 1953): 1. Fifteen issues of *Free Morocco* were published in New York, April 20, 1953 to June 25, 1955, to plead the cause of Moroccan independence. It had wide circulation: fifty thousand copies of each issue were printed and mailed to news media, United States officials, and formulators of public opinion. The first issue, April 20, 1953, said the decision to publish was occasioned by the establishment of the American bases in Morocco.

because, according to Bennouna, "We could facilitate their work and, by explaining the true nature of the nationalist movement, appease their apprehensions implanted by the protectorate authorities. My position in the personnel office during the construction of the broadcast facilities at Tangier gave me direct access to American official circles and was far more influential at policy level than my activities in the field of general information."[44] Allal El Fassi said that although Morocco had not been consulted on the decision to permit the United States to use the five air bases, a Morocco free of French rule would cooperate with the Atlantic Pact nations.[45] El Abed Bouhafa, in a letter to President Truman, denounced the violation of the territorial integrity of Morocco inherent in the construction of the bases.[46] When CBS correspondent David Schoenbrun asked King Mohammed V what the position of an independent Morocco toward the American bases would be, the king remained silent.[47] Schoenbrun, quoting a source from the king's immediate entourage, explained the apparent evasion: The king did not know "officially" that there were American bases in Morocco.[48]

King Mohammed V's silence on the subject of the Franco-American accord characterized his diplomacy; he made few statements, and those only after weighty consideration. He was content to watch the trial balloons launched by Balafrej, El Fassi, and others for a time to see which way the wind blew. His relationship with the resident-general became more and more strained, and the base agreement coincided with General Juin's attempt to dethrone him. He was unwilling to becloud the issue by precipitating a secondary crisis, but he nonetheless remained active on the diplomatic front, his position virtually unchanged throughout the Juin proconsulate.

Although the conflict between the king and the resident-general

[44] Interview, Mehdi Bennouna, Rabat, May 11, 1967; see also Rezette, *Les Partis Politiques Marocains,* p. 212.

[45] *New York Times,* February 24, 1951, p. 29.

[46] Ibid., April 12, 1951, p. 6.

[47] David Schoenbrun, "Les Américains sont au Maroc," in *La Nef: Maroc et Tunisie,* p. 82.

[48] Ibid.

involved internal affairs in Morocco,[49] the position the United States would take was crucial for two reasons: Morocco, despairing of a bilateral agreement with France had appealed her case to the conscience of the world, and France was in fact economically dependent upon the United States and therefore vulnerable to American pressure. Both sides renewed their efforts to secure support. The French Foreign Office rejected unconditionally the suggestion that the Franco-American accord was void because the king had not been consulted. It contended that the Treaty of Fez gave France authority to make all arrangements necessary for the defense of Morocco and to conduct its foreign relations.[50] It professed inability to understand why the United States should be concerned about the king for, after all, it was France that had provided the air base sites, a matter about which the king would have been "difficult,"[51] and appealed to the Department of State for support for Juin.[52] The general himself, after delivering an ultimatum on January 26, 1951, giving the king the Hobson's choice of abdication or forcible deposition, departed for Washington to buttress his position.

The North Africa Liberation Committee had also been active, urging the United States to make a "public declaration of its private assurances" that it did not support Juin, and apparently with some effect.[53] General Juin says in his memoirs that he found his friends in Washington using the same language with respect to North Africa as that used in Moscow—that France should get out. The objectives were different, Juin noted. The United States hoped that French withdrawal would restore order, while the Russians thought it would result in such chaos that communism would have

[49] See the following for detailed accounts of the conflict between the resident-general and the king: Bernard, *Le Conflit Franco-Marocain*, I, 93–120; Julien, *L'Afrique du Nord en marche*, pp. 364–386; and Robert Montagne, *Révolution au Maroc*.

[50] *New York Times*, April 12, 1951, p. 6. Mohammed Lahbabi, *Le gouvernement marocain à l'aube du XXeme siècle*, denies the thesis that the king was ever absolute in Moslem law and asserts that he was therefore unable to delegate his powers in the Treaty of Fez.

[51] Homer Bigart, "U.S. Slowness in Supporting Morocco Stand Irked French," *New York Herald Tribune*, Paris edition, December 17–20, 1951.

[52] *New York Times*, February 23, 1951, p. 4.

[53] Ibid., February 22, 1951.

little difficulty in taking over. No one would listen to him, Juin complained.[54]

Juin returned to Rabat via Paris where he received approval of his attempts to break the power of the Istiqlal party, but not of the deposition of the king. Foreign Minister Robert Schuman told him that the United States ambassador had warned against the ill effects of such an act upon the public order in Morocco, and that deposition was both strategically undesirable and, because of the probable adverse effects on French interests in Morocco, economically infeasible.[55] At Rabat, however, Juin found that he had set in motion forces he could hardly control. Opponents of the king, such as Thami El Glaoui and Civil Controller Phillipe Boniface, the spokesman for the violent French element recruited from the lower-class European immigrants attracted by the protectorate immigration policies after 1930, stepped up their pressure, pretending that a tribal revolt was imminent.[56] Finally, on February 25, Juin delivered an ultimatum to the king: denounce the Istiqlal party, renounce the ideology of violence, and render homage to the "generous action of the French Republic," or lose his throne.[57] The king submitted, affixing to the protocol, not his signature, but the notation, "It is known to us." What would have happened if the sultan had refused to sign the protocol? Mehdi Bennouna rhetorically asked in November, 1951, and in reply prophesied the exact course of events that did occur when the king was deposed in 1953.[58]

Juin's victory was a qualified one. The king was compelled to break officially with the Istiqlal party, but the *dahirs* remained unsigned, and the relations between the king and the resident-general were not improved by the humiliation that the latter had inflicted upon the monarch. The "used" tribes, previously apathetic, now joined the enemies of the protectorate. Even the victory

[54] Alphonse Juin, *Memoires*, II, 157–158.

[55] Bernard, *Le Conflit Franco-Marocain*, I, 112.

[56] See ibid., pp. 112–116; Julien, *L'Afrique du Nord en marche*, p. 380; and Parent, *The Truth about Morocco*, pp. 33–34, 72, for details of this campaign against the king. See Charles-André Julien, "Morocco: The End of an Era," *Foreign Affairs* 34, no. 2 (January, 1956): 202, for an analysis of the "petits blancs" and their influence on protectorate policies.

[57] Julien, *L'Afrique du Nord en marche*, p. 380.

[58] Bennouna, *Our Morocco*, p. 102.

was short-lived. The king had returned the protocol to Juin with the warning that forced signatures did not form bilateral accords,[59] and on March 27 in an interview published in the Egyptian newspaper, *Al Ahram*, he presented his case to the world.[60] *La Croix* (April 27, 1951) concluded that "perhaps [the king] is not weaker than Juin." General Juin, who had said in May that the French government did not have enough power to remove him, was transferred in August to a NATO command at the urging of the United States.[61] He was allowed to pick as his successor General Augustin Guillaume who assumed his duties on August 28, 1951.[62]

General Guillaume was no stranger to Morocco, nor to the Americans. He had served the Vichy regime in Morocco as director of political affairs under General Noguès; and General Patton, after a tour of the Berber country with him in 1942, remarked, "That man is worth two divisions by himself."[63] He had led Moroccan troops in the landings in South France in 1944 and had served as the French commander in chief in Germany after the war. He was a soldier but no politician, and he made no attempt to appease the troubled spirits in Morocco. "Fighting, that's my business, . . . and I know how to respond to insults," he declared publicly.[64] He said he would make the nationalists "eat dirt,"[65] and he characterized Allal El Fassi as a "traitor to his country, his master, and his religion, a serpent which from far-off Cairo spread his venom upon the world."[66]

Guillaume admitted no deficiencies in the French colonial regime in Morocco, and, fluent in English, he lectured American audiences on their own colonial deficiencies when the occasion presented itself. "The Moroccan is not your colonial ancestor," he insisted to one such group. "If you must draw a parallel, the Moroccan is your American Indian. We did not buy Casablanca for a string of glass beads, and we do not coop the Moroccans up on

[59] Ibid., p. 101.
[60] Text in *Cahiers de l'Orient contemporains* 23 (1951): 73–74.
[61] Bennouna, *Our Morocco*, p. 85.
[62] Bernard, *Le Conflit Franco-Marocain*, I, 121.
[63] Charles R. Codman, "French Morocco: Torch Plus Ten," *Atlantic Monthly* 190 (July, 1952), 52.
[64] *La Vigie Marocaine*, October 12, 1951.
[65] Ibid., author's translation of *manger de la paille*, literally, "eat chaff."
[66] *Ibid.*, October 12, 1951.

reservations. We build alongside them, showing them by example the way to progress . . . Do not criticize that which you do not understand."[67]

The change in residents-general did not mean a change in policy. The nationalists remained in the same relative position that they had held since 1944. The same individuals held the same offices under General Guillaume that they had held under Juin. The threats against the king and the penetration of the Moroccan government by French personnel continued. In spite of General Guillaume's soothing words to the United Nations General Assembly in November, 1951, that "complete peace reigns in Morocco among all elements of the population,"[68] it was at best a troubled peace emanating from fear and repression.

Although he was able to delay the inevitable for two more years by diplomatic maneuvering, the king was doomed.[69] The preservers of the status quo had no alternative except to attempt to arrest the development of the independence movement by decapitating it. That King Mohammed V's deposition did not occur until August, 1953, did not indicate the possibility or hope of accommodation; and an important factor in the delay was uncertainty as to what course the newly elected Eisenhower administration would take. The king hailed Eisenhower's election as "a victory for peace and the liberation of peoples," while General Guillaume said "if Eisenhower directly or indirectly aids the Moroccan nationalists, he will strike at the ties, already strained, which unite the partners of the North Atlantic Pact." He felt and hoped that Eisenhower and Dulles would not risk dislocating that alliance by any maneuver in North Africa.[70]

General Guillaume was apparently correct in his assumption. The interest of the United States was focused on Korea and the

[67] At the U.S. ambassador's reception in Paris, July 4, 1954. General Guillaume was then chief of staff of the French army. The author was present at the "lecture."

[68] Rezette, *Partis Politiques Marocains*, p. 49.

[69] See Bernard, *Le Conflit Franco-Marocain*, I, 131–148, and Robert Schuman, "Necessité d'une politique," in *La Nef: Maroc et Tunisie*, pp. 7–9, for an account of King Mohammed V's attempts to reach a diplomatic resolution of the differences.

[70] David Schoenbrun, "Les Américains sont au Maroc," in *La Nef: Maroc et Tunisie*, pp. 70–80, reports his interviews with the king and Guillaume.

cold war. In order to secure the adhesion of France to the European Defense Community, then pending, Secretary of State Dulles was willing to concede on issues not germane to the rearmament of West Germany, a provision to which the French vehemently objected. But the "blank check in North Africa" charge of Stephane Bernard and others may be premature.[71] Except for the intervention of Ambassador Bruce in February, 1951, against the deposition of King Mohammed V, the diplomatic records are silent, but the Moroccan nationalists did find a haven in the United States from which they effectively rallied world public opinion against France. Men like Ahmed Balafrej, Allal El Fassi, Mohammed Laghzaoui, Abderrahman Anegai, Dr. Mehdi Ben Aboud, and Mehdi Bennouna were not obscure figures, able to move about without being noticed. They came and went from the United States, yet their papers were never "in order." Balafrej used a Pakistani passport; Ben Aboud, a Yemeni one; Abderrahman Abdelali, Indonesian; and Anegai, Iraqi. Mehdi Bennouna had a Moroccan passport issued in the Spanish zone and also an American affidavit in lieu of a passport issued by the U.S. consul at Tangier. Allal El Fassi had an Egyptian *laissez-passer*, which immigration authorities questioned when he landed at Miami in the fall of 1952, following his propaganda tour of South America. He was detained for two days, then released on orders "from the very highest authority" in Washington in order that he might attend the Seventh General Assembly of the United Nations in New York.[72]

The Istiqlal party propaganda effort, directed by Ahmed Balafrej on a world-wide scale, paid off in the United Nations General Assembly Resolution of December 17, 1952, which affirmed the sovereignty and personality of Morocco, supported the nationalist demands for democratic reforms and the opening of negotiations, and asserted the competence of the United Nations to consider the Moroccan question as one of international character. The Istiqlal

---

[71] Bernard, *Le Conflit Franco-Marocain*, III, 335–339, 341–343. Abu Muhammad, "The Tragic Drama of Morocco," *Islamic Review* (May, 1951): 33–38, criticizing the United States policy of neutrality, asked what neutrality meant when one nation was powerful and the other weak.

[72] Information concerning the "accommodations" given the nationalist leaders furnished the author by Mehdi Bennouna in an interview at Rabat, May 11, 1967.

party received an additional dividend in the form of favorable treatment by the United States and international press. It is true that Phillip Jessup, the United States representative to the United Nations, supported the French position, but in the realm of practical politics what he said must be weighed with what the United States permitted the nationalists to accomplish.[73]

The question of free labor unions in Morocco had been an overriding issue throughout the six years of crisis. In that context the residency sought to secure approval in Western circles of its repressive policies by equating the Istiqlal party, which clamored for Moroccan labor unions, with the Communist party, which dominated the French labor unions in Morocco.[74] No one seriously believed the residency polemics. The king declared that communism was a "total contradiction to the principles of Islam and our national traditions,"[75] and with McCarthyism raging in the United States, the State Department hardly would have permitted free access to the United States for the nationalists if it had even slight evidence of their communist affiliation or sympathy. In fact the nationalist movement received its most powerful support in the United States from the American Federation of Labor. At its convention in San Francisco, September, 1951, it resolved that the developing free trade-union movements and genuine national independence movements should be aided and encouraged. On April 15, 1952, it joined with the CIO in a statement criticizing the neutrality position of the United States in the United Nations discussion of the Moroccan and Tunisian questions, and at its national convention in New York during September, 1952, in three of its foreign policy resolutions, it urged redoubled efforts to speed the extension of democracy, economic welfare, and national freedom to underdeveloped areas.[76] Until Moroccan independence was finally achieved, the AFL served as a distribution channel for nationalist propaganda.

[73] "Le problème est posé devant les Nations Unies," in *La Nef: Maroc et Tunisie*, pp. 29–50.

[74] *New York Times*, December 18, 1952, p. 18.

[75] To David Schoenbrun, quoted in Marjorie Rodes, *The Real Ruler of Morocco*, p. 10.

[76] Jay Povestone, "American Labor and the Struggle for National Freedom and Democracy," *Free Morocco*, no. 2 (May 25, 1953): 5.

Whatever may have been its contribution to the ultimate solution of the Moroccan question, the Istiqlal party leadership was not able to influence greatly the development of the conflict within Morocco. King Mohammed V must have seen the handwriting on the wall. Nor was there any hope from the French government. In Paris the Antoine Pinay government did not even raise the question of the disturbances in Morocco before its fall (on other issues) at the end of the month, and the succeeding René Mayer government appointed Georges Bidault, the advocate of General Juin, as foreign minister. The change in government actually meant little; the resident-general obeyed it only when he agreed with its instructions.[77] The protectorate administration was staffed at all levels with personnel hostile to the king, and it gave free rein to the French press in its outrageous campaign against the royal family but suppressed those papers favorable to it. The official *Bulletin de renseignement de la Direction de l'Interior* led the attack on the prestige of the king, treating each concession he made as a "capitulation" and each failure to concede as "further obstruction."[78] As the campaign developed, General Juin returned to Morocco to lend his personal prestige to the conspirators who planned to depose the king. Ahmed Balafrej protested to Secretary of State John Foster Dulles against the French maneuvers to depose the king, wipe out popular opposition by repression of the nationalists, and establish totalitarian rule by foreigners in Morocco.[79] His appeal fell on deaf ears. On August 20, under the exact circumstances predicted by Mehdi Bennouna in 1951, the king was placed aboard a French transport plane and flown to Corsica, then to Madagascar.

[77] Bernard, *Le Conflit Franco-Marocain*, I, 144–145, 191–194, and Schuman, "Necessité d'une politique," pp. 7–9.

[78] Bernard, *Le Conflit Franco-Marocain*, I, 163.

[79] Letter dated June 12, 1953, in *Free Morocco*, no. 3 (June 25, 1953): 2.

8. The Reign of Terror

THE MOROCCAN REVOLUTION, of which the war for independence was one aspect, began in 1953 with the confluence of several factors. The pressure of international politics focused world attention on Morocco because of its strategic location. The American presence, military and economic, established there as a legacy of World War II, weakened France's control of its restive protectorate. Moreover, the nature of the Moroccan quest for independence changed after 1950. The leadership of the nationalist movement broadened, and the new recruits brought ability and wealth. An activist, violence-prone base was added. The statesmanship of King Mohammed V had provided a framework within which all the disparate forces could be expressed, but the king failed to attract the support of the United States to his cause, and the French colonial forces, temporarily ascendant, deposed and exiled him. Bereft of moderate leadership, the Moroccan revolution entered a violent phase that lasted until the restoration of King Mohammed V to his throne in 1955.

According to the official French version of the crisis, the only serious problem after the deposition of King Mohammed V was the selection of a successor—as if one had not long since been designated! On the evening of August 20, four hours after the departure of the legitimate king and his two sons, Moulay Ben Arafa was proclaimed sultan. The new monarch, old and addicted to *kif*,[1] was only a tool of the French colonial interests and the Moroccan feudal lords who supported them. "Absolute calm reigned in all of the cities of Morocco," the report said, "and not just because of the measures taken to preserve public order, for the preventative arrests did not exceed seventy-two and the arrests for cause . . . not much more than the thousand mark."[2]

The resident-general's report was a bit sanguine. Even as the new sultan was being enthroned at Rabat, terrorists cells were meeting to plot his overthrow and the restoration of King Mohammed V. These cells were not "spontaneously" organized on August 20 as Stephane Bernard has indicated, nor did they emanate from the Istiqlal party.[3] They represented a new factor in Moroccan political life, one which has persisted to this day. The base was in the "uprooted" sector of Moroccan society—an urban proletariat, many of them laborers pulled to the coastal cities by the economic opportunities associated with the construction and operation of the United States military bases, and, later, rural but detribalized segments of the Moroccan population. The adherence of this new class to the cause of Moroccan independence resulted in a shift of the center of resistance from Fez to Casablanca and Port Lyautey and of tactics from reasoned protest to violence.

The leadership of the terrorist organization was not composed of

[1] Mahdi A. Bennouna, *Our Morocco: The True Story of a Just Cause*, p. 102 n. said Moulay Mohammed ben Arafa was "notorious for drunkenness." In an interview at Rabat, May 11, 1967, he clarified the statement: The intoxicating agent, he said, was *kif*, a plant of the cannabis family similar to hashish. Dr. Sadani, a neighbor of ben Arafa at Fez before his enthronement, said his addiction was such common knowledge that the children "mocked him on the streets" (interview, Rabat, May 28, 1967). Dr. Sadani was director of the North African Section of the Moroccan Foreign Ministry.

[2] Stephane Bernard, *Le Conflit Franco-Marocain, 1943–1956*, I, 185.

[3] Ibid., III, 261.

known Istiqlal party militants, none of whom had advocated violence,[4] but of individuals who, like the base, had not previously
been active politically. The terrorists merged into the Liberation
Army in 1954 and collaborated with the Istiqlal party in the quest
for independence, but after independence the individual members
more often than not opposed the old-guard Istiqlal.

Dr. Abdelkrim El Khatib, Majoubi Aherdan, Mohammed ben
Miloudi, and Attar Mohammed were typical of the new leadership. Majoubi Aherdan, an officer in the French army and married
to a French wife, was caid at Oulmes, a part of the protectorate
administration. He refused to sign the petition for the removal of
King Mohammed V in February, 1951, and was dismissed as caid.[5]
He became an officer of the Liberation Army in 1954, a cofounder
of the Popular Movement party in 1957, and minister of national
defense in 1961.

Dr. Khatib, of Algerian-Moroccan parentage, was practicing
medicine in Casablanca when the Carrières-Centrales riots occurred, and he cared for many of the wounded. He began organizing resistance to protectorate policies on August 20, 1953, as a
result of the deposition of King Mohammed V. In March, 1954, he
went to Europe, where he secured funds from North African workers in France, Belgium, and Germany to provide arms for the
Moroccan and Algerian revolutions. On November 1, 1954, at the
head of the so-called National Liberation Army in the Riff Mountains, he launched combat operations against the French occupants
in Morocco and Algeria. After independence was achieved in Morocco, he "presented the Army of Liberation to the King and it was
incorporated into the Royal Armed Forces of Morocco." Although
refusing public office at first, he participated in the organization

---

[4] Walter B. Cline, "Nationalism in Morocco," *Middle East Journal* 1 (1947):
18–28, predicted a dismal future for Moroccan nationalism. Its leaders, he said,
lacked the ability to formulate a plan of action and the courage to stage a
genuine riot, but sat around and moralized, harping incessantly on "Morocco's
rights" and typewriting petitions and manfestoes to slip under the doors of foreign consulates (p. 19). Cline, a professor of anthropology at the University of
Minnesota, served the last two years of the war in Morocco where, he said, he
observed the nationalist movement. His article expressed little sympathy or
understanding of it.

[5] Bernard, *Le Conflit Franco-Marocain*, I, 114–116. He is better known as
Majoubi than Mohammed Aherdan.

of the Popular Movement party with Aherdan and, at the request of the king, became minister of labor and social questions in May, 1960.[6]

Mohammed ben Miloudi ben Maati was a Berber farmer from the Khemisset region, forty miles east of Rabat. He too began his terrorist activities on August 20, but was captured in 1954, convicted of willful homicide, possession of arms, and association with criminals, and sentenced to prison in the Maison Centrale de Port Lyautey. He escaped on September 30, 1955, and joined the Liberation Army with the rank of lieutenant. Two years after independence was achieved, he led an armed uprising against the Istiqlal party government in Morocco "in support of the king," he insisted.[7] Gravely wounded when the rebellion was put down by the Royal Moroccan Army, he was hospitalized in Rabat. As a result of the intercession of Princess Lalla Amina, King Mohammed V's sister, and her husband, Prince Moulay Hassan ben Idriss, ben Miloudi was pardoned by the king and commissioned as a lieutenant in the Royal Moroccan Army.[8] Released to inactive duty in 1965, he was farming in 1967 near Kenitra.

Initially, the terrorist organization was composed of cells operating independently and for the most part unwittingly of each other. The operation at Port Lyautey is illustrative, but not exactly typical, for according to one observer, "everything starts in Kenitra because it is a new industrial city without traditions or hierarchy. The Kenitreans are hot-bloods."[9] The cell of which Arbab Ahmed was a member was recruited late in 1952 by agents from Casablanca, and it was one of the seven cells operating in Port Lyautey and among the thirty-two that, according to the *New York Times*, operated in the Carrières-Centrales *bidonville* of Casablanca.[10] Although the cells lacked overall strategic direction, all were similar

[6] "Autobiography of Dr. Abdelkrim El Khatib," a typed document given the author by M. Boejebar, Dr. Khatib's chief of cabinet at the Ministry of Labor and Social Questions, at Kenitra, June 15, 1960.

[7] Interview, Mohammed ben Miloudi ben Maati, tape recorded at Khemisset, May 17, 1967, with supporting documents furnished at that time by ben Miloudi.

[8] Interview, Mrs. Batoul Sbihi, tape recorded by the author at Rabat, May 13, 1967.

[9] Interview, Hassan Cherkaoui, Kenitra, May 5, 1967.

[10] *New York Times*, December 18, 1952, p. 18.

in composition and activity. Each cell consisted of six or seven men
and two or three women. The men engaged in sabotage, assassination, and like tactics. The women were couriers, fomenters of dis-
order, and procurers of arms.

The cellular organization was characteristic of the Istiqlal party,
but the new cells of the "resistants" bore as little resemblance to
the conventional Istiqlal cell as the Black Muslim movement in
the United States bears to the Islamic religion. The Istiqlal cells
were larger, organized in factories or schools, with occasional auxiliaries in the residential quarters; they had an office with a secretary and a treasurer and a literate guide who taught members to
read and write Arabic.[11] The members of the new cells were
young, often still in their teens, and illiterate. "If we had been
educated," one of them said, "we probably never would have
joined the Liberation Army [the terrorist organization of 1954–
1955]." If they were employed at all, it was generally only part-
time. They were street shoeshine boys, bazaar touts, pimps, and
"young toughs" of the sort that can be found in any society, although very few of them had police records. Many of them in Port
Lyautey spoke English learned "by experience" in their contact
with American soldiers and sailors, and they maintained that contact, not because they perceived a political advantage, but because
over the years they had developed a rude camaraderie with the
egalitarian American enlisted man. They were imbued with the
idea of independence popularized by the Koranic schools, but the
nationalist leaders of the 1940's made no effort to organize them
or to direct their activities.[12]

Arbab Ahmed, also known during the revolution under the
aliases of Ahmed ben Djilali and Sam, explained how the Americans unknowingly contributed to the Moroccan revolutionary effort. "My group acquired three pistols in June, 1953. I gave ninety
thousand francs to one of the girls [in his group] who worked as

[11] Robert Rezette, *Les Partis Politiques Marocains*, p. 293.

[12] Arbab Ahmed, alias Ahmed ben Djilali, alias Sam (during the revolution),
gathered together a group of the Port Lyautey "resistants," all identified by
their "Carte de Resistant," issued by the Moroccan government, at the patio of
the Bar de Tourisme, Port Lyautey, May 6, 1967, for an interview with the author. The foregoing profile is based upon that composite.

a bar girl at the Bar de Tourisme. She persuaded one of her American boyfriends to buy the guns, one Beretta and two Spanish pistols, in Portugal."[13]

According to Arbab, the terrorist cells did not want American arms—they might indicate American complicity and bring stricter controls. "It was absolutely forbidden to steal or even use American arms with traceable serial numbers because the presence of the Americans was our surest guarantee against massive reprisals by the French, and we could not risk exasperating them [the Americans]." But the flow of arms continued, and in all the cells the technique was about the same. One of the girls would make friends with an American sailor and, when she felt the time was right, ask him, "Cheri, you know what is going on here. I'm afraid. The next time you fly to Naples or Portugal, go to this address and buy me a Beretta pistol [or whatever weapon she could persuade him she needed for her security]." Arbab continued, "Since each girl had several boyfriends, we were able to get all the weapons we needed and were able to furnish weapons to cells in other places."

Latifa bint Mohammed, now married and the mother of three children, was a member of one of the Port Lyautey cells for over two years and she estimated she delivered "about a hundred" weapons to the "resistance." She indignantly denied the French charge that she was a prostitute: "I never slept with a man for money, and I never slept with a man whom I did not know and like. I never sold myself for a gun or anything else; it was not that kind of relationship." Latifa confessed that she at one time considered marrying an American; she felt they were kind and generous, but she said she was afraid she would not like America and "then all of this would seem bad."[14]

The American command never condoned the traffic in arms but was never able to stop it, nor were the French authorities. At least two major investigations were conducted in the early 1950's. At a court martial in December, 1953, James M. Bacon was convicted of the theft from the navy of three Colt .45 automatics, which he sold

[13] Interview, Arbab Ahmed, Kenitra, May 6, 1967.
[14] Interview, Latifa bint Mohammed, Kenitra, May 15, 1967.

to Abdelkadar ben Mohammed, alias Sfax. Bacon was sentenced to eight months' confinement and a fine of $285, and was not recommended for reenlistment in the navy.[15] Sfax was beyond the jurisdiction of the American authorities, and he was not tried by the French.

In another case, Frederick A. Farnsworth and John Anderson, both sailors from the Port Lyautey base, were tried and convicted by French authorities for the importation from Italy of seven Beretta 7.65 pistols and ammunition and their sale to six Europeans and one Moroccan Jew in Port Lyautey. They were fined ten thousand francs ($28.50), but they had been transferred from Morocco before the fine was affirmed, and they never paid it.[16]

In neither case was it even alleged that the arms went to the Moroccan terrorist organization, and the circumstances, considered in the light of Arbab's policy statement in the first case and the lenient sentence in the second, indicate they did not. Apparently neither the American nor the French authorities were aware of the arrangement by which the terrorists were getting arms, at least it was never proven, but the American base commander apparently suspected the truth, for he alerted all officers to prevent gunrunning from Italy. He cited six instances in which Beretta pistols had been brought in by personnel of Air Transport Squadron Twenty-Four and warned that the French authorities might start searching incoming planes unless the traffic was stopped.[17]

By 1954, although the Port Lyautey cells continued to operate autonomously, they identified themselves as part of the Liberation Army, openly wore its uniform, and cooperated with it in matters of escape and evasion and supply. Port Lyautey had become the principal distribution point for guns that were being provided not only by the Americans but also by Moroccan soldiers in the French army garrison there, and by smugglers from the Spanish zone.[18]

[15] CO USNAF, Navy 214, N.Y., letter serial 1509, January 17, 1954 to BUPERS, in Federal Records Center, New York, locator file 176899.

[16] USN file A-14-5; Subject: Frederick Arthur Farnsworth, 929 96 36, AM3, USN, in Federal Records Center, New York, locator file 141039A.

[17] Senior Officer Present Notice 8370 of March 4, 1954, Port Lyautey SOP Notice file, in Federal Records Center, New York, locator file 326148.

[18] See Bernard, *Le Conflit Franco-Marocain*, III, 261–263, for an account, essentially correct as far as it goes, of the terrorist operation at Port Lyautey.

The arms were distributed by a ruse almost unbelievable in its audacity.

Attar Mohammed, alias Cascade, was the Liberation Army ordnance officer for the region, and he explained how the system worked.[19] He had been employed at the United States Air Force base at Nouasseur, but was caught stealing grenades. Tried and convicted by a French tribunal, he was sentenced to death but escaped from prison and came to Rabat. There, he established contact with three U.S. Air Force officers by moving into the caretaker's room in an apartment house where they lived.[20] He began by washing their cars—without their knowledge or permission. "Sometimes they gave me five hundred francs, sometimes nothing, but they got used to me," Attar said. Then he made each of the three a business proposition: "For five thousand francs per month, I will wash your car each week at an agreed time. If it rains or the car otherwise gets dirty, I will wash it again. You will always have an impeccable car. If you need to have a flat fixed, or spark plugs changed, or any minor repairs, I will do that, too." Each of the three accepted and fixed a time for the weekly washing. On the appointed evening each officer in turn delivered his car to Attar who drove it around the corner, disconnected the speedometer, verified the amount of gasoline in the tank, and drove it to Port Lyautey. There he loaded guns or other materials in the trunk of the car and delivered them to Khemisset, perhaps, or some other locality, then returned to Rabat, washed the car, connected the speedometer, replenished the gasoline he had used, and the next morning returned it, "Voila, mon Colonel, votre voiture. Impeccable, n'est-ce pas!"

Attar, a personable young man with a light-olive skin and brown hair, apparently escaped detection by his sheer audacity. He had acquired a United States Air Force captain's uniform. He

[19] Interview, Attar Mohammed, Rabat, May 6, 1967. After hearing Attar's story, the author asked Abdallah Senhaji, a prominent figure in the Liberation Army, if the account were true. Senhaji replied, "It could be. He had the responsibility of distributing arms and he discharged his responsibility. In the Liberation Army, we never asked how." Attar now grows tomatoes near Bouznika, between Casablanca and Rabat.

[20] On Rue Dijon, near Bab Marrakech. The street has since been renamed Zankat Ibn Hagar.

always wore it while driving the impressive Buick or Pontiac automobile with the distinctive red license plates that indicated the automobile belonged to a member of the United States armed forces. In nineteen months, Attar said, he "slipped up" only once. "The colonel came down during the night on some urgent mission. His car was not there, and the next morning, he was furious. I told him, 'You know, Colonel, that I am not married. I have a girlfriend who lives in the *medina*. She comes out and cleans up for me sometimes. Last night it was late when she finished, and I used your car to take her home. Now I've lost a client . . .' The Colonel just said to forget it, but not to do it any more without his permission."

Attar was also a resourceful man. Although he wore an American uniform when driving an American car, he used other disguises, as a veiled woman and once, to get out of Casablanca, as a French officer in a stolen French car flying a French military flag. Asked to evaluate honestly his contribution to the Liberation Army, Cascade modestly deferred to the French evaluation—three times condemned to death (in absentia) and a price of seventeen million francs on his head. "They only offered thirty million for Abdallah Senhaji [commander of the Liberation Army in the Nador region]," Attar noted.

The terrorists had neither the experience nor the means to mount a sustained campaign. Their acts were expressions of opposition rather than a mode of combat. They intended the restoration of King Mohammed V, but the idea of political independence was a nebulous concept. Because the terrorist movement was unique in Morocco, the French police were never able to suppress it and the politicians never able to compromise with it. Before the decentralized and apparently irrational violence, the police were helpless. Accustomed to the demands of the Istiqlal party for independence a priori and probably, but not necessarily, restoration of the exiled king, both residency officials and the French government were unable to come to grips with the new organization or even to find a spokesman with whom they could discuss it.

Tactically, murder followed arson, which followed sabotage, repeated in random patterns. On August 25, 1953, the first sabotage occurred seven kilometers from Port Lyautey. The Mohammed Sefroui cell removed a rail from the track and wrecked the Casablanca-Tangier Express.[21] The same night another group set fire to the Mamora forest ten miles south of Port Lyautey. A few days later Allal ben Abdallah attempted to assassinate the new sultan but was himself cut down by the royal guard. And so it went throughout Morocco for three years. From August, 1953, to September, 1956, Morocco saw 1,407 acts of sabotage, 3,272 cases of arson, and 1,168 explosions. The casualties totaled 761 Moroccans killed and 1,409 wounded, and 159 Europeans killed and 598 wounded, totals that excluded losses to the European population during riots and losses by the French army.[22] The Jewish community seemingly was little involved. Only three Jews were killed in 1953–1954. Figures were not available for 1955–1956.

The paradox of a protestation against the French that produced three Moroccan victims for every European needs explanation. The Moslems marked for assassination were usually police informers or Moroccans compromised by their ties with French authorities and supporters of the new sultan. The terrorist organization deemed such assassinations necessary for its own security, and they served their purpose. The author of an attack simply melted into the crowd and found protection in a conspiracy of silence—the silence of approbation or the silence of fear.

In the face of the rising violence, the Istiqlal party was hard pressed to find a rationale. Ahmed Balafrej warned that violence was the only recourse left to the Moroccans when the Western powers blocked discussion of the deposition of Mohammed V in the United Nations Security Council,[23] and Allal El Fassi said, "Our commandos are doing their duty. They recently have killed thirty-three French and eighty-five Moroccan partisans of France."[24] At Paris, however, Moulay Ahmed Alaoui, director of the Istiqlal party's Bureau of Information and Propaganda, disassociated the party from El Fassi's position. He said the words attributed to El Fassi were contrary to fact and a contradiction of the Istiqlal party

---

[21] Interview, Arbab Ahmed, Kenitra, May 6, 1967.

[22] Bernard, *Le Conflit Franco-Marocain*, III, 260.

[23] Ahmed Balafrej, "Morocco Will Not Put Up with the Fait Accompli," in Moroccan Office of Information and Documentation [New York], *Free Morocco*, no. 5 (September 25, 1953): 1.

[24] To the Egyptian newspaper, *Rosa el Youssef*, quoted in Rezette, *Les Partis Politiques Marocains*, p. 221.

line, which had always reproached the use of violence and sought pacific means and political action to secure the national aspirations of Morocco.[25]

The French officials responded to the new situation with a three-pronged program designed to reassure the French colonial interests, break the opposition in Morocco, and placate world opinion. They failed on all counts. The new sultan immediately signed the legislation granting political rights to the French colony in Morocco and proclaimed "abolishment of the Day of the Throne, presentation of gifts to the Sultan, corruption, and absolutism." He also approved "modernization of justice, and the creation of democratic assemblies." He signed the *dahir* of August 31, 1953, delegating his authority to a "Limited Council," composed of the grand vizier and two deputies, the secretary-general of the protectorate, the counselor of the Cherifian government, and the director of the interior.[26] Henceforth, the office of the sultan was to be merely ornamental. The residency was all-powerful.

The French in Morocco replied to the Moroccan terrorism with both official and unofficial counterterrorism. Resident-General Francis Lacoste, who replaced General Guillaume on May 20, 1954, announced a decline of terrorist activity everywhere except Casablanca by September, 1954. He said the police and gendarmes had arrested 383 persons for terrorist crimes, and that the government, "faithful to France's traditions of humanity and generosity, has not deemed it possible to refuse the prisoners—in spite of the uncommon gravity and atrocity of the acts of which they are accused—the right to a defense and a fair trial, guaranteed by law to ordinary prisoners. However, certain steps which will substantially speed the process of examination and judgment have been taken at my request."[27] Pierre Parent described the subtle pressure to which he and other French opponents of the protectorate regime were subjected in the police headquarters in Casablanca, forced to sit all night and listen "wretchedly to the cries of Moroccan prison-

[25] *Le Monde*, October 9, 1953.
[26] Ambassade de France, Service de Presse et d'Information, New York, *Moroccan Affairs*, no. 3 (September 21, 1953).
[27] Ibid., no. 6 (September 22, 1954): 1.

ers not far away who were being tortured in order to obtain what are termed 'spontaneous confessions.' "[28]

The pressure on the Moroccans was less subtle. In a letter to the president of the Court of Appeals at Rabat, Abdallah ben Hassan ben Ahmed Layachi preferred charges against a French police official for assault and battery, barbarous acts, and abuse of authority. According to his affidavit, Layachi was arrested November 18, 1953, and taken to the police station of the Central Bureau of Investigation, Jean Courtin Avenue, Casablanca, at about 9:30 A.M. He was first beaten, as "an appetizer." Chief Inspector Garcette struck the first blow and directed each subsequent step of the interrogation. Layachi was then stripped naked and tied to a bench, stomach down, with his head hanging over one end. The end of the bench was raised and Layachi's head plunged into a tub of water. He had only to wiggle his hand to indicate his willingness to talk. An electric prod was applied to his chest, stomach, and genitals, and he was whipped on the soles of his feet with a wet riding crop. The treatment continued until noon when he was released and doused with cold water. He refused to obey the order to clean up the water from the floor and was forced to the floor, his mouth pried open with a broomstick, and the dirty water wrung from the rag used to clean the floor was poured into his mouth. The whipping, electric prod, and head-in-water treatment continued until 5 P.M. At that time, his hands and feet were tied behind him, and he was hung on an iron bar, the ends of which rested on two desks. The pain in his kidneys became intolerable and he lost consciousness. He was taken down until he regained consciousness, then suspended again and left until 10:30–11 P.M. He was then untied and permitted to spend the rest of the night sittting in a chair. He was released the next morning. Layachi urinated blood for the next two days, he said.[29]

The police brutality was too widely reported, given the censorship which existed in Morocco, to have been without foundation.

[28] Pierre Parent, *The Truth about Morocco*, trans. Eleanor Knight, p. 14.

[29] In the report of Robert Verdier, member of the French National Assembly Commission of Foreign Affairs and R. de Moustier, chairman of an investigation conducted in Morocco in 1954, published in *Free Morocco*, no. 10 (June 25, 1954), pp. 4–5.

Le Monde reported "various kinds of torture," including electricity, used by the French police.[30] Moroccans were punished for trivialities that the police said indicated nationalist sympathies—possession of outdated currency, failure to wear traditional dress or to shave the head.[31] Throughout Morocco the French police and army conducted *ratissages* (rakings-in). In Berkane, population 25,000, more than 2,000 men were imprisoned; in Ahfir, 18,000 population, 1,500 were imprisoned; in Tafoughalt, 23,000 population, 300 prisoners were squeezed into grain storage elevators—and this was all in Berber country supposedly loyal to France.[32]

A notorious *ratissage* took place in Port Lyautey on August 9, 1954. The Istiqlal party had called for a strike on August 7. When shopkeepers tried to close their shops, the police intervened to keep them open. A mob overwhelmed the police. The French army moved into the Arab sector and opened fire on the mob. According to the official report quoted in the *New York Times*, two European women and two Moroccan women were killed—their throats cut.[33] Frank White, a *Time* correspondent, gave an eyewitness account of the events of August 9, which was the day of the Feast of the Lamb commemorating Abraham's sacrifice. Most of the men were at home when the French army cordoned off the Arab quarter and legionnaires went through the *medina*, breaking down every door and driving them out. The women were driven back with rifle butts. The men were driven into the open square, the sheep market, where, according to White's report, a dozen policemen formed a gauntlet, six on either side. One by one the Arabs were thrust forward, each with his hands on his head.

"Entrez donc, Monsieur," said a reserve police colonel. "The session is about to begin." He smiled broadly, then hit a middle aged Arab with his right fist, below the belt. As the Arab went down, the colonel kneed him in the groin. The Arab tried to get up; another cop caught him across the jaw with a club. Down went the Arab and the next cop kicked him, twice. He got up again and ran into the arms of another

---

[30] J. A. Jaeger, *Le Monde*, May 6, 1954. Lest such incidents be considered isolated instances possible only in Morocco, see *La Gangrene*, for more than a half-dozen similar tortures in Paris in December, 1958.

[31] Henri Sartout, *Le Monde*, May 11, 1954.

[32] *Free Morocco*, no. 6 (October 25, 1954), 2–3.

[33] *New York Times*, August 8, 1954, pp. 1, 4, and August 9, 1954, pp. 1, 4.

policeman who poked him into a sitting position with the muzzle of a rifle.

More than 20,000 Arabs ran the gauntlet that day . . .

Later in the day those suspected of nationalist activity were separated from those against whom nothing was charged, and some six thousand of the suspects, including most of the men between seventeen and twenty-five were loaded into dump trucks and hauled away to the local prison. The police fired above the heads of the protesting women to keep them back, and Civil Controller Jean Husson, who had presided over the *ratissage*, made a speech to those left urging them to "resume your peaceful way of life. If you do not, the same thing that happened today will happen again. Only next time it will be worse . . . with jet airplanes shooting down on you from the sky." At that moment, White reported, a flight of French jets flew low over the crowd.

Husson told White that the show of force was necessary: "We know these people. To do anything less than we are doing would be to invite further disturbances." That night the residency tersely announced that a *ratissage* had been conducted in Port Lyautey and in the course of the roundup, "twenty Arabs died."[34]

Ali ben Mohammed, the U.S. Navy base commander's Berber cook, was one of the unfortunate "suspects." He told what happened next.

They took us in dump trucks to the prison. Inside the big wall they had a place about one hundred meters diameter [surrounded by accordion-rolled] barbed-wire. When we got there, they did not let us get off the trucks; they just dumped us like a load of rocks. Many people hurt—broken bones, bleeding, but they let no doctors come. When newspaper men come to see, they just throw them out. I was there two days—no food, no water, no nothing. When people start to holler, they drop bomb . . . smoke bomb that makes people cry on them.

My Captain, he was looking for me, and when my Captain tried to get me out, the French say it is not the American's business to come running to look for Moroccans . . . to stay out of it. But they let me and a lot of people go home.[35]

[34] Frank White, "Morocco: Running the Gauntlet," *Time* 64 (August 23, 1954): 27.

[35] Interview, Ali ben Mohammed, Kenitra, May 13, 1967. Ali has worked for

Captain Christian H. Duborg was then U.S. Navy base commander, and his intervention secured the release of at least a part of the prisoners. He did not rest his appeal on political legalism or humanistic considerations. He advised the French navy commandant, "You have my cook in jail and I am hungry and therefore in a foul mood. You also have about a hundred of my employees. They have not been involved in your political situation; they have been at work. You are welcome to check their time cards. I need them in order to operate the base, and unless I get them back immediately, I will be obliged to cut off your water and electricity."[36] There was a certain amount of jocularity in Captain Duborg's threat, but there was also a certain amount of gravity. The American navy furnished water and electricity for all of the French navy facilities, and the electricity was sixty-cycle current, whereas any current that the French navy might be able to get from the city of Port Lyautey would have been fifty cycle, and it would have played havoc with much of the French equipment calibrated for sixty cycles.

The French authorities in Morocco, accustomed to the tactics of the Istiqlal party did not realize until much too late that they were fighting two opponents, one weakening and the other growing stronger. The dual nature of the opposition is best illustrated by the events from November, 1954, when the Liberation Army "began combat operations," and the late summer of 1955 when the violence reached its crescendo. The political militants of the Istiqlal party had quit Morocco for New York, Cairo, Spain, and even Paris, to mobilize diplomatic pressure and public opinion against France. The second echelon of party, which remained in Morocco, either dropped out of the action or joined the terrorists. Mrs. Batoul Sbihi, for example, was a member of a prominent nationalist family and, unlike her brother, Abdelatif Sbihi, was a member of the Istiqlal. She organized a women's cell of the party in Salé, which conducted a school to teach girls to sew as a vocation, and to read and write. She was a lady-in-waiting to Princess Aisha and

the Americans all his adult life, first at the U.S. consulate at Casablanca, then as cook for the commander of U.S. naval activities at Port Lyautey, 1948–1962, then as head chef at the Port Lyautey Commissioned Officers Club.

[36] Interview, Captain Christian H. Duborg, USN, August 20, 1957, at NAS, Port Lyautey.

had unrestricted access to the palace through the women's quarters (the harem). Before the deposition of Mohammed V she had served as a courier between the king and the "command" cell of the Istiqlal party in Salé, which disseminated information and orders within Morocco. She had also been in contact with the terrorist organization and transmitted arms that she received from Lalla Rkia Awada, the mother of the personal secretary of Princess Aisha, to Azzouz Achourti, who distributed them.

On November 18, 1954, which the nationalists had designated "Independence Day" after Moulay ben Arafa abolished the Throne Day celebration, Mrs. Sbihi and the women of her cell in Salé decorated the mosques and minarets with flags and pictures of the exiled king. When the French attempted to arrest her, she fled to the Spanish zone, where she joined Dr. Khatib, Abdallah Senhaji, and others who were prominent in the terrorist organization. Thereafter, she was involved in the escape and evasion activities of the Liberation Army. She had abandoned the protest role for a more active one.[37]

A major objective of the Liberation Army was to extend the terror into the *bled* (rural areas). Here too the vehicle was the recruit driven into the resistance by French excesses. Mohammed ben Miloudi, for example, was never a member or a sympathizer of the Istiqlal party. He and fifty of his neighbors of the Khemisset region were arrested on mere suspicion and jailed, first at Meknes, then at Port Lyautey. They were able to escape from the maximum-security prison because they were given keys by one of the guards. They made their way on foot through the Mamora forest to the Spanish zone and joined Dr. Khatib and the Liberation Army. Thereafter, organized into small commando groups, they returned to the Khemisset-Oulmes region, burned crops and forests, and engaged in selective assassination. By the end of 1955, the revolt had spread from the coastal cities to the entire country.

Mrs. Sbihi, ben Miloudi, and many other prominent figures in the Liberation Army had been in contact socially with the Americans since 1943, but they never tried to involve them in the resistance activities of this period. Mohammed ben Miloudi said the

[37] Interview, Mrs. Batoul Sbihi, tape recorded by the author at Rabat, May 13, 1967.

Americans were not involved at all in his resistance activities "and perhaps were not even aware of them." They went hunting for birds and wild boar with him, for, as Russel Hope put it, "No one knew the Khemisset-Oulmes countryside and people as well as ben Miloudi." Small wonder. Ben Miloudi received medical treatment following an automobile accident in the U.S. Navy hospital at Port Lyautey and many people believe an American doctor, Captain Otto Schlicht, treated him for gunshot wounds incurred in one of his "actions," but that was not true, ben Miloudi said.[38] He did, however, accept a hunting rifle presented him by the base commander, Captain Christian H. Duborg, and presumably used it only for hunting wild boars.

In spite of their forty years of experience in Morocco, the French never understood the wave of violence, either urban or rural, and nowhere was the failure more evident than at Khouribga and Oued Zem, August 20–21, 1955. Khouribga, about one hundred miles south of Casablanca, was an important phosphate mining town and the site of a French naval air base. Violence was probable on August 20, the anniversary of the king's exile, yet the base was almost completely unprepared for the events to come. The commanding officer and many of the base personnel were in France on August leave and, of those not on leave, many had permission to be away from the base for the weekend; not more than 25 percent of the military personnel were actually present that Sunday. No intelligence reports had been received by the base indicating probable violence.

The first indication of something amiss came about 9 A.M. as an ominous, sullen roar wafted from the native Souk El Had[39] over the European section of Khouribga: "Ah-ash el malek [long live the king]." Commandant Palmesini (whose wife was American) alerted the base and posted French sailors armed with light machine guns along the railroad track that separated the European

---

[38] Interview, Mohammed ben Miloudi, tape recorded at his farm between Khemisset and Tiflet, May 17, 1967.

[39] Souk El Had is literally translated "Sunday market." At Khouribga it was no more than a farm market, but in other parts of North Africa sizable towns have grown up about the weekly market and are named for it, for example, Souk El Arba ("Wednesday market").

community from the Moroccan—tacit recognition of the animosity between the two races.

There were no incidents along the railroad, not a shot was fired; but seven kilometers to the east, half way between Khouribga and Oued Zem, aerial reconnaissance by a training plane from the air base located a crowd of about two thousand men, women, and children. No weapons were in evidence, only sticks. About noon the crowd split. Part of it headed toward Oued Zem, but the larger part headed toward Khouribga, herded along by outriders on bicycles. There were no horses. This was a city mob, not the "lean, hawk-nosed tribesmen" described in the ringing rhetoric of the popular press. It was deflected from the European section of the city by a couple of low passes by aircraft from the base, but it circled back around the European part and sacked and burned the native quarter—their own homes—and wrecked the phosphate company dispensary, built to serve the native workers themselves.

In Oued Zem, a massacre occurred—that much can be said, but the published reports of what actually happened are not very reliable or conclusive. According to *Time*, Oued Zem had a population of 4,600; according to *Le Monde*, 300 Europeans and 12,000 Moroccans. According to one source, 36 Europeans and 100 Arabs were killed; according to another, 37 Europeans and Moroccan Jews and more than 300 Arabs.[40] The only surviving journalist who was actually present, Barrett McGurn of the *New York Herald Tribune*, stumbled upon the carnage by accident while he was en route to Kenifra. He alerted the French legionnaires but was hardly in a position to gather statistics. But whether 136 or 337, doubling the number of dead would not make two nightmares of one, and, if such a rationale was used, how would the reprisal killings, said to be more than 300, be counted?

By Monday morning, the emotional "binge" was over and Khouribga was a city with a hangover. The streets were mostly deserted and many of the shops were still closed, steel shutters over their windows. In the Moroccan quarter of the city, the signs

---

[40] Barrett McGurn, *Decade in Europe*, is the most reliable account of the massacre at Oued Zem yet published. See also *Time* 66 (August 29, 1955): 22–23, and 66 (September 5, 1955): 18–19; *Newsweek* 46 (August 29, 1955), p. 26; *Le Monde*, August 21–22, 1955, pp. 1, 3.

of the weekend violence were everywhere. Many shops had been broken open and the wares scattered or stolen. Vegetables were not available at the farm market. The people seemed ashamed of their excesses—as if they had lost their reason for a time in the lower-order mentality of the mob.

The wonder is not the discrepancies in the various reports but at the persistence of certain errors. At a cocktail party in Khouribga that Sunday evening, fragmentary reports had begun to come in and there was much talk of the "tribes." News stories for several days spoke of "Berber horsemen from the Atlas," yet it was quite obvious that the rioters at Khouribga were local citizens, and the published photographs of captured suspects at Oued Zem show pedestrian townspeople in ragged *djellabas*. The Frenchmen apparently considered it more dignified to be killed by some unnamed "wild tribesman" than by their own gardeners.[41]

Although the French may not have realized the nature of the conflict in Morocco, they knew they were losing the sympathy of public opinion in both France and the United States. To counter the loss, even as they planned the deposition of King Mohammed V, residency officials also planned a be-nice-to-Americans program. They established Franco-American Clubs (for officers only), provided tour services, and expedited the issuance of automobile licenses and radio licenses,[42] lest "when these Americans go home they [spread] a great deal of ill will in America against France."[43] The Americans tried to cooperate. The Port Lyautey commander appointed a Military Community Relations Committee in July, 1953, and in December prescribed a detailed indoctrination program for naval personnel that included lectures on Moroccan geography, peoples, history, customs and traditions, currency and traffic regulations, and recreational facilities. The program emphasized the importance of the conduct of U.S. nationals upon the foreign relations of their country and urged the importance of

[41] The author was present at Khouribga, the guest of Commandant and Mrs. Palmesini.

[42] Resident-General, Information Service of Morocco, *Newsletter*, II, no. 1 (February 1, 1953).

[43] *New York World Telegram*, September 22, 1953.

"good community relations" with both the French and Moroccan local communities—a manifest impossibility.[44]

The program was a failure. Antagonisms were too old and too deep. Resentment of French obstruction of the base construction program permeated the upper echelons of the American military community in Morocco, and the G.I. resented the cavalier treatment accorded him in his day-to-day contacts with the French business community, the gouging on rents, and the price differential in stores between an American and a Frenchman. The Franco-American Clubs were seldom frequented by the Americans; they preferred their own clubs on the base. Except for a limited protocol contact, social contact between the French and American community was virtually nonexistent. Many Americans shared the sentiment of Major John Murphy, one of the U.S. Air Force officers stationed in Morocco: "After you're here awhile you got to keep reminding yourself it's the Russians who are our enemies and not the French."[45]

Airmen Ralph J. Polese and Robert Kern would not have been plagued by such doubt. Although the indoctrination program was nominally still in existence eighteen months later, they were attacked in a Rabat bar by "five or six French soldiers." They understood no French and said they knew of no reason for the assault. Polese suffered a concussion. Both he and Kern were arrested by the French police for disturbing the public order, but the French soldiers were not arrested—"another instance of our men being kicked around by the French and I don't like it," Captain Duborg, the American base commander, noted on the margin of the report.[46]

Nor would John T. Sommer have had any doubt—if he had lived. He and Kenneth J. Barnette were in Port Lyautey's red-light

[44] The efforts are reflected in Commander, U.S. Naval Activities Instruction 1620.3, dated July 30, 1953, and the subsequent modifications in the series, in Federal Records Center, New York, locator file 326148.

[45] *New York World Telegram*, September 22, 1953.

[46] CO PATRON 7 letter, "Investigative Report of Injuries sustained by Polese, Ralph J., AN, USN, on or about March 7, 1955, at La Renaissance Bar, Ave. Dar El Maghzen, Rabat," in USN file A-17-6, in Federal Records Center, New York, locator file 141039.

district one night about 3 A.M., although the gates to the district closed at midnight. They entered by climbing a light pole and jumping to the roof of one of the houses. The girls were still awake; it was *Ramadan*, and they were eating their last meal before beginning their fast of atonement. The two Americans were detected by the French policeman, Emile Hemard, making his rounds. According to Hemard, Sommer resisted arrest and was subdued by force. He died at the police station within the hour from blows on the head and neck.[47]

For these and other reasons the American military community was generally more sympathetic toward the Moroccans than toward the French, although their contact was limited to association with base industrial workers and domestic servants and occasional invitations to participate in one of the Moroccan festive occasions. But, predisposed by their own inherent anticolonialism and revulsion against French bullying, and confronted with the same patronizing air that the French exhibited to American and Moroccan alike, the Americans tended to identify with the Moroccans.

The identity was obvious in the sense of security that the Americans displayed. During the worst of the terrorism, they continued to hunt in the French-designated "Zone of Insecurity" in the mountains where the Liberation Army operated and to move about almost at will in the cities, although the various commands paid lip service to the many French curfews.[48] Their paramount concern was to avoid the possibility of being mistakenly identified as French. To that end, they wore uniforms at all times when they appeared in public and avoided crowds insofar as possible. Their automobiles already bore a distinctive license plate, white numbers on a red background. By the summer of 1954 every house in Port Lyautey occupied by an American family also bore a name plate,

[47] Chief of French Liaison Mission letter, Serial 2395 ML/1, dated May 18, 1955, in USN file A-14-5, Federal Records Center, New York, locator file 141039A.

[48] The restrictions on liberty for U.S. Navy personnel are detailed in COMNAVACTS Notice 1050, dated March 29, 1955, and modifications thereto, in Federal Records Center, New York, locator file 326148. Information on hunting and other activities that evaded the curfews provided for the author by interview, Russel Hope, Kenitra, June 1, 1967, and by Rear Admiral Thurston B. Clark letter to the author, dated St. Mary's City, Maryland, November 2, 1967.

white letters on a red background, prominently displayed on the premises. The latter precaution was perhaps more of a morale than a safety factor, for the terrorists knew where each American family lived, and, during the riots of 1954, they stationed a "soldier" before each American house to guard it against any inadvertent violence.[49]

France was more successful on the diplomatic front than the public front. The action of the Arab states in forcing the Moroccan question upon the United Nations also forced the United States to take sides between France and Morocco. The diplomats chose France. Foreign Minister Robert Schuman before the General Assembly in 1951 denied the competence of the United Nations to intervene in the "contractual relations" of France and Morocco, and the United States delegate supported his position. In 1952 the United States voted to put the Moroccan question on the agenda, but only after Secretary of State Acheson had mollified French Ambassador to the U.N. Henri Hoppenot with the assurance that the United States would support nothing stronger than hopes for continued talks.[50]

The United States support of France disillusioned the Moroccan nationalists. Ahmed Balafrej made a veiled threat of violence against the Americans in Morocco. The same day an unidentified Istiqlal party spokesman in New York recalled the warm welcome that the Moroccans had extended to the Americans in 1943 and the cordial relations that had existed until the United Nations vote in 1952, after which, he said "the first outbreaks against the Americans began . . . The people of Morocco have lost faith in the United States."[51] At Rabat, officials denounced the statement as Istiqlal "blackmail" and insisted that the Moroccan people had not lost faith, and that there would be no violence against the

[49] Interview, Captain Christian H. Duborg, Kenitra, Morocco, August 8, 1957. In an interview at Kenitra, May 20, 1967, Lieutenant Commander Carl Johnson, a retired naval officer now living in Kenitra, told the author that he frequently visited in the *medina* during the terrorism and had talked to "sentries" stationed before American homes by the Moroccans. Arbab Ahmed told the author, Kenitra, May 6, 1967, that he had "guarded" American homes the night of August 7, 1954.

[50] *New York Times*, October 23, 1952, p. 1.

[51] *New York Times*, November 4, 1953, p. 10.

United States by the Moroccan people.[52] At least the spokesman was correct in his prediction, if not in his assertion that the nation had rallied to the new sultan, for there was no violence against Americans.

The uncritical acceptance by the U.S. Air Force of the French interpretation of the "delicate political situation in Morocco" probably emanated from the political necessity of supporting France lest dissension disrupt NATO, but it led to mistakes in judgment. A U.S. Air Force intelligence estimate, for example, warned of the rise of anti-Americanism among younger elements of the nationalists who, the report said, had not yet been effective in stopping work, but might try to secure arms and explosives from the U.S. Air Force, and who "likely would be aided by the Communists" in any attacks on U.S. personnel or property.[53] The fact that no work stoppage had occurred, that no attempt to secure arms or explosives had been made, and that the nationalists were profoundly hostile to communism seems not to have precluded acceptance of the French diplomatic position.

The residency-imposed ceiling, which limited the U.S. Air Force to 7,400 personnel, civilian and military, weakened the French position vis-à-vis the terrorist organization. The air force, unable to operate even three of its five projected bases under such unrealistic conditions, resorted to "Project Native Son," a massive program to train and utilize Moroccan personnel to operate the service facilities and perform other nonmilitary duties.[54] The air force intelligence experts were wary of the native son project; they feared it would create an "area of vulnerability" of which the nationalists would take advantage.[55] They were correct in principle but not as to form. The indigenous personnel made little if any attempt to secure arms, but a part of their pay checks flowed into the coffers of the "resistance." Some of the contributions were vol-

[52] Ibid., November 5, 1953, p. 15.

[53] "History of the United States Air Force, Europe, January–June, 1954," vol. IV, appendix VII P, Air Intelligence Directorate Study no. 25, pp. 2–3, in USAF Archives, file no. K 570.01.

[54] "History of the Seventeenth Air Force, July 1 to December 31, 1954," vol. I, p. 13, in USAF Archives, file no. K 573.01.

[55] "History of the United States Air Force, Europe, January–June, 1954," vol. IV, Appendix VII P, Air Intelligence Directorate Study No. 25, pp. 2–3.

untary and some were extorted,[56] but, however come by, they constituted an important source of revenue for the Liberation Army.

Unfortunately, the United States chose the wrong bellwether for its military policymakers in Morocco. The navy position was always stronger with respect to both the French and Moroccan, yet command of the Moroccan area was vested in the United States commander in chief, Europe, an army command, and delegated by him to the commander of United States Air Forces in Europe. The arrangements "made pursuant to the agreement of December 22, 1950," were applied to the navy as well as to the air force, apparently oblivious to the existence of two agreements. By 1954 the French Liaison Mission controlled the "not purely military" affairs of the United States forces in Morocco, and "followed up on all questions which may have political consequences or reflect on the relationship with the local population." A stated function of the French Liaison Mission was "to help the American personnel employed for the construction and utilization of the bases while they stay in French Morocco, to give them all necessary information, and to promote good relationships between the French population and the American circles, enlightening the latter concerning the problems in France and Morocco."[57]

On January 22, 1955, General Orval R. Cook of the United States Air Force, deputy commander in chief of United States forces in Europe, signed an agreement at Paris with François Leduc, chief of the French Liaison Mission, which surrendered to the latter the responsibility for recruitment, security evaluation, administration, and payment of personnel hired by the French Service for the U.S. forces in the French Zone of Morocco. The conditions of employment, wage scales, supplementary payments, and conditions for the protection of the workers were to be henceforth the responsibility of the French. The United States was obligated to conform to "all local customs and practices," and to reimburse the French for disbursements and cost of administration.[58]

---

[56] Interview, Arbab Ahmed, Kenitra, May 6, 1967.

[57] "History of the United States Air Force, Europe, January–June, 1954," vol. IV, appendix VII P, Air Intelligence Directorate Study No. 25, pp. 26 ff.

[58] "Agreement For Recruitment, Administration, and Payment of Personnel Hired by the French Service for the United States Forces in the French Zone of Morocco," dated January 22, 1955, at Paris; copy in possession of the author.

The agreement was to have been incorporated in a status of forces agreement, then being negotiated but in fact never completed.[59] The control over its employees that the navy had exercised since 1942 was lost.

The status of forces agreement for Morocco was never completed because events simply moved too swiftly. By the late summer of 1955, Morocco was on the verge of anarchy. The Liberation Army exercised a shadowy control over the countryside and the terrorist cells at least disputed control of the cities with the French. French counterterrorist organizations formed. And the French police, powerless to control the situation, either resigned or collaborated with the French counterterrorists, an action counterbalanced by the defection of the Moroccan police auxiliaries to the "resistance." France had ceased to govern.[60]

As had been the history since the beginning of the terror, the American bases and the American personnel were little affected by the strife. Absenteeism at Nouasseur among the non-American employees, 29 percent of whom were Arab, was normal. Of the hundreds of non-Moroccan cars destroyed during the violence, only nine were American. The air force took fifty trailers out of storage and made them available to personnel who feared possible violence in Casablanca. Only three were occupied. The nationalists insisted, "We like Americans,"[61] and the more than twenty thousand Americans, seven thousand of them women and children, dependents of air force personnel, apparently believed them.[62] Even the French military high command recognized the sacrosanct position of the Americans in the face of the violence. The French air force commander in Morocco notified the American commander, Major General Frederick Glantzberg, that Moroccan tribesmen were attacking French outposts. He said they would possibly leave the American flag alone and authorized Glantzberg to fly it "as a matter of protection" at the American bases and outposts. He had twice previously denied American requests to fly the American flag

[59] Headquarters, United States European Command letter LFR 092.2 French Morocco (6), dated February 9, 1955, signed W. V. McGarity, LCOL, USAF; copy in possession of the author.

[60] Bernard, *Le Conflit Franco-Marocain*, vol. III, 278–285.

[61] *New York Times*, August 27, 1955, p. 3.

[62] Ibid., September 11, 1955, p. 9, for the personnel figures.

alongside that of the French.[63] The problems caused by the rapidly deteriorating situation throughout North Africa were by no means localized or categorized. The United States was torn between the irreconcilable necessities of building up French military strength to support NATO and, at the same time, of preventing France from using that strength in North Africa where most of her military training bases were located. The U.S. Military Assistance Advisory Group at Paris kept representatives almost constantly at the various French North African bases to survey the usage of the U.S.-provided equipment.[64]

The three French military services cooperated with the inspection teams, for they correctly surmised that they could focus attention on the effective use of the equipment and perhaps gain advocates in the United States Department of Defense. Not only were the various base commanders lavish in their reception of the inspectors, but the French ministries "buttered-up" higher-ranking officers with prestigious honors.[65] But when the situation became critical in the summer of 1955 because of the operations of the Liberation Army in Morocco and Algeria, the terrorism throughout North Africa, and the desertion of the native units to the resistance, the Frence Defense Ministry did not hesitate to transfer NATO-committed units into the breach. The United States tried to avoid involvement by refusing its assent to the use in North Africa of equipment provided for use in other areas. When the United States refused to agree to the transfer of helicopters from Indo-China to North Africa, Antoine Pinay visited the United States to explain "the positive aspects of the North African policies of France."[66] His mission was not entirely successful, but the United

[63] Ibid., September 2, 1955, p. 3.

[64] The author was one of them from June, 1954, to December, 1956.

[65] For example, Captain Robert Camera, USN, chief of the Navy Section, Military Assistance Advisory Group, received the Legion d'Honneur for services in World War II (since such honors were expressly forbidden for service in M.A.A.G.), and the author received the Medaille Aeronavale, the French navy pilot insignia, for "precious services . . . to the cooperation of the two allied navies." Aeronautique Navale letter no. 248 Aero/Maroc/Sec dated Casablanca, August 1, 1957.

[66] "Le problem Algerien," *Chronique de politique étrangère*, Vol. 8, No. 6 (November, 1955): 715–727.

States did resume the shipment of arms in categories not specifically adaptable for use against the North African rebels.[67]

United States caution reflected the recognition that a forcible solution of the North African problem was not possible. The only solution would be diplomatic and the exiled king would be the key to it, for he alone could calm the terrorists. The French majority in both Rabat and Paris was resolutely hostile to any arrangement involving Mohammed V, although it realized, certainly by the end of 1954, that the puppet ruler, sitting on his unwanted throne in the great walled gardens and court at Rabat, was more a liability than an asset. The more knowledgable of the Moroccan nationalists knew that no French government could restore Mohammed V, not in 1954, and survive. Both sides were willing to consider an alternative solution, but neither had reckoned with the tenacity of King Mohammed V nor with the unswerving loyalty of the Liberation Army to him.

Negotiations by the French government with the exiled king began in September, 1954, and were conducted through several intermediaries.[68] The king refused to abdicate, and he rejected a French proposal to grant internal autonomy to the Moroccan community in return for a guarantee of the "rights and major interests of France in strategic, political, diplomatic, economic, and cultural matters," and a recognized status for French settlers in Morocco "proportionate to the important contribution they have made."[69] He did, however, reiterate his consistent recognition as a matter of justice of the interests of the French settlers. The Edgar Faure government in France finally capitulated, and on September 29, 1955, Antoine Pinay announced to the General Assembly of the United Nations that Morocco was to be independent.[70]

[67] The author was instrumental in securing the release of AU-1 type, carrier-based attack aircraft to the French navy in July, 1955.

[68] Bernard, *Le Conflit Franco-Marocain*, 1, 227–389, is a detailed recital of the complex maneuvering in search of a solution. See also, Georges Izard, "Le secret d'Antisirabe," *Etudes mediterranéennes* 4 (Spring, 1958): 61 ff.; *L'Année Politique, 1955*, pp. 663–665, for the text of King Mohammed V's letter of December 26, 1955, to Georges Izard; and *Le Monde*, September 14, 1955.

[69] *Le Monde*, November 8, 1955, quoted in Bernard, *Le Conflit Franco-Marocain*, vol. I, 321.

[70] United Nations General Assembly, *Official Documents*, 10 Sess., 528 plenary meeting, September 29, 1955, p. 171.

The defenders of the status quo refused to accept the inevitableness of Moroccan independence. They might have brought down the government except for the crushing pressure of the terrorism in Morocco and the field operations of the Liberation Army in both Morocco and Algeria. Uniformed troops were attacking French outposts all through the Rif Mountains and in Algeria, and commando units were operating in the Middle Atlas Mountains south of Fez. A Liberation Army communiqué from Tetuan pledged to fight on until both Morocco and Algeria were "totally independent," and from Cairo, Allal El Fassi announced that the Liberation Army in Morocco and Algeria was operating under a single command.[71] The prospects were more frightening for the French settlers in North Africa and for the politicians in France than ever before. Before such pressure they capitulated, hoping to save what they could of their economic position, lest it be lost with their rapidly decaying political domination.

Extreme fluidity characterized the next six months, in Moroccan as well as French circles. All of Morocco rallied to King Mohammed V. Even Thami El Glaoui did an about-face; on October 25 he pronounced for the prompt restoration of Sidi Mohammed ben Youssef and his return to the throne, an act of political realism more than a change of heart.[72] On October 29, Moulay ben Arafa renounced all of his rights and asked his subjects to support Sidi Mohammed ben Youssef. The demonstrations throughout Morocco constituted a spontaneous plebiscite. On October 31, Mohammed V landed at Nice, his exile at an end, and immediately was escorted to Paris, where he spent two weeks engaged in political discussions. He returned to Morocco on November 16, and the three-day celebration that followed was unmarred by any unpleasant incident, but it was purely a Moroccan celebration. The French kept to their houses, a loaded shotgun behind the front door, as the Moroccan people paraded in the streets, singing and shouting.[73] All U.S. servicemen and their families were confined to their bases.[74]

On November 18 in his speech from the throne, the king "re-

[71] Pierre Boyer de Latour, *Verités sur l'Afrique du Nord*, pp. 171–173.

[72] *Le Monde*, October 27, 1955.

[73] The author spent those three days at Agadir as a guest of the home of the executive officer of the French Naval Air Station.

[74] *New York Times*, November 11, 1955, p. 8.

joiced to announce the end of the tutelary regime and protectorate and the beginning of an era of liberty and independence."[75] As a matter of practical fact, however, Morocco's problems as an independent nation were already showing on the horizon. Morocco's future relationship with France and the world remained undefined. The transitional Moroccan government was made up of political independents, and the Istiqlal party refused to support or to participate in it. Thus the political rivalry that was to devitalize the government of an independent Morocco existed before its first institution was created, a reflection of the different origin, nature, and degree of sophistication of the terrorist movement as contrasted with the Istiqlal party. The United States was inevitably caught up in those crosscurrents because of its military presence in Morocco.

[75] *Le Monde*, November 19, 1955.

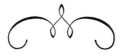

9. Sterile Diplomacy

WHEN KING MOHAMMED V RETURNED to Morocco in November, 1955, he was confronted with grave domestic and international problems, and the inflamed passions of his subjects gave him little time for his Sisyphean undertakings. Almost alone he had to organize a government from disparate, often conflicting, and almost totally inexperienced elements of the Moroccan population, salvage a disintegrating economy, and consolidate the tenuous grant of independence by establishing his sovereignty over the whole of Morocco. He faced the necessity of creating a Moroccan military organization and diplomatic service to take over functions previously performed by France. These problems were doubly difficult because of their interrelationship, and the United States was drawn into them from the very first because of its military bases in Morocco.

All of the negotiations and agreements leading to the restoration of King Mohammed V to his throne envisaged the appointment of a Moroccan government to direct its internal affairs and negotiate its new relationship with France. The king first devoted his attention to the organization of a government of national union. In the new government completed on December 7, only three weeks after the king's return to Morocco, Si Embarek Lahbil Bekkai was named prime minister. The Istiqlal party, which had agreed to participate in a government dedicated to national independence, territorial unity, constitutional monarchy, and responsible government, was represented with nine of the twenty ministerial posts. The Independent Democratic party (PDI) received six portfolios, and the ministry included five independents, one of whom was Jewish. Ahmed Reda Guedira, Mohammed Cherkaoui, Abderrahim Bouabid, and Driss M'Hammedi were named ministers of state and charged with negotiations with France.[1]

No individual prominently identified with the Liberation Army was included in the ministry, but then the Liberation Army was not essentially a political movement. However, the crucial posts of prime minister, interior (Lahcen Lyoussi), and national defense (Reda Guedira) were confided to individuals who more nearly shared its philosophy than did the Istiqlal. The participation of representatives of the various political groups did not result in political unity—only in endless bickering. The dominant Istiqlal party sought sole responsibility for government, and when it finally achieved this goal in 1958 the anti-Istiqlal elements reacted with an armed revolt that had to be put down by the Royal Moroccan Army.

To the average Moroccan, the king's return meant the war was over and independence was achieved. But the realities were less promising. As far as France was concerned, "interdependence" was a one-way street, as little different from her consistent policy toward Morocco for the past ten years as she could contrive to make it. France hoped to recoup by negotiation what she had lost in the revolution, but negotiations had to wait because the Faure government fell on November 29, not on the Moroccan question, but as a result of personality conflicts within the Radical party. The center parties, frightened by the gains of the Communists on

[1] Both Guedira and Cherkaoui were members of the Roosevelt Club, and Guedira was outspokenly pro-American.

the left and the followers of Pierre Poujade on the right in the elections of January 2, 1956, formed a coalition under Guy Mollet, who declared in his investiture speech that his government would begin immediate negotiations with the sultan of Morocco to define the ties that would unite the two countries.[2]

Both Bekkai and Mollet apparently believed that the issues over which France and Morocco had fought so long were settled, and only administrative details were left to be worked out. Mollet spoke of "negotiations based upon the recognized independence of the Sheriffian Empire,"[3] and Bekkai of an alliance with the "democratic and fundamentally anticolonialist" French people and of loyal and fruitful Franco-Moroccan cooperation in technical, economic, and defense matters. The aura of optimism was short-lived. Mollet became disenchanted with his North African policy when he flew to Algiers on February 6 and was greeted with a barrage of tomatoes hurled by a mob of "petits blancs." In the face of such defiance, Mollet gave up on his policy of conciliation and inaugurated in Algeria a state of siege, martial law, and strict censorship, the very formula that had just failed in Morocco. The "extraordinary powers" granted Mollet by the National Assembly to pursue "the dirty war" in Algeria augured ill for the relations between France and Morocco.[4]

When King Mohammed V led the Moroccan delegation to Paris on February 16 to negotiate the new relationship, a fundamental disagreement that had separated the two countries for the past year still existed. Morocco demanded unconditional independence, after which the nature of interdependence could be determined. France demanded that Moroccan sovereignty be limited by the terms of interdependence before independence would be recognized. Fortunately, perhaps for both France and Morocco, the unrelenting pressure of the Liberation Army forced the pace of negotiations and the Franco-Moroccan accords of March 2 were concluded before the Algerian war broke out in full force. On February 19 the Liberation Army announced the creation of the Great Atlas

[2] Stephane Bernard, *Le Conflit Franco-Marocain*, I, 363.

[3] Ibid.

[4] See Lorna Hahn, *North Africa: Nationalism to Nationhood*, pp. 163–165, for a discussion of the Mollet program in Algeria and its implications for Morocco.

Combat Zone and warned of a general insurrection unless Morocco was granted immediate independence. The war was spreading rapidly with fronts in the Rif Mountains and along the Algerian frontier, a "northern" front between Port Lyautey and Larache (in the Spanish zone), and a combat zone in the Middle Atlas Mountains.[5]

Success for the Liberation Army depended on circumstances. Although intensely loyal to King Mohammed V and formed to force his restoration, the army was not under his control. The king was not an advocate of violence for any purpose. King Hassan II recalled that "each bloody incident plunged my father into despair," and of the Oued Zem–Khouribga riots, "my father was sick for three days, and cried out, 'Can a man bear another murder committed in his name?' whereas another would have rejoiced at such proof of the attachment of the Moroccan people to him."[6] But the Liberation Army had little opposition in the interval between the king's return and the negotiations that began in late February. Although France surrendered the responsibility for internal security to the new Moroccan minister of interior, it retained control of the means of exercising it—the buildings, vehicles, communications equipment, and such. The Moroccan minister refused to accept the responsibility until France surrendered the public security infrastructure to his control. Under such circumstances the growing strength of the Liberation Army was more apparent than real.

The Franco-Moroccan negotiations culminated in a joint declaration of March 2, 1956, which did not abrogate the Treaty of Fez but which recognized that it was obsolete as a basis for Franco-Moroccan relations. The declaration specifically recognized the independence of Morocco and its right to provide for its own defense and diplomatic service. France declared its intention to respect and guarantee the territorial unity of Morocco and to aid in the creation of a Moroccan army. Both nations agreed to pro-

[5] *Le Petit Marocain*, February 19, 1956, p. 3; see the issues of January 28, and February 1, 6, 14, 26, 1956, for reports of terrorist acts, such as murders, grenade attacks, and burned farms.

[6] Quoted in Georges Vaucher, *Sous les cèdres d'Ifrane: Libres entretiens avec Hassan II, roi du Maroc*, p. 77.

ceed with negotiations to define "interdependence."[7] Finally, both nations recognized the necessity of a transitional stage and provided for it in a series of protocols embodied in letters exchanged between Si Bekkai and French Foreign Minister Christian Pineau.

One of those protocols, signed May 20 at Rabat and May 28 at Paris, stated that France would continue to conduct Moroccan foreign affairs until a new Franco-Moroccan diplomatic convention was negotiated. Article 11 provided that Morocco would assume the obligations of international treaties concluded by France in the name of Morocco, as well as those which resulted from international acts concerning Morocco on which it had made no reservations.[8] The article was therefore consistent with Mollet's declaration to the National Assembly that France would insist that international engagements concerning Morocco be respected.[9]

The conflict between the United States and Morocco over the American air bases in Morocco emanated from protocols supporting the agreement, for Foreign Minister Ahmed Balafrej "reserved" Morocco's position on the bases and French Foreign Minister Pineau agreed that Article 11 of the basic agreement did not apply.[10] The Moroccan reservation caused much speculation, and the United States' reaction to it remains incomprehensible, since the Moroccan position was well known. Moroccan Minister of State Mohammed Cherkaoui told the *New York Times* in January that the status of the U.S. air bases would have to be renegotiated as soon as Morocco became independent because neither the king nor the Moroccan people had been consulted and France had no right to cede land that did not belong to her. He said the question was only a legal one and the Moroccan position implied no hostility toward the United States.[11] Far from indicating hostility, the Moroccan action was a dramatic appeal to the United States to help

[7] *Le Monde*, March 4–5, 1956. In ibid., February 25, 1956, Pineau is quoted as saying he would not ask the National Assembly to abrogate the Treaty of Fez until he was able to lay before it the text of new accords defining relations between France and Morocco.

[8] Muhammed Khalil, *The Arab States and the Arab League: A Documentary Record*, vol. I, *Constitutional Developments*, doc. no. 50, p. 226.

[9] *Journal Officiel*, Debats parlementaires, Assemblée Nationale, February 1, 1956, p. 136.

[10] Khalil, *The Arab States*, vol. I, doc. no. 50.

[11] *New York Times*, January 18, 1956, p. 1.

Morocco consolidate its independence. Reda Guedira said the Moroccan negotiators recognized that the United States could not easily ignore its NATO treaty obligations to France, and by its reservation sought to remove France as an obstacle to bilateral negotiations between the United States and Morocco without forcing the United States to take an official position.[12]

The United States, however, was not anxious to enter into bilateral negotiations. The State Department insisted that the 1950 agreement establishing the bases was valid, and it expected Morocco as the successor authority to validate the French agreement.[13] United States Minister Plenipotentiary Julius C. Holmes (one of the negotiators of the 1942 agreement with General Giraud) said at Tangier that the bases were French, not American, and under French command and direction. He did not know, he said, whether they were even being discussed by the Franco-Moroccan negotiators at Paris.[14] Ahmed Balafrej made the Moroccan position crystal clear. He said the United States should negotiate as soon as possible with Morocco on the future of the bases and stop worrying about embarrassing France, which, he added, "has shown no parallel concern for the United States."[15]

France was desperately sensitive to any indication of American support for Morocco that might lessen Moroccan dependence on her. Alain Savary, French secretary of state for Moroccan and Tunisian affairs, warned that France would not respect any agreement between Morocco and the United States that did not respect the rights and interests of France,[16] apparently not quite believing the "private" assurances of the United States ambassador of con-

---

[12] Interview, Reda Ahmed Guedira, Rabat, May 20, 1967.

[13] *New York Times*, January 19, 1956, p. 7, and May 11, 1956, p. 4.

[14] *Le Petit Marocain*, February 24, 1956. According to Ahmed Taibi Benhima, director-general of the Royal Council, in an interview at Rabat, July 25, 1966, "The Moroccan position on the American bases was consistent from the very beginning. Together with Si Bekkai and M'Hammadi on March 2, 1956, I gave a note to Mr. Christian Pineau, the French foreign minister, saying Morocco would respect all treaties signed by France except the accord alienating Moroccan land and sovereignty to the United States [the bases]."

[15] *New York Times*, June 9, 1956, pp. 1, 3.

[16] Ibid., June 20, 1956, p. 4.

sistent American support for the French position in North Africa.[17] Balafrej said he regretted the inability of the United States to develop a clearly defined policy for North Africa. Economic and strategic considerations ought to compel it, he said.[18]

The United States position was indeed ambiguous, but it favored France rather than Morocco. Ambassador Douglas Dillon, in a speech in Paris, deplored the activities of "the few private American citizens who have anything to do with Morocco,"[19] an apparent reference to King Mohammed V's invitation to them to extend their capital investments and technical know-how to Morocco.[20]

American insistence on the status quo was also reflected in the State Department attitude toward the relinquishment of United States consular jurisdiction in Morocco, an action urged upon Congress in the summer of 1956 by Assistant Secretaries of State Robert Murphy and George V. Allen. The American community in Morocco protested that the Moroccan courts were in effect French consular courts, equipped with French judges and operating on French law.[21] Certainly the *Keil* case decision in 1952 indicated they were French courts,[22] and the French continued to claim responsibility under the terms of the Franco-Moroccan Agreement of March 2, 1956, for the operation of the modern court system in Morocco.[23] Allen nevertheless told Congress that United States military forces in Morocco were adequately protected by a Status

[17] Department of State, *American Foreign Policy: Current Documents, 1956*, pp. 703–707.

[18] Ahmed Balafrej, "Morocco Plans for Independence," *Foreign Affairs* 34 (April, 1956): 489.

[19] Department of State, *American Foreign Policy: 1956*, pp. 703–707.

[20] According to the *New York Times*, November 25, 1955, King Mohammed V received Robert C. Fisher, Harold S. Germain, Leo H. Lamprecht, Martin Parsowith, and Leon Judith at Rabat, and told them he would sincerely welcome American capital in Morocco because the United States had not only the financial means but also the technical know-how to contribute to the economic development of Morocco.

[21] *Relinquishment of Consular Jurisdiction in Morocco*, Senate Report No. 2297, 84 Cong., 2d Sess., 1956, testimony of Mr. Rodes on June 12, 1956.

[22] See pp. 157–158.

[23] "History of Detachment Two, Headquarters, United States Air Force, Europe (Moroccan Liaison Office)," August–December, 1956, p. 13, in USAF Archives file no. K-570.071c.

of Forces Agreement entered into with France in 1950 and still in effect,[24] and Raymund Yingling, a State Department legal advisor, said all Americans, including servicemen, would be tried in "pretty much the same courts as previously for some time to come."[25] The information was misleading, for a Status of Forces Agreement for Morocco never existed,[26] but Congress accepted the State Department recommendations and relinquished the jurisdiction granted by the Treaty of Meknes in 1836.

Moroccan overtures, United States coyness, and French petulance continued throughout 1956. On August 29 King Mohammed V called Morocco a meeting ground for the civilizations of the East and the West.[27] On October 6 when Ambassador Cavendish Cannon presented his letters of credence, the king eulogized the United States for its ideals, spiritual values, and historical friendship with Morocco, and expressed his desire to visit the United States and call upon the president.[28] There is little doubt that the United States could have "legalized" its military presence in Morocco in late 1956 by the simple expedient of adopting a foreign policy independent of France. The moment was never more propitious nor the prestige of the United States higher than the three months after the withdrawal of the Anglo-French expedition against the Suez Canal. That fleeting opportunity was lost in the lengthening shadows of the Algerian War.

More than one dream dissipated there. In their accord of May 26 France and Morocco mutually promised to coordinate their diplomacy in order to ensure concerted action in the domain of foreign policy.[29] King Mohammed V had faithfully observed his

[24] *Relinquishment of Consular Jurisdiction in Morocco*, House Report No. 2697, pp. 2–3, 84 Cong., 2d Sess., 1956; and "Relinquishment of Consular Jurisdiction," *Hearings on S. J. Resolution 165*, Senate Committee on Foreign Affairs, 84 Cong., 2d Sess., 1956.

[25] *Relinquishment of Consular Jurisdiction in Morocco*, Senate Report No. 2297, 84 Cong., 2d Sess., 1956, testimony on June 12, 1956.

[26] Headquarters, United States European Command letter LFR 092.2 French Morocco (6), dated APO 128, U.S. Army, February 9, 1955, copy in author's possession. The draft agreement was not completed until November 30, 1956, and it was never signed.

[27] To the Congress of Toumliline, August 29, 1956; text in Vaucher, *Sous les cèdres d'Ifrane*, pp. 260–262.

[28] *New York Times*, October 7, 1956, p. 6.

[29] Vaucher, *Sous les cèdres d'Ifrane*, p. 207.

promise to keep France informed as he attempted to mediate the two-year-old conflict in Algeria, but on October 22 the French military forces gratuitously insulted him by hijacking his personal plane en route to Tunisia, forcing it to land at Algiers, and kidnapping his guests, five of the Algerian leaders. The king was in Tunis at the time, but he canceled his talks with President Habib Bourgiba and returned to Morocco in a chartered Italian plane that landed at the U.S. Naval Air Station at Port Lyautey, a deliberate snub to the French, who controlled the civil airdromes in Morocco. According to the nationalist newspaper *Al Alam* it was a very important action that constituted de facto recognition of the American bases.[30] Two weeks later, on November 1, France ignored her treaty obligations to Morocco when without consultation or even notification she launched her attack on Egypt, not to defend the interests of the stockholders of the Suez Canal, but to end support from Cairo for the Algerian nationalists.[31]

Morocco and France severed diplomatic relations, and France suspended the economic aid promised in the independence agreements of March. Morocco turned to the United States. Prince Moulay Hassan and Princess Aisha flew to Washington to seek an economic arrangement that would permit Morocco to withstand French economic pressure. Since there was no commercial flight from Morocco to either London or New York except through Paris, the United States departed from its policy of "bending over backwards to avoid the appearance of interference with French aims in Morocco," as the *New York Times* put it, and the U.S. Air Force flew them from Nouasseur to London to allow them to catch a plane to New York without passing through Paris or using a French airline.[32] Their mission was successful, and Ahmed Balafrej announced on December 9 that the United States would extend aid that unofficial sources put at 28 million dollars.

Balafrej also announced that the solution of the question of the American bases in Morocco would "certainly encounter the under-

[30] *New York Times*, October 25, 1956, p. 1, and *Al Alam*, as quoted in ibid., October 26, 1956, p. 3.

[31] Vaucher, *Sous les cèdres d'Ifrane*, p. 209. The author was serving at the time as a technical advisor to the French navy and heard such a rationale ad infinitum.

[32] *New York Times*, November 21, 1956, p. 5.

standing of His Majesty the Sultan."[33] Later in the month he declared that the time was ripe for an agreement on the bases because
the king was decidedly sympathetic toward the presence of the
United States forces, the Moroccan government was favorable toward negotiations, and the United States bases constituted a guarantee of Moroccan liberty and security. He rejected the concept of
joint Franco-American occupation of Port Lyautey, which was, he
said, either an American base or a French base upon which the
French had introduced foreigners without consulting Moroccan
authorities. "We recognize the presence of the United States forces
as an existing fact," he added.[34]

The United States did not accept the invitation to begin negotiations. Neither was it administratively ready nor had it reached an
understanding with France as to objectives to be sought. The Department of Defense was partially responsible for the administrative delay. Ambassador Cavendish Cannon expected that he would
conduct the negotiations and would rely upon the military commanders in Morocco for technical and policy advice concerning
the bases,[35] but the view did not prevail in Washington and the
navy, which supported Ambassador Cannon's concept, was over-
ruled. William Lange was sent from Washington as the Department of Defense representative, and he did not arrive until the first
of May, 1957.

Differing points of view and delay reflected the confused military command structure existing in Morocco. Morocco was not a
part of the North Atlantic Treaty Organization and therefore coordination through SHAPE was not possible. The commander in
chief of United States forces in Europe was assigned area responsibility for Morocco, but for all practicable purposes there were no
U.S. Army forces in Morocco, and he delegated his authority not to
the navy, whose forces were under his command, but to the commander, United States Air Force, Europe. Since the Strategic Air
Command, user of the air force bases in Morocco, reported directly
to Strategic Air Command Headquarters, Offut Air Force Base,
Nebraska, the area authority was subdelegated to the Commander,
Detachment Two, Seventeenth U.S. Air Force. Thus the military

[33] Ibid., December 9, 1956, p. 9.
[34] Ibid., December 24, 1956, p. 4.
[35] Interview, Ambassador Cavendish W. Cannon, Port Lyautey, April 1, 1957.

commander in Morocco had no forces under his direct command and was junior to at least two of the military base commanders.

Detachment Two, the Moroccan Liaison Office, never particularly successful, was outmoded by the fact of Moroccan independence. It was created to represent the United States Air Force, Europe, administratively in Morocco, but it interpreted its responsibilities broadly to include "sole channel of communications between United States military agencies in Morocco and the Moroccan government, the French Liaison Mission at Rabat, and the United States Embassy."[36] The Moroccan officials regarded Detachment Two as a relic of the protectorate, an adjunct of the French Liaison Mission, and, when the protectorate administration was dismantled, Detachment Two lost its point of contact. It was never accredited to or recognized by the Moroccan government. The ambassador usually bypassed it for direct contact with the base commanders, and Detachment Two was reduced to writing plans that never were approved (the Status of Forces Agreement, for example), with the complaint that "other agencies" ignored its "prime responsibility."[37]

Diplomatically the situation was no better. The United States naval attaché disclaimed all functional responsibility for the U.S. naval forces in Morocco.[38] The army attaché's life was comparatively simple, since there were no U.S. Army forces in Morocco except for a small port detachment at Casablanca. There was no U.S. Air Force attaché and the Moroccan government refused to accredit one, since the naval attaché was also naval attaché for air. The Moroccan officials did not understand that the latter title was an administrative one, pertaining to eligibility for flight pay, and not a functional one.

Ambassador Cannon, an ex-marine himself, understood the military command structure, and he asked Captain Christian Duborg,

[36] "History of Headquarters, United States Air Force, Europe," January 1, to December 31, 1958, vol. I: Narrative, pp. 32–34, in USAF Archives file no. K-570.01, January–December, 1958, vol. I.

[37] "History of Detachment Two," July–December, 1957, p. 41. See ibid., August–December, 1956, p. 35, for complaint of navy's failure to coordinate intelligence matters.

[38] Interview, Captain H. K. Edwards, U.S. Naval Attaché, Rabat, to the author and Captain Christian H. Duborg, USN, Port Lyautey, July 8, 1957.

the navy commander at Port Lyautey, to designate an officer from his staff, preferably a French-speaking one with legal training and well briefed on the political situation in Morocco, to aid in the base negotiations. Captain Duborg wrote personal letters to two well-placed friends in the Navy Department asking that Lieutenant Commander Leon B. Blair be ordered to his staff to look after the navy's interests in the "forthcoming all-important U.S. base rights negotiations for Morocco."[39] Although the navy granted the request, the negotiations were actually directed from Washington and no naval representative from Morocco ever met with the negotiating group.

The time might have been right in December, 1956, for legalizing the status of the bases, but even then two forces were working against a solution satisfactory to the United States. The delay gave latent opposition time to coalesce. The more powerful of the two was public opinion, manipulated by the Union Marocaine du Travail, the national labor union, which identified the United States position with that of France. In a pressure move against France, the union refused to unload French military supplies at Casablanca. The ships came to Port Lyautey and unloaded at the U.S. Navy dock in spite of official "strenuous objections" by Captain Duborg, who pointed out that the arbitrary, unilateral decision was contrary to the technical agreements governing the base and would likely jeopardize the base's future.[40] The Moroccans established roadblocks to prevent trucks from hauling the supplies away from the dock. There was no overt hostility toward the Americans at Port Lyautey, but two weeks later at Casablanca the union refused to unload U.S. Air Force supplies from the S.S. *Norfolk Victory* as retaliation for "American complicity" in the French action. Ahmed Balafrej protested the French use of the American dock and

[39] Captain Christian H. Duborg letter dated at Port Lyautey, February 12, 1957, to Vice-Admiral W. V. Davis, Deputy Chief of Naval Operations (Air), and February 13, 1957, to Rear Admiral A. E. Hanegan, Bureau of Naval Personnel, Navy Department, Washington; copies in possession of author.

[40] See COMNAVACTS, Port Lyautey, letter of November 2, 1956 to the U.S. Embassy, Rabat; Troope française du Maroc, Chef d'arrondissement des travaux du genie, letter no. 92 of November 20, 1956; and COMNAVACTS, Port Lyautey, letter Serial 0029 to the Commandant, Base Principale Aeronavale, Port Lyautey, of November 24, 1956. All three letters are in the A-14 file, Federal Records Center, New York, file V 51.

called upon the Americans to take a stand.[41] Since they refused to do so publicly, they were increasingly identified with the French in the demand for total evacuation.

The United States discarded its best card on the very eve of negotiations. Morocco was in desperate financial straits as France tightened the economic screws. The United States' willingness to help had prompted the king and Balafrej to propose settlement of the base issue. But the United States soon made it clear that the two questions were not related. A mission from the U.S. International Cooperation Administration (ICA) visited Morocco in December, 1956, and in April it announced its readiness to provide twenty million dollars in economic aid to Morocco—without reference to the base issue. That action completely changed the psychological climate for the negotiations that began on May 9.

The primary concern of the United States was to reach an accord with Morocco that would be consistent with its other international security agreements. It first proposed a general statement defining a United States–Moroccan relationship "in defense of the Free World," or some similar formula. The Moroccan delegation was noncommittal and that proposal was quickly shelved. Agreement was then sought on specific details of jurisdiction, army and fleet post offices, customs exemptions, and post exchanges, again without success.[42] The negotiators had made no progress by May 29 and the negotiations were allowed to lapse until September.

The Americans, little concerned with the failure of the first round of negotiations, misinterpreted the Moroccan attitude, attributing it to lack of diplomatic personnel, diplomatic experience, and a clearly formulated foreign policy. Ambassador Cannon felt that these Moroccan deficiencies would correct themselves in time, and that it was therefore inadvisable to press for an agreement. The Moroccans, however, had a different scale of values. Their primary concern was the withdrawal of French and Spanish troops, not merely because they were a symbol of the hated protectorate but also because they posed a threat of future military intervention in Moroccan affairs. The Moroccans were aware of the Franco-American rapport but felt the United States would dissociate itself

[41] *New York Times*, December 24, 1956.
[42] Interview, Ambassador Cavendish W. Cannon, Rabat, May 11, 1957.

from French policies in Morocco in view of the changed political conditions. The apparent dawdling on the part of the Moroccan delegation was a deliberate maneuver to give the United States time to break loose from France.[43] Not only did the United States fail to respond to the Moroccan overture, but France and Spain used the conciliatory attitude toward the United States as a lever to demand equal consideration for their troops and bases.

Both the United States and Morocco sought to avoid any action that would force the pace of negotiations as each waited for the other to modify its position. For example, the death of John Wolf Bryan, Jr., about midnight on June 4, 1957, posed a potentially explosive question of jurisdiction. The infant's mother, accused of murder, was the seventeen-year-old wife of an American serviceman. Psychiatric examination indicated that she had the mentality of a ten-year-old child and would not be able to cooperate in her defense because of her mental condition.[44] The United States and Moroccan authorities desperately sought a formula that would obviate her trial in a Moroccan court with inevitable wide and unfavorable publicity, particularly in the U.S. press.

The facts of the case were not conclusive. Mrs. Bryan had "choked" the baby about 11:30 P.M. to stop his crying and turned him over on his stomach—her customary means of quieting him. She left him gasping in his crib, read awhile, and went to bed. Three hours later she arose to find the baby still and cold. She vainly tried to revive it by breathing into its mouth and manipu-

[43] Interview, Ahmed Taibi Benhima, director-general of the Royal Cabinet of Ministers, Rabat, June 25, 1966. Mr. Benhima has been personally involved in Moroccan diplomacy since its inception, and he reviewed all the notes pertinent to the base negotiations in the Moroccan Foreign Office in preparation for the interview. He said "the question was always one of law and politics. The United States position was illegal, and as long as you insisted that it was legal, negotiations were pointless. But we were willing to talk for we felt sure that you would see the logic of disassociating the United States position from that of France in time. Our intention was modified by a matter of practical politics. Spanish authorities told me in Madrid where I was negotiating for the Spanish withdrawal that they would withdraw when the others, meaning the United States, agreed to withdraw."

[44] Investigating Officer's Report, dated June 21, 1957, annex 15, in Federal Records Center, New York, file no. 148825B. Major Robert L. Williams, neurology and psychiatry consultant for the U. S. Air Force surgeon-general was flown to Morocco to conduct the examination.

lating it. Unsuccessful, she went upstairs to a neighbor couple, apologetically waked them, and asked them to call the police. She said she had killed her baby either by strangling or smothering him. On the basis of her statement she was charged with murder. The autopsy report indicated that the six-weeks-old child was physically defective. The left side of the brain showed old hemorrhaging and weighed only 60 percent as much as the right side. The pathologist was not able to determine whether the last hemorrhage would have caused death if the brain had been normal.[45]

The case was far more significant politically than legally because of the question of jurisdiction. The French authorities normally applied the Bidault-Caffrey Agreement of 1948 on civil affairs in cases involving Americans only and waived jurisdiction.[46] But the French were also negotiating with the Moroccan government, and they were hesitant to take action that might imperil their recently initiated (June 11, 1957) but still unsigned judicial convention. Nor were the French authorities in Morocco and Paris in agreement. Procureur-General Di Francesci at Rabat insisted that the 1948 agreement would be applied if only Americans were involved and if French officials handled the case. He disclaimed responsibility if Moroccan officials became involved.[47] The French Foreign Office at Paris advised that the New Franco-Moroccan convention did not alter the Bidault-Caffrey Agreement but did alter the Line of Communications Agreement of 1950, which extended the applicability of the Bidault-Caffrey Agreement to Morocco.[48] Moroccan officials, informed of the circumstances as a matter of routine by the navy commander at Port Lyautey, evinced no desire to "become involved."[49]

[45] Ibid., pp. 5–6.

[46] According to "History of Detachment Two," August–December, 1956, p. 15, the French officials of the Moroccan Ministry of Justice, holdovers from the old regime, granted waivers because of the expressed hope of establishing precedents that would operate to the advantage of French military forces stationed in Morocco.

[47] U.S. Embassy, Rabat, telegram 978 of June 14, 1957, to State Department, in Federal Records Center, New York, file no. 148825B.

[48] U.S. Embassy, Paris, telegram 912 of June 13, 1957 to State Department, in ibid.

[49] COMNAVACTS, Port Lyautey, telegram 961845Z of June 6, 1957, to CNO., in ibid.

Justice, blinded by political considerations, was perhaps more equitable than under more normal circumstances. On the basis of the psychiatric examination and "other circumstances involved," criminal proceedings were not instituted against Mrs. Bryan, and she was hastily transferred to the U.S. Naval Hospital at Bethesda, Maryland, for "complete study and treatment."[50] She was committed to Saint Elizabeth's Mental Hospital, Washington, for "further observation, evaluation, diagnosis, and treatment as indicated" on July 31.[51] American, French, and Moroccan officials breathed a sigh of relief.

Ambassador Cannon did not aggressively pursue the negotiations, because he felt time was on the side of the United States, but he realized that public opinion would be an important factor in the ultimate decision, and he encouraged the base commanders to be attentive to the image that the bases presented. The air force and the navy reacted oppositely to that advice. The air force withdrew inside the perimeter of its bases, hoping the presence of twenty thousand military and dependent personnel would not be noticed. The navy embarked upon a campaign to mold public opinion in its favor. The divergent concepts were never reconciled and resulted in friction between the two services during the next five years, but the navy's success enabled it to retain its Moroccan base when the air force bases were forced to close.

The navy campaign was successful because it was tailored to a unique situation and community. It could have succeeded only as a base-level program, for no higher headquarters would have approved in advance the composite program that did evolve. It was unprecedented, and precedent is usually the criterion for approval. To be successful the campaign had to avoid the active opposition of the French, which would bring inevitable diplomatic repercussions, establish a meaningful relationship with the Moroccan officialdom that sat uneasily and a bit suspiciously in places formerly occupied by the French, placate the rivalries in the American camp, and simultaneously create an effervescent interest among the naval personnel that would generate support and participation

[50] COMNAVACTS, Port Lyautey, letter dated July 15, 1956 to director of USAF Liaison Office, in ibid.
[51] COMNAVACTS, Port Lyautey, Memorandum, 30/amc A-17 of August 19, 1957, in ibid.

from individuals, apart from their assigned duties. The last criterion was important, for only in such a context could the dependents of military personnel be effective.

The first step in the navy community-relations program was the inauguration of public visiting aboard the base on Armed Forces Day (May 20, 1957). Captain Phillipe D'Arbois de Jubainville, the French commandant, interposed no objection; in fact, he offered to help with guides and interpreters and proposed flying the American flag alongside that of France at the entrance to the base. Captain Duborg declined the proffered assistance because he said time was running out for the French, and the United States would be caught in the same tide if it identified too closely with the French. As for the flag, he said it was "the most important emotional symbol, the most recognizable symbol of sovereignty existing in any country, and we will not raise that issue here at this time."[52]

The Armed Forces Day celebration was a substantial success. Over four thousand inhabitants of the local community who must have wondered what was behind the high fence and guarded gate found out. They walked through DC-4 airplanes, inspected fire trucks and rubber boats, and sampled hot dogs and ice cream. Local correspondents of Casablanca and Rabat newspapers provided extensive and perhaps the first favorable coverage any United States military installation in Morocco had yet received. The navy high command in London applauded the "accurate assessment of public response which was necessary for the advance planning of this event" and the "execution in detail."

Captain D'Arbois' cooperative attitude smoothed out some of the friction caused by the arbitrary decision of French authorities to use the U.S. Navy dock to unload their military supplies, and the two navies resumed their technical cooperation, particularly in antisubmarine warfare exercises. The new understanding had political overtones, for thereafter the U.S. Navy claimed the authority of its technical agreement of December, 1950, to use the local French commandant, and not the French liaison mission, for liaison with the local officials and community. Assuming a general authorization, the navy continued to handle routine matters—

[52] Interview, Captain Christian H. Duborg, Port Lyautey, May 10, 1957.

broadly interpreted—directly with the cognizant Moroccan authority.

The navy success with its Armed Forces Day revealed the lack of coordinated authority in the American diplomatic-military community. The navy had treated the question of public visitation on the base as a public-affairs matter and had secured the concurrence of the embassy public affairs officer for its plans. The air force had treated it as a political question and had secured the concurrence of the political affairs officer for its nonobservance of the day. In subsequent years the guidance for the air force and navy was consistent—no observance whatever of Armed Forces Day. But the crux of the issue, public visitation, was never resolved and the navy continued to invite the local populace to visit during Orphans' Benefit Day (for the local Moslem orphanages), American Friendship Day, and other days chosen to avoid further conflict or invidious comparison.[53]

Several attempts to foster mass people-to-people contacts between the American and Moroccan communities failed because the cultural differences between the two peoples were too great. For example, the American Boy Scout troops from Port Lyautey and the Sidi Slimane Air Force Base accepted an invitation from the Moroccan Ministry of Youth and Sports to participate in an international scout jamboree at Ras-El-Maa, high in the Atlas Mountains, in the summer of 1957, but the American scoutmasters withdrew their boys before the encampment was over because they said the shower facilities were inadequate and the food unsanitary. (The bread was delivered daily in long, unwrapped French loaves.) On another occasion the American high-school children joined the children from the high schools in Port Lyautey in planting the "Forest of Youth," as it was designated, between Port Lyautey and Rabat. The mobile canteens from the base furnished free hot dogs and cold drinks for all, but, because of the rumor that the hot dogs contained pork, most of the Moroccan children refused to eat them.

The gap between the two communities seemed unbridgeable because there were no institutions in which Americans could asso-

[53] See "History of the 3922 Combat Support Group," May 1–31, 1959, ex. 13, in USAF Archives, file no. K-GP-Supp 3822-H2 file, for measures "to play down in every possible way the existence of our bases," including "no publicity, on or off base . . . for Armed Forces Day."

ciate socially with Moroccans. The fact that Moroccan women did not participate with their husbands in social functions made the American concept of exchanging visits in the home awkward, and the sequestered status of most Moroccan girls, at least of the Islamic faith, precluded any social relationship between them and the American sailors. The differences in faith, except for a limited contact between American and Moroccan Jewish families, ruled out the church as a meeting place.

Mr. Seddik Abou Ibrahimi, the super-caid at Port Lyautey, tried unsuccessfully in the summer of 1957 to rejuvenate the defunct Franco-American Club as the Cercle d'Union Maroc–France–U.S.A. in order to provide a meeting place. The French had organized the club in 1953 and it had enjoyed a temporary success but the American members withdrew during the terrorism and it died. The club possessed an attractive building and adequate facilities in the Mamora Forest on the outskirts of town, but Seddik's efforts were in vain; the three nationalities found no bond of common interest. Only a few Moroccan officials attended the functions of the Cercle, and the Americans were about as welcome to the old French members as a new rooster in the barnyard.[54]

The only substantially significant contact between the Americans and Moroccans in Port Lyautey came through the Moroccan industrial and domestic employees of the military community. Most of them spoke English, and they frequently invited their supervisors, employers, and friends to attend marriages, christenings, or traditional feasts. The naturally curious Americans usually accepted. Their willingness to associate socially with "the servants" widened the gulf between the American and French community and focused American attention on viewpoints of the Moroccan proletariat rather than upon those of a comparable French or Moroccan social or economic class—where language

[54] In September, 1957, Naval Air Reserve Transport Squadron 702 was sent from its home base at Dallas, Texas, to Port Lyautey for a two-week active training period. It held a party at the Cercle to which the French and Moroccan communities were invited. Three Moroccans and about fifty French attended. Most of the expenses for the evening, which included a barbecue dinner, beer and wine, and a dance band, were paid from the squadron welfare fund; however, nonsquadron guests were charged $1.50. The French members of the governing board of the Cercle complained that they were overcharged. All money collected from the French community was then refunded.

would have been a barrier. This orientation resulted in a fundamental sympathy often reflected in navy attitudes, which differed from those of embassy personnel toward the Franco-Moroccan conflict.

The working relationship with Moroccan officials in Port Lyautey and the friendships that evolved were useful in arranging matters of routine importance, but obviously the king was the key to major questions—such as the future of the base itself. The navy therefore moved somewhat uncertainly in the summer of 1957 to establish contact with the royal family. The first opportunity came in June, when a fire destroyed a heavily populated slum suburb at Rabat. The navy base had a large quantity of clothing and bedding provided by World Church Service, which it immediately made available to Princess Aisha, the president of the Entr'aide Nationale, the Moroccan national welfare service. The gesture was well publicized throughout the local community, for the local base radio, certainly the most popular station with the Moroccans in the Port Lyautey area, broadcast news of the fire and made appeals every thirty minutes for American listeners to bring clothing and bedding for the victims to the chapel. The response was significant but perhaps not as massive as it appeared to be when two truckloads of material were delivered within twelve hours after the fire occurred. Thereafter, all of the numerous charitable contributions by the navy community were channeled through the princess, and the contact gradually broadened into a social relationship between the navy community and the princess and her associates.

The Entr'aide Nationale was placed under the supervision of the princess rather than one of the ministries in order to keep it nonpolitical, but the American support did not pass unnoticed by the king, and it led to political contact. Rumors were current early in June that Moulay Hassan, eldest son of the king, would be declared crown prince and successor to the throne on July 9, his twenty-eighth birthday.[55] Princess Aisha confirmed the rumors. How could the Americans appropriately recognize the historic occasion without involving the French? Arrangements were made with Admiral C. R. Brown, commander of the United States Sixth Fleet,

---

[55] Traditionally the *ulema*, a religious electoral college, selected the succeeding monarch from several eligibles when the throne became vacant.

for a naval salute at sea off the Moroccan coast. Ambassador Cannon tendered Admiral Brown's invitation and it was accepted for July 12. Three small transport planes from the aircraft carrier U.S.S. *Forrestal* were flown to Rabat to pick up the crown prince and his party. Press representatives flown from Port Lyautey the evening before were on board to report his arrival, which was delayed two hours because of the pea-soup fog that covered the Rabat airport at the scheduled takeoff time.

The visit and the aerial salute by the air groups on the *Forrestal* were a scintillating success.[56] The press coverage was massive and favorable. Ambassador Cannon said he received the compliments of the entire diplomatic corps in Rabat for days thereafter. Some indication of the impact upon the crown prince is to be found in his decision a year later to adopt the U.S. Navy summer uniform for the newly created Royal Moroccan Navy. The uniforms and accessories, less insignia, were purchased through the Navy Exchange Store at Port Lyautey.[57]

The visible good will expressed in the American relationship with the Entr'aide Nationale and in the public recognition of the crown prince set the stage for contact with King Mohammed V and the evolution of a formula of "nonpolitical" cooperation with Morocco's foremost political figure to achieve distinctly separate but nonconflicting Moroccan and American objectives. The pro-

[56] Ambassador Cavendish W. Cannon letter to Captain Duborg, dated Rabat, August 5, 1957; copy in possession of the author. The only sour note was the intelligence report, filed by the U.S. naval attaché, Captain H. K. Edwards, indicating that the prince was two hours late; the report failed to explain why. Captain Edwards had opposed the visit from the first because he said there was not enough time to prepare for it, and he told the author at the Rabat airport on the morning of July 12, 1957, "I've said all along there wasn't enough time to arrange this affair properly."

[57] A temporary problem in the sale of the uniforms resulted from lack of authorization to accept payment in Moroccan francs. Captain Duborg sent the author to Washington to work out a solution with the United States Treasury Department. In an exchange of letters, both dated August 14, 1957, between the commander of U.S. naval activities, Port Lyautey (signed Leon B. Blair, By Direction), and the comptroller of the navy, the former was authorized to exchange $1,000 per month in Military Payment Certificates for francs, thus legalizing a practice that had existed for more than six months. Copies of the letters are in "Report of Investigation, U.S. Navy Exchange, Port Lyautey," Exhibits 61 and 62, in Federal Records, Center, New York, file no. 148825B.

gram lasted for over three years, long after the conditions for which it was created had changed. It depended upon the U.S. Naval Air Reserve, whose squadrons came monthly from various naval air stations in the United States to Port Lyautey to perform two weeks of required active-duty training. These squadrons needed extensive and glamorizing publicity in their home communities in order to stimulate the recruitment and retention of personnel. The king and palace officials recognized that Morocco lacked a national news service and had no effective voice in the United States. Even Associated Press and United Press International stories emanating from Morocco were edited in Paris before transmission to the United States. The United States needed to create for its bases in Morocco an image that would emphasize a humanitarian and social role and play down the strictly military aspect of its presence. The cooperative program that was developed with the Naval Air Reserve satisfied all three needs.

Operation Tom-Tom (Training Operational Mission to Orphanages in Morocco) of Naval Air Reserve Transport Squadron 702 from Dallas, Texas, was typical. The squadron appealed to the citizens of North Texas through press, radio, and television to give blue jeans and cowboy boots for four thousand orphans in Morocco. The humanitarian aspect resulted in wide coverage, not just in the metropolitan areas but also in the county weekly, college, and even high-school newspapers, calling attention to the fact that someone from the community was flying to a far-off, exotic land with the local Naval Air Reserve squadron. It was an oblique but certain appeal to join the Naval Air Reserve and see the world without a long separation from family, friends, job, or school. In Morocco the reservists were accepted by even the critics of the United States' presence as "different" from the professional military personnel permanently stationed at the bases, and their activities could be publicized without commitment on the question of the bases. The shipment of blue jeans and boots, most of it donated by manufacturers and such service organizations at the Dallas Junior Chamber of Commerce,[58] also contained as presentation items a

[58] The appeal resulted in the donation of much clean, usable, discarded clothing, which was given without publicity to the Entr'aide Nationale to avoid the probable charge by critics of the United States that the gifts were nothing of value. All items presented publicly were new.

Texas hat from Governor Price Daniel for the king and a blue-jean-clad doll for Princess Amina, his four-year-old daughter. The symbolic presentation to the king on September 3, 1957, placed receipt of the entire shipment within the competence of the palace press attaché and his releases assured wide publicity in the Moroccan press, publicity that necessarily included the Port Lyautey naval base, since Captain Duborg appeared in uniform with the king in the photographs. The warm reception given the reservists and the information and facilities that palace officials placed at the disposition of the newsmen accompanying the squadron resulted in substantial reporting in the American press on Moroccan politics, social development, and touristic opportunities after the squadron returned home.[59]

King Mohammed V thanked the Texans personally and sent a letter of gratitude to Governor Price Daniel.[60] But the full impact of the program is better evidenced by the fact that when the king visited the United States in November–December, 1957, he arranged his itinerary so that all stops but one (Offut Air Force Base) were in communities from which a Naval Air Reserve squadron had visited Morocco during the preceding six months. When he stepped from his plane at Dallas' Love Field on November 29, he

---

[59] The scrapbook in the office of the Public Affairs Officer, Naval Air Station, Dallas, Texas, contains twenty-odd stories pertaining to Operation Tom-Tom.

The efforts of Moroccan officials were not always appreciated by diplomatic officials at the United States Embassy. Mr. Mehdi Bennouna, cultural attaché in the Moroccan Royal Cabinet, told Mr. John Treen, of the *Detroit Times*, on July 18, 1958, that he could not understand why the United States would spend millions on the Voice of America radio station at Tangier, which broadcast on such a high frequency that not even 3 percent of the Moroccan radios could receive it, and yet allow the American school at Tangier, the student body of which was more than half Moroccan, to close for lack of funds. Mr. Bennouna, a director of the school, made his statement to a representative of a Detroit newspaper as a deliberate play for Ford Foundation funds for the school, but when diplomatic officials challenged his account as published in the *Detroit Times*, he refused to modify his statement or say he was misquoted. "I've said the same thing to you, Mr. Ambassador, and I have said it to Mr. Dulles, himself," he insisted. The interview took place in the author's home, and Mr. Bennouna related the repercussions to the author in an interview at Rabat, July 25, 1957.

[60] Mohammed ben Youssef, king of Morocco, letter to Governor Price Daniel of Texas, dated Rabat, September 3, 1957; copy in possession of the author.

said his visit to Texas was "not something that just happened," that he had yearned to visit Texas since "some months ago [when] Governor Price Daniel sent me a cowboy hat and regalia for my little girl."[61]

Variations on Operation Tom-Tom included three prize-winning Columbia sheep, a ram, and two ewes donated by the Future Farmers of America and accepted by Prime Minister Bekkai for the Moroccan nation. Moroccan ewes were added to this unit to see if the flocking instinct for which the Columbia breed was created would be transmitted to the crossbred Moroccan sheep. The king responded to the gift with a deep-pile Moroccan carpet, woven while the squadron from Minneapolis, Minnesota, was in Morocco for Governor Orville Freeman of Minnesota. The design in Arabic script spelled out a message: "A remembrance to the people of Minnesota."

Other gifts were a ton of Northrup-King hybrid corn seed, which was used to provide experimental data for the production of hybrid corn in the Doukkala region of Morocco; budded paper-shell pecan trees and native nuts for seedlings as the basis for new agricultural production in the Rif Mountains; an Onan generator for a back-country hospital; fifty thousand pencils for Moroccan schoolchildren; seven tons of "Multi-Purpose Food," a high-protein food supplement produced by the Meals for Millions Foundation, for Algerian refugee camps and tuberculosis hospitals; antibiotics; and Braille equipment for the blind. Almost every shipment contained some item well suited to public presentation; for example, a Western riding outfit from Neiman-Marcus in Dallas was presented to Princess Aisha with a shipment of clothing for Entr'aide Nationale and a chronometer to Princess Malika with a shipment of antibiotics for the Moroccan Red Crescent (similar to the Red Cross).[62]

The coordination of the visits of the reserve squadrons led to a closer association between palace officials and navy officials at Port Lyautey, as the former turned to the latter for information and

[61] The *Dallas Morning News, Washington Post,* and *New York Times,* all of November 30, 1957.

[62] See Commander, Naval Activities, Port Lyautey, Kenitra, Morocco, *People to People Report,* for reproductions of Moroccan news coverage of the gift of the sheep and carpet. *Time* 75 (June 6, 1969): 30, refers to such presentations, but without identifying them as a part of a much larger presentation.

sometimes advice. For example, the navy made suggestions and furnished information concerning the king's itinerary in the United States during his visit, and Lieutenant Commander Blair spent four evenings at the palace in the fortnight prior to the king's departure helping Mr. Abderrahman Anegai, the chief of the Royal Cabinet, polish up the English-language text of the major speeches that the king would deliver in the United States. The speeches had been prepared in Arabic and Mr. Anegai had translated them into English, but the language was sometimes a bit stilted for press release. Another problem resulted from the printer's delay in completing the king's official biography.[63] It did not come off the presses until November 20, less than a week before his scheduled departure, and there was no way to get it to Washington in time for distribution before his arrival except by a navy transport plane out of Port Lyautey. From such association extended over the next three years an identity emerged for the navy base that was distinct from the air force bases and from the United States Embassy.

The press was the key to the changing image. The French newspapers in Morocco had been consistently hostile toward the Americans. *Le Petit Marocain*, for example, had reported the "rape" of a French prostitute—four times in one hour—by a drunken Marine in much the same terms it probably would have reported the burning of Joan of Arc by the English.[64] The favorable coverage given the Sixth Fleet venture indicated the possibility of a more cooperative relationship. The navy at Port Lyautey proposed to invite reporters from Moroccan newspapers and radio stations, French-language as well as Arabic, to travel to Washington as guests of the United States Navy to cover the arrival and state visit of King Mohammed V. After the king's departure from Washington the journalists would have a week free to do as they liked and then return to Port Lyautey aboard another navy transport plane. All expenses except transportation and en route conveniences would be the individual's responsibility. The Navy Department in Washington initially rejected the proposal because of "foreseeable complications," but agreed to Captain Duborg's second proposal, which

63 Rom Landau, *Mohammed V, King of Morocco.*

64 "Odious Aggression in the Mamora Forest against a Young Girl Kidnapped in Rabat," *Le Petit Marocain*, September 23, 1953. The rape charge was dismissed, but the defendant was fined for disorderly conduct.

argued the advantages in "protecting this hundred million dollar investment," provided he would send an escort charged with "full responsibility for those invited."

Fourteen newspapers and radio stations accepted the invitation.[65] None of the journalists had been in the United States previously. Seven of them spoke English, and all but one spoke French. They were about equally divided between the three major press centers in Morocco—Casablanca, Rabat, and Tangier. For a time it appeared that the palace press attaché might veto participation by the Arabic-language press if the French papers were invited but he finally accepted the idea of allowing the various editors to nominate "suitable" reporters. Upon arrival at Norfolk the group was given a briefing on the mission and capabilities of the United States Navy and a visit through the naval base, but no attempt was made to guide or influence their reporting.

At Washington they followed closely the king's itinerary, but did little reporting. The wire services would have beaten them with the factual stories anyway, and the cable charges were too expensive for interpretative reporting. Upon their return to Morocco they provided the most extensive and laudatory coverage of the American scene ever to appear in the press of a foreign country.

Ambassador Cannon recognized the Moroccan journalists' contribution: "I have become acutely aware of the important role which the Navy has played in making this visit a success. I find that at least twenty-five per cent of the total coverage given the King's tour in the Moroccan press and radio, including five major series of newspaper articles and four series of radio programs, resulted directly from the group of fourteen Moroccan journalists which were sent to the United States under Navy auspices."[66]

[65] They were Mustapha Abdallah of Radio Tangier; Moulay Mustapha El Alaoui, editor of *Al Ahd El Jadiid*; Mustapha El Alaoui, editor of *El Machaaid*; Ahmed Benghitti, *Er Rai El Am*; Mehdi At Tazi of Radio Africa; Tayeb Filali, *Al Ataalia*; Kacem Zhiri, director of Radio Maroc; Bertrand Bellaigue, Radio Africa/Agence France Presse; Pierre Guillemot, Agence Central Presse; Jacques Latscha, *Le Petit Casablancais*; Michel Oger, *L'Echo du Maroc*; Marcel Herzog, *La Vigie Marocaine*; Gilbert De Simpel, *Le Petit Marocain*; and Ahmed Benzacour, *Seanfilm*.

[66] Ambassador Cavendish W. Cannon letter to Captain C. H. Duborg, dated Rabat, January 14, 1958, copy in possession of the author. The articles concerned such diverse subjects as the makeup and content of a Sunday newspaper

The importance of the navy's role was not apparent in 1957, nor were the consequences predictable because the anti-American forces had not yet surfaced. But the indications were there. The coalition that had won Moroccan independence began to crack almost as soon as independence became a reality, and the rift was clearly evident during the National Consultative Assembly debate on foreign policy on the eve of the king's departure. The Istiqlal party reasserted its demand for a government of "party responsibility" from which nonparty members would be excluded. The focus of the attack was upon Reda Guedira and Rachid Moline, both Liberal Independents, both members of the old Roosevelt Club, and both pro-American.[67] In such a context it was not surprising to see the Istiqlal party zero in on the American bases.

Ahmed Balafrej was torn between the two factions. A party leader since the very birth of the Istiqlal, he too desired a single-party government, but he was also the foreign minister whose policy was being criticized. He tried to prevent a rupture on the base question, which after all was only incidental to the party rivalry. He said it was possible to regulate the problem of foreign troops and bases, but that Morocco did not intend to be tied to problems of mutual defense, "as has been proposed" [by Ambassador Cannon in May]. For the first time he spoke in terms, no longer of "legalizing" the status of the bases, but of "the basic problem: the existence of the bases themselves."[68] He did not specifically link the

---

in Washington, an interview with Admiral Arleigh Burke, chief of naval operations, at the Pentagon, and American attitudes toward drinking whiskey on Sunday, the racial question, and communism. Gilbert De Simpel, in the last of a series of thirteen articles totaling about thirty columns in *Le Petit Marocain*, December 22, 1957, concluded that the trip would never be over for him because of the memories engendered. He noted his surprise at the openness of the American society, "the absence of any iron curtain, . . . the concern for the liberty of others . . . and the sense of fair play that the Americans seem to possess to a high degree." He said "the American is very clearly anti-Communist," but not anti-Russian, and that "he absolutely does not desire war, but he will not hesitate to fight one if he feels that his liberty is menaced, for he loves it as much as he loves his country, and that is saying a great deal."

[67] See *Al Istiqlal*, October 19, and *Al Alam*, October 20, 1957, for criticism of Moline's statement praising the American bases as an element of equilibrium in Morocco.

[68] *Realisations et perspectives*, pp. 128–131.

American bases to the oft-repeated demand for the withdrawal of French and Spanish troops, but two weeks later he indicated the direction the wind blew when he spoke to newsmen of a "temporary solution" for two or three years that would leave Morocco with "freedom of choice." He sought to placate American concern with the assurance that Morocco would remain uncommitted to any bloc. He recognized that a demand for immediate evacuation would be tantamount to an alliance with the Soviet bloc.[69]

The debate in the Consultative Assembly was a challenge not only to the leadership of Ahmed Balafrej, but also to that of the king, who hoped to resolve the debate with a speedy agreement between himself and President Eisenhower.[70] Mohammed V failed to achieve any of his objectives. He was overwhelmingly disillusioned when he asked for United States support for Franco-Algerian negotiations on the basis of self-determination and got only Secretary of State Dulles' vague expression of hope for a "peaceful, democratic, and just solution" to the problem.[71] Nor had he reached an agreement on the bases, or on economic and technical aid for Morocco, including help in establishing a small-arms manufacturing capacity and a plant for making uniforms for the Royal Moroccan Army. He came home, a politician in trouble in his own country, with empty hands.

At the Washington airport upon his arrival, November 25, King Mohammed V again spoke of Morocco as a bridge between the East and the West; it was his last use of that metaphor. When he returned to Morocco, he turned to an "African policy" for Morocco. In retrospect, President Eisenhower's illness during the visit was perhaps a blessing. Mohammed V, who tended to measure the authority of the president by his own yardstick, remained unshaken in his conviction that his failure occurred only because he was not able to discuss the problems directly with the other chief of state.[72]

Mohammed V's new policy did not imply hostility toward the United States or toward the bases; it was simply a realistic appraisal of what was possible and a revision of priorities. His paramount concern was the impact of the Algerian war upon Morocco's

[69] *New York Times*, November 23, 1957, p. 3.
[70] Ibid., November 25, 1957, p. 1.
[71] Ibid., November 28, 1957, p. 2.
[72] His Majesty so indicated several times to the author in 1958–1959.

new and precarious independence. He had little time or energy for that which did not contribute directly and visibly to its consolidation. He was content to leave less important questions to subordinates. His apparent lack of interest, however, was interpreted in American circles as vacillating weakness at best and perhaps as downright unfriendliness,[73] and the inherent republican attitudes of the American diplomatic colony gradually hardened into an antimonarchial position. Mohammed V's failure at personal diplomacy threw the question of the American bases into the political arena and Moroccan-American relations entered a negative phase that lasted for the next two years.

[73] Interview, Ambassador Charles W. Yost, Rabat, October 27, 1958, and Ambassador Yost's telegram to the State Department of November 25, 1958, doc. no. 48, in "History of Headquarters United States Air Force in Europe," January 1–December 31, 1958, vol. III: Supporting Documents, USAF Archives, file no. K 570.01.

10. Anti-Americanism?

MOST ANALYSES OF RELATIONS between the United States and Morocco after the latter gained its independence in 1956 have been in terms of the American military bases, and these studies generally have equated the pressure for evacuation with a growth of anti-American sentiment in the Moroccan masses. Such oversimplification is misleading. Anti-Americanism was never significant in Morocco. The pressure for evacuation resulted from the failure of traditional diplomacy to understand and cope with the unusual conditions created by the presence of the large American military community in Morocco.

As the United States' diplomatic position worsened, schisms appeared in the politico-military relationships in Morocco. They emanated from personality clashes, inadequately defined objectives, and uncertain authority resulting in the various United States agencies in Morocco working at cross-purposes. These schisms began, coincidentally, in December, 1957, and thus complicated the diplomatic situation produced by the failure of King Mohammed V's mission to the United States. They began with the retirement of Captain Christian H. Duborg as the commander of U.S. naval activities at Port Lyautey.

Captain Duborg was a naval aviator, a graduate of the United States Naval Academy in the class of 1924. An experienced and senior navy commander, he was rushed in April, 1954, into the double command of all naval activities at Port Lyautey and of the U.S. Naval Air Station, the largest of more than a dozen subordinate commands, in order to preempt the top job for the aviation branch of the navy.[1] During the turbulent years of the terrorism, he had managed to retain the esteem of the French and also to develop friendships with some of the leading Moroccan nationalists. He was scheduled for retirement on June 30, 1957, upon completion of thirty years of commissioned service. Ahmed Balafrej, perhaps unduly apprehensive of new faces, asked Ambassador Cannon to intervene with the United States government in order that Captain Duborg might remain at his post until the status of the bases was settled. The ambassador relayed the foreign minister's request to Washington where the Navy Department requested and received congressional authorization to continue him in command beyond his statutory retirement date.[2]

Captain Duborg had repeatedly recommended that command of the naval activities be divorced from that of any subordinate command, and in June his recommendation was approved. Captain Eugene Dare was ordered in as commander of the Naval Air Station. Inexperienced in command and plagued by personal problems, Captain Dare found it difficult to work for a superior who knew the details of the operation of the Naval Air Station far more intimately than he, and Captain Duborg perhaps found it difficult to relinquish the habit of command at the time he surrendered the

[1] Captain Duborg's date of rank preceded that of Captain J. A. H. Tuthill, USNR, who was commander of the naval communications facility, the second largest subordinate command. Captain Tuthill was not an aviator and was, in addition, a reserve officer, which did not disqualify him for the top command but evoked no enthusiasm from regular navy officers.

[2] See *Navy Times*, June 4, 1957, for a report of the congressional action. Captain Duborg was termed "just too valuable to let go . . . because he is taking a vital part in negotiations for military base rights in Morocco."

authority. The two were not on good terms, and in September
Captain Dare reported irregularities in the operation of the Navy
Exchange Store that reflected upon Captain Duborg's personal integrity. A navy board of investigation cleared Captain Duborg of
any personal wrongdoing, but "slapped him on the wrist" for inadequate supervision of the Navy Exchange and belatedly retired
him. Captain Dare was relieved of his command a few weeks later, and a new team took over at Port Lyautey.

Captain John L. Counihan, the new commander of naval activities, was an outspoken individual who was openly critical of the
ambassador's role in retaining Captain Duborg in command at
Port Lyautey. Ron Moxness, the embassy press officer, at a public
affairs conference in Paris in early 1958, informally brought the
resulting conflict to the attention of Admiral J. L. Holloway, the
navy commander for Europe. Admiral Holloway wrote a caution-
ary letter to Captain Counihan.

The incident destroyed the rather informal working relationship
that had previously existed at staff levels in the embassy and at
Port Lyautey. It evoked the question of the authority of subordinate embassy officials over base programs that might have political
consequences that would be reflected in the Moroccan press. The
basic conflict was never resolved, and questions that subsequently
arose, if not important enough to be referred to the embassy, were
usually left in limbo.

The navy proposal to expand the interpretative reporting of the
American scene began by the navy-sponsored visit of the Moroccan
journalists at the time of King Mohammed V's visit to the United
States was an example. The navy proposed to invite two Moroccan
journalists to accompany one of the Naval Air Reserve Squadrons
back to its home community, where they would spend a week, then
be flown by the Naval Air Reserve to the home station of the
squadron next scheduled for deployment to Morocco. There they
would participate in the precruise publicity and become familiar
with a second American community. Upon their return to Morocco with the second squadron they would be able to aid the
American newspapermen accompanying the squadron in interpreting Moroccan events and scenes for American audiences. All of
the Moroccan journalists would have been on assignment from
their papers or radio stations; the navy was only proposing to fur-

nish transportation on planes already scheduled and extend normal courtesies en route. Both the United States and Morocco would benefit from the greater understanding of each other.

The State Department blocked the proposal, and, for good measure, discontinued further visits by American newsmen to Morocco. According to a departmental spokesman, "it has been our policy to block most Defense-sponsored trips of American news media to Morocco," because "even with the best briefing in the world . . . one can't control what the press actually will write."[3] The prohibition was not totally effective, because some of the uniformed reservists were working newspapermen in civilian life, and they continued to report, but the scale of coverage was reduced.

The United States also missed an opportunity to help shape the Moroccan labor movement, because of ill-defined objectives and lack of decisive leadership. The labor movement was new and lacked deep-rooted traditions. French unions had existed since 1943, but they were communist dominated and therefore repugnant to the Moroccans—who were legally ineligible to join, anyway. French noncommunist unions had significant membership but it was almost all French; if the unions had any Moroccan members, the leadership was always French, and it provided no training to the Moroccan element in union methods or procedures.

The Union Marocaine du Travail (UMT), like Topsy, "just grew" out of clandestine Istiqlal unions organized by Tayeb ben Bouazza and Mahjoub ben Seddik in 1954 and thereafter. The movement remained under cover until January, 1955, when Tayeb ben Bouazza, as spokesman for an "organization committee for the establishment of trade unionism in Morocco," published a demand for legislation permitting all workers to form trade unions and to select their representatives "in conformance with the principles of the international convention on the liberty of trade union organizations." A later release proclaimed membership open to all workers regardless of creed or nationality. On March 21, 1955, the UMT was organized in Casablanca with Mahjoub ben Seddik as president and Tayeb ben Bouazza as secretary-general. It de-

3 Rupert Prohme letter to Les Squires, public affairs officer at the U.S. Embassy, Rabat, undated, Department of State, Washington, in reply to Mr. Squires' letter of April 28, 1959, and written prior to Mr. Prohme's departure for Alexandria, Egypt, "at the end of June"; copy in possession of the author.

clared its intention of affiliating with the International Confederation of Free Trade Unions and not with the World Confederation of Trade Unions, which was "of Communist persuasion," the press release said. On May 15, the ICFTU international congress, meeting in Vienna under the chairmanship of Irving Brown, an American, officially recognized the UMT as a member.[4]

On September 12, Resident-General Boyer de Latour promulgated a *dahir* authorizing the establishment of Moroccan trade unions, and the UMT embarked on a concentrated membership drive that succeeded in emptying the French unions of their Moroccan membership. The new unions were handicapped by lack of experience and were dependent upon European leadership and training. Their communiqués were couched in Marxist terminology of "the working class and the capitalist companies," but the UMT was not communist dominated.

In early 1956 the UMT organized the Union Syndical des Bases Americains (USBA), which, in February, presented the Americans with the first demands by organized labor.[5] Mahjoub ben Seddik requested a meeting with General Frederick Glantzberg, commander of the Seventeenth Air Force, who sought the advice of United States Consul William Porter, at Rabat as to who should receive Seddik. Should it be Glantzberg, his representative, the French Liaison Office, or the French intendant? He sought Porter's advice instead of that of higher military headquarters because Porter had direct access to the State Department, while decisions concerning Morocco were usually "short-circuited" in Paris if the question was submitted via the complicated chain of military command. But Porter as usual "shied away from military problems," and the State Department "was unable to help with advice."[6] Glantzberg met Seddik, but required him to submit his demands through the

[4] All information concerning the trade-union movement, not otherwise identified, is from "History of the Seventeenth Air Force," January–December, 1956, vol. III, appendix 3, document 10 ("The Labor Movement in Morocco") in USAF Archives, file no. K 573.01. A detailed account of the growth of the labor movement in Morocco is contained in Douglas E. Ashford, *Political Change in Morocco*, pp. 270–300.

[5] "History of the Seventeenth Air Force," January–December, 1956, vol. 3, app. 3, doc. no. 7.

[6] "History of the Seventeenth Air Force," January–December, 1956, vol. III, app. 3, doc. no. 6, report no. 4, dated January 11, 1956.

French intendant and the French Liaison Office. He refused Seddik's request to "treat directly with the Americans."[7]

Seddik's demands related to the "innate dignity of the workers" —protests against racial discrimination in salaries and employment, family benefits, and increases in salaries and fringe benefits. The French residency officials took the position that the demanded wage raises to 120 francs (thirty cents) per hour would bankrupt the economy. The United States refused to exceed the local economy wage rate or to recognize any one union as the sole bargaining agent, but compromised on the wage demand at sixty-seven francs per hour, an increase of ten francs.[8]

The accord was short-lived. In April the USBA was back with demands for a flat salary increase of 5,000 francs ($14.30) per month for all workers, a 34 percent raise for the lowest paid workers and an average raise of 17 percent. The increases would cost the United States armed forces about one million dollars per year. The strike from April 9–13 was almost 100 percent effective and resulted in an agreement to begin negotiations on a new wage scale and a two-year contract specifying wages parallel to those paid by local industry. The strikers were to be paid for the four days they were out on strike. They finally received an increase of about 10 percent.[9]

In January, 1956, the Seventeenth Air Force Standing Policy Advisory Committee tried to bring the navy into line with the air force on labor policy. The navy had resisted indirect hire through a French intendant until forced by the decision of Secretary of Defense Wilson to accept the Cook-Leduc Agreement of January 22, 1955. The navy was not particularly enthusiastic about labor unions, and the Cook-Leduc Agreement made no provision for them, but obviously a policy was now necessary. The air force recognized the USBA, but set up advisory councils for those individuals who did not wish to join a union—a concession to the non-Moroccans who held the higher-paying jobs. The navy opposed recognition of the USBA, the establishment of advisory councils,

[7] Ibid., report nos. 9, dated February 8, and 10, dated March 2, 1956.

[8] Ibid., report no. 9, dated February 8, and doc. no. 7, dated March 25, 1956; see also *Le Petit Marocain*, February 19, 1956.

[9] *New York Times*, April 9, 1956, p. 5, April 13, 1956, p. 3, and June 22, 1956, p. 3.

and the operation by the Moroccan government of an indirect hire system. The navy contended such steps would involve the union in the selection of employees, discriminate against French and Jewish employees, and not work anyway because the Moroccan government lacked the administrative experience to operate it.[10] Although the navy never established the advisory councils, it was compelled to accept a Moroccan government-operated indirect hire system similar to the Cook-Leduc Agreement when the French intendant system was dismantled on June 30, 1959.

The changing mood of the Moroccan nation was mirrored in the attitudes of the labor leaders. In November, 1956, Abdelhadi Bel Hadj, secretary-general of the USBA, said in connection with a strike threat against use of "French Morocco" on signs on the bases and on the base radio broadcasts, "We are interested in our demands, but we do not want the Americans to leave Morocco. They have done a great deal for our country."[11] Abdallah Ibrahim, Moroccan minister of labor and social questions, opposed a reduction in the labor forces at the bases because of the economic crisis and unemployment.[12] Eighteen months later Abdallah Ibrahim was a vocal advocate of evacuation, and Bel Hadj, although still demanding a stop in the reduction of forces, urged the workers to accept without protest their dismissals as a patriotic duty.[13]

A great part of the labor unrest in the USBA and the UMT was not associated with wage demands or working conditions, but was a reflection of the national inferiority complex emanating from racial discrimination by the French. Complaints and threats of strikes because of alleged slights to Moroccan honor or insulting treatment of Moroccan workers were common.[14] Some of the incidents that ought to have been settled locally reached international proportions.

One incident occurred on January 31, 1958, when a B-47

10 "History of the Seventeenth Air Force," January–December, 1956, vol. III, app. 3, doc. no. 6, and "History of Detachment Two," January–June, 1957, pp. 44–49, in USAF Archives, file no. K 570.071c.

11 *New York Times*, November 10, 1956, p. 9.

12 "History of Detachment Two," January–June, 1957, pp. 47–48.

13 "History of the Seventeenth Air Force," 1958, vol. III, letter in appendix dated July 28, 1958, signed by A. T. Wellborn, counselor of the embassy, Rabat.

14 See *New York Times*, August 9, 1957, p. 4, and December 30, 1957, for examples.

crashed and burned at Sidi Slimane Air Force Base. American, but not the Moroccan, workers were evacuated from the base. The roads were clogged in all directions with bumper-to-bumper traffic—heavy American automobiles. That something was amiss seemed obvious, but the Moroccan authorities were not informed. Rumors of an atomic bomb in the burning wreckage soon reached Rabat. King Mohammed V called the super-caid at Kenitra and asked him to investigate. Mr. Seddik immediately drove thirty miles to Sidi Slimane and asked to see Colonel Williams, the base commander, but was refused admission. Chagrined, he was compelled to report the circumstances of his failure.[15]

The Sidi Slimane incident was a turning point in the Moroccan attitude toward the bases. The air force and the embassy press releases treated the evacuation as a practice alert. The American press killed the story. The French-language press accepted the official version, although perhaps with tongue in cheek. *L'Echo du Maroc* congratulated the Americans on their sense of realism. Who else, it said a few days after the accident, would burn a B-47 on the runway and close the field for three days for the sake of realism in a practice alert. The Arabic-language press treated the matter as an atomic catastrophe fraught with danger, the peg upon which advocates of closing the bases hung their propaganda.[16]

Local criticism of the incident might have been weathered if it had not been coupled with other irritants. Sidi Slimane was a small town in a relatively isolated part of the Rharb Valley, and the bomber incident was over before it became general knowledge. There was no explosion, and radioactivity was beyond the comprehension of the average Moroccan, but a flag incident in Casablanca, less serious but better known, weighed heavily on Moroccan public opinion. Prior to 1958, a United States naval ship operated by the Military Sea Transportation Service flew the Moroccan flag while in port, just as if it had been a civil commercial vessel.[17] In Jan-

15 Interview, Seddik Abou Ibrahimi, Kenitra, February 1, 1958. See "History of Headquarters United States Air Force, Europe," January 1–December 31, 1958, vol. 3, doc. nos. 32-A and 32-C for confirmation.

16 *New York Times*, May 23, 1958, p. 3.

17 According to a Department of Navy, Military Sea Transportation Service letter to the author, dated Washington, December 31, 1964, no USN ship ever flew the Moroccan flag, but that information apparently is in error.

uary, 1958, Commander Bernard M. Kassell assumed command of the Military Sea Transportation Service office in Casablanca. He was aware of MSTS policy that classified the United States naval ships in the same category as warships; they therefore were not required or expected under international law to fly the Moroccan flag in port. Commander Kassell requested advice from the embassy and, failing to receive it, ordered the U.S.N.S. *Callan*, which arrived on February 3, not to hoist the Moroccan flag. The ship unloaded and departed without incident. On February 7 the MSTS tanker U.S.N.S. *Mission Loreto* unloaded under similar circumstances, although a ship chandler in the port warned the master of the vessel that he "would get no work done" without hoisting the flag. Thereafter none of the USNS ships hoisted the Moroccan flag, but there were no protests until the arrival of the U.S.N.S. *Short Splice* at the end of May. [18] It too might have been unloaded without incident except for the governmental crisis of April 17, which forced the resignation of Si Bekkai and the pro-American members of his government. Ahmed Balafrej was appointed prime minister on May 12. The longshoremen sought an issue to use against him. They treated the refusal to fly the Moroccan flag as an insult to the national honor and refused to unload the ship, nor would they accept an explanation of the previous American policy as a mistake.

The consequences were grave. Mr. Balafrej considered the squabble of little importance. He suggested that the USNS ships be diverted into Port Lyautey until the matter was settled, and, when told that such a measure was not practicable,[19] offered to unload the ships with service troops from the Moroccan army.[20] The United States was not willing to compromise its new-found sense of rectitude. Ambassador Cannon feared that the United States would be caught in the middle of a showdown between the union, bent on embarrassing its own government, and the govern-

[18] Bernard M. Kassell letter to the author, dated Washington, February 26, 1965, in which he quotes his diary of the events recorded as they happened.

[19] "History of Headquarters United States Air Force, Europe," January 1–December 31, 1958, vol. III: Supporting Documents, document no. 43, dated June 6, 1958, in USAF Archives, file no. K 570.01.

[20] Ibid., doc. no. 44, dated June 26, 1958.

ment of Morocco.[21] The U.S. Air Force feared the spread of labor unrest from the port to the bases themselves and considered the ship stoppages as less threatening.[22] The navy felt that economic pressure generated by the loss of employment for the longshoremen would bring the union to terms.[23] The *Short Splice* departed without unloading, and the *Maurice Rose*, scheduled to dock at Casablanca on June 12, was diverted to Gibraltar. No further ships were to be scheduled into Casablanca "until the labor situation returned to normal."[24] It never did. The United States' action presented a victory to that element in Morocco most hostile to the monarchy, most divisive in the Istiqlal party, and most insistent on the evacuation of the American bases, and it was a factor in the progressive alienation of the king and of more moderate Istiqlal leaders, such as Balafrej.[25]

Lack of mutual support between agencies of the United States government was nowhere more evident than with respect to the labor situation on the bases. From the time that Americans first set foot on the beaches at Mehdia, the wage differential between Moroccan and French employees at the American bases had been a sore point with the Moroccans. The non-Moroccan work force was not only better paid for the same work but also monopolized most of the better jobs. At Nouasseur Air Force Base non-American employees constituted 55 percent of the work force; 41 percent Moroccan, 9 percent French, and 5 percent non-French European. Moroccan Moslems held only 2 of the 60 highest paying jobs; Moroccan Jews, 11; non-French Europeans, 16; and French, 31. Of the 647 lowest-paying jobs, Moroccan Moslems held 99 percent; Moroccan Jews, less than 1 percent; and Europeans, only one of the 647.[26]

[21] Ibid.

[22] Ibid., doc. no. 43.

[23] Conference at the Naval Air Station, Port Lyautey, June 6, 1958, at which the author was present.

[24] Department of the Navy, Military Sea Transportation Service, letter to the author dated Washington, December 31, 1964.

[25] For less critical interpretations, which ignore the change of policy aspect, see I. William Zartman, *Morocco: Problems of New Power*, pp. 41–42, and *New York Times*, June 12, 1958, p. 62.

[26] "History of the Seventeenth Air Force," January–December, 1956, vol. III, app. 3, doc. no. 8, dated December 12, 1955.

The French intendant justified the discrimination on the grounds that Moroccans were "untrainable," an untenable position, for the growing economic nationalism in Morocco doomed the existing labor policies. Moroccans had to be trained, and the Americans had sufficient experience to know that they were readily trainable.

In the fall of 1957, in order to demonstrate training methods, the navy literally picked seven eighteen-year-old Moroccans off the streets in Kenitra and offered them a course in motor mechanics. The only criteria for selection were age, at least six years of schooling, and a physical examination. They were promised instruction, their noon meal, and work clothes. If they completed the course satisfactorily, they were to receive their chauffeur's license, but the navy accepted no obligation to provide employment, nor were the students obligated to the navy in any way. The standard course for navy construction driver, third class, was used as the basis of instruction, but it was expanded from four to five weeks in order to provide time for two hours per day of instruction in English. At the end of the five weeks all had completed the course and received the chauffeur's license, and all could understand simple instructions in English.[27]

The school attracted considerable attention. Representative Frances Bolton of the House Committee on Foreign Affairs visited it and concluded that it represented an effective and economical way of providing much-needed technical training for Morocco. A training mission from the United States Agency for International Development headed by Edward Lull studied the school as a prototype for a technical training school programmed by that agency for Morocco. He observed that, since the navy was not training for its own use, the legality of the school was doubtful; such training should be provided if at all by the AID mission. Using the Port Lyautey experience, AID established a school in Casablanca, completely divorced from any of the bases and facilities that could have been provided at infinitely less cost. A year later the school had a building, equipment, and staff, but few students. The entrance requirements were so high that candidates with enough education to qualify did not apply. They were not interested in becoming mechanics.

[27] See Commander Naval Activities, Port Lyautey, Kenitra, Morocco, *People to People Report*, p. 44, for photograph and description of the class.

The failure to make the military bases a prime objective of American foreign policy resulted in a general lack of cooperation by the other executive departments. The United States Information Service consistently rejected appeals for a USIS library in Kenitra, although it operated others in Casablanca, Marrakech, Rabat, Tangier, and Fez. Logic indicated that Kenitra should have been the first. It had the largest American population and probably the largest English-speaking Moroccan population of any Moroccan city. The city officials had frequently appealed for one, even offering to furnish the building and utilities, but were rebuffed with the statement that no funds were available. The USIS was, however, struggling to open a library in Fez, where the city officials were indifferent and the French population hostile to the penetration of American culture. To navy appeals USIS officials replied, "We leave that to the navy."[28] Eventually the library was built upon a site provided by the city of Kenitra, from materials provided jointly by the city and navy surplus, and with labor paid for by individual contributions from the American community of Kenitra. Most of the books were provided by communities in the United States and were transported to Morocco by the Naval Air Reserve squadrons. The librarian, a Moroccan, was paid from funds generated at the Navy Exchange Store on purchases by Moroccan army and other Moroccan government officials. The reluctance of USIS to establish a library in Kenitra is perhaps best explained by a comment of Ron Moxness to Mustapha Alaoui, editor of *El Machaaid*, a monthly picture magazine similar to *Look* or *Life*. Alaoui asked why USIS did not caption their window displays in English as well as French and Arabic "so I can get my daily English lessons as I walk by." Moxness told him, "You'd never get up to the window; there would be too many Americans around it."[29]

Although the library served a useful function in Kenitra, the most effective agency for establishing contact between the American and Moroccan-French community was the American Red Cross Center, located in an old Moroccan U-shaped house built

[28] Both Les Squires, embassy public affairs officer, and Ron Moxness, embassy press officer, so expressed themselves to the author many times in 1958–1959.

[29] The author was present.

around a courtyard-garden across the street from the Lycée Abdelmalek as Saadi. The director of the center had to minimize the international aspect, for the center was primarily a recreational facility for enlisted American servicemen, and most of its activities were directed to their interests.

The concept of the recreation center as an organ of international understanding, justified with the passage of time, originated with Mary Louise Dowling, national director of the Supplemental Recreational Activities Overseas (SRAO) program and her staff and Department of the Air Force personnel who were interested in strengthening community relations. The World War II Red Cross rest and recreation camps had been phased out during 1946–1947 and closed by 1948. General MacArthur in Korea and the U.S. Air Force in England, France, and Morocco asked that they be reestablished, but the Red Cross felt the basic need had changed. Learning to live in a new and strange culture or in isolation (as in Korea) and not combat fatigue was the nemesis of the single serviceman or one whose family did not come overseas with him in the mid-1950's.[30] The Red Cross SRAO program helped meet both needs. It was officially ratified by the Pentagon in September, 1954, although it was actually operating earlier in Korea.[31]

In developing a program that would appeal to the single serviceman, the Red Cross used people rather than props and equipment to build a successful program within a limited budget.[32] The center was therefore located, not on the base where access by the local community would have been restricted, but in Kenitra, where transportation could readily be provided for the users. The center profited from its location near the lycée because it drew alert, educated, late-teen-age visitors, and the community tended to place this new, strange activity in a cultural and not a military context —otherwise, it rationalized, why was it across from the school? The Kenitra Center[33] opened in March, 1954, and had 378 visitors that month. In May it had 3,500, and it reached its peak of 5,496 in

[30] Interview, Mary Louise Dowling, Washington, D.C., March 22, 1967.

[31] Department of Defense Directive 1330.5, dated September 27, 1954, in American Red Cross Archives, Washington, D.C.

[32] Interview, Mary Louise Dowling, March 22, 1967.

[33] Similar centers operated in Marrakech, July 31, 1954, to May 1, 1957, and Rabat, August, 1955, to May 1, 1959.

January, 1956. It operated seven days a week from 1–11 P.M. except
on Saturdays, Sundays, and holidays when it opened at 10 A.M.
Political tensions affected attendance, as in July, 1954, when terrorist activity in Kenitra dropped attendance to 146 visitors, or in February, 1956, when the navy and the air force, anticipating violence, restricted their personnel to the bases. But the average
monthly level of attendance was about 3,500. A typical breakdown
of the visitors (in December, 1959) showed that 2,157 of them
were U.S. servicemen; 41 were servicemen of other forces, presumably French and Moroccan; 271 were U.S. civilians, including
teachers and service dependents; and 872 were civilian personnel
from the local community.[34]

The activities of the centers were diversified. Servicemen and
guests learned to sing, cook, and cha-cha-cha. Overcoming the language barrier, they staged musical and dramatic productions, parties, and dances; played pinochle, bridge, and Scrabble; and went
on excursions. If a visitor simply wanted to sit in the garden and
meditate or listen to a record, the facilities were available. If he
wanted to ride a bicycle or strum a guitar, he could check one out.
If he or she wanted to learn Arabic, French, or English, volunteer
instructors were available. Whole organizations, ranging from
Moroccan, French, and American musical combos to the Kenitra
Fencing Club, participated in the center's program. In the month
of January, 1956, seventy events were provided for the 5,496 visitors, and coffee and cool soft drinks helped to establish a friendly
atmosphere.[35]

The American Red Cross assigned a director and three or four
assistants to meet the needs of the Kenitra Center, and the center
employed five or six local people for administrative and housekeep-
ing duties. The assigned personnel concentrated on planning and
supervision, depending on volunteer workers for the bulk of detail.
The volunteers came from the American service community and
included single servicemen, husband-and-wife teams, dependents,
and people with many talents and skills from the local community.
The French-Moroccan groups presented unique problems. Their
social structure and philosophy were far different from those of

[34] Each center filed a monthly SRAO Operations Report. They are available
in the Red Cross Archives.

[35] SRAO, Kenitra, Operations Report, January, 1956.

the American. The very idea of volunteering was foreign to both French and Moroccan, and community support had to be earned by demonstration.[36] About twenty single French girls seventeen to twenty-five years old were recruited and persuaded to partici- pate as *jeunes aides*. Although the center had the support of several Moroccan men and couples, single Moroccan girls were not re- cruited. Moroccan government and Red Cross officials alike agreed that, although the emancipation of Moroccan women had come a long way in the last few years, it had not come that far.[37]

Red Cross officials regularly reviewed the concept of the SRAO centers. Were they providing worthwhile leisure-time activities for the servicemen? Miss Dowling found her answer in the changing response of the base commanders. One of them told her in 1957, "If he can get to town, he's going to go there when he's off duty. You can figure that 10 percent are going to get into trouble anyway regardless of what we all plan; 60 percent are on the fence and could go either way; 30 percent want to do things that are whole- some and good . . . 90 percent need the center."[38] Miss Dowling privately deplored the negative approach. "Our mission was not to keep servicemen out of trouble," she said, "but to provide worth- while and interesting opportunities for learning about the country and the people."[39] By 1960 the base commanders and the military community looked upon the centers as positive assets. They were reaching almost 80 percent of the single servicemen on an irregular basis (one to three visits per month) and about 50 percent on a regular basis (three visits per week). Many American military personnel using the centers were studying the local language and trying to use it. Anti-Americanism and antimilitary sentiment in the community were decreasing. Miss Dowling concluded that the centers had played a part in helping develop friendship and under- standing between the American servicemen and the people of the host community. They had gained the support of the military

[36] Mary Louise Dowling, "Report of Supervisory Visit to the European Area," dated August 10, 1960, in the Red Cross Archives.

[37] Interview between Mary Louise Dowling and Dr. Djebli El Aydouni, vice- president of the Moroccan Red Crescent, at Rabat, December 2, 1963, quoted in Dowling, "Report of Supervisory Visit," dated February 20, 1964.

[38] Dowling, "Report of Supervisory Visit," dated January 14, 1958.

[39] Interview, Mary Louise Dowling, March 22, 1967.

brass, the G.I., the local government officials, the French Red Cross, and the Moroccan Red Crescent—which planned but never instituted a similar program. The center personnel had learned how to hold the interest of the serviceman while simultaneously directing his interest to the other nationality group.[40]

In 1962 Miss Dowling referred to the "People to People" program and to President Eisenhower's letter to service personnel, which indicated that "service men and women are the largest group of official U.S. personnel stationed in foreign countries and, as a result, people form their personal attitudes towards our country and our way of life by what they see and hear about American service personnel." But she could find no reliable study that had been made to evaluate progress in strengthening U.S. military–host country relations.[41] Therefore the American Red Cross Office of Research Information prepared a statistical analysis of the activities of the SRAO centers in France, Turkey, and Kenitra, Morocco. The pattern of replies at all the centers was similar. Whereas most servicemen went to the centers for relaxation and enjoyment (to meet girls), an overwhelming majority of the local community participants came to "better understand the U.S. customs and way of life," and "to meet some American people."[42] The replies on how to strengthen American-Moroccan relationships were more idealistic than practical. Sixty-seven percent thought it might be done through "better international understanding," while only 6 percent proposed building personal friendships.[43] The survey showed that most visitors returned and became regular participants —except for one poor soul who complained, "I met my wife at the center. Now I am not allowed to visit the center any mo [*sic*]."[44]

Ambassador Yost was a frequent visitor at the Red Cross Center and at Moroccan functions in Kenitra. He also visited the Rabat center and some fourteen embassy staff personnel served there as volunteers, but the contact of embassy officials in communities

[40] Dowling, "Report of Supervisory Visit," dated August 10, 1960.
[41] Ibid., pp. 3–4.
[42] "1962 SRAO Center Survey—Questionnaire, and Replies re Activities of Each of the Five Centers—Verdun, Chateauroux, and Nancy, France; Adana, Turkey; and Kenitra, Morocco," pp. 16, 29, in Red Cross Archives.
[43] Ibid., p. 5.
[44] Ibid., p. 39.

surrounding the bases was negligible. They seldom came to Kenitra except to shop at the Navy Exchange and Commissary Store or
to obtain medical services at the base hospital. And the apparent
diffidence was not merely toward the base communities. At the
Spring Ball of the Royal Guard at Rabat in April, 1959, the best
and most prominent table in the ballroom was set aside for the
United States Embassy. The function lasted from nine in the evening until five the next morning, but none of the Embassy personnel came; the table was completely unused the entire evening.[45]

The isolation of the American diplomatic colony from Moroccan
society, initially self-imposed, and the ready acceptance of the
naval personnel from Kenitra led to an estrangement between the
two American groups. The American diplomatic group did not
come to the Royal Guard Ball; they were not invited to the birthday party of Prince Moulay Abdallah on May 30. The party had
been tentatively arranged by the king and left in the hands of
Princess Aisha while the king and his retinue were on a visit to
the Moroccan Sahara. Three days before the party the orchestra
that had been engaged canceled its appearance. Princess Aisha
asked if a combo of sailors that she had heard on the base would
play for the party. She explained that she had not gone to the ambassador because the request was personal and not official. Had it
been otherwise, she would have been obliged to go through the
Moroccan Foreign Office; under the circumstances, with her father
and the crown prince away, there simply was not time. "Besides,"
she added, "the ambassador doesn't have an orchestra and you
do."[46]

Fortunately the Seventeenth Air Force Band was scheduled to
visit Morocco for a series of concerts under the auspices of the
USIS. A telephone call from the base commander at Port Lyautey
to General Palmer, commander in chief, Europe, sufficed to get
their arrival date in Morocco moved up a day; in addition, the win-
ners of the U.S. Army talent competition in Europe flew down on
the courier flight from France. The entertainers were lavishly en-
tertained at the palace, a treat the band missed, since it did not
arrive until the afternoon of the party. The ball was an enormous

45 The author, his wife, and Commander Robert Curts, visiting in Morocco
from Washington, were guests of Princess Aisha and sat at her table.

46 Interview, Princess Aisha, Sidi Bouknadel, May 27, 1959.

success. The next day the band departed on its concert tour and the entertainers spent the day recording for Radio Maroc, then caught the shuttle plane back to their bases in Europe.

The repercussions were not long in coming. An unidentified member of the embassy staff, piqued because embassy personnel were not invited to the party, gave a story to the *New York Times* resident correspondent (who also was not invited)[47] that indicated the United States military forces spent an estimated $35,000 importing fifty entertainers for one midnight show for about one hundred royal guests. The story indicated the project was "undertaken without consultation with the Embassy or the Ambassador" and added the *non sequitur* conclusion that the party had not dissipated the atmosphere of antagonism toward the bases in left-wing, labor, and government circles.[48]

The lack of contact extended beyond social niceties into official matters. For example, no naval attaché made even a courtesy call upon Crown Prince Moulay Hassan, chief of staff of the Royal Moroccan armed forces, during the period from the organization of the Moroccan army in 1956 until sometime after 1960. Captain Jesse Pennell perhaps expressed the mood of all when he explained why he had never called upon "the arrogant little bastard . . . he kept the Sixth Fleet waiting three hours."[49] The ascribed reason was in fact a rationalization of the antimonarchial feeling endemic in the embassy. As a consequence of the failure to call, however, the names of the attachés did not appear on the protocol list of the Royal Moroccan armed forces and they did not receive invitations

[47] According to Dr. Francis Hammond, cultural affairs officer at the embassy, interview with the author, June 10, 1959.

[48] The story in the *New York Times*, June 7, 1959, p. 25, is inaccurate in fact and totally false in its implication. Thomas Brady, who wrote it, was angry at the navy because it had refused him authorization to make purchases at the Navy Exchange Store. The military forces spent no money on the party, and USCINCEUR telegram 281630Z of May 28 (copy in possession of the author) not only informed the embassy but requested USIA to review the proposed entertainment and handle the publicity, if any, in connection with the military participation at the palace. The *New York Times* story served as the basis for a savage attack on Princess Aisha by Edward Wakin, "Veiled Revolution," *Midstream: A Quarterly Jewish Review* 5 (Autumn, 1959); 79–85.

[49] The remark to the author and Mr. Mac Johnson, embassy political affairs officer, in June, 1960, at Rabat, referred to Captain Hal Edwards' intelligence report of the visit of the crown prince to the Sixth Fleet, July 12, 1957.

to such official functions as the Royal Armed Forces Day celebration on May 14, 1960, to which the attachés of most other nations and several officers from the navy base were invited.[50]

Intergovernmental negotiations for the future of the air bases were thus resumed against a background of dissension in both the American diplomatic-military colony in Morocco and the Moroccan government, where the deepening split between the republican and monarchial wings of the Istiqlal party distracted and preoccupied the negotiating personnel. Balafrej was unwilling to make any concession to the Americans that might serve as a precedent for the French. He had urged the United States to dissociate itself from France when Secretary of State John Foster Dulles passed through Morocco on January 23, 1959, but the Americans cited tenancy and security agreements that they said made dissociation impossible. Both sides had concluded that only a temporary agreement was possible. The Moroccans thought in terms of three years; the Americans, twenty, or until a permanent agreement could be reached.[51]

The king introduced a new element into the negotiations in April, when a royal cabinet communiqué announced that any new military agreement with a foreign country must be preceded by recognition of the principle of withdrawal of foreign troops.[52] At an Istiqlal party rally in Casablanca a few days later, Balafrej identified the evacuation of foreign troops as Morocco's principal problem. He said France had been asked to get out, and intimated that Spain and the United States would be next. He said that other Moroccan problems were the determination of Morocco's frontiers, the reorganization of the colonial economy, the Algerian War,

[50] The author discovered the omission and secured five invitations from Colonel Moulay Hafid, director of the Military Cabinet of the Crown Prince. The invitations for the naval attaché and military attaché and the senior air force base commanders were delivered to the embassy the evening of May 13, and the individuals notified by telephone to pick them up. The attachés attended with the ambassador—at his request, but the air force base commanders did not attend. Embassy-military relations became so strained that the Moroccan Liaison Office was denied access to embassy files and thus handicapped in reporting essential information, according to "History of Detachment Two," July–December, 1959, p. 15.

[51] *New York Times*, April 2, 1958, p. 10.

[52] Ibid., April 9, 1958, p. 4.

and the establishment of a united North Africa.[53] Quite obviously, however, Morocco was not yet ready to commit itself on the American bases, for in May Balafrej urged the countries of North Africa to refrain from making unilateral commitments in defense and foreign affairs pending the establishment of federal institutions uniting Morocco, Algeria, and Tunisia.[54]

On May 8, the king named Ahmed Balafrej as prime minister, replacing Si Bekkai, and promulgated a royal charter guaranteeing organizational and press freedom, individual and collective responsibility for the appointed ministers, and an indirectly elected deliberative assembly that would vote on budgetary matters. He also announced plans for a national assembly whose members would be directly elected by universal suffrage.

Balafrej announced his new economic program on May 24. It depended largely on $50 million in economic aid from the United States.[55] On June 10 the United States granted an additional $10 million, bringing the total for the year of 1960 alone to $30.5 million.[56] The major part of the funds was to be used for antilocust campaigns, reforestation, livestock improvement, public housing, and highway construction. Apparently the economic aid had some impact upon Balafrej, for almost coincidentally with the signing of the aid program he again announced that Morocco did not recognize the accords for the American bases, because they were concluded without Moroccan consultation, but he demanded changes in certain clauses of the agreements rather than evacuation.[57]

Many scholars base their interpretations of this aspect of United States–Moroccan relations upon the actions and declarations of the republican element in Morocco and tend to ignore the less flamboyant actions of the king. Every government of independent Morocco, even that of Abdallah Ibrahim (December 24, 1958, to May 20, 1960), tried to find a modus vivendi for the American bases that would be politically acceptable to the Moroccan nation. That was the significant concept in the king's statement concern-

[53] Ibid., April 12, 1958, p. 3.
[54] Ibid., May 8, 1958, p. 12.
[55] Ibid., May 24, 1958, p. 4.
[56] Ibid., June 10, 1959, p. 3.
[57] *Le Petit Marocain*, May 29, 1958.

ing "the principle of evacuation" and Balafrej's statement concerning "changes in certain clauses." The king and Balafrej sought to disarm their opponents to some extent by changing the image of the bases—calling them something besides strategic atomic bases.

The air force, instead, emphasized the strategic concept. The Southern Air Material Command, the huge supply depot that the air force operated at Nouasseur, had been phasing out for over a year and, on June 30, it was turned over to Strategic Air Command Headquarters at Omaha for operational control, and to the Sixteenth Air Force at Torrejon, Spain, for administrative control. Abderrahim Bouabid, minister of the national economy and a spokesman for the leftist groups, denounced the change as an attempt to integrate Nouasseur indirectly into the North Atlantic Treaty Organization defense system, and the foreign ministry protested the supposed change in function without prior advice or consultation at a time when the Moroccans were involved in negotiation with the French on evacuation. "Present operating procedures [maintenance of the status quo] did not envisage such change," Mohammed Jaidi told Counselor of the Embassy Alfred T. Wellborn.[58]

Balafrej's attempt was further complicated by the United States intervention in Lebanon. The Moroccan National Consultative Assembly denounced it as intervention of foreign armed forces in the internal affairs of countries of the Middle East and a blow to their sovereignty, as colonialist aggression, and as a grave threat to world peace.[59] Although the king took no action on the assembly resolution inviting him to protest the aggression and the use of Moroccan territory as a base for attack against peoples who were fighting for their liberty and independence, Balafrej said he personally did not approve of United States intervention in the internal affairs of Lebanon and Jordan. He accepted, however, as unquestionably true Mr. Wellborn's denial of a report that United States troops had been sent from Casablanca to a NATO base at Adana, Turkey.[60]

Balafrej found a "lack of comprehension" on the part of the Americans, he said in an interview on July 21, and added that he

[58] *New York Times*, June 30, 1958, pp. 1, 6, and July 1, 1958, p. 10.
[59] Ibid., July 19, 1958, p. 6.
[60] Ibid., July 22, 1958, p. 16.

did not know if Morocco and the United States could still negotiate a temporary status for the bases in view of "recent events." He cited the Lebanese intervention, the failure of the United States to reply to Moroccan queries on the status of United States airmen and sailors who lived "in an enclave beyond Moroccan influence," and the French agreement to withdraw from the American bases. "If the French tenants of the bases leave, the American guests must follow," Balafrej remarked, and he must have restrained himself with difficulty from adding that he frequently had urged the Americans to "dissociate" themselves from the French.[61]

Another six weeks elapsed before the United States was prepared to negotiate seriously. On September 10, Charles W. Yost, the new ambassador who had presented his credentials in August, handed Mr. Balafrej a reply to his proposal of March. He indicated that the United States accepted the principle of evacuation and asked for seven years of continued use of the bases. Thereafter the discussions centered on the time period, although *Al Alam* and the other nationalist organs continued to harp on nonaggression and nonstrategic usage for the bases.[62] The king, in what was generally considered an attempt to placate the antimonarchial group, told the National Consultative Assembly on November 18 he was determined to obtain total and unconditional evacuation of United States bases as well as French and Spanish troops.[63]

The king's declaration evoked no enthusiasm from Ambassador Yost. He said the king, the prime minister, and the crown prince all had said an arrangement favorable to the United States could have been worked out at the time of the king's visit to the United States, but that psychologically favorable moment had passed and the king, a "weakling," would adopt extreme nationalist goals to avoid being outstripped and isolated. He recommended a "nimble, flexible, conciliatory" diplomacy that included dissociation from the French, "fuzzing up" the strategic concept of the bases, em-

[61] Ibid.

[62] Ibid., September 17, 1958, p. 5, for comment on attitudes expressed by Radio Maroc and *Al Alam*.

[63] *New York Times*, November 19, 1958, p. 4. That same evening, King Mohammed V told the author, at Rabat, "In your country, a politician who loses favor with his people is simply no longer elected. Here it is different. . . . My people expect me to lead them."

phasizing instead the defensive nature, stepping up the economic contribution of the bases by expanding technical training, on-the-job training, and technical schools, and by permitting Nouasseur to be used for civil aviation. He recommended a $40-million aid program and a cash payment of $10 million in lieu of customs because, he said, withholding economic aid would be a dangerous tactic that would leave the Moroccan leaders, already aware of their dependence, open to opposition charges that they had sold out to the United States.[64]

The navy command at Port Lyautey did not agree with Yost's evaluation of King Mohammed V or with his defeatist outlook on the bases. The suspicion that the ambassador considered the bases an impediment to the untroubled functioning of his diplomatic mission was heightened by the presentation of the Moroccan Country Team Report to a Europe-wide Public Affairs Conference at Paris on October 6. The report was prepared by Les Squires, the embassy public affairs officer, and, contrary to the implications inherent in the title, did not represent concurrence by the military community in the views expressed. In fact the very existence of such a report was unknown to the military members of the Country Team until it was read at the conference by Dr. Francis Hammond, Squires' assistant. In discussing public attitudes in Morocco, Squires emphasized the rather negligible communist dissent in Morocco, then stated that the Communists had no current objectives in Morocco that could not be effectively countered by the evacuation of the American bases. Introduction of a communist issue, although it played on the sensitivities of the conferees from Washington and other areas, was in fact a red herring insofar as Morocco was concerned. Communism was never an issue there nor did it ever become one.

Ambassador Yost's recommendations did not touch upon the Algerian War, the issue of prime concern to the king, and his views concerning foreign aid were debatable, but those concerning the image of the bases before the Moroccan people were almost exactly the concessions sought by the king, the crown prince, and Prime Ministers Bekkai and Balafrej since 1956. They were not imple-

    [64] "History of Headquarters, United States Air Force Europe," January 1–December 31, 1958, vol. III: Supporting Documents, doc. nos. 48 and 49.

mented, neither before nor after the recommendation, because the executive branch of the United States government was not able to resolve the departmental conflicts involved. The problem was money and "empire." Whose responsibility was it, and whose budget was to be charged for expanded technical training and technical schools when the objective was political and not technical? The headquarters for the U.S. naval forces in the eastern Atlantic and Mediterranean, rejected a navy, Port Lyautey, request for $5,000 to be used in "fuzzing up" the strategic concept of its base with the comment, "I wonder if you intended to be serious," but did authorize payment for subscriptions to local newspapers from official funds.[65] The navy had instituted and operated a technical school a year earlier but discontinued it because such training fell within the competence of the AID mission and not that of the navy. AID divorced the continuance of the school from the support of the base.

When the Lebanese crisis broke, Morocco and all the rest of the Arab world was deluged with anti–U.S. propaganda that, in Morocco, was associated with the air bases. Explanations by an American were futile in countering the Egyptian-originated screams of "colonialism" and "imperialism." The navy flew Mustapha Alaoui and a photographer from *El Machaaid* out to the Sixth Fleet, off the Lebanese coast, and allowed them to observe the naval operations and to discuss the objective and nature of the intervention with Admiral C. R. Brown, the fleet commander. The two were then flown into Beirut where, insofar as the Americans were concerned, they were at complete liberty to go where they wished and talk to whomever they desired. Alaoui visited the United States Embassy and discussed the matter with the chargé d'affaires (the ambassador was not in town); then he went to the United States military encampment at the edge of town and talked with General Gray. He visited the headquarters of the two opposition factions in Beirut, and he made substantial soundings of the opinion of the man-in-the-street. Upon his return to Morocco, editor Alaoui and his photographer put together a thirteen-page story that was unmatched for objectivity in the Arab press. Alaoui reported his interviews and observations without editorializing, and he used his

[65] Letter signed Richard Lane, dated August 14, 1957, to the author.

pictures and also the public information handouts of the U.S. armed forces. He reported the concensus of the man-in-the-street when asked why the fighting between two Lebanese factions had not stopped with the election of General Chehab as president: "The problem of Lebanon has become more complicated . . . and I see that the propaganda of Gamal Abdel Nasser has made the problem more complicated and encouraged the people to keep Arabism and their arms. . . . Above all, the bitter truth is this Lebanese problem is much more personal than religious and political."[66]

The attitude of the U.S. Embassy toward the navy venture was summed up in the remark of Les Squires, the public affairs officer: "That will teach you to mess around with these Arab journalists. He says your Admiral Brown is insane." He was referring to a picture caption, "Admiral Brown . . . Commander of the U.S. Sixth Fleet . . . Khrushchev said: 'He is insane.'" Admiral Brown himself gave Alaoui that information.

During the time the diplomats were searching for a political solution to the problem of the bases, Crown Prince Hassan was also searching for a "technical" formula that would permit continued American utilization of the bases in a context acceptable to the Moroccan people. He envisaged the creation of a Royal Moroccan Air Force, which would use American equipment and training, but he encountered the opposition of the French, who cited the terms of the Franco-Moroccan independence accords of 1956 by which France agreed to aid in the creation of the Moroccan royal armed forces. The French interpreted the accords as a limitation on Moroccan freedom of action and were jealous of any thought of American infringement.[67] The United States did not entirely agree with the French interpretation, but neither did the Americans furnish any encouragement to the prince. The Americans pleaded language and "other" difficulties.

Nor did more come of another grandiose plan for the development of a major port at Kenitra. Marshal Lyautey had envisaged such development thirty years earlier, and French engineers had

66 *El Machaaid*, no. 23, 1958, published in Rabat in November, 1958. This publication does not bear a monthly calendar date.

67 "History of Headquarters, United States Air Force Europe," July–December, 1958, vol. III, doc. no. 22.

amassed detailed data on the characteristics of the Sebou River. The need for the port was quite evident; the port of Kenitra, the third in Morocco measured by the tonnage handled, was working at capacity with as many as fifteen ships frequently waiting to enter. The richness of the hinterland promised substantial growth when additional facilities became available. A port at Mehdia would be of great value to the Naval Air Station; it would save a six-mile trip up the river.

Seddik Abou Ibrahimi, the super-caid at Kenitra, broached the idea in late 1958 and asked for United States technical help. Resident navy engineers at Port Lyautey considered the concept feasible, and the commander of naval activities forwarded it to the Navy Department at Washington, where it was discussed at almost all echelons.[68] In essence, Seddik's proposal envisaged a developmental program spread over a period of ten to fifteen years and based at the U.S. Naval Air Station. He suggested that the work be done in small increments beginning with a technical survey by U.S. Navy engineers, rather than with an announcement of a grandiose program. The United States Navy would provide engineering and specialized technical assistance, and the Moroccan army would assume responsibility for the ordinary, dirt-moving type of work. When asked about the "ten to fifteen years," in view of the expected demand for evacuation within a period of five years, he replied with characteristic Moroccan symbolism, "Domestic politics. No Moroccan will insist on severing the root that nourishes the tree."

The proposal was a serious attempt to find a nonpolitical framework in which the Port Lyautey Naval Air Station would be placed in the position of visibly contributing to Moroccan development, and thus defer political plans for evacuation. But the navy deferred to the State Department, which was unwilling to consider it in the absence of a political agreement on the bases themselves. When Secretary of the Navy Thomas S. Gates visited Morocco in April,

[68] The author discussed this proposal and urged favorable consideration with Defense Department officials, including Admiral Arleigh Burke, chief of naval operations, and General Graves B. Erskine, director of the Department of Defense Special Operations Branch; also, contact was made with Mr. Tye Woods of the Draper committee, then in session; and with officials of the Agency for International Development, in Washington, May 1–10, 1959.

1959, Mr. Seddik urged the merits of the plan on him. Mr. Gates told him, "You are talking to the wrong people. You ought to be talking to our friend the ambassador here." (Mr. Yost was doing the interpreting.) Seddik replied, "We have been talking to the ambassador but we expect nothing will ever come of it. On the other hand, we know the U.S. Navy has built ports all over the world and that if it will undertake this one, we will get the port that we need."[69]

Another proposal being discussed during the same period sought to respond to what the Moroccans considered their most critical need: educational facilities. A few American children had been attending the schools in Port Lyautey rather than the American Dependents School on the base. They did as well or better in the French-language schools than they had done in American schools. Their presence was favorably noted by both the French and Moroccan community. *L'Echo du Maroc* congratulated the French teachers at the parochial Ecole de la Sainte Famille for their success in implanting a "solid notion of our culture" in these young Americans who were thus "brought in contact with our students of different nationalities, different races, and different religions. All of these children are learning to better understand and love each other in order to make a better world," the report concluded, and rhetorically asked,

> Is that not our role?
> To learn to understand and to love . . .
> Yes, my Sister, you are in your role. You serve God and France.[70]

Another student, Christopher Blair, won the Prix d'excellence in the local Lycée Abdelmalek as Saadi, a feat so remarkable that it attracted comment in both the local and international press and inspired Princess Aisha to send him a magnificent Arabian stallion as a reward "to a young foreigner who has made the effort to learn our language and customs."[71]

The success of the American students in Moroccan schools had its counterpart with Moroccan students in the base Dependents School. That program began in September, 1956, with the admis-

[69] Interview at the home of Captain John L. Counihan, commander of naval activities, Port Lyautey, first week in April, 1959. The author was present.
[70] *L'Echo du Maroc*, October 25, 1957.
[71] See, for examples, *Stars and Stripes*, March 16, 1960, p. 11.

sion of the daughters of Abdelatif Sbihi and Mohammed Laghzaoui, and, as it expanded during the next four years, it included children from other social classes. As in any new program, there were difficulties to be worked out, but they had been largely overcome by 1958.

One problem was political. Faiza Sbihi and Aisha Laghzaoui[72] sought admission to the American school because of their fathers' fundamental antipathy to anything French. For the same reason, the Egyptian Ambassador at Rabat requested the admission of his daughter. She was accepted, but the French security forces refused her admission to the base.[73] The Suez crisis had poisoned French attitudes.

Another problem was administrative. The navy operated the Dependents School at Port Lyautey; the air force and other services paid a tuition fee of about $250 to the navy for each of their dependents who attended. In other parts of the world the air force or perhaps the army operated the school and the navy paid tuition. In fact, the tuition payments represented little more than a bookkeeping transaction in Washington. Since the United States Embassy at Rabat had requested the admission of the Sbihi and Laghzaoui girls, the navy assumed the embassy would pay the tuition fee. When the bills came due, however, the embassy protested that it had no money budgeted for such expenses and asked the navy to absorb the cost.

Navy school administrators meanwhile had discovered a positive benefit to their American charges in having Moroccans, in spite of the novelty of their situation, compete on even terms in circumstances that the Americans took for granted—and in three languages. The navy command and the diplomatic experts perceived a political advantage. The Moroccans saw an opportunity for some relief in an area of critical shortage, and any expansion of educational opportunity was welcome. Each group wanted to expand the numbers of Moroccan students in the American schools.

Washington officialdom debated the question of fiscal responsibility for almost two years. There was little disagreement as to

[72] Upon graduation in 1960, Aisha Laghzaoui married Abderrahaman Abdelali, Moroccan minister of public works, and after his death, Ahmed Taibi Benhima, who is presently Moroccan ambassador to the United Nations.

[73] *New York Times*, March 25, 1957, p. 26.

objective or desirability. The whole question, debated by officials to whom a $25 million budget would have been commonplace, concerned whose budget was to be charged approximately $2,500 for the tuition of ten Moroccan students. The navy, the State Department, and the International Cooperation Administration each insisted that some other agency had primary responsibility.[74] Secretary of the Navy Gates finally resolved the differences when he authorized the commander of naval activities of Port Lyautey to admit such children as he deemed desirable, without tuition if space was available, and to refer any question of such procedures to the secretary.

Actually the debate was somewhat academic. The ten children started attending classes in September, 1958. From Rabat they included Faiza Sbihi and Aisha Laghzaoui, the two children of Mehdi Bennouna, and Farid and Kamel Belkacem, sons of one of the Algerian chieftains, and four boys from the local orphanage in Kenitra. A few weeks later the daughter of Mohammed Bel Hadj, director of the Takadoum School in Kenitra, was admitted.

Mohammed Hasnaoui Ben Laabdia was one of the orphans, and his case is illustrative. He was born in the Rharb Plain area about 1944, the son of a Spanish father and an Arab-Berber mother who died when he was a baby. His father died when he was six years old. By some providential fate he was taken into the Société Musulmane de Bienfaisance, the Moslem orphanage. As a Spanish child he would have been ineligible, so his name was changed to Mohammed and he was given the name of his mother's tribe, Hasnaoui, and his mother's nickname, Laabdia. Mohammed was a bright child, and the orphanage sent him to school where he was consistently on the honor roll until he was fifteen years old. At that time, according to the institution rules, he was old enough to take care of himself, and his place in the orphanage was needed for a younger child. The practical effect of being forced to make a

[74] Interviews, E. G. Lansdale, asistant to the secretary of defense; Tye Woods, Draper committee; Captain George R. Raring, USN, Office of the Chief of Naval Operations (OP-607); Marjorie Belcher, Office of Comptroller, ICA; and the Honorable George Mahon, House Committee on Appropriations, United States Congress, May 1–10, 1959. See also George R. Raring letter to the commander of U.S. naval activities, Port Lyautey, dated Washington, February 25, 1959, in Navy Department (OP-607) files, Washington, D.C.

living for himself was his leaving school. Through an American classmate, Christopher Blair, his plight came to the attention of the U.S. Navy community. Captain and Mrs. John Fridell took him into their home and the U.S. Marine Corps (Fridell was a marine) chipped in to buy his clothing and other needs. Hasnaoui completed high school at Port Lyautey, then came to Fort Worth, Texas, where the Fort Worth Downtown Optimists Club sponsored him to a Bachelor of Arts degree at Texas Wesleyan College. He returned to Morocco in 1966 as an executive of an international hotel chain where, in the educational and administrative vacuum existing in his country, he will rise rapidly. Whatever the vicissitudes of the future may be, they can hardly shake the faith of Hasnaoui ben Laabdia in the innate goodness of the American people.

What was true of Hasnaoui was also true in varying degrees of the others. All the orphans lived in American homes and for all practical purposes as Americans. Masrour Hammadi ultimately received his Bachelor of Arts degree from Ripon College; Mohammed Amraoui from Southwestern Missouri State; Mohammed Bel Hadj attended Arlington (Texas) State College; Faizi Sbihi went to Dana Hall on a scholarship arranged by Mrs. Franklin D. Roosevelt. Farid and Kamel Belkacem went home to Algeria when that war ended. They and others who followed them were afforded a unique opportunity to observe American society.

The navy was completely unsuccessful in securing funds for a project to "fuzz up" the strategic nature of the base, a step that the ambassador had regarded as indispensable to retention. The project envisaged the creation of a department of vocational argiculture in the Dependents High School that would utilize land within the perimeter of the base for project farming. The school needed a vocational department for its own accreditation purposes. At least half of the 3,400 acres that made up the Naval Air Station could be farmed without interfering with the military usage—grow alfalfa between the runways instead of weeds. The Naval Air Station was able to support such a school with classroom facilities, machinery, water, and practical training help. If implemented either as a crop-dairy, crop-beef, or crop-poultry program, the American community provided a ready market at the Navy Exchange Store; and if implemented on a pure crop basis, a partial market existed with the base Special Services Division, which operated the riding stable on the base. In either case, such a program was bound to appeal to the Moroccan's love for a well-appointed farm, and with an expected twenty-five Moroccan students in the school the Moroccan community, hopefully, might come to look upon the base as a type of agricultural school from which they visibly benefited. This proposal was debated concurrently with the tuition question but found no financial sponsor in Washington. The mixed American-Moroccan nature of the student body would exclude it both from the purely American Dependents School program and from the cultural programs administered by the State Department for foreign nationals. The International Cooperation Administration rejected the idea as being too small to justify its attention. According to Comptroller Marjorie Belcher, "We could not even hire an administrator for the twenty thousand dollars you say you need for the whole project."[75]

Navy interest in education was not limited to the exchange program. The most persistent Moroccan complaint against the French for two decades had been lack of educational facilities. After independence was achieved, the Moroccan government moved rapidly to augment them. The school system expanded by four times in four years.[76] The explosive expansion demanded additional classrooms and additional teachers. Both the navy and the air force donated surplus Quonset huts and Dallas huts, portable buildings developed by the armed forces during World War II, to be moved to new or expanded school sites in Moroccan communities. The sight of a navy tractor-trailer carrying a 20 by 48 foot Quonset hut, followed by a navy mobile crane to lift it onto its new foundation, was commonplace in Kenitra in September, 1959.[77] The

[75] Interview, Marjorie Belcher, Washington, D.C., May 7, 1959.

[76] According to Mehdi Ben Barka, *Problèmes d'édification du Maroc et du Maghreb*, p. 63, quoting Moroccan Ministry of Education figures, 215,000 Moslem children of the 2,265,000 in the five-to-fourteen age group and 7,300 of the 980,000 in the fifteen-to-nineteen age group were in school in 1955–1956, the last year of the protectorate. According to Ministry of Education figures quoted in Zartman, *Morocco: Problems of New Power*, p. 173, more than 850,000 Moslem children were in school in 1960–1961 and the total school population was 910,000. Zartman discusses in detail, pp. 155–195, the problems of education in Morocco in the immediate postindependence period.

[77] In his letter no. 8A47 of September, 1959, to Captain Counihan, Comman-

Naval Air Reserve squadron brought technical equipment, cutaway engines, and tools.[78] The American community furnished teachers.

The teaching program was probably the most ambitious undertaken by the navy, and probably of most lasting consequence. The Moroccan curriculum included English as a recommended foreign language, but Morocco did not have enough English-language instructors nor enough money to pay them if they had been available. The Officers' Wives Club from the navy base volunteered to fill the gap in the local community. Initially a cooperative venture was envisaged in which the English-language teaching program of United States Information Service would provide instructional materials and technical assistance. The latter, however, "had no funds available for a program in Kenitra," and the technical advice only pointed out the obvious difficulties without suggesting solutions. The ladies decided to rely upon their own resources. An appeal to the Regents Publishing Company produced an immediate donation of the requested textbooks,[79] and the teachers, many of them experienced in American classrooms before their marriage, fashioned their own instructional materials. The program continued until 1962–1963, and its impact is indicated by the request of Mohammed Bel Hadj, director of Takadoum School, for the admission of his daughter to the American Dependents School because of the example of humanitarian competence displayed by these women.[80]

---

dant les Forces Armées Américaines de Kenitra (copy in possession of the author), the pasha of Kenitra acknowledged receipt of the building and expressed the gratitude of the Moroccan authorities for the American assistance.

[78] See Commander, U.S. Naval Activities Port Lyautey, Kenitra, Morocco, *People to People Report*, 1960, for a description of navy assistance to Moroccan education in 1959–1960. The author retains in his possession the documentation pertaining to the development of the programs. According to "History of Detachments Two," July–December, 1959, the USAF donated 1,600 huts to the Moroccan government.

[79] T. L. Lebow, Regents Publishing Company, letter to author, dated New York, January 22, 1959, concerning the donation of 160 copies of Fisher and Dixon, *Beginning Lessons in English*.

[80] See Paul H. Spiers, "The ABCs are Shipshape," *Stars and Stripes*, November 22, 1958, for a story concerning the participation in this project of Susan Montalbine, Mercedes Perry, Susan Ruffini, Mattielou Armenaki, Ruth Wal-

Technical assistance was given when requested to many agencies of the Moroccan government. Generally the request was prompted by an unforeseen circumstance and the need was urgent. For example, the governor of the Meknes province discovered only three days before the opening of the International Ski Festival at Michliffen in February, 1959, that his electrical system was not functioning properly and his technicians were not able to diagnose the trouble. He sought the help of a U.S. Navy engineer. One was dispatched to the scene and he determined that two small fifteen-kilowatt generators available for operating the ski lift were inadequate to illuminate the crater for the night phases of the festival, which were to be attended by the king and many European dignitaries. The navy sent a seventy-five–kilowatt mobile generator and, cutting the fifteen-kilowatt, fifty-cycle generators off the circuit, carried the entire electrical load at a navy-standard sixty cycles—the only possible solution in the time available.

Diplomacy will never be the same again in Morocco. The tent in which His Majesty received the foreign dignitaries was pitched on one side at the end of the only hard-surfaced road leading into the crater. The huge generator with "US NAVY" in letters a foot high was parked in front of it. (It did not obstruct the view, but its diesel engine was a bit noisy.) The technicians in work uniform were obliged to use the same access route as the impeccably dressed diplomats. For a time M. Hajouji, a young official of the Moroccan Protocol Office, attempted to keep the two groups separated, but he soon gave up. "Inch-Allah [it is the will of God]," he said, and before the festival was over he was serving them tea from the same pot from which he served the king.

Another example involved the Moroccan Sûreté Nationale, the national police force, which wanted to protect the identification cards of its personnel with a laminated plastic cover similar to that used by the United States armed forces. The navy laminating machines would take the Moroccan cards but the precut plastic used for the American cards was too small for the Moroccan cards. To locate a supplier in the United States and negotiate a contract would be the work of months. The matter was arranged by a per-

---

dron, Alice Milner, and Portia Schlicht, among others who contributed of their time, money, and talents.

sonal letter from the navy base liaison officer to a United States manufacturer who agreed to ship the twenty thousand sheets of plastic via parcel post to the base at a price no higher than that charged the United States government and to accept payment by personal check from the liaison officer, who was in turn reimbursed by the Moroccan government. The whole matter was resolved in three weeks.[81]

Technical assistance to the local municipality was furnished almost as a matter of routine. When the pump in the local waterworks broke down, a new part was manufactured in the base machine shop. When a winter storm piled sand across the highway at Mehdia Beach, the navy sent bulldozers and graders to clear the mile-long stretch and also graded the beach for the approaching summer season. The most dramatic testimonial to the worth of the navy as a good neighbor came during the Christmas week of 1958, when unusually heavy rains sent rivers out of their banks and flooded the 100,000-acre Rharb Plain.

Floods were common at one time in the area; in fact before the French came to Morocco it was more marsh than plain, but the French constructed an elaborate system of canals and dikes and transformed the Rharb into a garden spot of orange groves and rich fields. As the French technicians left after Morocco regained its independence, the canals silted up and the dikes deteriorated. The system was not able to handle the deluge when it came.

The rains began on December 19 and continued until Christmas Day. Beginning on December 20 the navy twice-daily flew surveillance patrols over the area, watching the rising waters with increasing alarm. On Christmas Eve the dikes on the Oued Beth, a tributary of the Sebou River, broke and sent a three-foot wall of water into the Rharb Plain, portions of which were already isolated because the dirt roads were impassable for wheeled vehicles, and the water was not yet deep enough for boats.

Rescue operations began during the night as a company of Moroccan soldiers with high-wheeled trucks and motor launches start-

[81] Direction Générale, Sûreté Nationale letter to author, No. 8990, dated Rabat, February 5, 1959; author's letter to the president, Tommy Tucker Plastic Company, Dallas, Texas, dated Kenitra, February 6, 1959, and reply, dated Dallas, February 12, 1959; and Sûreté Nationale receipt for the plastic, dated March 5, 1959; all correspondence in possession of the author.

ed moving the people and livestock out of the low-lying areas. At
first light on Christmas Day navy helicopters went into action
from an advanced base near Allal At Tazi, at the very edge of the
flood waters and were joined during the day by others from the
Sidi Slimane Air Force Base. Under a ragged five-hundred-foot
ceiling and in a drizzling rain, they lifted 134 persons from crum-
bling mud houses, isolated rooftops, and trees.

The rescue operations were a contest against the sinister dynam-
ics of the flood. Allal At Tazi was selected as the advanced base
of operations for several reasons. It was near the most gravely
threatened area. It had some facilities for taking care of the refugees. It should remain above water, according to the charts. Most
important of all, the access road would be flooded, if at all, only
after the town. The base could always move back as the waters
advanced. At daybreak the section of the main, hard-surfaced highway, blocked off as a landing area for the helicopters, was at least
one hundred yards from the water's edge. By midmorning the
water was running in the bar-ditches, and on the east side of the
road, dammed back by a ridge of dirt under the fence row, the field
became a sheet of water. Soon a trickle no bigger than a finger
poked through the weed stubble on the dam. In just a few minutes
it was a hand-wide rivulet, then the dam crumpled and water
lapped at the edge of the pavement. The gasoline trucks and helicopters moved back about a mile toward Port Lyautey and continued operations.

Helicopter operations continued for three days, the first in actual
evacuation, and the next two in dropping food parcels to people
isolated on high ground. The first food parcels contained flour,
sugar, beans, and milk powder and a can of water; but upon the
advice of some of the refugees the parcels were soon revised to include bread, sugar, tea, and charcoal. Without charcoal they could
not cook; their ovens were under water and they could not bake;
they had never seen milk powder and did not know how to use it;
and they did not feel a need for additional water. When the use of
milk powder was explained, the inevitable question was, "Can
lambs (or calves) drink it?"

The news of the flood and the role of the United States armed
forces completely dominated the Moroccan press for a week. The
navy furnished aerial photographs. As the tempo of operations

slacked off on December 27, the navy also allowed reporters to go along on the reconnaissance flights. The theme of the navy news releases, which was generally accepted by the Moroccan press, was "in the absence of Moroccan rescue services of its own, the United States Navy is always ready to lend a helping hand."

The flood was the last of a series of five rescue operations in 1958 that normally would have been performed by a Moroccan coast guard—if Morocco had possessed one. They included the rescue of the crews of two ships stranded on the Moroccan coast during storms, the French cargo vessel *Pei-Ho* and the Moroccan trawler *Al Widad*; the crew of the Norwegian tanker *Seirstad*, which broke apart in the Mediterranean off the Moroccan coast, was saved as were the snowbound villagers in Djebel Katma in the Rif Mountains.

The navy efforts to create an image of Port Lyautey as something more than a self-serving instrument of United States policy received no financial support from any other agency of the U.S. government and the limited program that it was able to mount with its own resources was inadequate to modify the trend of diplomatic negotiations in 1959. Only the king possessed enough prestige to stem the clamor of the antimonarchial group for evacuation and he was unwilling to risk that prestige and possibly the dynasty to bolster a Franco-American position. Only a dramatic reversal of the American attitude toward the Algerian War could have given him a commanding voice.[82] Short of that, he was willing for popular opinion to have its way.

The United States lost its last influential supporting voice in the Moroccan government when Ahmed Balafrej resigned as prime minister in November in a sharpening domestic crisis. In December, even as the American helicopters worked over the flooded waters of the Rharb, the king appointed Abdallah Ibrahim, an outspoken proponent of evacuation, as prime minister. In mid-May, 1959, Ibrahim asked Ambassador Yost for a public statement by the United States affirming the principle of evacuation, recog-

---

[82] According to Dir., Seventeenth Air Force (MLO) letter to Commander, Seventeenth Air Force (M2 INT-25-H 230C), dated August 27, 1958, in "History of the Seventeenth Air Force," 1958, vol. III, quoting Mohammed Laghzaoui, one of the king's closest associates and the United States' firmest supporters.

nizing Moroccan sovereignty over the bases, and giving a definite schedule of withdrawal. Ambassador Yost concluded that the sentiment for evacuation was irreversible.[83]

The French belatedly agreed to the dissociation of United States and French policies and agreed to phase out the French Liaison Mission and remove the French guards from the air force bases, but continued to insist on the validity of the 1950 agreements.[84] They claimed the right to use the air force bases at any time without prior notification and the right of first refusal on any surplus property of which the United States might dispose. Both demands were associated with the Algerian War. French intelligence purportedly had discovered materials sold as surplus by Port Lyautey in the hands of Algerian rebels,[85] and, according to the U.S. Air Force, the Moroccan government was reluctant to prosecute the perpetrators of the theft because of the "possible involvement of Government of Morocco officials in material for the Algeria War."[86] Mohammed Laghzaoui, director of Sûreté Nationale, was aware of the thefts but he refused to investigate unless guaranteed the right to investigate on joint U.S.–French bases and have jurisdiction of the culprits regardless of nationality. "No such authority could be given," the air force concluded.[87] The French finally abandoned both demands. They relinquished command of Nouasseur, Ben Guerir, Sidi Slimane, and Bouhaut, hauled down their flag, withdrew their security guards, and disestablished the French Liaison Mission by June 30, 1959.[88] The changes affected Port Lyautey only insofar as an agency of the Moroccan government was substituted for the French intendant in the management of non–U.S. employees of the base. The question of surplus materials was avoided by giving the Moroccan government an oppor-

[83] "History of the United States Air Force, Europe," January–June, 1959, I, 65.

[84] Ibid., June–December, 1958, vol. III, doc. no. 8, dated October 28, 1958.

[85] See "History of Detachment Two, Headquarters, United States Air Force, Europe (Moroccan Liaison Office)," January–June, 1957, p. 21, in USAF Archives, file no. K-570.071c.

[86] "History of United States Air Force, Europe," July–December, 1957, vol. II, doc. no. 57, and ibid., January–June, 1959, I, 52–54.

[87] "History of Detachment Two," January–June, 1957, p. 24.

[88] "History of United States Air Force, Europe," January–June, 1959, I, 46–54. See also vol. 3, doc. no. 40, para. 11.

tunity to purchase the material before it was declared surplus,[89] but after the French had screened it to indicate "sensitive" material, which was then not offered for sale.[90]

Abdallah Ibrahim and his followers sought issues by which they could enhance their political power rather than solutions to the economic and political problems confronting Morocco. The economic crisis was grave, and growing worse. The U.S. forces had pumped $68 million into the Moroccan economy over and above the U.S. economic aid in 1958–1959.[91] They employed more than eight thousand people in a country where one in four employables had no job,[92] but Ibrahim insisted the Moroccans were eager for evacuation. He said that acceptance of economic aid from the United States was an act of courage—but he was a courageous man. He accepted $40 million without political, military, or strategic conditions attached. According to his finance minister, "no question was raised about the American military bases in Morocco" while the program was being worked out.[93]

While accepting the economic aid with one hand, Ibrahim continued his harassment of the American bases with the other. He forbade radio transmissions in Morocco from any station except Radio Maroc. A measure aimed primarily against Radio Tangier, it also affected military base radio operations.[94] It was never enforced against the bases, but it remained a constant threat, and the ban on "ham" radio transmitters was enforced. Ibrahim rejected Yost's "inference" that the aid was "quid pro quo" for any concession on his demand for immediate withdrawal of the American forces. The Moroccans, he said, considered it payment due for the special privileges that the American forces enjoyed.[95] To put an end to alleged "black-marketing" from the bases, he established customs agents at the gates. His inspectors were invited to examine the navy's financial records and procedures to guard against black-marketing. They did so and professed to be satisfied, but returned apologetically two days later with instructions to establish the

[89] Ibid., pp. 52–54.
[90] "History of Detachment Two," January–July, 1957, p. 21.
[91] Ibid., July–December, 1959, pp. 24–25.
[92] "History of United States Air Force, Europe," January–June, 1959, I, 66.
[93] *New York Times*, June 25, 1959, and July 11, 1959, p. 2.
[94] Ibid., May 28, 1959, p. 1.
[95] "History of United States Air Force, Europe," January–June, 1959, I, 66.

customs checkpoints anyway. The navy then invited the customs service to at least come inside the gate where water, electricity, shelter, and sanitary facilities were available. They became a permanent fixture on the base and caused almost no inconvenience to the Americans going in and out.

When Ibrahim was appointed, the king gave him the mission of preparing the nation for elections. Six months later he had made no appreciable progress, and the king suggested that he resign. He refused and, seeking an easy popular issue, stepped up his campaign for immediate evacuation. The principle had already been decided; the only question to be resolved was when the evacuation would take place. At Washington in October, Ibrahim proposed a two-year withdrawal period to Secretary of State Herter, a proposal that the Pentagon rejected. But the joint communiqué drawn up at the end of his visit reaffirmed the principle of withdrawal and continuing recognition of Moroccan sovereignty over the bases. Upon his return to Rabat, Ibrahim promised to fix an evacuation date by negotiation within two weeks. He was not able to do so, and King Mohammed V again took an active part in reaching an agreement.

In September, the U.S. Air Force decided to withdraw from Morocco within five years,[96] but rejected Ibrahim's proposal for two years. The ground for compromise lay somewhere between, and the compromise came during the visit of President Eisenhower to Casablanca on December 22, 1959. In a conversation of about one and a half hours, the king and President Eisenhower agreed that the United States forces would be withdrawn by the end of 1963, and that Boulhaut—just completed and never used because of the French troop limitation—would be surrendered by March 31, 1960.[97] The negotiations for the United States Air Force bases had ended, and those for the navy base entered a new phase. In the general jubilation over the presidential visit, his amicable reception, and a settlement of the problem, Crown Prince Hassan's statement that discussions were continuing on the status of the navy base at Kenitra passed virtually unnoticed.[98]

---

[96] *New York Times*, September 13, and October 31, 1959.
[97] Ibid., December 23, 1959, p. 10.
[98] *L'Echo du Maroc*, December 26, 1959.

11. The Worth of a Good Neighbor

MOROCCANS REGARD 1959 as their "year of troubles." In a period of fourteen months they suffered a series of overwhelming disasters —the flood in December, 1958; the death of Abderrahman Anegai, chief of the Royal Cabinet, killed in an automobile accident on January 28, 1959; a nation-wide epidemic of paralysis caused by the use of toxic cooking oil in the autumn; another flood in the Rharb in January, 1960; and an earthquake that destroyed the city of Agadir and killed more than twenty thousand people in February.

The nation was ill prepared to face these disasters, for at the outset the strained political fabric of Morocco ripped. Sporadic uprisings occurred in the rural areas where the Liberation Army had been strong in 1955, and they continued well into 1959. Paradoxically the revolts were against the government in support of the king. Not only had the old rural-urban antagonism reappeared but the Istiqlal party itself had split. On January 25, 1959, Mehdi Ben

Barka and the republican element of the party seceded and went
into opposition. Initially, the new group directed its fire against
the "Old Guard" leaders, but before the year was out it became
increasingly critical of the king. Several of its leaders were implicated in the plot to assassinate the crown prince in December.

By its very presence the United States was involved in Morocco's troubles. Public opinion associated the Americans with each
of the natural disasters, with three of them favorably and with
one unfavorably. The ambassador and his staff tried to help whenever possible without becoming involved in political dissension.
Moroccan government officials interpreted "neutrality" toward the
antigovernment group as sympathy for their goals,[1] and Abderrahman Anegai, who understood the apparent inconsistencies of
American attitudes better than any other palace official, was no
longer around to explain them.

The 1958 flood coincided with the investiture of the Abdallah
Ibrahim government. The American rescue operations provoked
some criticism of preceding governments for failing to keep the
Rharb drainage system in good repair and for leaving Morocco
unprepared to handle its own emergencies. During the "year of
troubles," however, Ibrahim was prime minister. His presence
logically should have muted the criticism by his followers of
American humanitarian efforts, even though the bases themselves
remained a political issue. But Ibrahim, neither a statesman nor
a distinguished administrator, was in a situation that demanded
statesmanship and ability. He obviously was failing to prepare the
nation for elections. His foreign policy was bankrupt and the national economy almost so. He had designated the American bases
as a "whipping boy," and, reasonable or not, the criticism of even
innocuous events continued.

The second tragic development was a widespread epidemic of oil

---

[1] For example, two reporters from High School News Service asked the help
of Mr. Ron Moxness, the embassy press officer, in preparing a story on education in Morocco. Moxness, unaware of the Moroccan political situation, asked
Moulay Ahmed Alaoui, the palace press attaché, if he would arrange an interview for them with Mehdi Ben Barka, who spoke English and possessed adequate credentials as an educator. Mr. Alaoui was evasive, suggesting that Mr.
Ben Barka was not in town and was very busy, anyway. He suggested instead
an interview with the minister of education. Mr. Moxness then arranged the
interview directly, and Mr. Alaoui never again even spoke to Moxness.

poisoning. The poisoning agent came from the U.S. Air Force base at Nouasseur. In closing out its operations, the Southern Air Matériel Command sold vast quantities of surplus matériel on the Casablanca market for whatever it would bring. A dealer in Casablanca bought a forty-ton lot of lubricating oil and sold it in smaller lots to twenty-five other merchants, purportedly garage owners, but actually purveyors of cooking oil. They mixed one part of the lubricating oil with three parts of olive oil and sold the mixture as cooking oil. The lubricating oil contained triortho cresyl phosphate, an anticorrosive agent, two grams of which taken orally can cause paralysis of the arms and legs. By November ten thousand people were paralyzed and at least thirty thousand destitute, physically unable to work and earn a living for themselves and their families.[2]

The Moroccan government traced the poison to its source and the twenty-five merchants were arrested, tried under an ex post facto law, and assessed the death penalty. The Moroccan government, neither at the ministerial nor palace level, considered the U.S. Air Force culpable. *Al Alam*, in its April 27, 1960, issue complained that, if the United States had not established bases in Morocco in the first place, the whole series of events could not have happened, a criticism to which Abdelatif Sbihi replied by pointing out that except for pressure by "certain parties" the air force would not have been phasing out and selling surplus matériel.

The suffering posed a delicate question both for the United States government and for the Americans as individuals. The almost instinctive American response in the presence of such tragedy is to help, and yet any substantial aid might very well be misinterpreted as the response of a guilty conscience. Moroccan people and those in many other parts of the world do not understand spontaneous generosity.[3] The air force at Nouasseur offered to pro-

---

[2] See Youssef ben Abbes, Moroccan minister of public health, "The Malady of Meknes," *Time* 74 (November 30, 1959): 24, for a description of the epidemic, worst in the vicinity of the city of Meknes, that affected the victims very much as the same poison in Jamaica "jake" affected its victims during Prohibition in the United States—those able to move at all could do so only in a jerky, uncoordinated manner.

[3] Abdelhamid El Alaoui, pasha of Kenitra, told the author in September, 1959, in connection with the gift of surplus navy buildings to the city, "We must find a formula by which the city can buy these buildings at a nominal

vide food and other badly needed relief supplies if the ambassador declared a disaster and provided funds to pay for them.[4] The ambassador, having had some experience with air force prices, declined to do so[5] and recommended instead that United States aid be channeled through the American Red Cross and the International Red Cross.[6] The navy personnel at Kenitra provided to the Entr'aid Nationale one thousand sheets, a substantial quantity of clothing, and 250,000 francs to be used at the discretion of Princess Aisha and her technical advisors.

The third blow, the second major flood in the Rharb, came hard on the heels of the oil poisoning. It differed from the 1958 flood because the bulk of the flood water came down the Oued Ouerrha from the Rif Mountains rather than down the Sebou and Oued Beth from the Atlas Mountains. The area of operations was therefore farther from Port Lyautey and more difficult to support, but, on the other hand, both the navy and the Moroccan officials, profiting from their experience thirteen months earlier, were better prepared. For one thing, the Fleet Weather Central at Port Lyautey had been keeping a close watch on the amount of precipitation in the Sebou River watershed. As the rain approached abnormal levels, the navy made one or more flights daily over the area and, if the weather at all permitted, photographed the terrain. By using photographic analysis, Moroccan hydrographic officials were able to predict accurately the pattern of flooding and to move out most of the endangered population and livestock well in advance

---

cost. No one will understand why you would just give them away, and they will conclude that something suspicious is going on between the pasha and the Americans."

[4] "History of the Sixteenth Air Force," July 1–December 31, 1959, vol. IV, exhibit 99, in USAF Archives, file no. K 569.01. The air force was able to recoup $50,000 in 1960 from "cold war" funds provided for impact propaganda projects in Morocco, according to "History of United States Air Force, Europe," January 1–June 30, 1960, I, 8–9.

[5] "History of the Sixteenth Air Force," July 1–December 31, 1959, vol. IV, exhibit 100. The air force had furnished surplus supplies for the Unity Road Project in the summer of 1957, and they were charged off to foreign aid appropriations at prices substantially above those that they would have brought on the surplus market in Casablanca. The transaction drew considerable criticism from the Moroccan officials who charged "toothbrushes without bristles and overage antibiotics."

[6] U.S. Embassy, Rabat, telegram 212 of November 21, 1959, in ibid.

of the rising water. Also Moroccan officials, such as the governor of the Fez province and the super-caid at Kenitra, had learned to work with American flight crews and to appreciate the limitations and capabilities of the helicopters and other equipment.

Although the rescue operations were conducted more efficiently in 1960 than in 1958, the public impact of the American help was lost in a welter of interdepartmental and interservice rivalries. In 1958 the local navy commander, responding to a disaster situation in his area of responsibility, ordered the helicopters into action in order to save human life. He had the authority to do so without reference to higher authority. He had no time to await a request from the Moroccan government or from the United States ambassador. His representative was physically present in the operating area to coordinate and resolve immediately any difficulties arising from language or communications. In accordance with standard navy procedures he made complete press releases supported with pictures to all news media represented in Morocco and telegraphed navy press releases to higher headquarters where they were picked up by the wire services. Immediate world-wide coverage resulted, and the feedback served to keep the story prominent in the Moroccan press. Although competing in the news with a government crisis, the navy action broke as the lead story on the front pages and continued there substantially throughout the week. Perhaps coincidentally, nothing more was heard of "base tenure" until early summer.

Within the United States military establishment, the success of the navy operation won official commendations and unofficial kudos, but also evoked the question: "Where was the air force while all this was going on?" The air force was in fact working alongside the navy. Two helicopters from the Sidi Slimane base performed more evacuations than the smaller navy helicopters. But it was a navy operation in the public view.

Following the 1958 flood the staff of the commander in chief, Europe, prepared a master plan for foreign disaster relief operations and it arrived in Morocco on January 15, 1960, the first day of the second flood. The coincidental arrival provoked problems that probably would have been worked out if there had been time to study the plan. Essentially, there were three problem areas in the new concept: finance, command, and the press. The traditional authority of the local commander was suspended. Neither navy nor air force units could begin operations until the ambassador declared that an emergency existed and requested assistance from the U.S. military forces. Once he did that he was obligated to provide funds to reimburse the military units. The effect was to delay decision until the disaster was full-blown before sending United States forces into action. In this case, the embassy complained, urgent rescue operations were delayed thirty-six hours "pending clarification and guarantee of reimbursement by the Embassy to the USAF."[7]

In 1960 coordination control was no longer a function of an officer present with the operating forces. The disaster relief officer on the staff of the commander in chief of the U.S. Air Force in Europe directed operations from Wiesbaden, Germany, through the Moroccan Liaison Office in Rabat. The Moroccan Liaison Office was not accredited to the Moroccan government and was thus ineffective, but even if it had been accredited, the time-lag and transmission difficulties would have made such long-distance coordination unwieldy.

In the new plan, the responsibility for press releases was assigned to the United States Information Service, which was directed to avoid "overemphasizing" the assistance provided by the military services and "to attempt to generate a feeling of mutual cooperation among all nations." Although the USIS personnel made an effort to be useful, they were inadequate. Throughout their tenure in Morocco, they had studiously avoided identification with the bases. Now they incurred the resentment of the Kenitra representatives of the Rabat and Casablanca press, upon whom the bases depended for desirable but less sensational stories, by releasing all information at Rabat. They were basically unfamiliar with military operations and therefore unable to foresee the dramatic episodes of the operation. Stories and pictures were released piecemeal. The releases were uniform, statistically oriented, impersonal, late, and unprinted for the most part. American military partici-

[7] U.S. Embassy, Rabat, telegram 1449 to State Department, dated January 17, 1960, in "History of the United States Air Force, Europe," January 1–June 30, 1960, vol. II: Supporting Documents, chapter 1, doc. no. 18, in USAF Archives, file no. K 570.01.

pation in the flood rescue operations was buried on page five. Pictures made by the military forces were not used in the Moroccan press until the third day of the crisis, and then they were credited to USIS. And finally, USIS was unable to transmit electronically their releases to the military communications channels except through the United States Information Agency, Washington, another unacceptable delay. Such was the price of consensus and coordination.

The rescue operation went smoothly, once it started. Navy Lieutenant Commander James Buchanan was in charge of the operating helicopters, as he had been in 1958. He spoke neither Arabic nor French but was able to work effectively with the governor of the Fez province, who spoke no English. The exigencies of the crisis seemed to furnish a common understanding. If Buchanan was aware of the dissension in Rabat, he ignored it as he went about the business of picking three people out of a treetop here, someone off a rooftop there, and hauling food to a collection point that was cut off to access by road.

The aftermath of the flood was again complicated by bickering between the navy and the air force with the embassy caught in the middle. The subject was money. The navy asked no reimbursement for its efforts in the flood relief, saying in effect, "Forget it. The bookkeeping will cost more than the gasoline burnt." Under navy procedures, any reimbursement would not be to the Naval Air Station, which would have to do the accounting, but to the navy general fund. When directed by the headquarters of U.S. forces in Europe, the navy did submit a report of expenditures covering the materials used, such as aviation gasoline, lubricants, food supplies expended from navy stores, and other items. The air force report was based upon different criteria, which included aircraft depreciation, per diem, and other overhead factors. The air force expenditure, although reflecting less aircraft flight time, was therefore ten times that of the navy. Understandably the embassy preferred to reimburse, if at all, on navy criteria. A steady procession of planning experts from Paris visited Morocco during the next few weeks "to get this mess straightened out," but they had not succeeded when Morocco's heaviest blow fell.

At seven minutes before midnight, February 29, 1960, a shallow earthquake hit Agadir, Morocco's southernmost major city. It utterly destroyed the town, hardly leaving one stone atop another. Twenty thousand people—half the population—were killed.

Agadir was one of Morocco's oldest cities. Pliny, the Roman historian, wrote about it in the first century, A.D., and an old map (1565) shows a Portuguese town at the end of the bay. In the eighteenth century Moroccans traded sugar from Agadir for marble from Italy. Sugar cane is no longer grown in the Sous Valley, but the marble still adorns the whole of Morocco. In 1911 Agadir was on every tongue, a pawn in the checkmate of European politics as Germany "protected her interests" by sending a "cruiser" about the size of a modern PT boat to Agadir. The world was on the verge of war because of the "Agadir Incident." After World War II, European capital financed a string of gleaming, multistory hotels around the throat of the bay. And Agadir, although it retained importance as a port for the agricultural produce of the Sous Valley and for sardines from its coastal waters, became best known as a winter resort city where one could either loll on the beach or ski in the nearby Atlas Mountains.

Agadir was at the height of its tourist season when the earthquake struck, and several Americans were known to be in the city. Ambassador Yost flew into Agadir on a navy plane from Port Lyautey at dawn on March 1. Upon his return he officially declared Agadir a disaster situation and requested maximum assistance from the United States armed forces. He named Lieutenant Commander Leon B. Blair, the navy politico-military liaison officer, as his personal representative at the scene with instructions to coordinate and direct the American effort, which "was being placed at the entire disposition of the Moroccan government."

Rear Admiral Frank Akers, the navy fleet air commander for the eastern Atlantic and Mediterranean, was at Port Lyautey conducting an annual military inspection. He canceled all schedules and ordered his transport planes to asemble at Port Lyautey. Most of them arrived within eighteen hours. Rescue squads were organized at the Port Lyautey, Sidi Slimane, Ben Guerir, and Nouasseur air bases, and all of them were working in Agadir within twenty-four hours after the quake. French planes from the French Naval Air Station five miles east of the city evacuated the first wounded, but navy planes were shuttling in and out of Agadir before the day was over, bringing in rescue squads and flying wounded out to hospitals in Casablanca, Marrakech, and Port Lyautey. As the nearer hospitals filled, those at Meknes and Tangier were used. By noon, March 2, eight navy and two marine transport planes had flown thirty-seven sorties and had evacuated 393 injured victims to permanent hospitals.[8]

About twenty hours after the quake the Americans arrived in Agadir. The first American rescue squad was under the command of marine Lieutenant Colonel Walter Williams. Since French military personnel from the naval air base five miles east of the city were already working in the rubble of the French sector, the Americans took over the Talborjt sector inhabited primarily by Moroccans. During that first night the American rescue parties dug out five survivors and took out another dozen bodies but concluded that without floodlights their efforts were largely ineffective and unacceptably hazardous to the rescue personnel. Fortunately they suffered no casualties although the rubble shifted several times as they bored into it.

The nature of the rescue operation was dictated by circumstances. The earthquake had destroyed the city, killed nearly all of the Moroccan army unit stationed there, destroyed all power sources and disrupted the distribution system beyond usage, and knocked out all communications facilities. Most of the city and provincial officials were either killed or wounded, and the surviving population was in a state of shock. No one exercised any authority until the crown prince arrived during the night of March 1; thereafter some order began to emerge.

Moulay Hassan made his presence felt. He cordoned off the disaster area with Moroccan troops trucked in from the closest garrisons and later flown in from points as far distant as Oujda.[9] He established refugee camps about five miles away from the city and

[8] Headquarters, United States European Command, "After Action Report Agadir Disaster," dated May 13, 1960, p. 24, in Naval Air Station, Port Lyautey files.

[9] Leon Blair, "Order Book," a chronological account of events from March 1 to March 6, contains this entry: "Inezgane, March 3, '60. Request you send planes to Oujda. Departure of troops scheduled for morning, March 4. 800 men. Destination, Agadir. Signed, Oufkir." Colonel Oufkir was King Mohammed V's military aide. "Order Book" in possession of author.

allowed no one to enter the disaster area without a special permit. He ordered looters shot. From 9 A.M. until dark he was in the city, perhaps at one of the command posts but more often with one of the working parties. At 10 P.M. he received the daily reports of the various units at an informal session in his tent at Inezgane, on the outskirts of Agadir, then flew back to Rabat to report to the king. He returned to Inezgane in time for the morning briefing at 4:30 A.M., issued orders for the day, breakfasted and slept for three hours or so, and then returned to the city.

He has been criticized for his decisions,[10] particularly the arbitrary order to shoot looters and to exclude residents from their ruined homes, but there was no looting and his rationale for cordoning off the city had a certain logic. He said the residents were in a state of shock and weakened by exposure and hunger after the quake. If permitted to enter the city, they would simply return to their homes where they would be unable to accomplish anything not already being done more efficiently. He felt admission without restriction would encourage looting and that, since most of the people were ignorant of sanitary precautions in such a situation, they risked infection that would threaten the area with a possible epidemic. It was, he said, a situation that called for trained, disciplined men.

The first rescue parties entered Agadir with only hand tools and light equipment, clearly inadequate for the undertaking. The only communications were provided by "ham" radio operators, dragooned at Port Lyautey with their equipment.[11] Their communication log indicates the evolution of the rescue work; a transmission during the morning of March 2 said: "Most urgent needs in order of priority: disinfectants for morgues; emergency rations—bread, milk, cheese; at least 100 more men with compressors, jackhammers, acetylene torches, generators and lights. FYI [For Your Information]. Next 200 being evacuated to Kenitra. Alert Pasha and

[10] Major General Hewitt, USAF, urged formation of rescue parties from the refugees because "it creates a bad impression when the international press sees American, French, and Moroccan soldiers working under such conditions and five thousand able-bodied Moroccans sitting out at the edge of town doing nothing" (Major General Hewitt to author, Agadir, March 4, 1960).

[11] Navy Petty Officers William Wright and [first name not available] Jones. Lieutenant Commander David Minton and others at Port Lyautey provided the other end of the link.

Super Caid. Pass to A.F. and Embassy." That message reflected both the experience of the first night's operation and the novelty of disaster operations in general. Who would have thought of disinfectants except a doctor? The planning had been done by line officers.

The headquarters of the U.S. Army in Europe, "went on standby basis pending receipts of funds and approval by the Ambassador"[12] on March 2, but sent no help until March 3. Upon arrival the European-based troops found "the time for rescue operations . . . practically past,"[13] according to Air Force Major General Hewitt. This was a too-severe judgment, for the army's Company A, Seventy-ninth Engineer Battalion, from Pirmasens, Germany, performed magnificently upon arrival. The battalion unloaded three DC-8 caterpillar tractors, one turnadozer, eleven five-ton dump trucks, one front-loader, and one wrecker during the night of March 3, and started work the next morning. Their mission was to save lives, not clear away debris, but they performed admirably at both. As they lifted out a concrete floor to get at the spaces underneath, the crane did not simply lay it to one side; it put it on a dump truck to be hauled away. They razed structures whose walls were so unstable as to be hazardous and hauled away the debris. They cleared the streets and filled fissures so that vehicles could get through. On the hill overlooking the city they bulldozed the remains of the ancient *kasbah* into a rounded mound—a burial mound. Saddest of all, in a field southeast of the city their bulldozers opened five long graves, twelve feet wide and six to eight feet deep. In each grave Moroccan troops laid to rest three thousand unidentified victims, side by side, Moslem, Jew, and Christian. There were no shrouds or coffins; they buried them in the clothes they happened to be wearing, or, more often, in the blanket from the bed in which they had been sleeping, then covered the bodies with quicklime, and the bulldozer came again and covered them with earth.

The U.S.S. *Newport News*, a 21,000-ton cruiser from the Sixth

---

[12] "After Action Report Agadir Disaster," p. 14.

[13] General Hewitt's criticism to General Barcus was not of the slow start but of the routine fifteen-hour crew rest that the air force planes made in Madrid en route, just three hours short of their destination. "I don't think we look very good in this one," he concluded. Ibid., p. 33.

Fleet, also arrived during the night of March 3 after a forced-draft voyage from Italy—1,255 miles in forty hours, an average speed of thirty-one knots. Her condensers supplied vitally needed fresh water and her bakers were able to supply ten thousand loaves of bread upon arrival. Her storerooms provided cotton uniforms for Moroccan army personnel working in unaccustomed heat and under conditions where washable uniforms were a must. Admiral Gallatin made his helicopter available to Moulay Hassan for reconnaissance of the area.

Most of the rescue squads from the United States air bases in Morocco were pulled out of Agadir on March 6, their life-saving mission completed. The U.S. Army Engineers and some of the heavy equipment operators and medical personnel from Port Lyautey stayed another week. Lieutenant Davis, a navy doctor from Rota, Spain, stayed three weeks working on a delousing and inoculation program in the Sous Valley. But the story of the Agadir earthquake, so briefly sketched here, did not end with the withdrawal.

When the news of the earthquake broke in the press in the United States it generated a tremendous wave of sympathy for the unfortunate victims.[14] The Job's Daughters organization of Los Altos, California, and the students of Arroyo High School of San Lorenzo collected four tons of children's clothing. The Meals for Millions Foundation in Los Angeles gave three tons of their Multi-Purpose Food concentrate. Three planes from Naval Air Reserve Transport Squadron flew the donations four thousand miles from Oakland to Agadir on March 17. Tom King of the *San Francisco Examiner* and Jean Paulson of the *Berkeley Gazette* accompanied the flight and reported the presentation to Princess Malika, King

[14] Probably few stories in the history of modern journalism have been more inaccurately reported. See, for example, the *New York Times*, March 2, 1960, p. 1, 18, and March 7, 1960, p. 10. No tidal wave or fire occurred and Lieutenant (junior grade) Norman Lefton, reported "on his honeymoon in Agadir," was not even married. No submarine volcano formed, the sea bottom did not undergo major change, and Crown Prince Moulay Hassan did not confirm reports of a "boiling sea when he flew over the spot in a helicopter late this afternoon." The mass graves were not two feet deep as reported in *Time* 85 (March 14, 1960). The pictures in *Life* 48 (March 14, 1960): 36, show them to be at least six feet deep. Most of the fictional report writers never got south of Casablanca.

Mohammed V's third daughter and president of the Moroccan Red Crescent, at Agadir. She said: "You have brought what we need most, food and clothing for the babies. In situations such as this people are inclined to think in general terms—in terms of adults. These children have lost everything, even their adults. What you have brought today will satisfy at least half of our present needs."[15]

The story was widely printed in the United States newspapers on March 19–20, and the result was electrifying. From across the nation offers to help poured into navy offices. Three days after the story was first printed, Admiral Allen Smith, Jr., sent out a message to all navy stations: "Cease collections *Angels for Agadir* [the code name for the operation]. Present response exceeds lift capacity." A few days later three transports from the Naval Air Station, Memphis, Tennessee, discharged twenty-three tons of clothing at the Naval Air Station, Kenitra, for delivery to the king's residence at Dar-es-Salaam, where it was sorted and distributed through Entr'aide Nationale channels. On April 23 Commander T. F. Byrnes brought the U.S.S. *Opportune,* a navy rescue ship, into the harbor at Agadir with the remainder of the clothing —fifty-five tons—and presented it to Princess Lalla Aisha.

The navy part in the Agadir disaster brought the usual criticisms of confusion in command responsibility, funding, communications, and "a tendency of certain forces engaged to work unilaterally within a joint operation." Specifically, "the Navy rescue party conducted rescue operations throughout the night of March 1 without coordination with other U.S. forces [which had not yet arrived]." The same old unresolved question of ambassadorial versus military authority was again raised: "CINCUSAFE [Commander in Chief, U.S. Air Force, Europe] had been given responsibility by USCINCEUR [United States Commander in Chief, Europe] for the Agadir operation but the U.S. Navy apparently was running the operation."[16] The air force "monitored the operations cost to insure that the disaster relief would not exceed authorized funds,"[17] but missed the essential point—the timeliness of

[15] Copy of the story as transmitted over U.S. Navy communication system in possession of the author.

[16] "After Action Report Agadir Disaster," pp. 1–2, 20.

[17] "History United States Air Force, Europe," January 1–June 30, 1960, vol. I: Narrative, pp. 6–7, gives the cost incurred by U.S. military services in the

response is frequently more significant than the magnitude. In an unprecedented and chaotic disaster situation the Moroccan nation was reassured by the knowledge that competent help from the United States was a reality.

Agadir could have been a turning point in Moroccan-American relations. The nation was tired of internal political bickering and was inclined to regard the series of misfortunes as God's punishment for their political sins. They rallied to the royal family. King Mohammed V, conscious of the fact that only the Western world had jumped to Morocco's aid, spoke of the help his people had received from the United States. He said, "When a few hours [after the quake] I arrived at the scene, our friends were already at work in the ruins. . . . The American knowhow became a miracle of wonder to our people."[18]

On March 6 at a luncheon at Agadir the crown prince asked Ambassador Yost to request President Eisenhower to lend Lieutenant Commander Blair to the Royal Moroccan armed forces as a technical and liaison officer. "Many questions with respect to the bases remain unsettled," said the prince. The ambassador received the proposal with little enthusiasm and his staff even less so, but the Department of Defense approved the request. The embassy not only refused to take advantage of the new "technical" approach but worked actively to negate it.[19] The naval attaché, determined "to break any connection between the palace and Port Lyautey," insisted that Blair be administratively assigned as assistant naval attaché and, when that was done, wrote his orders in such a manner that he could not be paid mileage and pay allowances.[20] The

---

Agadir Operation as USAF, $727,705.02; USN, $81,248.14; and the U.S. Army $14,465.35. The air force flew fifty-two missions to airlift 575 tons of cargo and 481 personnel. Total missions by the navy are not given, but by noon, March 2, totaled thirty-seven. Port Lyautey–based aircraft evacuated 417 victims, 27 to the Port Lyautey base hospital, lifted 279 tons of cargo into Agadir, and flew 605 relief workers into Agadir and out again. U.S.-based planes of the U.S. Naval Air Reserve flew six missions with 27 tons of cargo into Agadir.

[18] King Mohammed V, as told to Christine Hotchkiss, "Why I Like Americans," *This Week*, September 11, 1960, p. 34.

[19] The embassy sought instead accreditation of an air force attaché in its letter no. 702 of May 10, 1960, to the Moroccan minister of foreign affairs. The request was refused. Correspondence in possession of the author.

[20] Initial orders envisaged continued permanent assignment at Port Lyautey

ambassador refused to become "involved in administrative detail" when the inequity was brought to his attention. Not only was the connection with Port Lyautey broken, the naval attaché opined that Blair should stay away from his assigned office in the palace "as much as possible in order to avoid being used as a link with the Embassy. We have established channels," he said.[21]

The modified orders precipitated a grave crisis in the Moroccan government. In December, 1958, the king had disarmed his leftist opposition by giving it the responsibiliy of government. It had failed in its mission, but it refused to resign, and the king had not yet dismissed it. Prime Minister Ibrahim and Minister of National Economy Bouabid were identified in the popular mind with Mehdi Ben Barka's Union Nationale des Forces Populaires, which had split from the Istiqlal party and was suspected of sympathy with, if not complicity in, the assassination plot against the crown prince.[22] Protocol demanded that an assistant naval attaché be accredited to the Moroccan Foreign Office. The ambassador accordingly submitted a request for accreditation and diplomatic status on May 11, and on May 16 Ibrahim (who was also foreign minister) replied that "such a position [at the General Staff of the Royal Armed Forces] does not permit the minister of foreign affairs to consider this officer as *persona grata*,"[23] the last of several unmistakable slaps at the crown prince and the king.

Seeking to make an issue that would appeal to the country of

with temporary duty orders to the ambassador for policy guidance. The naval attaché's endorsement to the modified orders indicated that "Government Quarters were available at NAS, Port Lyautey, and were utilized in the execution of these orders," precluded payment of per diem for lodging and food at Rabat, but authorized only one round trip between Rabat and Port Lyautey, thirty-five miles away—no commuting. The purpose of such an endorsement was to put pressure on the recipient to seek termination of the orders in order to avoid the additional expense.

[21] Verbal orders, Captain Jesse Pennell to author at the U.S. Embassy, Rabat, April 29, 1960.

[22] See *New York Times*, April 3, p. 10; March 30, p. 13; March 25, p. 3; and March 20, 1960, p. 26, for references to the assassination plot. General Hamou ben Kettani told the author in an interview at Rabat, April 10, 1960, that the plot included several leading members of palace and government staffs, including himself.

[23] Moroccan Ministry of Foreign Affairs letter to the United States Ambassador, dated Rabat, May 16, 1960; copy in possession of author.

"foreign domination" of the Moroccan army, Ibrahim issued a press release on May 20,[24] the day his reply was actually delivered to the U.S. Embassy, justifying his action. It was his last official act; four hours later the king announced via Radio Maroc that Prime Minister Abdallah Ibrahim, having completed the mission entrusted to him more than a year before, had resigned and that a new government would shortly be constituted.[25]

The new government that took office May 24 was Morocco's first royal government since independence. The king also served as prime minister, and the crown prince was deputy prime minister and still chief of staff of the royal armed forces. Si Bekkai, the ex-prime minister, was named minister of interior, and Colonel Mohammed Oufkir became director of the National Police. The king thus retained all military and police power in his own hands or in those followers of unquestionable loyalty. Reda Guedira became director-general of the Royal Cabinet, and Mohammed Cherkaoui, minister of post, telephone, and telegraph. Both were members of the old Roosevelt Club. Abderrahman Abdelali, so prominently associated with the Moroccan Office of Information in New York during the fight for independence, was minister of public works. Dr. Abdelkrim El Khatib, the ex-commander of the Liberation Army in the Rif Mountains, accepted his first governmental post as minister of labor and social questions. The Istiqlal party was represented only by the minister of public health, Youssef Bel Abbes, although several of the ministers at one time had been party members. The king had sought to include all parties but it "became difficult to establish such a government today," hence "I prefer to take the matter in hand and direct the affairs of state through the Crown Prince in the interest of stability and national union."[26] The new "Government of National Union around the Throne"

---

[24] *L'Avant-Garde*, June 18 and 26, 1960; *L'Express* (Paris), June 2, 1960; *Er Rai El Am*, May 21, 1960; *Time* 75 (June 6, 1960): 30; *American Universities Field Staff Reports Service, North Africa Series* 4, no. 2 (May, 1960): 9; and *New York Times*, May 23, 1960, all comment on the "Blair Affair."

[25] *New York Times*, May 21, 1960, p. 11. The *Times* attributed the dismissal to Ibrahim's demand for a reorganization of the Interior Ministry and the National Police System, and that was certainly an important factor because it, too, was a challenge to the Crown.

[26] Ibid., May 24, 1960, p. 1.

was unquestionably the most pro-American government since the Bekkai governments, if not since independence.

In his speech announcing the new government, the king promised a constitution before the end of 1962. He called upon the people to end demagoguery and remain orderly and tranquil while the constitution was being drafted.[27] A few weeks later he explained to an American journalist, "I could be a dictator, if I chose. . . . My people wish me to rule them, because they have very little tradition of self-rule. But . . . dictatorship does not pay." Then he added this mystical but characteristic allegory: "I am building a house for you, my children. I am going to put furniture in it—even though you may not wish me to do so. Oh, I know, you may prefer to sleep on the floor, our ancestors have done so and survived, but my duty is to show you better ways." His legacy to his people and to the future would be democratic institutions, and again he resorted to symbolism: "The schoolboys from your naval air base have helped our Moroccan youths to plant the Forest of Youth [in November, 1957] on the bare hills outside our capital city of Rabat. I enjoyed driving by and watching the young eucalyptus saplings turn into slim, healthy trees. This is a good augury for our friendship. This is how the ideas which you have imparted to us will take shape."[28]

In spite of the promise of the new political situation, the United States failed to respond. Proposals concerning the American bases fell like rain during the next few weeks, but they were ignored or rejected out of hand. The crown prince had decided before the change of government to take a hand in the American base situation. On February 12 he had proposed a visit to the U.S. Air Force base at Boulhaut, which King Mohammed V and President Eisenhower had agreed would be turned over to the Moroccan government by March 31. He flew into the base with General Kettani and four other officers that afternoon.[29] The flight control tower

[27] Ibid.

[28] To Christine Hotchkiss on July 3, 1960, at Rabat, reported in "Why I Like Americans," *This Week*, September 11, 1960. The appearance of the article by the chief of state of a "nonaligned" nation just before the session of the United Nations at which Khrushchev distinguished himself by pounding on his desk with his shoe caused considerable comment.

[29] The author was one; the others were Commandant N'Michi, later com-

was not manned; the line crew that should have parked his air-craft was not alerted; no one met him. After a fifteen-minute wait, an air force major arrived who explained that he had received no "official" notice [from U.S.A.F. command authorities] that the prince and his party were coming, although he had been unofficially advised that he might "drop in." The prince, miffed by the dis-courtesy, departed immediately but left General Kettani and the others to inspect the base. Boulhaut was evacuated March 4, 1960, without ceremony—and with no notification to the Moroccan gov-ernment.[30]

The first proposal by the new government was offered by Si Bekkai. He would turn the Port Lyautey naval base into a school for the Moroccan navy (which did not yet exist). He would send two hundred Moroccan naval trainees to Kenitra and place them under the command of the American commandant to be trained as the cadre of a navy. His proposal was never forwarded from the embassy to Washington.[31]

Dr. Abdelkrim El Khatib, minister of labor and social questions, had his eye on Site Y-11, the air defense headquarters at the Rabat-Salé air field. Critical of the impersonality and vagueness of the existing American programs, he proposed the creation after evacu-ation of a "Boystown" at Site Y-11, which would be administered by Americans—"four young university graduates who need in-ternational experience and one man of experience, perhaps in retirement from the military or business." Boystown, Morocco, would be for children of the poorer classes who would otherwise have no chance for an education. They would receive an acceler-ated, rudimentary education and "at some point, when they have learned English and are otherwise ready, some of them will be sent to the United States, some to work on a prosperous farm where they would learn to mix fertilizers and repair machinery; others to a stock raiser where they would learn to mix feeds and castrate

---

mander of the Royal Moroccan air force, Major Serghini, and M. Alami. The author retains a copy of his report to the ambassador concerning the visit.

[30] "History of United States Air Force, Europe," January 1–June 30, 1960, vol. II, chap. II, doc. no. 30 (U.S. Embassy, Rabat, telegram 1511, to State Dept.).

[31] The author gave Mr. Bekkai's proposal to the U.S. naval attaché on June 1, 1960.

cattle. When they returned to Morocco they would be able to teach rural cadres the fundamentals of modern agriculture—they would be a rural intelligentsia rather than a rural proletariat."

Dr. Khatib did not envisage Boystown as a one-way street. He felt that Americans might want to come to Morocco to perfect their knowledge of Arabic or French or to participate in some phase of Moroccan life that interested them, or simply to learn by living with a Moroccan family.[32] Nothing came of the proposal.

Site Y-11 was evacuated June 23. The crown prince had asked that a "dignified and honorable modality for transfer" be worked out on an "army-to-army" basis, a much simpler procedure, since all of the political problems had been resolved. His suggestion was rejected, and the American garrison simply departed during the night of June 22; when the Moroccans arrived the next day, no one was there.

The American discourtesy toward the Moroccan government was out of concern for the French, who insisted that, even though they could no longer deliver their part of the contract, the 1950–1951 agreements were still valid and that the United States was obligated to turn over the bases and their fixed installations to the French air force.[33] The Moroccans did not ask the United States to take a position vis-à-vis France, but did insist that the United States give advance notice and provide an inventory of the matériel left behind. Ambassador Yost was not willing to accept the French contention, but neither was he willing to meet the Moroccan demand. He said the agreement to evacuate did not oblige the United States to notify Morocco of U.S. troop movements.[34] He preferred a unilateral withdrawal, leaving the French and Moroccans to fight out the question between themselves.

The closing of Site Y-11, the largest air defense site in Morocco, resulted in the transfer away from Rabat of about 450 military

[32] Dr. Khatib's proposal was initially advanced in conversation with a group of naval air reservists and newspapermen from Kansas City at the home of his brother-in-law, Pasha Abdelhamid El Alaoui, at Kenitra, on June 15, 1960, and was presented in a memorandum dated June 17, 1960, to the U.S. Embassy. See *The Independence Examiner*, June 25, 1960, for a report on the Boystown idea proposed by Dr. Khatib.

[33] "History of the United States Air Force, Europe," January 1–June 30, 1960, vol. I: Narrative, pp. 61–66.

[34] *New York Times*, April 26, 1960, p. 11.

personnel (half of whom had dependents living in town), the release of several large buildings in the city including two hotels, and the discharge of about two hundred employees and as many more domestic servants. The French opposed the evacuation because it would immediately pose the question of land titles and of air defense and would encourage greater demands on the French, but Ambassador Yost was adamant. He felt that the visible evidence of evacuation from the national capital would give the Moroccan government a political advantage that would outweigh the economic disadvantages.[35]

The most promising of the Moroccan overtures, however, was only peripherally associated with the bases. On May 2, General Kettani requested United States assistance in planning a Moroccan navy whose function would be essentially that of a coast guard with helicopters capable of rescue missions, "such as those in the Rharb with which you are certainly familiar," and coastal patrol craft to prevent smuggling and "to enable Morocco to fulfill her international obligations." He requested the help of U.S. Navy engineers in the development of Alhucemas as an antismuggling port in the Mediterranean. General Kettani said Morocco had asked the United States for such assistance the preceding fall, when the military mission headed by Colonel Anderson visited Morocco in connection with the sale of United States–manufactured support and communications equipment.[36]

General Kettani's proposal, if it had been adopted, would have provided a face-saving cover for the U.S. Navy at Port Lyautey. A Moroccan navy could have been based there without the slightest inconvenience to functional use by the U.S. Navy. The cover would have been good for years; it takes time to build and train a navy. It was an opportunity to draw the attention of Morocco away from Algeria, away from Nasser, away from Mauritania— all African sores—and to the Atlantic and its community of nations. By lending available surplus U.S. Navy patrol vessels to a Moroccan navy and by providing U.S. Navy training to the crews, the whole future Moroccan navy might have been oriented toward

[35] "History of the United States Air Force, Europe," January 1–June 30, 1959, vol. I: Narrative, pp. 54–56.

[36] General Kettani's proposal was submitted to the United States ambassador in a memorandum dated May 12, 1960; copy in the possession of the author.

U.S. Navy strategic and tactical concepts. In view of the strategic significance of Morocco's geographical position the advantages of responding favorably appeared glaringly obvious, but Ambassador Yost merely suggested that Morocco "get on with current programs" before attempting something new.

The royal Moroccan armed forces were interested in a jet air force as well as a navy. Morocco had little apparent need for jet airplanes; it had neither the airfields for their use, the technical personnel for their maintenance, the supply organization for their provisioning, nor the pilots to fly them. There were only four pilots, including the crown prince, in the royal Moroccan armed forces who were jet-qualified, and jet planes delivered in 1960 would have been obsolete before all of the deficiencies were corrected. The Moroccan need, however, was political rather than military. "We are competing for leadership in Africa," the crown prince said, "with Egypt, with Ghana, with Guinea. Somebody has to hold the reins or the Communists will take all. We need jets as a prestige factor. Our competition already has them."[37]

Crown Prince Hassan proposed to buy F-100-D, or better, planes from the United States, and he was prepared to pay the same prices for which the United States had sold F-84's to France some three years earlier. He broached the proposition to the embassy and also directly to Secretary of the Army Wilbur Brucker upon the latter's visit to Morocco in the summer. The United States demurred, anticipating a protest from France that would have been couched in terms of the Algerian War but that would have really been concerned with preemption of the supply prerogative for the Moroccan military and the incidental inhibition of Moroccan prestige. In October at the United Nations when Nikita Khrushchev offered MIG's to Prince Hassan, he still wanted U.S.-built airplanes. He advised the Department of Defense of the Soviet offer and suggested that, unless the United States indicated before he returned to Morocco a willingness to sell them, he would buy the Soviet planes.[38] He received no definitive answer at all.

[37] Crown Prince Moulay Hassan to the author, Rabat, February 12, 1960. General Kettani again raised the question as posed to the Anderson survey group in November, 1959, to Colonel Keisler, the U.S. army attaché on May 6, and by memorandum transmitted by the author to the ambassador on May 7.

[38] The information was relayed by the author by telephone on October 6 to

The failure of the United States to respond to the various proposals of the crown prince resulted from several factors. The ambassador and his diplomatic staff were reluctant to recognize an
approach through any except the traditional Foreign Office–to–
Embassy channel. The "technical" approach served well in 1947
when the United States and France had been unable to reach diplomatic agreement on Port Lyautey, but when the crown prince
suggested that a Moroccan commander (instead of a French commander) be named at each base as a symbol, the possibility was
rejected as impracticable.[39] The decision assumed a general incom-
petence on the part of the Moroccan armed forces as well as hostility toward the crown prince.

The misevaluation of the Moroccan military establishment was
an indictment of the anachronistic military attaché system that,
based on European tradition, was unworkable in Morocco. The
attachés were too old, too protocol conscious, and too senior in
rank to be able to establish any sort of meaningful relationship
with individuals in the royal Moroccan armed forces. The ambassador accepted the attaché system as part of the accoutrement of
an embassy, but neither supported it nor demanded responsibility
from it. He condoned what amounted to insubordination.[40] Both
the army and naval attachés felt that the commander of naval
activities at Port Lyautey was usurping their function—and probably that of the ambassador as well. Therefore they ignored any
question that was not passed "officially" through channels that

---

Commander Allan Slaff, personal aide to the chief of naval operations, and
confirmed by letter on October 7. See also *New York Times*, February 19, 1961,
pp. iv–61.

[39] "History of the United States Air Force, Europe," January 1–June 30,
1960, vol. II: Supporting Documents, doc. no. 18.

[40] For example, Ambassador Yost asked the author on May 3 to find an
American proposal for the sale of military equipment to the Moroccan army,
submitted two weeks earlier to the headquarters, Royal Moroccan Army, and
to expedite action on it if possible. The author located it and hand-carried it
through to General Kettani, who presented it to the crown prince for signature
on May 5. It was signed and returned to the U.S. army attaché on May 6. The
army attaché complained to the Department of the Army of navy interference
in army affairs. When the matter was brought to Ambassador Yost's attention
as something he had specifically directed, he said he had not known of Colonel
Keisler's telegram, that he had no control over the attaché communications
channels.

they recognized, whether the Moroccans recognized them or not.[41]

The Blair mission obviously had no chance of success and it was terminated June 28. Ambassador Yost explained to the prince that the unceasing attacks in the republican press of "foreign influence" in the Moroccan army was embarrassing to the United States, and that after the assassination attempt of June 15—two sticks of dynamite that did not explode in his car—it was dangerous for Lieutenant Commander Blair to remain longer in Morocco. The month of July was spent in a series of good-bye parties, and the Blair family departed Morocco on August 8. The antimonarchial *L'Avant-Garde* editorially paid its respects: "The famous Commandant Blair is finally leaving Morocco. . . . We wish him good-bye . . . and hope he never comes back."[42]

Crown Prince Hassan had tried for eight months to find an acceptable context for the American bases when, in October, he led the Moroccan delegation to the United Nations General Assembly. While in the United States he discussed Moroccan-American relations with Secretary of Defense Thomas S. Gates, Chairman of the Joint Chiefs of Staff General Nathan F. Twining, Under Secretary of State Douglas Dillon, the secretary of navy, and high-ranking officers of the Department of Defense. He paid tribute to the "magnificent and deeply appreciated contribution" of the U.S. armed forces at Agadir. He said the U.S. forces in Morocco were "respected because of their obvious lack of aggressive intentions, colonial traditions, or occupational role," but as "foreign troops" were not desired on Moroccan soil. He suggested instead that Sidi Yahia (the communications station dependent on the Naval Air Station) be operated by U.S. civilian personnel augmented by some Moroccan personnel. He pledged that the American-built bases would never be used by a third power.

As to general foreign policy, Moulay Hassan said that Morocco

[41] For example, the refusal of the commanding officer of the U.S. Air Force base at Boulhaut to meet the crown prince and General Kettani on May 12, and the refusal of the naval attaché to meet the U.S.S. *Opportune* and Princess Aisha at Agadir on April 23.

[42] *L'Avant-Garde*, July 30, 1960. The paper had somehow secured an invitation to the farewell cocktail party at the naval base and printed a facsimile. The sentries at the gate had been instructed to pass anyone with an invitation. About fifty welcome but unexpected friends attended the reception with the invitation clipped from the newspaper.

could contribute little to the West by openly backing it, that Morocco must remain neutral, but that the United States risked losing the respect and backing of the neutral nations at the United Nations if it persisted in regarding neutral votes as a sign of enmity. With Algeria obviously in mind, he urged the United States to exercise "dynamic" leadership in order to present effectively the United States' case, which he said was essentially "correct and moral."

The crown prince was no more successful in Washington than he had been in Morocco. The United States military chieftains concluded that he was "haughty and weak . . . but that his fallacious, mystic, neutral psychology could be modified by a determined effort to win his confidence," and, correctly, that "military leaders have not established effective relations with top Moroccans."[43] No responsible individual had ever before accused Moulay Hassan of weakness. His critics complained that he was trying to consolidate the dynasty and his own succession against republican tendencies,[44] which undoubtedly was true. Abderrahim Bouabid, the leftist-leaning minister of national economy under Ibrahim and the two preceding governments, said he was a "brilliant and intelligent man, but he does not share my political and economic ideas."[45] Both Bouabid and Ibrahim charged "fascist dictatorship" and the exchange of "colonial overlords for Moroccan overlords" against the government of May 24,[46] and Mehdi Ben Barka accused the king and crown prince of seeking to reestablish a "theocratic, feudal regime" that would "revive or maintain medieval social structures" in Morocco.[47] The journalist Jean Lacouture asked rhetorically why such an exceptional person, brilliant, well educated, courageous, successful within and outside the country in diplomatic matters, should cause such debate. He concluded there were three reasons: his very assurance indisposed many—princes

[43] "Memo for the record," dated October 18, 1960, concerning the conversations of October 12, in "History of the United States Air Force, Europe," July 1–December 31, 1960, vol. 3, chap. 2, doc. no. 61.

[44] *New York Times*, March 30, 1960, p. 13.

[45] Ibid., April 3, 1960, p. 10.

[46] Ibid., May 28, 1960, p. 8.

[47] Ibid., May 29, 1960, p. 7.

ought not to have such virtues—his habitual lateness, and his entourage of playboys, rumored without foundation to be in public employ.[48]

The appearance of the criticism belied the dictatorship charge; Morocco was probably the freest country on the African continent, and the new "Government of Union around the Throne" made notable progress. Mohammed El Basri and others implicated in the 1959 assassination plot against the crown prince were pardoned for Aid el Kebir in June. Municipal and communal elections were held on May 29. Ninety-two percent of the eligible voters, men and women over the age of twenty-one, were registered, and 75 percent of them voted. The party affiliations of those elected were disputed, but the official figures indicated that the Istiqlal party won 44 percent of the 10,200 places; the National Union of Popular Forces (the Mehdi Ben Barka schism), 23 percent; the independents, 22 percent; the Popular movement (the Khatib-Aherdan group), 7 percent; and the Constitutional Democratic party (the old Ouezzani group), 3 percent.[49] The antimonarchist strength was greatest in the industrialized cities, but the interior seemed safe for the Crown.

On August 27, true to his promise as he assumed personal power in May, King Mohammed V appointed a constitutional committee of seventy-eight members that included almost every politician of note except those of the Ben Barka faction.[50] Forty of them were chosen by the king from professional and technical groups and the other thirty-six represented the sixteen provinces of Morocco, four each from Casablanca and Rabat, and two from each of the other provinces. The king bypassed the political parties, for the draft-constitution had to be approved first by the king and then by the people in a direct referendum.

Paradoxically the American diplomatic colony in Morocco saw the government, considered fundamentally right-wing if not re-

[48] Jean and Simone Lacouture, *Le Maroc à l'épreuve*, p. 124.

[49] Quoted in Roger Le Tourneau, *Evolution Politique de L'Afrique du Nord Musulmane: 1920–1961*, p. 271.

[50] See the *Bulletin Officiel du Royaume du Maroc*, no. 2,506 (November 4, 1960), p. 1898, for the *dahir* creating the constitutional committee, and no. 2,507 (November 11, 1960), p. 1930, for the list and affiliation of the members.

actionary, drifting to the left in foreign policy. The *New York Times*, reporting that drift, cited the Moroccan support for Patrice Lumumba in the Congo and the cooperation of General Kettani, commander of the Moroccan forces and deputy supreme commander of the United Nations forces in the Congo, with Colonel Joseph Mobuto, chief of staff of the Congolese army, who took over when Lumumba was deposed. But the *New York Times* also cited the seizure five times in one week of *Rai El Amm*, a leftist newspaper, for articles critical of the United States military aid program for Morocco.[51]

The leftward drift seemed confirmed when the Moroccan government announced conclusion of a military aid agreement with the Soviet Union for twelve MIG-17 fighters, two Ilyushin bombers, and other military equipment. The American reaction was confused. The *New York Times* reported Western diplomatic quarters "stunned by the announcement of the Soviet gift," and a "high-level Western diplomat" said that Morocco had opened its doors to the cold war.[52] American diplomatic officials in Rabat spoke of a "friendly disengagement" in Morocco as the result of Moroccan acceptance of Soviet aid but, when challenged, categorically denied the report that the United States had threatened to cut off spare parts for American equipment provided to Morocco.[53] Military observers expressed the fear that the Soviet planes might compromise the security of the U.S. bases in Spain as well as Morocco. American displeasure was evidenced by scaling down economic aid from $50 million to $40 million.[54]

The Moroccan action should have surprised no one in view of the position the crown prince had taken a month earlier, but then his "threat" had been regarded as a bluff. The American resentment was laid squarely at the palace door and relations became cooler, if possible, than before. Embassy officials openly predicted that the dynasty was on its last leg, that it could not last "longer than two years."[55] The fact that acceptance of the Soviet aid would

[51] *New York Times*, September 19, 1960, p. 11.

[52] Ibid., November 16, 1960, pp. 1, 4, and November 17, 1960, p. 5.

[53] See ibid., February 13, 1961, pp. 1, 9, for the report, and February 14, 1961, p. 6, for the denial.

[54] Ibid., December 4, 1960, p. 35.

[55] Mr. Laurence Hall, public affairs officer, to Mrs. Robert Roberts and other

appeal to the group that had been most critical of the monarchy apparently escaped the prophets.

On January 24, 1961, the crown prince again asked for jet aircraft from the United States, making his approach this time to General Horace Wade, the ranking air force officer in Morocco. He said that he had made the request earlier to the embassy but had received an evasive answer concerning "budget considerations." When General Wade informed the embassy of the approach, he was advised that "the Chief of Mission [the Ambassador] is the personal representative of the President"—or, keep out of diplomatic affairs. The embassy took a negative view of the request in view of "the Prince's precarious position politically, his undependable, contradictory, emotional attitude, and the dearth of advantage."[56]

Conceivably, except for one of those accidents of history, Crown Prince Moulay Hassan might have remained an irritant in American-Moroccan relations for a long period, an irritant that could not be ignored because of his position as chief of staff of the royal Moroccan armed forces. That accident, the death of King Mohammed V on February 26, 1961, during the course of a minor nasal operation, elevated him to the throne. The Moroccan nation had lost its beloved leader and the world one of its towering statesmen, one who in six short years had negotiated the independence and reunification of his country, unified its economy and monetary system, inaugurated profound social changes, and laid the foundation for the settlement of the Algerian War.[57] As chief of state, King Hassan II could no longer be dismissed as an inconsequential playboy.

The extent to which the United States had misjudged Hassan rapidly became apparent. The international press anticipated the overthrow of the monarchy,[58] and American diplomatic officials

---

members of the Dallas Council on World Affairs, at Dallas, Texas, December 6, 1960.

[56] "History of the United States Air Force, Europe," January 1–June 30, 1961, vol. V, doc. no. 207, and 7416 supp. sq., Rabat (MLO) telegram 5557 to USAFE, attached.

[57] Si Bekkai, author architect of Moroccan independence and one of Mohammed V's closest associates, also died of a heart attack on April 13.

[58] *Fort Worth Star Telegram*, February 28, 1961, story by Thomas Brady, *New York Times* News Service, and the *Dallas Morning News*, March 5, 1961.

predicted a coup "within forty-eight hours."[59] But the Moroccan nation only mourned its dead king and accepted as the natural order the succession of his son to the throne. Not only did the "left" not revolt, but it joined the rest of the nation in mourning and acceptance. The very idea of revolt was unrealistic because it ignored the tradition of monarchial rule, the conservatism and attachment to Islam of the larger part of the Moroccan people, and the elemental fact that the army and the national police were undeniably and unquestionably loyal to the throne. The international press and the diplomats had been bemused by the polemics of the leftist press in Morocco.

Hassan II as king produced no immediate change in policy toward the military bases. The director-general of the Royal Cabinet, Reda Guedira, had suggested in October that the United States, if dissatisfied with its agreement concerning Kenitra, should make counterproposals—"You haven't asked for any more than you are getting."[60] On May 23, 1961, Minister of Public Works Abderrahman Abdelali, in Boston for a minor operation, said, "The bases have represented over the years a point of contact between your people and ours. We should search for a means of maintaining that contact. We don't want to see them go like Boulhaut [with MIG's]. I am authorized by His Majesty to discuss and explore this question should any responsible American authority desire to do so." That information was transmitted to the chief of naval operations on May 24,[61] but the overture was completely ignored.

Morocco received its Soviet-built MIG's in early 1961 and based them at the U.S.-built Boulhaut air base. The air force, stung by that decision, sought to develop a program that would permit retention of the rest of its bases if possible, or, if not, deny their usage to others and provide for reentry if necessitated by world conditions. The program would emphasize the advantage of continued

[59] In an interview at Kenitra, October 4, 1961, Captain R. D. Cox, USN, commander of the U.S. naval activities at Kenitra, said, "My standard greeting to the Rabat crowd these days is, 'When is the forty-eight–hour period up?' "

[60] Transmitted by the author, letter dated Washington, October 7, 1960, to Commander Allan Slaff, personal aide to the chief of naval operations.

[61] By author, letter dated May 24, 1961, at Washington, to Commander Allan Slaff, personal aide to the chief of naval operations.

association with the United States, including the favorable climate for investment that would result from "mutual understanding." Belatedly the air force was willing to adopt the "technical solution" that the crown prince had been harping on for a year—the improvement of civil air facilities at Nouasseur, expanded training of Moroccan pilots, and the provision of jet aircraft.[62] Unfortunately the program was never funded, but the objective was partially achieved by other agencies.[63]

By the end of 1961 the question of the American bases had been settled. All except Kenitra would be evacuated by the end of 1963, as agreed, but with provisions for reentry. "Our accords then [in 1959] and now [in 1966] foresee the possibility that the United States will again need the bases—and we do not reject the idea. That is why in the reconversion of Nouasseur we are using American material. If the United States needs Nouasseur urgently, there will be no need to change the equipment in the installation."[64] In providing for the disposition of the bases, a nine-member team headed by William O. Baxter from the U.S. Department of State studied with Moroccan officials the possibility of converting the U.S. Air Force bases to civilian use. On December 24, Moroccan officials indicated that Nouasseur would become an international airport, and its housing facilities would be used to resettle Casablanca slum dwellers. The industrial facilities would be used to decentralize Casablanca industry. Sidi Slimane was to become an agricultural training school and farming center. Ben Guerir, "half-way between New York and New Delhi, half-way between Oslo and Johannesburg," was to be an international air maintenance

[62] "History of the United States Air Force, Europe," January 1–June 30, 1961, vol. V, doc. no. 201, dated June 5, 1961.

[63] The change in attitude of the executive department of the U.S. government was prompted in part by heightened congressional interest in the diplomatic blundering in Morocco. That concern is reflected in correspondence (in possession of the author) with President Kennedy, Vice-President Johnson, Congressman George Mahon, and Senator Thomas Dodd between December, 1960, and November, 1961, and culminating with the author's testimony before the Senate Foreign Relations Committee in a hearing before Senator Dodd, and others, on November 15, 1961.

[64] Interview, Ahmed Taibi Benhima, director-general of the Royal Council of Ministers, Rabat, July 25, 1966.

depot. Kenitra was to be a naval air station for the royal armed forces, and its hospital, schools, and other buildings were to be the nucleus of a new civilian settlement.[65]

The year of 1962 was a period of watchful waiting for the Americans in Morocco. The Moroccan flirtation with the Soviet Union apparently accomplished its objective. Moroccan Defense Minister Majoubi Aherdan said Morocco purchased Soviet arms because of her urgent defense needs, but would have purchased them from the United States if they had been obtainable quickly. "When there is a fire at the border we cannot wait around for our friends to make up their minds whether it is politically expedient to help," he added.[66] In July King Hassan, tired of long-range dickering, said he would discuss Moroccan-American military questions only with President Kennedy or his direct representative. Ambassador Phillip Bonsal, whose short stay had been neither pleasurable nor productive, tendered the president's invitation to visit Washington in March, 1963, and then resigned.[67]

Conditions were favorable for King Hassan's first state visit outside Africa. He had been able to consolidate his domestic position. His "Fundamental Law" of June 2, 1961, had defined the nature and duties of the Moroccan state and its economic and social role and had confirmed the guarantee of individual and public liberties and the position of "nonengagement" in foreign policy.[68] The constitution outlined in his Independence Day speech of November 18, 1962, was approved in a national referendum on December 7 by an overwhelming 97 percent of the voters.[69] The king's opponents charged that a generous distribution of American wheat swayed the elections.[70] And the Egyptian press interpreted the constitution as evidence of the king's pro-west, pro-European sympathy and the nation's support of it as a break in "Arab solidarity"

[65] *New York Times*, December 24, 1961, p. 15, and "History of 4310th Air Division, 3922nd Combat Support Group," February 1–28, 1962, in USAF Archives, file no. K-Div-4310-HI.

[66] *New York Times*, March 4, 1962, p. 22.

[67] Ibid., July 17, 1962, p. 12, and "History of the Sixteenth Air Force," July–December, 1962, vol. I, pp. 71–72, in USAF Archives, file no. K 569.01.

[68] See Vaucher, *Sous les cèdres d'Ifrane*, pp. 266–268, for the text.

[69] See *Le Maroc en Marche: Discours de S.M. Le Roi Hassan II depuis son Intrônisation*, pp. 541–542.

[70] *New York Times*, December 22, 1962, p. 3.

that had strengthened the king's grip on his country and caused him to look less to the East.[71]

International circumstances had also improved. The Algerian War was over, and the Algerian refugees were going home. The French and Spanish troops had been evacuated, thus removing much of the pressure from the Americans. And in January, 1963, the Rharb Valley suffered its third flood in five years and the American rescue operations were again prompt and effective. The king asked the U.S. ambassador to express his personal thanks to President Kennedy for the timely American response.[72]

King Hassan arrived in Washington on March 28 to the warmest welcome he had ever received in the United States. He "toured the horizon" with President Kennedy on such topics as conversion of the bases, Morocco's economic development, and its role in Africa. They decided the bases would be evacuated on schedule— except that skeleton crews would remain beyond the deadline to operate the facilities, and United States "officers and technicians" would remain at Kenitra to train Moroccans and to operate the navy communication facilities.[73] *Time* reported, "The State Department liked the intelligence and competence displayed by King Hassan throughout the sessions, his serious preoccupation with his own region of North Africa. . . . The Washington consensus: King Hassan is a 'modern reformist' in the tradition of the Shah of Iran."[74]

King Hassan's improved image was reflected in more concrete terms as well. On April 6 President Kennedy approved the creation of a Joint U.S.–Moroccan Liaison Mission, which immediately

[71] Ibid., December 11, 1962, p. 2.

[72] "History of the Sixteenth Air Force," January–June, 1963, vol. III, exhibit 88. The flood presented the identical problems of command and policy as in 1958 and 1960. The navy began operations January 8 when the danger became apparent; the air force on January 10, after the ambassador had guaranteed funds. Ibid., vol. I, pp. 123–132. The air force bill amounted to $452,918 of the $500,000 provided for the operations by the Agency for International Development.

[73] *New York Times*, March 29, 1963, p. 2, and March 30, 1963, p. 1.

[74] *Time* 81 (April 5, 1963): 37. A letter from Frank R. Shea, office of the publisher of *Time*, to the author, dated April 11, 1963, inclosing a clipping of the report, said, "Your predictions have come true or, at least, are in the course of coming true."

moved to provide substantial help to the royal Moroccan air force.[75] The most urgent need at that time was a troop carrier capability, a need glaringly obvious following the Algerian attack along the Moroccan frontier in October, 1963.[76] The aircraft provided were mostly World War II vintage, six C-119's, six C-47's, three 12-E Hiller helicopters, and two H-43B helicopters, all with spare parts and support items, but Morocco was not able effectively to use more modern equipment. The long-range plan also envisaged an English-language training program that would do much to relieve Moroccan dependence on France for its military needs. The military liaison program would preserve an American-Moroccan contact after the evacuation of the bases.

The agreement for evacuation was not wholly without advantage to the United States. The air force bases had been built because war with the Soviet Union loomed as a towering danger in 1950–1951, but that danger had abated by 1963. Morocco retained its strategic importance, the "other leaf of the Mediterranean gate"— equally true whether by sea or by air corridor, but the repeated assurances that the bases would never be used against the United States and would indeed be available in case of urgent need mitigated that consideration. The bases were expensive to operate,[77] and the evacuation agreement necessitated a regrouping of facilities that in fact resulted in operating economies.

Most of the operating units and the supporting administrative facilities that logically ought to remain in the Mediterranean area were simply moved across the Strait of Gibraltar into the newly completed Spanish base network. That move had been going on since 1959, and some of the dispersal would have been made regardless of the Moroccan political question. The air force units moved to Torrejon Air Force Base, outside Madrid, and the navy ordnance facilities, the antisubmarine patrol squadron, the fleet air

[75] "History of the United States Air Force, Europe," January 1–June 30, 1963, vol. I, pp. 104–105.

[76] According to King Hassan the question was not simply a dispute over frontiers but an attempt to overthrow the Moroccan dynasty. See King Hassan's analysis of the problem in *Le Maroc en marche*, pp. 322–332, and specifically, pp. 329–330.

[77] The payroll for the 4,900 civilian employees at Nouasseur, Ben Guerir, Sidi Slimane and Kenitra for the last six months of 1959 was 1,900,000,000 francs ($3,800,000) according to *New York Times*, March 13, 1960, p. 7.

logistics squadron, the fleet air service squadron, and other air units moved to the new naval air base at Rota, across the bay from Cadiz, where they had the advantage of a deep-water port. The facilities for stocking and distributing maps and other intelligence information were moved to Jacksonville, Florida. The moves were completed in 1963. By September 1, the air force had withdrawn the last of its aircraft and combat personnel from Nouasseur and closed its service facilities for the 7,948 military personnel and their dependents.[78] On December 16 Ambassador John Ferguson presented a symbolic key to Moroccan Foreign Minister Reda Guedira at Kenitra, and the United States flag was lowered as the Moroccan flag was raised over the historic ground of the first American amphibious landing of World War II. At noon the same day Colonel Robert T. Calhoun handed over Nouasseur.[79] But the story of the American presence in Morocco was not ended and, really, it would never end. At Kenitra, the title of the American commander was changed from Commander, U.S. Naval Activities, to Commander, U.S. Naval Training Command—Morocco, but the function remained. The spaces vacated by the departing air units were utilized in part by the U.S. Navy for training Moroccan military personnel, but the vital U.S. military functions continued, unimpaired. The former French facilities were occupied by the royal Moroccan armed forces, and the base as a whole passed to Moroccan command, paralleling the 1947 arrangement with the French navy. More than one thousand United States Navy personnel and their dependents remained at Kenitra, more than in 1947–1950, and on December 1 the United States commander in chief in Europe assigned military responsibility for Morocco to the navy instead of the air force,[80] responsibility that the navy had exercised until 1950. More importantly, hundreds of thousands of Americans "whose bodies no longer walked the other side of the Atlantic remained there in their thoughts and memories."[81]

[78] Ibid., September 1, 1963, p. 15.

[79] Ibid., December 17, 1963, p. 3.

[80] "History of the United States Air Force, Europe," July 1–December 31, 1963, vol. I, p. 17.

[81] A slight paraphrase of the language, but not the concept, of Gilbert De Simpel, *Le Petit Marocain*, December 22, 1957, concerning his voyage to the United States.

12. Conclusion

"FROM THE WHEELS OF CHANCE come many strange combinations. Your military detachments have been cast in a day-to-day role of contact with various segments of my people. They have imparted to us some of their ways . . . and I hope that they in turn have learned something from us and from our way of life. A strong bridge of friendship has been built—and it will last because its beginnings go far back into history." Thus spoke Mohammed V, king of Morocco.[1]

What did the king mean to say? Was he speaking of techniques, of forestry, soil conservation, or scientific breeding of cattle, for he used those examples. "No," said the man who knew him more intimately than any other—his son, now King Hassan II. "He meant spiritual values. The Americans are technically competent, but they are a great deal like the Moroccans in their outlook on

[1] Mohammed V, king of Morocco, as told to Christine Hotchkiss, "Why I Like Americans," *This Week*, September 11, 1960, pp. 32–33.

life. We can learn from you how to use technical competence without losing spirituality."[2] "No," said his daughter, Princess Aisha, whom he had cast into a humanistic symbol for the nation and for the Arab world. "He meant compassion. You never asked how much it would cost at Agadir, neither in money nor in effort. I saw your soldiers there work until they literally dropped from exhaustion and they never asked if it was dangerous—only if they perhaps can save one more."[3] "No," said General Mezzian, an experienced soldier and diplomat and confidant of the king. "He meant democracy."[4]

If these consistent analyses by people who knew him well are accepted, then the meaning is clear. The king of Morocco, and probably the Moroccan nation, shared to a large degree the image that the American held of himself. The evidence is impressive that such is the case. Most Moroccans think in terms of liberty of the individual and of the nation, and they vicariously identify with liberty by evoking the United States experience rather than that of France. In explaining why, in spite of differences in language and civilization, King Hassan II said: "I think I have found the answer in your heroic combat over the generations and in the heroic combat that my people as well have fought for generations. One sacred and unique quest unites us: love of liberty."[5]

King Mohammed V and King Hassan II are only two of the many Moroccans who are quick to point out that Morocco was the first—or one of the first—nations to recognize the independence of the United States.[6] Mohammed V's children and their associates in school were taught American political history, and in 1963 King Hassan drew upon that knowledge to explain the "nonalignment" aspect of Moroccan foreign policy: "By strange coincidence this policy is identical to that followed by the United States at the be-

[2] Interview, King Hassan II, New York, April 6, 1963.

[3] Interview, Princess Aisha, Rabat, July 23, 1966.

[4] Interview, General Mezzian, Moroccan ambassador to Spain, Madrid, May 3, 1967.

[5] King Hassan II, *Le Maroc en marche*, p. 256.

[6] King Mohammed V, "Why I Like Americans," *This Week*, September 11, 1960, and King Hassan II, *Le Maroc en marche*, p. 260. *Time* 81 (April 5, 1963): 37, quotes President Kennedy in the same sense and points out that Morocco was first in intent but that France "slipped in ahead" on February 6, 1778, while the Moroccan recognition did not arrive until February 20.

ginning of its history." And he followed with illustrations from
the foreign policies of George Washington and Thomas Jefferson.[7]
The French, in denying that the Moroccan revolution was comparable to the American revolution, tacitly recognized the validity
of the Moroccan concept.

The American landing on the shores of Morocco in 1942 was
more than just another wartime amphibious operation, it was a
symbol of liberty of the Moroccan people and nation from an oppressive regime. It shattered the myth of French power, not just
on the battlefield of Europe, but on the beaches of Morocco where
all could see and talk about it. Liberty was attainable, not in some
distant future, but now.

The Moroccans, however, were looking further ahead than the
Americans, whose objective was not the categorical preservation
of liberty, but the preservation of the world status quo. The dis-
parity between the quest for liberty and the quest for status quo
is nowhere more glaring than in United States foreign policy toward Morocco. In the name of military expediency, based upon
erroneous intelligence estimates, the United States cooperated with
a reprehensible regime in North Africa during World War II.
Those responsible could not plead ignorance, for the discrimination against the "natives" was obvious, and the anti-Semitism of
the French colonial officials was a matter of record as a point of
difference between them and King Mohammed V. Because of the
political need for French recovery after the war, those same powerful officials in Washington continued to support French colonial
policies in North Africa.

The glaring failure of United States foreign policy over a period
of two decades was the apparent inability to reconcile the concept
of "absolute monarch" with "liberalism," both of which were ex-
emplified in the person of King Mohammed V. In both he was
impotent under the protectorate, but myriad indications reveal the
liberal: his ringing support of France's fight against nazism in
1939; his refusal to permit enforcement of the Vichy anti-Semitism
laws in 1941; his reception of the American armies in 1942; his
insistence on the creation of labor unions in 1946–1947; his speech
at Tangier in 1947; his insistence on purifying the Islamic religion

[7] King Hassan II, in *Le Maroc en marche*, pp. 261–262.

of its medieval traditions; his insistence on ameliorating the status of women; his insistence on education for his people; and finally the acceptance of deposition rather than the surrender of principle. When he returned to the throne, every progress and every pronouncement was toward constitutional liberalism, equality before the law, and man's natural right to happiness and liberty.[8]

Mohammed V was the victim of biased reporting. The Arabic press, often incoherent and illogical, was in any event little read in the West. Much of the French press, understandably, sought to justify the protectorate, and the American press in its scant reporting of Moroccan news tended to follow the French lead during the protectorate period. After 1956 American press coverage was still thin and, oriented toward the processes of functioning representative government as understood in the West, tended to focus on fresher, emerging political personalities like Mehdi Ben Barka, Abdallah Ibrahim, Abderrahim Bouabid, and other opponents of royal policies. Under such circumstances, the fact that the dynasty has been the unifying influence throughout Moroccan history, and that Mohammed V remained the central figure in Moroccan politics, certainly after 1942, was obscured.

Whether from conviction in ultimate justice or the want of a better alternative, Mohammed V preserved his confidence in the rectitude of the United States. There is no evidence that President Franklin D. Roosevelt had any more than a casual concern for Moroccan independence. He had made no study of the background of Moroccan nationalism, nor had he planned for the postwar world. His dinner for Mohammed V at Casablanca on January 22, 1943, which looms as a landmark in Moroccan history, would never have occurred if General De Gaulle had arrived in Casablanca on January 20, as planned; it was something to do while waiting. Roosevelt's lack of concern for Moroccan independence was indicated by his ratification at Casablanca of the Murphy-Giraud Agreement, pledging United States support for the restoration of the French colonial empire. Nevertheless the Roosevelt tradition persists. As late as May 24, 1961, when King Hassan with good reason might have showed some hostility toward the United

[8] See King Mohammed's New Year's message, 1957, in Rom Landau, *Mohammed V, King of Morocco*, p. 125, and many other pronouncements, *ibid.*, pp. 123–136.

States for its attitude toward his own person, he said that Roosevelt understood the Moroccan situation and, "if he had not died, the United States would not have failed to accelerate the process of liberation of Morocco."[9]

The Moroccans viewed the Americans in the perspective of roseate tradition, and they overlooked inconsistencies. They respected American military personnel for their deportment, kindliness, and egalitarianism—in short, their personal qualities, for these were not inconsistent with the dream of liberty, but in fact neither the military personnel nor their dependents after they came ever established significant social contact with the Moroccan people. The tendency of the American community to isolate itself was unfortunate, for Moroccan institutions were nebulous when independence came in 1956 and therefore susceptible to American influence. American civilian employees of the various bases might have shaped the Moroccan labor movement if they had only joined the union serving their base. The United States armed forces might have averted the diplomatic crisis concerning the bases if it had accepted a social responsibility in Morocco similar to that discharged by the U.S. Army Corps of Engineers in the United States. But these were policy failures, not personal shortcomings, and they did not lessen the respect—not fear, as of the French, and not a familial relationship, as with other Arab nations—that the Moroccan people held for the Americans.

Any valid interpretation of Moroccan-American relations during the last quarter century must consider the United States military bases and must answer the question: Why was the United States Air Force compelled against its will to abandon its bases in Morocco and not the United States Navy? Conventional diplomacy was not able to provide a solution to the problem of all of the bases, because the diplomats were unwilling to match United States imperatives against Moroccan imperatives and seek a bilateral solution in that context. Instead, they subordinated U.S. needs in North Africa to French desires, vainly hoping thus to secure greater French cooperation in Europe. They were unwilling to concede Moroccan demands on details, customs, for example, lest the concessions create precedent for other areas of the world, and they

9 King Hassan II, in *Le Maroc en marche*, p. 42.

regarded the Moroccan refusal to accept precedents established elsewhere as a somewhat hostile manifestation. Ultimately, both nations were forced to bypass the traditional diplomatic apparatus. Both major decisions concerning the bases were made by the chiefs of state.

I. William Zartman, among others, has studied the impact of the Navy's "people-to-people" program and concluded that it caused problems for the ministers in the Moroccan government and "bought not one day of reprieve for the bases," but he made no attempt to explain the paradox of the continued existence of the navy base. He said that "any program designed to win over friends would have been effective in keeping the bases for the Americans only if the targets of the program had been the ministerial level or the leaders of the opposition."[10] There was a third alternative, the king, and he was willing to give as much as public opinion would allow, but for the navy to have cultivated the leaders of the opposition would have been an affront both to the king and to the overwhelming body of opinion that supported him. The navy did not make that mistake.

Ambassador John H. Ferguson, who participated in the conversations between King Hassan II and President Kennedy in 1963, said the president was able to obtain the "unique concessions" for "strictly military requirements which must be met" only because of the "exemplary behavior of the Navy in Morocco since 1942." He said public opinion was the final determinant and in spite of the efforts of the Russians and Chinese who "left no stone unturned to develop this emotional state of mind [for evacuation] in the newly independent countries [of Asia and Africa]," the conduct and attitude of the officers and men at Kenitra had tipped the scales of public opinion in favor of the United States. "You have been here many years with never any serious complaint. . . . You have conducted yourself with dignity, friendliness, and a spirit of generosity," and that made the difference, Ambassador Ferguson concluded.[11]

The officers and men at Kenitra and their dependents were nei-

[10] I. William Zartman, *Morocco: Problems of New Power*, p. 58.

[11] Ambassador John H. Ferguson, speech at Kenitra, April 22, 1964, copy in "History of Commander Naval Activities, Morocco," a loose-leaf notebook in the office of the public affairs officer, USNTC-Morocco.

ther individually nor collectively conscious agents in a campaign
to modify Moroccan public opinion. They were simply a Western
window in the Arab world, through which two civilizations might
look at each other. The American landing in 1942 crystallized the
concept of "liberty now" in the Moroccan mentality, and the continued American presence evoked the desire and provided the example for social and economic evolution. That is the story of the
"americanization" of Morocco—or any other area of the world
where large bodies of American military personnel are stationed
for a long period of time. In the long run, they make a greater contribution in peace than in war, and it is a potential that is inherent
only in the military service, for it is the only agency of the United
States with enough personnel in a foreign land to produce a
measurable transformation.

SOURCE MATERIAL

Notes on Sources

General

Bibliographical material in the English language concerning Morocco is very limited, but to understand the vagaries of contemporary Moroccan history a basic familiarity is necessary. One of the best recent general histories is Neville Barbour, *Morocco* (New York: Walker, 1965). The Moroccan Ministry of Information published *Morocco: A Glimpse of History* (Rabat, 1966), highly readable but concerning only positive achievements. Marcel Peyrouton, *Histoire générale du Maghreb: Maroc, Algérie, Tunisie, des origines à nos jours* (Paris: Albin Michel, 1966), is knowledgeable and quite objective, considering Peyrouton's personal involvement as an official of the French colonial regime.

Official Documents

The records of neither the United States Department of State nor the French Foreign Office are yet open for the period after 1942. However, U.S. Department of State, *Documents on German Foreign Policy, 1918–1945* (Washington: Government Printing Office, 1956), Series D, Volumes X, XI, XII, provides valuable information concerning French policy and problems in North Africa for the years immediately preceding the American invasion, and some additional material is contained in its *American Foreign Policy, 1950–1955* (2 vols., Washington: Government Printing Office, 1957), and in *Treaties and Other International Acts Series 6132* (Washington: Government Printing Office, no date).

The Public Papers of Franklin D. Roosevelt, Samuel I. Rosenman, ed. (13 vols., New York: Harper & Bros., 1938–1950), particularly the 1943 volume, *The Tide Turns*, 1950, provides insights into the Moroccan political attitudes at the time of the Casablanca conference. The Franklin D. Roosevelt Library at Hyde Park has additional material available on microfilm.

The United States Congress held extensive hearings on the construction of the U.S. Air Force bases in Morocco. The congressional interest was primarily fiscal, but the testimony reflects the social and political conflict existing in Morocco. The hearings have been published as "Moroccan Air Base Construction," Parts 4 and 4-2, in *Hearings, Investigation of Military Public Works*, Subcommittee on Appropriations, 82 Cong., 2d Sess., 1952. Additional insight is provided in "Relinquishment of Consular Jurisdiction of the United States in Morocco," in *Hearings on S.J. Resolution 165*, Senate Committee on Foreign Relations, 84 Cong., 2d Sess., 1956.

The trial of the "Action of the French Republic on its own behalf and as the protecting power of Morocco against the United States concerning the rights of American nationals in Morocco" before the International Court of Justice did much to clarify French protectorate policies. Details are found in *American Foreign Policy, 1950–1955*, previously cited; in International Court of Justice, *Report of Judgments, Advisory Opinions, and Orders*, 1951; and in various Department of State bulletins of 1951–1952.

The archives of the United States armed forces are rich in source material that has not been previously considered in examining U.S.-Moroccan relations. The Modern Military Records Division, National Archives and Record Service, King and Union Streets, Alexandria, Virginia, has the "Final Report on Operation Torch, 8–11 November 1942," the *Logistical History of NATOUSA-MTOUSA*, Naples, Montanino, 1945, and a substantial collection of uncatalogued documents relating to Morocco. The United States Air Force Archives at Maxwell Air Force Base, Alabama, have the "History of the Twelfth Air Force," which gives an account of its participation in the Moroccan campaign, "Pertinent Data on French Morocco," dated October 25, 1942, which includes intelligence estimates of political attitudes and conditions, and "Miscellaneous Material Dealing with the Moroccan Landings." The archival material for the period of World War II has not been catalogued and is difficult to use, but the material after the return of the air force to Morocco in 1950 is superbly organized in unit histories, most of which use a standard format prescribed by the air force with footnotes in the narrative volume also identifying the supporting documents in a supplementary volume. They include "History of Headquarters, United States Air Force, Europe," "History of Detachment Two, Headquarters, United States Air Force, Europe (Moroccan Liaison Office)," and its successor organizations classified under the same file number, "History of the Sixteenth Air Force," and "History of the Seventeenth Air Force." All have material pertaining to Morocco, as does the "History of the Southern Air Material Command," and other local unit histories.

The U.S. Navy Archives in Washington have "Commander Moroccan Sea Frontier War Diary," and several partial histories of the United States naval activities in Morocco, dated in 1944, 1946, 1951, and 1959. All are in the Port Lyautey–Northwest Africa file. In addition the Office of Aviation History, Navy Department, Washington, has material on Port Lyautey in its Port Lyautey Shore Establishment file. Two publications of Commander, U.S. Naval Activities, Port Lyautey, Kenitra, Morocco, bearing the same title, *People to People Report*, one published by Iframar at Rabat in 1959, and the other by USIA at Beirut in 1960, give information concerning the navy's public relations program in those years. The Library of Congress and the New York Library hold copies.

The largest collection of documentary source material on the military bases in Morocco are the records in the various navy units at Port Lyautey stored at the Federal Records Center, New York. They are filed according to the navy filing system and are difficult to work with unless the researcher is familiar with it.

The Archives of the American Red Cross in Washington contains valuable information on relief operations in North Africa in 1942–1943, and on Red Cross Centers in Morocco during the period 1955–1961. For the earlier period, see "French Africa–War Relief," the *American Red Cross Report for the Year ending June 30, 1943* (Washington, 1943), and "Foreign War Relief Operations," Senate Document No. 228, 78 Cong., 2d Sess. For the later period, see the monthly "Report of Supplemental Recreational Activities Overseas," prepared by the Red Cross centers at Kenitra, Rabat, and Marrakech, and correspondence pertaining thereto.

The French archives are not yet open for the period from 1942–1963. For the establishment of the protectorate, see France, Ministère des Affaires Etrangères, *Documents diplomatiques français, 1871–1914*, 2 Serie 1901–1915, V (Paris: Imprimerie Nationale, 1932), and the *Journal Officiel*, 1912, and thereafter. André P. G. A. Tardieu, *La Conférence d'Algéciras, Histoire diplomatique de la crise marocaine (15 janvier–7 avril, 1906)* (Paris: F. Alcan), 1906, is an exhaustive examination by a participant. Maurice Beaumont, *L'essor industriel et l'impérialisme colonial, 1878–1904* (Paris: Presses Universitaires, 1937), gives valuable background on the French penetration of Morocco, and Mohammed Lahbabi, *Le Gouvernement Marocain à l'aube du XXeme Siècle* (Rabat: Editions Techniques Nord-Africaines, 1958), on the circumstances that made that penetration possible. M. Toudelas, "L'Espagne au Maroc," *Cahiers Internationaux: Revue internationale du monde du travail* (Paris), no. 71 (December, 1955), gives a generally socialist and specifically Spanish reaction to the establishment of the Spanish protectorate in Morocco. George E. Mowry, *The Era of Theo-*

dore Roosevelt and the Birth of Modern America, 1900–1921 (New York: Harper Torchbooks, 1958), provides some information on early United States interest in Morocco, associated largely with the Algeciras Conference.

The official Moroccan documents are relatively scarce. The most valuable are Mohammed V, *Le Maroc à l'heure de l'indépendance* (Rabat: Ministère de l'Information, 1957), and Hassan II, *Le Maroc en marche. Discours de S.M. Le Roi Hassan II depuis son Intrônisation* (Rabat: Ministère de l'Information, 1965). Georges Vaucher, *Sous les cèdres d'Ifrane. Libres entretiens avec Hassan II, Roi du Maroc* (Paris: Julliard, 1962), is unofficial but authoritative. Ministère de l'Information, *Réalisations et Perspectives, 16 Novembre 1955–18 Novembre 1957* (Rabat: Iframar, 1957), contains a substantial collection of documents and policy statements by prominent Moroccan officials. The Ministry of Foreign Affairs has made much of the same material available in English in *Morocco* (Rabat, 1957). Youssef Ben Abbes, Ministre de la Santé Publique, *Conférence Nationale de la Santé* (Rabat, 1959), reveals the deficiencies in the public health infrastructure left by the French.

Memoirs

Perhaps few periods in history have been as rich in memoirs and, subject to customary caution in the use of self-serving writings, they are valuable. One of the best is Paul Auphan and Jacques Mordal, trans. Captain A. C. J. Sabalot, USN (Ret.), *The French Navy in World War II* (Annapolis, 1959). Rear Admiral Auphan was minister of the French navy in 1942, and Mordal, his aide. *The War Memoirs of Charles De Gaulle: Unity, 1942–1943*, trans. Richard Howard (2 vols., New York: Simon & Schuster, 1959), gives one side of the Vichy–De Gaulle conflict, and Henri Giraud, *Tout pour la victoire* (Algiers, 1942), gives an opposing view. Fleet Admiral William D. Leahy, *I Was There* (New York: McGraw-Hill, 1950), relates the author's experience as ambassador to Vichy France, and Robert Murphy, *Diplomat among Warriors* (Garden City, Doubleday, 1964), writes of his experiences as chargé d'affaires in Vichy France and as President Roosevelt's personal representative and General Eisenhower's political advisor in North Africa. Kenneth W. Pendar, *Adventures in Diplomacy* (New York: Dodd, Mead, and Co., 1945) is an autobiographical narrative by one of the control officers in North Africa who provided planning information from Morocco for Operation Torch. Elliott Roosevelt, in *As He Saw It* (New York: Duel, Sloan, and Pearce, 1946), writes of his father's attitude toward colonialism and gives the most complete account existent of the famous Casablanca meeting between

President Roosevelt and King Mohammed V. *The Memoirs of Cordell Hull* (2 vols., New York: Macmillan, 1948), give much information about the diplomatic maneuvering associated with General De Gaulle's capture of power in North Africa.

Three memoirs of value concerning Operation Torch by military participants are Harry C. Butcher, *My Three Years with Eisenhower* (New York: Simon & Schuster, 1946); Major General George S. Patton, Jr., *War As I Knew It* (Boston: Houghton Mifflin, 1947); and Lieutenant General Lucien K. Truscott, Jr., *Command Missions: A Personal Story* (New York: E. P. Dutton, 1954). Butcher was General Eisenhower's aide, and he kept a daily diary of events in Eisenhower's headquarters. General Patton was commander of the Western Task Force, and General Truscott was the commander of the attack on Mehdia Beach–Port Lyautey.

Several of the French residents-general in Morocco wrote memoirs. The following are pertinent: Louis Hubert Gonzalve Lyautey, *Paroles d'Action: Madagascar, Sud-Oranais, Oran, Maroc, 1900–1926* (Paris: Armand Colin, 1926); Maréchal Alphonse Pierre Juin, *Mémoires* (2 vols., Paris: A. Fayard, 1959–1960) and also *Le Maghreb en Feu* (Paris: Plon, 1957); Gilbert Grandval, *Ma Mission au Maroc* (Paris: Plon, 1956); and Pierre Boyer de Latour, *Vérités sur L'Afrique du Nord* (Paris: Plon, 1956). In the same defensive vein, see Robert Montagne, *Révolution au Maroc* (Paris: France-Empire, 1953), and *Naissance du Prolétariat Marocain* (Paris: Peyronnet, 1952). Montagne lived in Morocco many years and worked with the protectorate authorities. Both works seek to exculpate the residency in the Franco-Marocain conflict. François Mitterrand, *Présence française et abandon* (Paris: A. Colin, 1959), generally opposes residential policy in Morocco. One of the earliest French colonists, Dr. Fritz Weisgerber, in *Au Seuil du Maroc Moderne* (Rabat: Laporte, 1947), gives a good account of early Moroccan resistance to the French protectorate. Although more a collection of documents by contemporaries than a memoir, René Richard and Alain de Serigny, *La bissectrice de la guerre: Alger, 8 Novembre 1942* (Algiers: Maison des Livres, 1946), is extremely valuable. It is pro-Vichy and pro-Giraud, but it contains the text of documents, the Murphy-Giraud Agreement, and the Bethouart Paper, for example, and the minutes of meetings in which French support for the American landings was planned. Only five hundred copies were printed, and most of those were seized, so the book is rare. The Bibliothèque Générale at Rabat holds a copy.

The state of siege and the censorship in Morocco during the proconsulship of Marshal Juin and General Guillaume inhibited political commentaries. Most of the works of that period by French writers are technical studies. Eugene Guenier, *Maroc* (Paris: Encyclopédie coloniale et maritime, 1947), is a geographic and demographic study. Albert Guillaume, *L'Evolution économique de la société rurale marocaine* (Paris, 1955), is an agricultural-sociological study. Syedah Fatima Sadeque, *Baybars I of Egypt* (Dacca, Pakistan: Oxford University Press, 1956), makes no mention of Morocco, but it does have a good description of the Islamic fiscal system, which does have a bearing on Morocco. Several works provide understanding of the sociological evolution of Morocco. They include Georges Hardy, *Histoire sociale de la colonisation française* (Paris: Larose, 1953); Jacques Berque, *Structures Sociales du Haut-Atlas* (Paris, 1955), and *Le Maghreb entre deux guerres* (Paris: Editions du Sueil, 1962); Jean d'Etienne, Louis Villeme, and Stephane Delisle, *L'Evolution sociale du Maroc* (Paris: Peyronnet, 1950); and Robert Rezette, *Les Partis Politiques Marocain* (Paris: A. Colin, 1955). Although old, L. Sonolet and A. Peres, *Moussa et Gi-Gli: Histoire de deux petits noires* (Paris: A. Colin, 1919), provides valuable insight into the racism that was such an integral part of the French colonial system. "Le Scoutisme musulman," Part I in Centre d'études de politique étrangère, *Entretiens sur l'évolution des pays de civilisation arabe* (Paris: Hartman, 1937), discusses the paramilitary nature of the scouting movement in Arab countries. Angelus Keller, *Essai sur l'esprit du berbère marocain* (Fribourg, Switzerland: Franciscaines, 1949), seeks to justify the proselyting of the Berbers, a factor that figured importantly in the rise of Moroccan nationalism.

Morocco and World War II

Except for the memoirs previously cited, most published studies of World War II in Morocco are by American authors. Herbert Feis, *Churchill, Roosevelt, and Stalin: The War They Waged and the Peace They Sought* (Princeton: Princeton University Press, 1957), gives diplomatic background, as does William L. Langer, *Our Vichy Gamble* (New York: Norton, 1947). Four semiofficial military histories are concerned with North Africa: Samuel Eliot Morison, *Operations in North African Waters: October, 1942–June, 1943* (Boston: Little, Brown, 1947); George F. Howe, *Northwest Africa: Seizing the Initiative in the West* (Washington: Government Printing Office, 1957), an army history; Harry L. Coles and Albert K. Weinberg, *Civil Affairs: Soldiers Become Governors* (Washington: Government Printing Office, 1964); and Wesley F. Craven and James L. Cate, eds. *The Army Air Force in World War II. Europe: Torch to Pointblank, August 1942 to December 1943* (Chicago: University of Chicago Press, 1949). A journalist, Waverly Root, in *Casablanca to Katyn: The Secret History of the War* (New York: Scribner's, 1946), gives a critical pro-De Gaulle interpretation of wartime diplomacy and events in Morocco. Henry S. Villard, "Action in North Africa," *American Foreign Service Journal* 19 (December 1924), seems to be the only account of the actions of the control officers prior to the landing aside from Pendar's *Adventures in Diplomacy*, previously cited. Villard was chief of the African Division, Department of State. Jacques Lemaigre-Dubreuil, "Giraud et De Gaulle à Alger," *Revue de Paris* (July, 1949), is indispensable on the policy conflict that divided U.S. councils.

The Growth of Moroccan Nationalism

Several authors deal specifically with the growth of Moroccan nationalism. Rom Landau has written with such a pro-Moroccan bias that he has almost attained the status of a court historian; see *Moroccan Drama: 1900–1955* (San Francisco: American Academy of Asian Studies, 1956); *Mohammed V, King of Morocco* (Rabat: Ministry of Foreign Affairs, 1957); and *Hassan II, King of Morocco* (London: George Allen & Unwin, 1962). For other works sympathetic to the nationalist cause, see Edmund Stevens, *North African Powder Keg* (New York: Coward-McCann, 1955), and Lorna Hahn, *North Africa: Nationalism to Nationhood* (Washington, Public Affairs Press, 1960). Two authoritative accounts by leading participants in the nationalist movement are Allal El Fassi, *The Independence Movement in Arab North Africa*, translated from the Arabic version published in Cairo in 1949 by Hazem Zaki Nuseibeh (Washington: American Council of Learned Societies, 1954), and Mahdi A. Bennouna, *Our Morocco: The True Story of a Just Cause*, printed clandestinely in Morocco in 1951. The Istiqlal party was actively propagandizing its viewpoint in the early 1950's; see *Morocco under the Protectorate: Forty Years of French Administration* (New York: Moroccan Office of Information and Documentation, 1953); Pierre Parent, *The Truth about Morocco*, trans. Eleanor Knight (New York: Moroccan Office of Information and Documentation, 1952). Earlier, the Istiqlal published *Plan de Réformes Marocains, élaboré et présenté à S.M. le Sultan, au Gouvernement de la République française, et le Résident-Général au Maroc par le Comité d'Action Marocain*, n.p., or name of ed., 1935. Allal El Fassi has published a collection of documents and commentary on the nationalist movement in *Livre rouge et documentaires* (Tangier: Editions Marocaines Internationales [c. 1959]), as has Muhammad Khalil, *The Arab States and the Arab League: A Documentary Record* (2 vols., Beirut: Khayats, 1962). Marjorie Rodes, wife of an American businessman in Casablanca, in *The Real Ruler of Morocco* (New York, 1954), gives an account very favorable to Mohammed V. *Free Morocco*, a series of excellently done pamphlets published in New

York by the Moroccan Office of Information and Documentation from 1953 to 1955, effectively propagandized the nationalist viewpoint. Copies of the whole series are held by the New York Public Library.

French-language works critical of the protectorate regimes in North Africa are almost as numerous as in English. Ferhat Abbas, the Algerian nationalist, in *La Nuit Coloniale: Guerre et Révolution d'Algérie* (Paris: Julliard, 1962), and Jean Rous, the French Socialist editor of *Franc-Tireur*, in *Chronique de la Décolonisation* (Paris: Présence Africaine, 1965), write from the broader viewpoint of decolonization rather than narrow nationalism. Albert Ayache, a Communist, in *Le Maroc* (Paris: Editions Sociales, 1956), gives statistical data on the Moroccan economy and demography that most writers accept as valid and valuable. Nobel prize winning Albert Camus is harshly critical of French racial and cultural policies in "the Arab countries"; see *Actuelles III: Chronique Algérienne, 1939–1958* (Paris: Gallimard, 1958). Jean Dresch, "Lyautey," in *Les Techniciens de la colonisation* (Paris, 1947), is a mildly critical account of Lyautey's proconsulship. Most subsequent writers consider Charles-André Julien, *L'Afrique du Nord en marche* (Paris: R. Julliard, 1952), a valid indictment of the protectorate.

Although the resident-general attempted a general rebuttal of the Istiqlal party charges through Public Relations Service of Morocco, *News Bulletin*, and replied to *Morocco under the Protectorate* with Centre d'études marocaines, *Morocco: Truth versus Fiction* (Casablanca, 1952), most writers assumed the failure of protectorate policies. The most exhaustive study is Stephane Bernard, *Le Conflit Franco-Marocain, 1943–1956* (3 vols., Brussels: L'Institut de Sociologie de l'université libre de Bruxelles, 1963). A single-volume work with much the same general approach is Roger Le Tourneau, *Evolution Politique de L'Afrique du Nord Musulmane* (Paris, Armand Colin, 1962). Two eminent French journalists pioneered that approach, Jean and Simone Lacouture, *Le Maroc à l'épreuve* (Paris: Editions de Seuil, 1958). *La Nef: Maroc et Tunisie, le problème du protectorat* (Paris: Julliard, 1953), is a collection of essays by competent observers, including French Foreign Minister Schuman, which attempt to delineate the most important reasons for the failure.

Recent scholarship on contemporary Morocco includes Douglas E. Ashford, *Political Change in Morocco* (Princeton: Princeton University Press, 1961), and I. William Zartman, *Morocco: Problems of New Power* (New York: Atherton, 1964). Both share the disadvantages of lack of access to official sources and the advantages of personal knowledge and the opportunity to discuss many of the events with still-living participants.

Periodical Literature

The periodical literature during the last quarter century concerning Morocco must be used with caution. The press in Morocco was never free during the protectorate. The Pierre Mas trust dominated the French-language daily newspapers with *Le Petit Marocain* and *La Vigie Marocaine* at Casablanca, *L'Echo du Maroc* at Rabat, and *Le Courrier du Maroc* at Fez. Mas lost control of *Le Petit Marocain* to the Communist party from 1945 to 1950, but whether communist or French *ultra*, all four papers were hostile to the United States' presence in Morocco. The *Maroc-Presse*, owned by Jean Walter, championed a liberal pronationalist policy for France toward Morocco and was less hostile toward the United States than the Mas papers, but its circulation was small and its influence slight.

The Moroccan press was divided into two parts, one in French and the other in Arabic. It had little influence. The Europeans ignored the Moroccan papers and only a small fraction of the Moroccan population was able to read them. The residency officials tolerated a Moroccan press, although they kept it strictly censored, because its limited circulation and influence presented little danger. Most of the Moroccan newspapers ceased publication after a few years as a result of both economic and political pressures. The principal French-language papers were *La Voix Nationale*, an independent paper published from 1938 to 1943, and *L'Opinion du Peuple*, the weekly organ of the Istiqlal party, founded in 1947 and succeeded by *Al Istiqlal* in 1951. *Al Istiqlal* was suspended with the rest of the nationalist press in 1952 but reappeared after Morocco became independent. The principal newspapers written in Arabic were *Al Alam*, also of the Istiqlal party, which published from 1946 to 1952 and reappeared with *Al Istiqlal* after independence, and *Er Rai el Am*, the organ of the Independent Democratic party (PDI), which published intermittently from 1948 to 1952 and also reappeared in 1956.

The political circumstances of the French and Moroccan press were reversed when Morocco became independent. Before independence the Moroccan editors were forced to hew a fine line between free expression and suspension, while the French editors had almost unrestricted liberty as long as they supported the protectorate—which they were inclined to do in any event. After independence, the French editors considered it prudent to avoid politics. They published official communiqués as released and generally without editorial comment. The Moroccan editors on the other hand gave free rein to political expression—as might be expected of the editorial organs of political parties. However, the Moroccan papers before independence and the French papers after independence are generally more reliable sources for the researcher on topics other than political opinion.

American periodicals were handicapped in reporting events in Morocco by the lack of a permanent news-gathering organization. The *New York Times* maintained a permanent bureau in Rabat, but its representative was also assigned responsibility for Algeria and Tunisia, a large territory for one man to cover adequately. Except for occasional reportorial visits, the other American papers used wire-service reports emanating from French sources.

The press in France constitutes the richest source of periodical information concerning Morocco. The French people were interested in and demanded news of Morocco, and the French press was free to criticize or applaud governmental policies. Generally speaking, *Le Monde* and *Le Figaro* provided extensive coverage that was either noncommital or favored government policies toward Morocco, while *Combat, Franc-Tireur*, and *L'Observateur* opposed them. The Bibliothèque Générale at Rabat, which has long subscribed to clipping services of the international press, has extensive holdings of periodical literature of all political colorations.

Articles worthy of specific mention include Georges Marey, "Le réarmament française en Afrique du Nord, 1942-44," *Revue politique et parlementaire* 193 (October, 1947), and the entire issue of *Revue de la France d'outremer*, Numéro Spécial, *Maroc, terre d'avenir, 1948.* Other publications that feature material on Morocco are *La Revue des Deux Mondes, Revue de défense nationale, The Middle East Journal,* and *The Islamic Review.* Charles R. Codman, "French Morocco: Torch plus Ten," *The Atlantic*, June 11, 1952, was useful concerning the establishment of the American presence in Morocco, and Mohammed V, King of Morocco, "Why I Like Americans," *This Week*, September 11, 1960, is essential in estimating the impact.

Many individuals furnished material either in interviews with the author or by letters. Most of the interviews were recorded on tape and remain in possession of the author, as do many unpublished documents and letters.

Works Cited

Abu Muhammad. "The Tragic Drama of Morocco." *Islamic Review*, May, 1951, pp. 33–38.

Auphan, Paul, and Mordal, Jacques. *The French Navy in World War II.* Translated by A. C. J. Sabalot. Annapolis: U.S. Naval Institute, 1959.

Ayache, Albert. *Le Maroc.* Paris: Editions Sociales, 1956.

Balafrej, Ahmed. "Morocco Plans for Independence." *Foreign Affairs* 34 (April, 1956): 489.

Barbour, Nevill. *Morocco*. New York: Walker and Co., 1965.

Beaumont, Maurice. *L'Essor industriel et l'imperialisme colonial, 1878–1904*. Peuples et Civilisations, vol. 18. Paris: Presses universitaires de France, 1937.

Ben Abbes, Youssef. *Conférence Nationale de la Santé*. Rabat: Ministère de la Santé, 1959.

———. "The Malady of Meknes." *Time* 74 (November 30, 1959): 24.

Ben Barka, Mehdi. *Problèmes d'édification du Maroc et du Maghreb*. Paris: Plon, 1959.

Bennouna, Mahdi A. *Our Morocco: The True Story of a Just Cause*. Morocco, 1951.

Bernard, Stéphane. *Le Conflit Franco-Marocain, 1943–1956*. 3 vols. Brussels: L'Université Libre, 1963.

Blair, Leon B. "The Origin and Development of the Arabian Horse." *Southwestern Historical Quarterly* 68 (January, 1965): 303–316.

Butcher, Harry C. *My Three Years with Eisenhower*. New York: Simon & Schuster, 1946.

Camus, Albert. *Actuelles III: Chronique Algerienne, 1939–1958*. Paris: Gallimard, 1958.

Centre d'études de politique étrangère. *Entretiens sur l'évolution des pays de civilisation arabe*. Paris: Hartman, 1937.

———. *Industrialisation de l'Afrique du Nord*. Paris: Armand Colin, 1952.

Centre d'études marocaines. *Morocco: Truth versus Fiction*. Casablanca, 1952.

Churchill, Winston S. *The Hinge of Fate*. Boston: Houghton Mifflin, 1950.

Cline, Walter B. "Nationalism in Morocco." *Middle East Journal* 1 (1947): 18–28.

Codman, Charles R. *La documentation française: Articles et documents*, August 20, 1952.

———. "French Morocco: Torch Plus Ten." *Atlantic Monthly* 190 (July, 1952):52.

Coles, Harry L., and Weinberg, Albert K. *Civil Affairs: Soldiers Become Governors*. Washington, D.C.: Government Printing Office, 1964.

Commander, U.S. Naval Activities, Port Lyautey. *People to People Report*. Rabat: Iframar, 1959.

———. *People to People Report*. Beirut: USIA, 1960.

Craven, Wesley F., and Cate, James Lea, eds. *Europe: Torch to Point-blank, August 1942 to December 1943*. The Army Air Forces in World War II, vol. 2. 7 vols. Chicago: University of Chicago Press, 1948–1958.

DeLatour, Pierre Boyer. *Vérités sur l'Afrique du Nord*. Paris: Plon, 1956.

d'Etienne, Jean; Villème, Louis; and Delisle, Stephane. *L'évolution sociale du Maroc*. Paris: Peyronnet, n.d.

De Gaulle, Charles. *The War Memoirs of Charles De Gaulle: Unity, 1942–1944*. Translated by Richard Howard. 2 vols. New York: Simon & Schuster, 1959.

Dresch, Jean. "Lyautey." In *Les Techniciens de la colonisation, XIX–XX siècles*. Paris: Presses Universitaires, 1947.

El Fassi, Allal. *Livre rouge et documentaires*. Tangier: Editions Marocaines Internationales, n.d.

———. *The Independence Movements in Arab North Africa*. Translated by Hazem Zaki Nuseibeh. Washington, D.C.: American Council of Learned Societies, 1954.

Guedira, Reda Ahmed [El Mathar]. "Chewing Gum." *La Voix Nationale*, January 10, 1943.

Feis, Herbert. *Churchill, Roosevelt, and Stalin: The War They Waged and the Peace They Sought*. Princeton: Princeton University Press, 1957.

Guenier, Eugène. *Maroc*. Paris: Encyclopédie coloniale et maritime, 1947.

Guillaume, Albert. *L'Evolution économique de la société rurale marocaine*. Collection de Centres d'Etudes Juridiques, vol. 48. Paris: Librarie Générale de Droit et de Jurisprudence.

Hahn, Lorna. *North Africa: Nationalism to Nationhood*. Washington, D.C.: Public Affairs Press, 1960.

Halstead, John P. *Rebirth of a Nation: The Origins and Rise of Moroccan Nationalism, 1912–1944*. Harvard Middle Eastern Monograph Series. Cambridge: Harvard University Press, 1967.

Hardy, Georges. *Histoire sociale de la colonisation française*. Paris: Larose, 1953.

Hassan II. *Le Maroc en Marche: Discours de S. M. Le Roi Hassan II depuis son Intrônisation*. Rabat: Ministère de l'Information, 1965.

Howe, George F. *Northwest Africa: Seizing the Initiative in the West*. Washington, D.C.: U.S. Government Printing Office, 1957.

Istiqlal party. *Documents: 1944–46*. Paris: Imprimerie Centrale Croissant, 1946.

———. *Morocco under the Protectorate: Forty Years of French Administration*. New York, 1953.

Juin, Alphonse. *Mémoires*. 2 vols. Paris: Arthème Fayard, 1960.

Julien, Charles-André. *L'Afrique du Nord en marche*. Paris: René Julliard, 1952.

———. "Morocco: The End of an Era." *Foreign Affairs* 34, no. 2 (January, 1956): 202.

Khalil, Muhammed. *The Arab States and the Arab League: A Documentary Record*. 2 vols. Beirut: Khayats, 1962.

Lacouture, Jean and Simone. *Le Maroc à l'épreuve*. Paris: Editions de seuil, 1958.

Lahbabi, Mohammed. *Le gouvernement marocain à l'aube du XXeme siecle*. Rabat: Editions techniques Nord-Africains, 1958.

Landau, Rom. *Mohammed V, King of Morocco*. Rabat: Ministry of Foreign Affairs, 1957.

Langer, William L. *Our Vichy Gamble*. New York: Norton and Company, 1947.

Lauriac, R. "La guerre secrète au Maroc." *La Vigie Marocaine*, January 8, 1946.

Leahy, William D. *I Was There*. New York: McGraw-Hill, 1950.

Lemaigre-Dubreuil, Jacques. "Giraud et De Gaulle à Alger." *Revue de Paris*, July, 1949.

Le Tourneau, Roger. *Evolution Politique de l'Afrique du Nord Musulmane: 1920–1962*.

Lyautey, Louis Hubert Gonzalve. *Paroles d'action: Madagascar, Sud-Oranais, Oran, Maroc (1900–1926)*. Paris: Armand Colin, 1927.

Marey, Georges. "Le réarmament français en Afrique du Nord, 1942–1944." *Revue politique et parlementaire* 193 (October, 1947): 48–49.

Marty, Paul. "La politique berbère du protectorat." *Bulletin du Comité de l'Afrique française*. July, 1925.

McGurn, Barrett. *Decade in Europe*. New York: Dutton, 1959.

Millis, Walter, ed. *The Forrestal Diaries*. New York: Viking Press, 1951.

Mohammed V. "Why I Like Americans." *This Week*. September 11, 1960.

Montagne, Robert. *Révolution au Maroc*. Paris: Editions France Empire, 1953.

Morison, Samuel Eliot. *Operations in North African Waters: October, 1942–June, 1943.* History of United States Naval Operations in World War II, vol. 2. 15 vols. Boston: Little, Brown and Co., 1947–1961.

Mowry, George E. *The Era of Theodore Roosevelt and the Birth of Modern America, 1900–1921.* New York: Harper Torchbooks, 1958.

Murphy, Robert D. *Diplomat among Warriors.* Garden City: Doubleday, 1964.

Parent, Pierre. *The Truth about Morocco.* Translated by Eleanor Knight. New York: Moroccan Office of Information and Documentation, 1952.

Patton, George S., Jr. *War As I Knew It.* Boston: Houghton Mifflin Company, 1947.

Pendar, Kenneth. *Adventures in Diplomacy: Our French Dilemma.* New York: Dodd, Mead & Company, 1945.

Peyrouton, Marcel. *Histoire Générale du Maghreb.* Paris: Albin Michel, 1966.

Pavestone, Jay. "American Labor and the Struggle for National Freedom and Democracy." *Free Morocco* 2 (May 25, 1953): 5.

Réalisations et perspectives. Rabat: Ministry of Information, 1957.

Rezette, Robert. *Les Partis Politiques Marocains.* Paris: Armand Colin, 1955.

Richard, René, and Serigny, Alain. *La bissectrice de la guerre.* Algiers: Maison de Livres, 1946.

Rodes, Marjorie. *The Real Ruler of Morocco.* New York: Moroccan Office of Information and Documentation, 1954.

Roosevelt, Elliott. *As He Saw It.* New York: Duell, Sloan, and Pearce, 1946.

Root, Waverly. *Casablanca to Katyn: The Secret History of the War.* New York: Charles Scribner's Sons, 1946.

Rosenman, Samuel I., ed. *The Public Papers and Addresses of Franklin D. Roosevelt.* 13 vols. New York: Harper and Bros., 1938–1950.

Sadeque, Syedah Fatima. *Baybars I of Egypt.* Dacca, Pakistan: Oxford University Press, 1956.

Schuman, Robert. "Necessité d'une politique." In *La Nef: Maroc et Tunisie.* Paris: Julliard, 1953.

Sherwood, Robert E. *Roosevelt and Hopkins: An Intimate History.* New York: Harper & Bros., 1948.

Sonolet, L., and Peres, A. *Moussa et Gi-Gli: Histoire de deux petits noirs.* Paris: A. Colin, 1919.

Tardieu, André P. G. A. *La conférence d'Algéciras: Histoire diplomatique de la crise marocaine (15 janvier–7 avril, 1906).* Paris: F. Alcan, 1906.

Toudelas, M. "L'Espagne au Maroc." *Cahiers Internationaux: Revue international du monde du travail*, no. 71 (December, 1955).

Toussaint, Frantz. "Chants of War of Islam." *Revue d'outre-mer*, 1948.

Truscott, Lucian K., Jr. *Command Missions: A Personal Story*. New York: E. P. Dutton and Company, 1954.

United States, State Department. *American Foreign Policy, 1950–1955*. 2 vols. Washington, D.C.: Government Printing Office, 1957.

———. *American Foreign Policy: Current Documents, 1956*. Washington, D.C.: Government Printing Office, 1959.

———. *Documents on German Foreign Policy, 1918–1945*. Washington, D.C.: Government Printing Office, 1956.

Vaucher, Georges. *Sous les cèdres d'Ifrane: Libres entretienes avec Hassan II, roi du Maroc*. Paris: Julliard, 1962.

Villard, Henry. "Action in North Africa." *American Foreign Service Journal* 19 (December, 1942): 637ff.

Weisgerber, Fritz. *Au seuil du Maroc moderne*. Rabat: Editions Laporte, 1947.

White, Frank. "Morocco: Running the Gauntlet." *Time* 64 (August 23, 1954): 27.

Zartman, I. William. "The Moroccan-American Base Negotiations." *Middle East Journal* 18 (1964): 27–40.

———. *Morocco: Problems of New Power*. New York: Atherton Press, 1964.

Interviews

Arbab, Ahmed (Kenitra, Morocco), May 6, 15, 1967.

Attar, Mohammed (Rabat, Morocco), May 6, 1967.

Princess Aisha (Sidi Bouknadel, Morocco), May 27, 1959; (Rabat, Morocco), July 23, 1966.

Amraoui, M'hammed (Fort Worth, Texas), March 26, 1967.

Bargach, Ali (Rabat, Morocco), May 20, 1967.

Belcher, Marjorie (Washington, D.C.), May 7, 1959.

Ben Barka, Mohammed (Kenitra, Morocco), May 9, 13, 1967.

Benhima, Taibi (Rabat, Morocco), July 25, 1966.

ben Ibrahim, Abdallah (Mehdia Beach, Morocco), May 13, 1967.

ben Miloudi ben Maati, Mohammed (Khemisset, Morocco), May 17, 1967.

ben Mohammed, Ali (Kenitra, Morocco), May 13, 1967.

Bennouna, Mehdi A. (Rabat, Morocco), May 11, 1967.

Ben Simon, Lucien (New York), April 13, 1963.

bint Mohammed, Latifa (Kenitra, Morocco), May 15, 1967.
Boniface, Marius (Mehdia Beach, Morocco), May 25, 1967.
Cannon, Cavendish W. (Port Lyautey, Morocco), April 1, 1957.
Cherkaoui, Hassan (Kenitra, Morocco), May 5, 1967.
Counihan, John L. (Port Lyautey), April, 1959.
Cox, R. D. (Kenitra, Morocco), October 4, 1961.
Dowling, Mary Louise (Washington, D.C.), March 22, 1967.
Duborg, Christian H. (Port Lyautey, Morocco), August 20, 1956; May 10, August 8, 1957.
Dudley, Paul L. (Washington, D.C.), September 11, 1967.
El Fasi, Mohammed (Rabat, Morocco), May 26, 1967.
Feste, Adrien (Casablanca, Morocco), May 23, 1967.
Guedira, Reda Ahmed (Rabat, Morocco), May 20, 1967.
Hammond, Francis, June 10, 1959.
King Hassan II (New York), April 6, 1963.
Hope, Russel (Kenitra, Morocco), June 1, 1967.
Johnson, Carl (Kenitra, Morocco), May 20, 1967.
Kaslowski, C. F. (Kenitra, Morocco), May 21, 1967.
Krijanowsky, C. W. (Casablanca, Morocco), May 23, 1967.
Labbancz, John (Kenitra, Morocco), May 21, 1967.
Mchiche, Mlah, May 30, 1967.
Medford, Richard Carl (Kenitra, Morocco), May 28, 1967.
Mohammed V (Rabat, Morocco), November 20, 1957.
Mortier, Jeanne (Kenitra, Morocco), May 21, 1967.
Nourani, Nony, née Campillo (Kenitra, Morocco), May 21, 1967.
Omar, Youssef (Kenitra, Morocco), May 5, 1967.
Peyrouton, Marcel (Casablanca, Morocco), May 23, 1967.
Sbihi, Mrs. Batoul (Rabat, Morocco), May 13, 1967.
Serghini, Embarek (Madrid, Spain), May 3, 1967.
Smith, Cyril Barton (Casablanca, Morocco), May 23, 1967.
Walton, Helène, née Campillo (Kenitra, Morocco), June 4, 1967.
Yost, Charles W. (Rabat, Morocco), October 27, 1958.
Zeghari, M'hamid (Kenitra, Morocco), June 1, 1967.
Zizi, Mohammed (Kenitra, Morocco), May 19, 1967.

INDEX

Murphy-Weygand Agreement: provisions of, 39–40, 41–42
Mussolini, Benito: and French fleet, 34

Naciri, Mekki: and Moroccan United party, 28
National Action Committee: consolidates nationalist groups, 22, 27
National Reform party: takes fascist bent, 28
nationalism, Moroccan: organization and objectives of, 21–22
nationalists: look to United States, 79, 96–97, 124, 129, 144, 159, 165, 192; tactics of, 24, 25, 26, 28–29, 79, 101, 102–103, 123, 125, 137, 194
NATO: effect of, on Moroccan-U.S. relations, 144, 190, 193, 206
Naval Air Reserve: develops people-to-people program, 218–221, 237, 257, 276–277
Naval Air Station, Port Lyautey: status of, 106–108, 126
Noguès, Auguste: as resident general, 28, 39, 45, 68, 89, 90, 91–92, 93, 95–96, 100, 118, 123
Nomy, H. M.: and Moroccan facilities, 127–128
Norstad, Lauris: signs technical agreement, 150
Norstad-Lechères Agreement: provisions of, 150, 152–153
North Africa: as a military reserve, 37
North Africa Liberation Committee: SEE Bouhafa, El Abed
Northrup-King Co.: provides hybrid corn, 220

Olds, General: on Norstad-Lechères Agreement, 153
Operation Torch: evolution of, 3, 38, 42, 50, 52, 54–62, 113–114; reaction of people at Port Lyautey to, 72–73; assessed, 300
Oued Zem: massacre at, described, 184–186
Ouezzani, Mohammed bel Hassan: as Moroccan nationalist, 22, 28, 29
Ouezzani, Sherif Moulay Hassan El: promises aid against French, 120
Oufkir, Mohammed: as director of national police, 280

Palmesini, Commandant: and Khouribga, riots, 184–185

Parent, Pierre: on French counter-terrorism, 178–179
Patton, George C., Jr.: role of, as military commander in Morocco, 54, 61, 69, 91, 92, 93, 94, 118, 163
Paulson, Jean: reports on Agadir, 276
Pennell, Jesse: as U.S. Naval Attaché in Morocco, 243, 278–279
Penney, Truman C., Captain: in Franco-Moroccan conflict, 119–120
people-to-people program. SEE Ferguson, John H.; Naval Air Reserve; Zartman, I. William
Perry, John P.: on U.S. air bases in Morocco, 146, 148
Perry, Mercedes: in Takkadoum school, 257 n.
Pétain, Marshal: forms government, 32, 34
"petit blancs": influence of, 142, 199
Peyrouton, Marcel: role of, in North Africa, 27, 43 n., 45–46, 89
Phillips, Lloyd Earl: operates black market, 77
Pick, Lewis A.: on costs of air bases, 149
Pinay, Antoine: explains French North African policy, 193
Pineau, Christian: on U.S. air bases, 201
Plan of Reforms: published, 27
Plitt, Edwin A.: role of, in base agreements, 147, 158
Polese, Ralph J.: mistreated by French police, 187
Porter, William: on Moroccan labor demands, 230
Port Lyautey Base Technical Agreement: signed, 128
Puaux, Gabriel: on French position in Morocco, 123, 124

Ragsdale, V. H.: negotiates agreement, 128 n.
Recoing, Henri: to welcome invasion, 52
Rigault, Jean: in "Group of Five," 42
Rodes, Robert E.: protests French discrimination, 156–157
Rommel, Erwin, General: and Seventh Panzer division in France, 32
Roosevelt Club: organized, goals of, 98–99, 135, 280
Roosevelt, Franklin D.: North Afri-